Praise for the Eighteenth Edition

"A political parties textbook needs to cover a tremendous amount of ground—from party organizations to nomination contests to partisan attitudes in the electorate and beyond. Marjorie Randon Hershey's *Party Politics in America* does it all superbly. Combing fresh insights, the latest scholarship, and current politics in a highly engaging text, this new edition is indispensable for classes."
—*Bruce Larson, Gettysburg College*

"Hershey gives a remarkable update to her classic book on political parties. The new additions are timely and represent the current trends in this evolving field. This book continues to be the standard for teaching about American political parties."
—*Beth Ginsberg, University of Connecticut—Stamford*

Praise for the Seventeenth Edition

"Why should you use this book to guide you in the search for understanding democratic politics in America? The short answer is that this book is the best guide you can have."
—*John H. Aldrich, Duke University, from the Foreword*

"This new edition of *Party Politics in America* continues its tradition of combining the most comprehensive coverage of scholarly research with an up-to-date treatment of the rapidly-changing party and electoral landscape. The 2016 election cycle has produced more drama and change for American parties than any in decades, and Marjorie Randon Hershey chronicles it especially well. Between its readability and stellar integration of scholarship and current politics, this book will appeal to students and instructors alike. I look forward to using it in my course, and to learning from it in my own research."
—*Paul A. Beck, The Ohio State University*

"In the midst of unprecedented events and personalities in American politics, one thing remains unchanged: *Party Politics in America* is an unparalleled resource for understanding the central role of political parties in American democracy. With clear, accessible language and organization, Marjorie Randon Hershey covers every aspect of American party politics in a way that enables readers to make sense of and identify patterns in what appears to be a messy, even irrational, system."
—*Christina Wolbrecht, University of Notre Dame*

"This text continues to be the gold standard for courses on American political parties. In clearly written and engaging prose, these chapters reflect enduring wisdom alongside newly developed analytical insights from the best scholars. Marjorie Randon Hershey also does a wonderful job of contextualizing parties in the American political climate, documenting the challenges they face, and pointing out the myriad ways parties structure and influence behavior and policy."
Kyle Saunders, Colorado State University

PARTY POLITICS IN AMERICA

Considered the "gold standard" of political parties texts, this new, Eighteenth Edition of *Party Politics in America* moves its comprehensive and authoritative coverage into the age of deepened partisan conflict, expanded presidential power, and global health threats. Marjorie Randon Hershey builds on the book's three-pronged coverage of party organization, party in the electorate, and party in government and integrates important developments in racial politics, social media use, and battles over access to the vote. The book uses contemporary examples to bring to life the fascinating story of how parties shape our political system.

New to the Eighteenth Edition:

- Fully updated through the 2020 election, including changes in virtually all of the boxed materials, the chapters, and the data presented.
- Examines the impact of the Trump presidency on the Republican Party's supporting coalition and issue positions, changes in party and ideological polarization, and the return to the world of campaign finance of "interested money" from big (and often anonymous) donors.
- Explores political attitudes and voter turnout among college-age and other young voters in light of dramatic changes in American politics and the economy.
- Expanded online Instructor's Resources, including author-written test banks, essay questions, relevant websites with correlated sample assignments, the book's appendix, and links to a collection of course syllabi.

Marjorie Randon Hershey is Professor of Political Science Emerita at Indiana University, USA.

EIGHTEENTH EDITION

Party Politics in America

MARJORIE RANDON HERSHEY

Indiana University

Foreword by

JOHN H. ALDRICH

Duke University

Routledge
Taylor & Francis Group

NEW YORK AND LONDON

Eighteenth edition published 2021
by Routledge
605 Third Avenue, New York, NY 10158

and by Routledge
2 Park Square, Milton Park, Abingdon, Oxon, OX14 4RN

Routledge is an imprint of the Taylor & Francis Group, an informa business

Tenth edition published by Pearson Education, Inc., 2002
Sixteenth edition published by Pearson Education, Inc. 2014, and Routledge, 2016
Seventeenth edition published by Routledge, 2017

Library of Congress Cataloging-in-Publication Data
Names: Hershey, Marjorie Randon, author.
Title: Party politics in America / Marjorie Randon Hershey, Indiana University;
Foreword by John H. Aldrich, Duke University.
Description: Eighteenth edition. | New York: Routledge Taylor & Francis Group, 2021. |
Includes bibliographical references and index. Identifiers: LCCN 2020024448 (print) |
LCCN 2020024449 (ebook) | ISBN 9780367472597 (hardback) |
ISBN 9780367472573 (paperback) | ISBN 9781003034452 (ebook)
Subjects: LCSH: Political parties—United States.
Classification: LCC JK2265 .H477 2021 (print) |
LCC JK2265 (ebook) | DDC 324.273—dc23
LC record available at https://lccn.loc.gov/2020024448
LC ebook record available at https://lccn.loc.gov/2020024449

ISBN: 978-0-367-47259-7 (hbk)
ISBN: 978-0-367-47257-3 (pbk)
ISBN: 978-1-003-03445-2 (ebk)

Typeset in Sabon
by codeMantra

Visit the eResources: www.routledge.com/ 9780367472573

BRIEF CONTENTS

PART V   THE PARTY IN GOVERNMENT

CONTENTS

PART I PARTIES AND PARTY SYSTEMS

PART IV PARTIES, NOMINATIONS, AND ELECTIONS

PART V THE PARTY IN GOVERNMENT

FIGURES

TABLES

BOXES

FOREWORD

Why should you be interested in studying political parties? The short answer is that virtually everything important in America's "Great Experiment" in democracy is rooted in party politics. Political parties are at the core of American politics and make it what it is today—just as they have virtually from the Founding.

A slightly longer answer is that, today as I write this during the 2020 elections, the parties are newsworthy on several major fronts. First, they are the major structuring feature of the elections—indeed more so over this current generation than in generations preceding today. It is common to describe partisans in the public as holding "tribal loyalties," and the growth of antipathy with the other party is stark.

Second, each has recently weathered internal divisions in elections and in Washington. The Republicans had faced internal stresses from the so-called Tea Party Republicans (starting in 2010) and their successor, the House Freedom Caucus, which led to even Republican congressional leaders being "primaried" by little-known opponents. This discontent spilled over to the House, in particular, leading John Boehner to resign as Speaker and his successor Paul Ryan to retire in 2018 rather than continue to have to deal with divisions within their party. Both parties had contentious contests for their party's presidential nomination in 2016, and the 2018 congressional elections, even though returning the Democrats to majority in the House, were widely expected to divide between progressive liberals and more moderate Democrats.

And yet, today, President Donald J. Trump appears to have quelled dissent in his party, and of course was unchallenged for renomination. Speaker Nancy Pelosi has unified her party to handle such contentious issues as impeachment. As of this writing, Joe Biden, the presumptive nominee for the Democrats defeated Sen. Bernie Sanders for nomination much more easily than did Hillary Clinton four years earlier.

All this means that we should anticipate the 2020 elections to be particularly contentious contests between the two parties. No one can say what consequences the COVID-19 pandemic will have on the presidential contest, but it seems as though it is entirely overshadowing House and even Senate campaigns. The best guess at the moment is that this catastrophe and the reelection bid of the president will lead to new heights of nationalization of all partisan elections.

The stakes are unusually high this year, and we can be confident that political parties will be at the center of these disputes. This begs the question: Why should you use this book to guide you in the search for understanding democratic politics in America? The short answer is that this book is the best guide you can have, and it has been the best guide in this search for quite a long time.

A longer answer for this question is that I first encountered this text at the same stage in my life you are in now: as an undergraduate, although in my case that was back in the 1960s. At that point, the book was authored by an up-and-coming scholar named Frank Sorauf.[1] Following on the heels of his important study of the effect of political parties on the Pennsylvania legislature,[2] *Party Politics in America* established him as arguably the leading scholar of political parties of his generation. In those days—less so today—it was common for a "textbook" (i.e., a book designed to be used in class) to do more than just tell you what others had written about its subject. Rather, books written for undergraduates were also designed to make a coherent argument about its subject matter—to engage you, the reader, intellectually. So it was then, and with this book, so it remains today.

In the sixth edition, published in 1988, Frank brought in Paul Allen Beck as coauthor. Paul took over the authorial duties beginning with that edition, and Marjorie Randon Hershey did so beginning with the ninth edition in 2001, leading to the book that you are about to read today. Each did so with considerable respect for the substance and the perspective that characterized the previous editions. This has brought a high degree of intellectual continuity to *Party Politics in America*. Sorauf, Beck, and Hershey achieve this through the use of a three-part division in the discussion of political parties, considering the political party in its electoral, governing, and organizational roles. These three aspects of a party create a coherent system that (sometimes loosely, sometimes more tightly) provides a degree of integration to the diverse workings of any one political party.

When Sorauf first wrote, the three pieces were rather loosely integrated. Partisanship in the public, for example, was nearly as strongly held as today, but the party in government was deeply divided, especially the majority party, the Democrats (into North and South, or pro- and anti-civil rights), but also the minority Republican Party (into "Wall Street" and "Main Street" Republicans). Today, partisanship is as strong as always. Democratic officeholders, however, are much more strongly united than they were then, and so too are the Republicans, perhaps a quarreling family, but one that has been forged together by the President and Mitch McConnell, the majority party leader in the Senate. In addition, the party organizations are much stronger than they were then (and vastly better financed) making their ability to conduct highly partisan campaigns ever more effective.

The second continuity is that Sorauf, Beck, and Hershey see the two major political parties together in the U.S. as a system. The two-party system has long played a central role in the evolution of American politics (see especially Chapter 7). Although this two-party system has important implications for political dynamics, they also see the two-party system as a part of the intermediary groups in society. By this, the authors mean that the parties serve as points of contact between the public and its government (see Figure 1.2, a figure that I believe has graced this book for all of its editions now).

The third continuity is that each author is a terrific scholar of political parties, and although these continuities have allowed this book to keep its unique intellectual stamp, the transition among authors has also allowed each to bring to the work his or her particular strengths. In the end, this has made this edition of the book richer and stronger than ever before. As I noted earlier, Frank Sorauf used his expertise to explain the role of the political party in government. Since then, he became one of the nation's leading experts on the role of money in politics and in later editions reflected that increasingly important but perennially controversial subject.[3] Paul Beck brought a distinguished career of scholarship, examining the role of political parties in the electorate and adding nicely to Frank's expertise about the governing role.[4] Paul is, like Frank and Marjorie Hershey, an expert on American politics. However, Paul is also, more than most of us who study American politics, genuinely knowledgeable about comparative politics.

Marjorie Randon Hershey, through her expertise, has made important contributions to one of the most difficult questions to study: How do candidates and their campaigns shape and how are they shaped by electoral forces?[5] This interaction links the two most important components of the party, elections and governance, into a more coherent whole. It has allowed her to bring clarity to what has become an increasingly confused portion of the field. Marjorie has also closely studied the role of gender in politics, a dimension of party politics that not only has been of long-standing importance from at least the granting of women's suffrage but has also become especially critical with the emergence and growth of the "gender gap," something that recent events has made even more telling.[6] Finally, she has made a long series of contributions to help us understand how to bring meaning to complex events.[7] One special feature of this book is the increased use of narratives from well-known and little-known party figures alike, narratives that serve to bring the subject matter to life.

Not only does each author add a unique and innovative understanding to political parties as they join the continuity of leading scholars who have shaped this book, but also each edition adds new life to the text by considering the politics of the time. This edition is not an exception. Here, then, are some of the facets of particular relevance to contemporary politics that I find particularly worth considering (by you that is).

One issue that is critical to all who study American politics is the way that an understanding of politics matters in your life. This is your government, and the political parties are ways in which you can help shape what your government and elected officials do. This is one of the most important meanings of American political parties. They, and the government that they create, are the consequences of you and your political actions. So saying allows me to move more directly to the longer answer about the study of political parties themselves.

At the outset, I mentioned that you should want to study political parties because they are so important to virtually everything that happens in American politics and because political parties are so central to the workings of any democracy. Great, but you are probably asking, "So what questions should I keep in mind as I read this book? What questions will help me understand the material better?" Let me propose as guidelines three questions that are neither too specific nor too general. We are looking, that is, for questions somewhere in between "Are parties good?" on the one hand and "What role did Boehner's violation of the informal 'Hastert Rule' play in his decision to resign as Speaker in late 2015?" on the other hand.

You are well aware that today politicians can appear magnanimous and statesmanlike if they say that they will be nonpartisan and if they call for Congress to "rise above" partisan politics to be bipartisan. Yet, essentially every elected official is a partisan, and essentially every elected official chooses to act in a partisan way much of the time. Why do politicians today, you might ask, speak as if they are of two minds about political parties? Perhaps they actually are. Even if you dismiss this rhetoric as just words, it is the case that the public is of two minds about parties, too. This book, like virtually all written about American political parties, includes quotes from the Founding Fathers warning about the dangers of party and faction, often quoting such luminaries as John Adams, Thomas Jefferson, and James Madison. Yet these very same men not only worried about the dangers of party but were the founders and leaders of our first political parties. So the first question is, "Why are people—leaders and followers, founders and contemporary figures alike— both attracted to and repulsed by political parties?"

Let me suggest two books that might give you additional ways to think about this question. One is Richard Hofstadter's *The Idea of a Party System: The Rise of Legitimate Opposition in the United States, 1780–1840* (Berkeley, CA: University of California Press, 1969). This book is a series of public lectures that Hofstadter gave in which he roots political parties deeply in the American democratic tradition, arguing that they represent the outward manifestation of a change in philosophic understanding of the relationship between citizens and leaders in this, the world's first practicing democracy. Another is Thomas E. Mann and Norman J. Ornstein, *It's Even Worse than It Looks: How the American Constitutional System Collided with the New Politics of Extremism* (New York: Basic Books, 2016). Mann and Ornstein are both political scientists who also worked at major think tanks (The Brookings Institution and the American Enterprise Institute, respectively) applying scholarship to practical politics. In this book, they have made one of the strongest cases for the dangers of hyper partisanship in politics in a partisan-polarized era, adding a contemporary account of the classic question of the "idea of a party system."

This question of the purpose of parties in our democracy, both theoretical and practical, leads easily to a second major question that should be in your mind as you work through this book and your course: "How does the individual connect to the political party?" There are two aspects to this question. One is fairly direct—what do parties mean to the individual and how, if at all, has this changed over time? The great work that laid out this relationship in the modern era is *The American Voter* by Angus Campbell, Philip E. Converse, Warren E. Miller, and Donald E. Stokes (New York: John Wiley & Sons, 1960). Many argue that this connection has changed fundamentally. Green, Palmquist, and Schickler, for example, and even more recently Lilliana Mason have shown that partisanship is perhaps as or more influential in shaping the vote as ever.[8]

It is certainly the case that today we hear people say, "The government, they …," and not "The government, we …" I suspect that few of us think that way. It is certainly common to hear politicians call for a tax cut by claiming that doing so will give the people back their money. Such a statement would not make sense if we thought of the government as being composed of us, ourselves, and thus thought of *our* taxes as using our money to work in *our* government, doing *our* bidding by enacting *our* preferences into legislation selected by *our* representatives whom *we* chose. The question can, however, be cast even more broadly, asking whether the people feel removed from social, cultural, economic, and political institutions, generally, with political parties and the government therefore only one more symptom of a larger ill. This is certainly a part of the concerns that motivated Robert D. Putnam in his *Bowling Alone: The Collapse and Revival of American Community* (New York: Simon & Schuster, 2000). Today that sometimes comes out in the sense that the debate among the politicians in Washington seems to be more about scoring points over the partisan opposition and less about working in the public's interest. This sense of remove peaked during the summer of 2011 in the debate over whether to raise the debt ceiling, in which the elected figures in each party appeared to put the country's economic recovery at risk merely to win their side of a policy dispute.[9]

The change from a trusting, supportive, identified public to one apparently dramatically less so is one of the great changes that took place in American politics over the past half century. A second great change is "polarization," a growing distance between the elected officials of the two parties. That is, compared with 50 years ago, today the Democrats are more liberal and consistently more so than Republicans, who in turn are much more conservative. Although this is not to say that there is anything close to an identical set of beliefs by the members of either party, there is a greater coherence of opinion and belief in, say, the congressional delegations of each party than in earlier times. Even more undeniable is a much clearer divergence between the policy interests and choices of the two parties in Washington than, say, 50 years ago. You might refer to *Polarized Politics: Congress and the President in a Partisan Era* (Washington, DC: CQ Press, 2000), edited by Jon R. Bond and Richard Fleisher, for a variety of fairly early indications of this fact. The question, then, is not whether there is greater polarization today; the question is whether this relative clarity of polarization matters. As usual, there are at least two ways to understand the question. One is simply to ask whether a more polarized Congress yields policies very different from a less polarized one. The readings in Bond and Fleisher generally support that position. Others, for example Keith Krehbiel and David W. Brady and Craig Volden, argue that the Founders' creation of checks and balances makes polarization relatively ineffectual in shaping legislation due to vetoes, compromises necessary between the two chambers, and so on.[10] Even more generally, however, David R. Mayhew has argued that our system generates important legislation regardless of which party is in control or whether they share power under divided partisan control of government.[11] As you might expect, there has been considerable interest in the challenge that Mayhew, Krehbiel, Brady, and Volden have raised. One set of responses can be seen in the Bond and Fleisher volume, another can be found in *The Macro Polity*.[12]

However, this returns us to one of the original questions: Just how closely does the party in the electorate align with the party in government? On this, too, there is considerable disagreement. On the one hand, Alan Abramowitz argues that the partisan public follows only at a degree of lag the polarization of the partisan elite in Washington, while on the other hand, Morris Fiorina argues that the public remains primarily, even overwhelmingly, moderate, and sees the polarization in Washington, but does not follow it. There is, in his words, a "disconnect," presumably caused by political parties and their leaders.[13] And this, of course connects to politics today in a vast number of ways, such as those just discussed. But it also shapes many other aspects of politics: Will the new voter identification laws serve to reduce fraudulent voting or reduce, instead, voter turnout by minorities, young people, and the elderly?

More recently, scholarship has tended to focus on the negative consequences of partisan polarization. For example, Danielle Thomsen finds that polarization affects just who will run for Congress, tending to attract more polarized and discourage less polarizing and more moderate candidates from even trying.[14] Jamie Druckman et al. show how political polarization shapes public opinion in a more polarized way.[15] On the other hand, David Jones finds that polarization has led to a degree of increase in collective accountability of its congressional affiliates in elections.[16] And Gary Jacobson extends that line of argument, in a way, by showing how partisan polarization has also generated increasingly partisan polarization in the public in terms of their evaluations of the incumbent president—and changed how they determine their votes for Congress.[17]

As you can see, we have now gone from writing about the Founding of the American republic and now reached the point of recently published work. That is, we are asking questions that are motivating the work of scholars today and problems that are motivating the public and its leaders today. So, let's get on with it and turn to the book and the study of political parties themselves.

John H. Aldrich
Duke University

Notes

1 Frank Sorauf passed away on September 6, 2013. We miss him.
2 Frank J. Sorauf, *Party and Representation: Legislative Politics in Pennsylvania* (New York: Atherton Press, 1963).
3 See, for example, Frank J. Sorauf, *Money in American Elections* (Glenview, IL: Scott Foresman/Little, Brown College Division, 1988) or *Inside Campaign Finance: Myths and Realities* (New Haven, CT: Yale University Press, 1992).
4 He has written a great deal on this subject. One illustration that has long been one of my favorites is his "A Socialization Theory of Partisan Alignment," which was originally published in *The Politics of Future Citizens*, edited by Richard Niemi (San Francisco, CA: Jossey-Bass, 1974, pp. 199–219) and reprinted in *Classics in Voting Behavior*, edited by Richard Niemi and Herbert Weisberg (Washington, DC: CQ Press, 1992).
5 See especially her books, *Running for Office: The Political Education of Campaigners* (Chatham, NJ: Chatham House, 1984) and *The Making of Campaign Strategy* (Lexington, MA: D.C. Heath-Lexington, 1974).

6 Especially interesting accounts of the ways the political parties reacted to female suffrage can be found in Anna L. Harvey, *Votes Without Leverage: Women in American Electoral Politics 1920–1970* (Cambridge: Cambridge University Press, 1998) and J. Kevin Corder and Christina Wolbrecht, *Counting Women's Ballots: Female Voters from Suffrage through the New Deal* (Cambridge: Cambridge University Press, 2016).

7 See, for example, "Constructing Explanations for the U.S. State Governors' Races: The Abortion Issue and the 1990 Gubernatorial Elections," *Political Communication* 17 (July–September 2000): 239–262; "The Meaning of a Mandate: Interpretations of 'Mandate' in 1984 Presidential Election Coverage," *Polity* (Winter 1995): 225–254; and "Support for Political Women: Sex Roles," in John C. Pierce and John L. Sullivan, eds., *The Electorate Reconsidered* (Beverly Hills, CA: Sage, 1980), pp. 179–198.

8 Donald Green, Bradley Palmquist, and Eric Schickler, *Partisan Hearts and Minds: Political Parties and the Social Identities of Voters* (New Haven, CT: Yale University Press, 2002). Lilliana Mason, *Uncivil Agreement: How Politics became Our Identity.* (Chicago, IL: University of Chicago Press, 2018).

9 See the discussion of poll reports in the height of the debate over this concern (July 14, 2001) at http://people-press.org/2011/07/14/the-debt-ceiling-show-down-%E2%80%93-where-the-public-stands (accessed November 29, 2011).

10 Keith Krehbiel, *Pivotal Politics: A Theory of U.S. Lawmaking* (Chicago: University of Chicago Press, 1998); David W. Brady and Craig Volden, *Revolving Gridlock: Politics and Policy from Jimmy Carter to George W. Bush* (Boulder, CO: Westview Press, 2006).

11 David R. Mayhew, *Divided We Govern: Party Control, Lawmaking and Investigations, 1946–1990* (New Haven, CT: Yale University Press, 1991) and *Partisan Balance: Why Political Parties Don't Kill the U.S. Constitutional System* (Princeton, NJ: Princeton University Press, 2011).

12 Robert S. Erikson, Michael B. MacKuen, and James A. Stimson, *The Macro Polity* (Cambridge: Cambridge University Press, 2002).

13 Alan I. Abramowitz, *The Disappearing Center: Engaged Citizens, Polarization and American Democracy* (New Haven, CT: Yale University Press, 2010); Morris P. Fiorina, *Culture War: The Myth of a Polarized America,* 3rd ed., with Samuel J. Abrams and Jeremy C. Pope (New York: Longman, 2011); and *Disconnect: The Breakdown of Representation in American Politics* with Samuel J. Abrams (Norman, OK: University of Oklahoma Press, 2009).

14 Danielle M. Thomsen, "Ideological Moderates Won't Run: How Party Fit Matters for Partisan Polarization in Congress," *The Journal of Politics* 76, 3 (2014): 786–797.

15 James N. Druckman, Erik Peterson, and Rune Slothuus, "How Elite Partisan Polarization Affects Public Opinion Formation," *American Political Science Review* 107, 1 (2013): 57–79.

16 David R. Jones, "Partisan Polarization and Congressional Accountability in House Elections," *American Journal of Political Science* 54, 2 (2010): 323–337.

17 Gary C. Jacobson, "Partisan Polarization in Presidential Support: The Electoral Connection," *Congress & the Presidency: A Journal of Capital Studies* 30, 1 (2003). Jacobson, Gary C. "It's nothing personal: The decline of the incumbency advantage in US House elections." *The Journal of Politics* 77, 3 (2015): 861–873.

PREFACE

Politics has always been personal. But when seven in ten unmarried Democrats say they would not consider having a committed relationship with a Trump voter, and when a majority of Republicans describe Democrats as unpatriotic and even immoral, it's clear that American party politics in the 2020s have changed dramatically from the time when most faculty members grew up. Just as our students' personal lives have been up-ended, so have their perceptions about politics and their relationship with government.

The disruptions of 2020 have been especially unsettling, but change in contemporary American politics has become a feature, not a bug. That's why books about political parties produce new editions with every new election. Although calculus workbooks and Spanish texts may not become outdated quickly, books about American politics do. Think about what changed just between the 2016 and 2018 elections. Republicans had won the trifecta in 2016: control of both houses of Congress and an Electoral College victory for the presidency. Yet in 2018, Democrats took back the House, eight state legislative chambers, and seven governorships in a midterm that was largely a negative reaction to the president elected two years earlier. At times, change led to surprising levels of inter-party agreement, as was the case when both parties in Congress supported trillion-dollar stimulus programs even at a time of intense party polarization. At other times, partisan conflict reached into areas most of us had not anticipated, as when supporters of the 2020 Democratic presidential candidate circulated this meme on social media: "Biden: He Won't Inject You with Bleach."

The job of this new edition of *Party Politics in America* is to explain how these rapid changes, and the drama of the 2020 elections, affect American politics and governance. But the story of 2020 isn't limited to change.

The two major parties continue to be closely balanced at the national level. Although both parties are far from beloved even by many of their own supporters, minor parties have not gained ground. The Democratic and Republican coalitions have remained relatively constant, with non-college-educated white males a bit more prominent among Republican supporters and white suburban women a slightly bigger portion of the Democratic coalition. Party and ideological polarization reigns. And most worrisome, the harsh rhetoric and barely veiled calls to violence in the presidential race infused party identification with unprecedented hostility.

New to This Edition

Here are some of the new features of the eighteenth edition:

* For those of us dealing with the brave new world of online teaching, the book is available online. To hold students' interest, we've used color and made the layout even more readable.

- Every chapter is updated to include material about the 2020 elections, including election results and campaign finance data incorporated immediately after the election.
- Donald Trump's preferences for tariffs on imported goods, greatly reduced immigration, and ballooning federal spending have challenged the Republican Party's traditional issue stands and led to some changes in the party's coalition of supporting groups, as Chapters 1, 7, and 11 show.
- Have college-age people really increased their political activity recently? If so, what difference has it made? You'll find answers in Chapters 5 and 8.
- How can we reconcile the widespread notion that party "bosses" control parties' choices with evidence that state and local party organizations lack important sources of power? See Chapters 3, 4, and 16.
- Chapter 11 demonstrates how the corona virus pandemic changed campaigning in 2020, ranging from its impact on door-to-door canvassing to its effects on voting methods and turnout.
- Elections in 2020 were also threatened by legislative efforts to restrict access to the vote and online interference by Russia and other nations, as discussed in Chapter 8.
- More women are running for office – and winning. In what ways has that affected the two parties' coalitions of supporters? See Chapters 7 and 11.
- Immigration became even more of a hot-button issue during the Trump administration. How has that affected Hispanic and Latino Americans' party preferences? In particular, how can the Republicans respond to demographic change while retaining their white, rural, and exurban base? See Chapters 6–8 and 16.
- New and updated Instructor's Resources on the book's webpage (www.routledge.com/9781138683686) include test banks for each chapter with multiple-choice, short answer/identification, and essay questions; an annotated list of websites and correlated sample assignments; the book's appendix incorporating the 2020 election results; and links to a collection of syllabi (including my own).

This book, long known as the "gold standard" of political parties texts, has developed and adapted over a long time period, just as the American parties have. Frank J. Sorauf, a pioneer of modern political science, had the vision to create *Party Politics in America* in 1968, and Paul Allen Beck brought the book into the late 1980s and 1990s, with the intellectual mastery and comparative perspective that has marked his research on parties and voting behavior. Their goal for each new edition was to provide students with the clearest, most comprehensive and engaging understanding of political parties and partisanship, which in turn are key to understanding the workings of elections, public opinion, policy making, and leadership.

Features of This Text

This new edition continues that effort by adding new and updated versions of the features that were so well received in recent editions. The boxes titled

"A Day in the Life" tell the personal stories of individuals whose experiences help to illustrate recent changes in the parties. Many of my students see political parties as remote, abstract, and a bit underhanded—something that might interest elderly people, but not teens and 20-somethings. I hope these compelling stories—including that of Alexandria Ocasio-Cortez, who ran for Congress less than a decade after completing college—can show readers why studying party politics is worth their time.

In other chapters, the feature titled "Which Would You Choose?" illustrates major debates about party politics in summary form: for example, whether encouraging greater voter turnout would help or harm American democracy (see Chapter 8). These mini-essays can provoke thoughts and debate on fundamental concerns about political parties.

Additional special feature boxes portray examples of "real politics" in action and are strategically distributed throughout the text.

As in previous editions, I've tried to make the reader's job easier by putting important terms in boldface and clearly defining them, emphasizing the vital points, and illustrating them with engaging examples. In addition, for instructors, I have written each chapter to stand alone, so that teachers can assign chapters in any order they choose without leaving their students puzzled because relevant concepts were explained elsewhere.

As elected officials know, good representatives need detailed information about what their constituents want. I've really appreciated hearing from instructors and students about their reactions to *Party Politics in America* and what they'd like to see changed. I'd like to hear from you as well. You can reach me at hershey@indiana.edu; I'll be happy to respond.

ACKNOWLEDGMENTS

I am so grateful for all the help I've received in researching, writing, and revising this volume: from my graduate and undergraduate students; present and former colleagues at Indiana University, particularly Ted Carmines and Bob Huckfeldt, Bill Bianco, Eileen Braman, Chris DeSante, Mike Ensley, Bernard Fraga, Matthew Hayes, Yanna Krupnikov, Elinor Ostrom, Leroy Rieselbach, John Williams, and Jerry Wright; and departmental staff members Jess Coulter, Jackie Gentry, Chris McCann, Jan Peterson, and Jessica Williams.

Austin Ranney, Leon Epstein, Jack Dennis, and Murray Edelman stimulated my interest in party politics and convinced me of the value of political science. Murray Edelman deserves special mention in that group, not only as a mentor and model for so many of us but also as a much-beloved friend. John Aldrich, one of the most insightful and systematic analysts of political parties, has been kind enough to write the Foreword to the book. I've learned so much as well from Alan Abramowitz, John Aldrich, Paul Beck, Nate Birkhead, Rachel Blum, Tony Broh, Philip Bump, Tom Carsey, Heather Evans, Richard Fenno, Audrey Haynes, Paul Herrnson, John Hibbing, Jennifer Hochschild, David Karol, David Kimball, Geoff Layman, Burdett Loomis, Michael Malbin, Seth Masket, Scott McClurg, Hans Noel, Bruce Oppenheimer, Chuck Prysby, Doug Roscoe, Kyle Saunders, Kay Schlozman, Brian Silver, Paul Sniderman, Jim Stimson, Brad Warren, Christina Wolbrecht, and John Zaller.

A large group of talented people have also offered suggestions on revision for this edition: Lawrence Bensky, California State University-East Bay; David Darmofal, University of South Carolina-Columbia; John Davis, University of Arkansas-Monticello; Michael Hagen, Temple University; Adam Lawrence, Millersville University; Geoff Peterson, University of Wisconsin-Eau Claire; Robert Postic, University of Findlay; Charles Prysby, University of North Carolina-Greensboro; Douglas Roscoe, University of Massachusetts-Dartmouth; Priscilla Southwell, University of Oregon. They and reviewers of previous editions have been central to my efforts to keep the book relevant to students' and instructors' changing needs. And it is a great pleasure to work with the people at Routledge: Jennifer Knerr, Ze'ev Sudry, Jacqueline Dorsey, and the members of the production team, including Philip Stirups and Jeanine Pirro.

Most of all, I am very grateful to my family: my husband, Howard, and our daughters, Katie, Lissa, Lani, and Hannah; their partners Jim, David, Andrew, and Michael, and grandkiddos Chloe, Parker, Dae'yana, Talan, Jade, Jack, Seamus, and Liam. Everything I do has been made possible by their love and support.

Marjorie Randon Hershey

PART ONE

Parties and Party Systems

The Democratic-controlled U.S. House of Representatives voted to impeach President Donald Trump on December 18, 2019. Trump called the vote a "scam" and a "brazen and unlawful attempt to overturn the results of the 2016 election." The Democratic managers of the impeachment process replied, "The Framers deliberately drafted a Constitution that allows the Senate to remove Presidents who, like President Trump, abuse their power to cheat in elections, betray our national security, and ignore checks and balances."[1]

Was this dramatic story simply "politics as usual"? Or was it evidence of a working two-party system, offering voters two alternative choices for governing? Just as the two major parties had different views of Trump's impeachment, they also put forward contrasting policies on other matters that affect your daily life, from whether the beer or water you drink should be tested for contaminants to whether the electricity that powers your smartphone should come from coal or from wind energy. National, state, and local governments make decisions that bear on almost everything you do.

Because these governmental decisions have such great impact, large numbers of groups have mobilized to try to influence the men and women in public office who will make them. In a democracy, the political party is one of the oldest and most powerful of these groups. Parties have a lot of competition, however. Organized interests such as the National Rifle Association and the Gay and Lesbian Victory Fund also work to get the government policies they want, as do pro-life groups and the National Organization for the Reform of Marijuana Laws (NORML). Even organizations whose main purpose is nonpolitical, such as universities, Walmart, and Facebook, try to influence the many government decisions that affect them.

These groups serve as **intermediaries**—links between citizens and the people in government who make the decisions that affect our lives (Figure I.1). They raise issues that they want the government to address. They tell people what the government is doing. By bringing together people with shared interests, they amplify these people's voices in speaking to the government. They keep an eye on one another as well as on the actions of public officials. Different intermediaries specialize in different political activities. Parties focus on nominating candidates, helping to elect them, and organizing those who win. Most organized interests represent narrower groups; they are not likely to win majority support, so they try instead to influence the views of candidates who do win office—and of appointed officials, such as bureaucrats and judges. In other democracies, parties

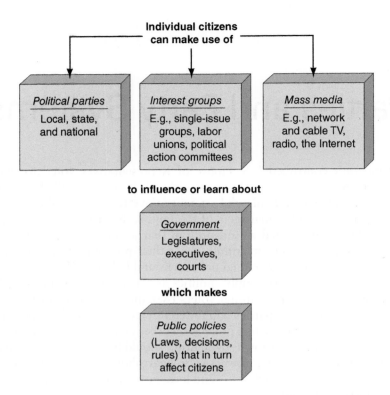

FIGURE I.1 Parties and Other Intermediaries between Citizens and Government

may behave differently. The American parties, for example, concentrate on election activities, whereas many parties in Europe have been more committed to keeping their elected officials faithful to the party's program.

Parties compete fiercely with one another. They also vie with interest groups for money, expertise, and volunteer help and then, with those resources in hand, for the support of individual citizens and elected officials. Parties must even fight for a major role in political campaigns; the American parties are not nearly as dominant in the business of campaigning as they were a century ago. Yet most Americans continue to identify with either the Democrats or the Republicans. In fact, if we knew the party you feel closer to, and the party affiliation of your representatives in government, we could predict your and their votes about 90 percent of the time.

Therefore, political parties continue to be important features of the American political landscape. Even so, parties have always been viewed with suspicion in the U.S., since even before the American Revolution. Leaders ranging from Washington and Madison to the Progressive movement to current critics have equated parties with "boss rule" and tried to reform or weaken them. The resultant public hostility has led state legislatures to restrict what parties can do and how they can organize. Party leaders have coped with these challenges over time by adapting their organizations and activities, adopting conventions, primary elections, superdelegates, independent spending campaigns, data bases, Twitter feeds, and micro- and nano-targeting. Politicians who lived a century ago would hardly recognize the political parties of the 2020s, and the parties we know today will probably change dramatically in the coming decades as we create new information technology and move toward a more diverse society.

What will those changes look like? President Trump has set the Republican Party on a different path from the Republicans of half a century ago. His preference for tariffs (taxes) on imported goods differs from the traditional Republican commitment to free trade. His "America First" suspicion of the international alliances that Republicans once valued and his stands on such issues as immigration and deficit spending have posed a choice for many Republican elected officials: Should they accept these changes in the principles they used to campaign on, or alienate Trump's base of support, which showed up in large numbers in 2016 and to a lesser extent in 2018 and 2020? Will the Republicans continue to be the Trump Party? And if so, how will the Democrats respond?

By the time you finish this book, you'll be able to explain how the American parties developed, the many ways in which they affect your life, and what they are capable of contributing to a democratic politics. What you read will challenge your ideas about whether political parties are essential to the survival of a democracy, whether they benefit you as a citizen, and how you intend to act as a mover of a representative political system.

Note

1 Jeremy Herb, "House Democrats Call Trump Filing on Impeachment 'Dead Wrong' in New Brief for Senate Trial," January 20, 2020, https://www.cnn.com/2020/01/20/politics/house-democrats-impeachment-brief/index.html (accessed August 12, 2020).

CHAPTER 1

What Are Political Parties?

Twitter was bursting with political commentary as the 2020 election campaign started. Here is a sampling:

> Democrats are the party of hate!!!—Ryan, 9/24/19
> This Republican Party, the party of hate, greed, corruption and division...—Diane, 9/15/19
> Democrat women don't deserve respect. Look at the way they dress?—Linda, 9/16/19
> Do I really hate myself enough to date a republican... hmmmm—Pate, 9/15/19
> How America works? Republicans hate Democrats and Democrats hate Republicans—Camilo, 9/19/19

At the center of this storm of party conflict was Donald J. Trump. President Trump did not invent these conflicts, but his controversial statements calling African-American-dominated cities "a disaster" and "rat infested" and referring to Mexican immigrants as "rapists" and "drug dealers" deepened the divisions among Americans that had been festering since even before the Constitution was drafted.

American politics is more deeply divided along party lines now than it has been in more than a century. Shortly after entering the White House, President Trump had a record 90 percent approval rating among Republicans but a record-low 14 percent approval among Democrats.[1] Four years later, that remarkable level of partisan division had seeped into almost every corner of American life; Republican and Democratic identifiers differed markedly even on whether they considered the COVID-19 pandemic a major threat to their own personal health and whether they were willing to wear a face mask to protect themselves.[2]

Substantial proportions of Americans not only disagree with the other party's policies, but even view them as "so misguided that they threaten the nation's well-being."[3] In a recent survey, most Republicans say that Democrats are more closed-minded and unpatriotic than other Americans, and smaller percentages of Democrats describe Republicans in the same terms. These proportions have been increasing even since 2016, as have the proportions of partisans viewing the other party as "immoral" and "lazy" (see Figure 1.1). In short, more and more Americans have come to believe that the other political party is the enemy,

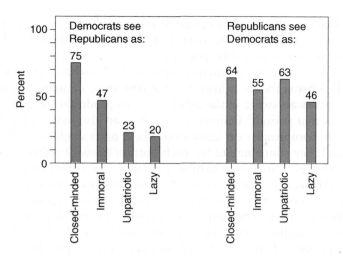

FIGURE 1.1 Partisans See the Other Party in Increasingly Harsh Terms

Note: Bars show the percentage of respondents who say the other party is more likely to have these characteristics, compared with other Americans.

Source: Adapted from Pew Research Center, "Partisan Antipathy: More Intense, More Personal," October 10, 2019, https://www.people-press.org/2019/10/10/partisan-antipathy-more-intense-more-personal/.

not just an alternative choice, and that government can't be trusted when the other side holds power.[4]

Such striking partisan divisions are not unique to modern politics. Over time, the American parties have been polarized more often than not. Yet party polarization is unusually intense in the 2020s. One reason is that party lines have hardened as they have become reinforced by other societal differences. Younger people are more likely now to vote Democratic, and older people lean more Republican. Democrats tend to live in cities, while Republicans congregate in rural areas and churches. People of color vote Democratic much more than do white Americans. Consider the fact that African-Americans now support Democratic presidential candidates at rates higher than 90 percent, whereas a majority of white Americans last voted Democratic for president in 1964—more than half a century ago. (Chapter 7 explores the roots of this "partisan sorting.")

These group differences in party loyalties are linked closely with attitudes toward major issues. Not only in Congress but also in state legislatures and even in courtrooms, Democrats typically hold different views from Republicans about guns, same-sex marriage, taxes, immigration, and other issues. The gulf between the parties in government has grown so dramatically wider that recent Congresses have been among the most polarized in U.S. history.[5] Active Republicans in the larger population also differ from active Democrats in their views on issues.[6] Perhaps because these group and issue differences reinforce one another, partisanship generates stronger emotions than most survey respondents reported about the parties 50 years ago.[7]

How does this affect you? Because of these marked party divisions, a shift from Democratic to Republican control of Congress and the White House can lead to major changes in public policies, from rules on repayment of student loans to action or inaction on climate change. In 2008 and 2009, the Democratic-majority House was the most liberal in the past three decades. Yet, just a year later, the Republican swing in the 2010 elections produced the most conservative House in that period.[8] Differences this big can also make it harder for the two parties to compromise on legislation. These party conflicts may be painful to watch, and they contribute to the rock-bottom levels of public confidence in Congress.[9] However, they also help us to clarify our voting choices and hold elected officials accountable to the people. That benefits a democracy.[10]

Americans have expressed suspicion of political parties, if not outright hostility, long before the current partisan polarization. George Washington declared in his Farewell Address that "the spirit of party" was the "worst enemy" of popular government. Parties, he feared, would encourage people to pursue their narrow self-interest at other people's expense and cause jealousy, division, and revenge. Without parties, in his view, we'd be more likely to get noble and uncorrupted leaders who could speak for the nation as a whole. Washington's dream of a government "above parties" has long been widely shared. Then, if so many are disgusted by partisan conflict, why do we still have political parties?

The main reason is simply that political parties do necessary things for us that would not get done otherwise. Most people are not very interested in politics, so how would they decide on a candidate without the guidance that party labels provide? Will they spend hours researching the backgrounds and issue stands of dozens of candidates? Would you?

Without parties, how would Americans choose a president? With no party primaries and caucuses, who would be able to winnow the thousands of presidential wannabes to the very few who will run in the general election? Could members of Congress make that decision? Not in a system designed to separate legislative from executive powers. How about nomination by the nation's mayors and other elected officials, as happens in France? A new version of the television series *Survivor?*

Strong party organizations bring voters to the polls. Without political parties, would voter turnout, already lower in the U.S. than in most other industrialized democracies, drop even further? How would members of Congress elected as 535 individuals, with no party loyalties to guide them, put together majorities to pass packages of legislation?

We wouldn't eliminate conflict by abolishing parties. Although most Americans agree on such lofty goals as freedom and national security, we naturally differ on how to reach those goals. Is national security best achieved by higher military spending or by strong international alliances? Is excellent education more likely when we funnel tax money only into public schools or when we divert some of those funds into vouchers to support private and religious schools?

Who runs this political organization that is so needed and yet so distrusted? Does "the party" include only the politicians who share a party label when running for and holding public office? Does it also include activists who work on campaigns, citizens who vote for a party's candidates, or interest groups that share a party's aims? Or is a party any group that chooses to call itself a party, whether Democratic, Republican, or Tea?

The Three Parts of Parties

Most scholars would agree that *a party is a group organized to nominate candidates, to try to win political power through elections, and to promote ideas about public policies.* For many analysts, the central figures in a political party are the candidates and elected officials who share a party's label. Anthony Downs, for example, sees a political party as "a coalition ... seeking to control the governing apparatus by legal means ... [through] duly constituted elections or legitimate influence."[11] Many parties in democratic nations, including the U.S., began as groups of political leaders who organized to advance certain policies by winning elections.

Most observers, however, see the American parties as including more than just candidates and officeholders. As John Aldrich points out, parties are organizations—institutions with a life and a set of rules of their own, beyond that of their candidates.[12] Interested individuals can become active in political parties and help set their directions and strategies, just as one would do in a sports team or a student group. These activists and organizations are central parts of the party, too.

Some researchers urge us to define "party" even more broadly, to include other groups that ally with a party's elected officials and organization, such as interest groups and even media organizations. The Republican Party, then, would be seen as encompassing small business lobbies, conservative Christian groups, and media people such as Laura Ingraham and Sean Hannity, whereas the Democratic Party's umbrella would cover labor unions, environmental and feminist groups, and media outlets with a liberal slant (see "Extended Party Networks" below). These groups are "policy demanders" who work in tandem with party organizations to achieve mutual aims.[13]

It is tempting to close our definition at this point and to view the American parties solely as teams of political specialists—elected officials, candidates, party leaders, activists, and organizations—who compete for power and then exercise it. That leaves the rest of the population on the outside of the parties, which many citizens may prefer. Yet this would ignore an important reality: Parties are rooted in the lives and feelings of citizens as well as candidates and political activists. Even though the American parties do not have formal, dues-paying "members," most voters develop such strong and enduring attachments to a particular party that they are willing to tell a pollster, "I'm a Democrat" or "I'm a Republican," and to develop strong negative feelings about the other party. And when writers refer to a "Democratic sweep" or a "Republican area," they see parties that include voters and other supporters as well as officeholders, office seekers, and activists.

The Progressive movement of the late 1800s and early 1900s, which promoted voter registration and the use of primary elections to nominate candidates, strengthened the case for including a citizen base in a definition of American parties. Voters in primary elections make the single most important decision for their party: who its candidates will be. In most other democracies, only party leaders and activists have the power to make this choice.

Because American voters have the right to nominate the parties' candidates, the line that separates party leaders from followers in most other nations becomes blurred in the U.S. American voters are not only consumers who choose among the parties' "products" (candidates) in the political marketplace but also managers who decide which products will be introduced in the first place. Making consumers into managers has transformed political parties, just as it would revolutionize the market economy. So it makes sense to include citizen-supporters as parts of the parties, because they are not just the targets of party activity but also hold the power to tell the party organization who its candidates will be.[14]

In short, the major American parties are composed of three interacting and overlapping parts, comprising the **party organization,** which includes party leaders and the activists who work for party causes and candidates; the **party in government,** composed of the men and women who run for and hold public office on the party's label; and the **party in the electorate,** or those citizens who express an attachment to the party (see Figure 1.2).[15] We explore each of these parts separately, keeping in mind that the character of the American parties is defined by the ways in which they intersect and overlap.[16]

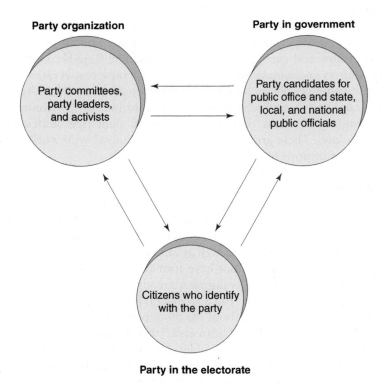

Party organization

Party committees, party leaders, and activists

Party in government

Party candidates for public office and state, local, and national public officials

Citizens who identify with the party

Party in the electorate

FIGURE 1.2 The Three Parts of American Political Parties

The Party Organizations

Party organizations write the party's rules and raise its funds. They are made up of people who hold party jobs with titles—the national and state party chairs and other officers; the county, city, ward, and precinct leaders and committee people (see Chapters 3 and 4)—and other supporters who are devoted enough to volunteer their time, money, and skills to advancing the party's aims (see Chapter 5). These groups are charged with promoting *all* of the party's candidates and its stands on major issues, not just an individual candidate or two. Some party leaders or activists may be waiting for the right time to run for public office (and thus cross over into the party in government). Others have been pressed into service as candidates for Congress or city clerks when nobody else wanted the job.

Party in Government

The party in government consists of the candidates for public office and those who hold office, whether elected or appointed, who share a party label (see Chapters 13 and 14). The major figures here are presidents, governors, judges, Congress members, state legislators, bureaucrats, mayors, and other officials who hold the same party affiliation.

Members of the party in government do not always cooperate smoothly with people in the party organization.[17] They often work together to meet shared goals, but they may have different priorities in reaching those goals. A senator, for example, may be trying to raise as much campaign money as possible, because she believes that a landslide victory will improve her chances of running for president later. At the same time, the party organization's leaders may be hoping that some of the senator's campaign contributors will donate money to other, more vulnerable party candidates instead, so the party can get or keep a majority in Congress.

These two parts of the parties also contend for leadership of the party as a whole. When reporters want to get a "Republican view" on an issue such as immigration, they will often interview a source in the White House, if the president is a Republican, or a Republican leader in Congress; these members of the party in government are often assumed to speak for the party. Leaders of the party's organization, such as the Texas state Republican Party chair, might want to put a different spin on the issue. However, presidents and congressional party leaders do not have to clear their pronouncements with the party organization, nor can they be controlled by it. These tensions and the competition for scarce resources show why it is helpful to treat the party organization and the party in government as separate parts of the party.

The Party in the Electorate

The party in the electorate consists of the women and men who *see themselves* as Democrats or Republicans: citizens who feel some degree of loyalty to the party, even if they have never set foot in the party's headquarters or met its candidates.

We call them **partisans** or **party identifiers.** As you'll see in Chapter 6, the great majority of Americans consider themselves partisans. Many of these partisans declared themselves to be a Democrat or Republican when they registered to vote; more than half of the states require citizens to register by party. Others see themselves as partisans even if they never cast a ballot.

Partisans usually support their party's candidates and issue stands, but nothing forces them to do so. In general elections, they may vote for one of their party's candidates and reject another; in primaries, they may decide to saddle the party with a candidate that the organization can't stand. However, they are vitally important as the core of the party's electoral support. Without this reliable base, the party would have to work much harder to win and keep power. The Trump presidency has offered an especially vivid example of the influence of a party's base on its leaders.

This relationship between the party organization and the party in government, on the one hand, and the electoral party, on the other, is one of the most striking characteristics of the major American parties. Other political organizations—interest groups such as teachers' unions and oil companies—try to attract public support, but these supporters remain outside the group's organization. In contrast, in the American parties, the party in the electorate is not just an external target to be mobilized. In addition to its power to choose the parties' candidates by voting in primaries, in many states, the electoral party selects local *party* officials, such as precinct committee leaders. Thus, the major American party is an open, inclusive, permeable organization. The extent to which citizens can affect the choice of its leaders and candidates sets it apart from parties in most other democracies.

What Parties Do

Political parties in every democracy engage in three sets of activities to at least some degree. They select candidates and contest elections; they try to educate citizens about issues important to the party; and they work to influence government to provide certain policies and other benefits.[18] Parties and party systems differ in the degree to which they emphasize each of these activities, but no party can completely ignore any of them.

Elect Candidates

Parties often seem completely absorbed by their efforts to elect candidates. In the 2020 elections, for instance, the two national parties raised $2 billion and employed many hundreds of people to capture the White House, the U.S. House, and the Senate. Parties are goal-oriented, and in American politics, achieving goals depends on winning elections. The need to elect candidates links the three parts of the parties. Party leaders and activists committed to a particular elected official join with other members of the party in government and with party identifiers to return that official to office.[19]

Educate (or Propagandize) Citizens

Parties also try to teach or propagandize citizens. (If you like their message, you might call it "voter education." If not, it may sound like propaganda.) They work to focus voter attention on the issues that bind the party together and downplay issues that might split their adherents. The Democrats and Republicans do not promote all-inclusive ideologies like those of a fundamentalist Islamic party. They do, however, represent the beliefs and interests of the groups that identify with and support them. In this sense, the Republicans are usually linked with business and conservative Christians, and Democrats are often seen as the party of minorities and liberals.

Govern

Almost all American national and state elected officials run for office as either Democrats or Republicans, and their partisanship affects every aspect of the way the government works. The legislatures of 49 states[20] and the U.S. Congress are organized along party lines. Although some issues may divide a party, there has been an impressive amount of party discipline in legislative voting in recent decades. In executive branches, presidents and governors usually choose cabinet officers and agency heads of their own party. Even the courts show evidence of the guiding hand of partisanship, though in more subtle ways, as you'll see in Chapter 14.

Extended Party Networks

The American parties do not have a monopoly on educating citizens, working to elect candidates, or governing. Interest groups such as the National Rifle Association (NRA), other organizations such as churches and corporations, and media organizations ranging from networks to bloggers try to affect at least one of these goals. Sometimes parties compete with these groups, even those within their own party network. For example, Fox News has been regarded as a Republican-leaning media outlet, but it drew sharp criticism from President Trump when Fox aired interviews with Democratic officials in 2019. In many local elections, groups backing or opposing a new sports stadium or a referendum on school tax rates try to influence primaries or urge candidates to run. Parties also cooperate with other like-minded political and nonpolitical organizations to achieve particular policy aims, to the point where (as noted on page 7) some observers view these groups as part of the party itself. At the least, parties often maintain long-lasting alliances with nonparty groups and some media outlets. Civil rights groups work closely with the Democratic Party and gun rights groups with the Republicans, even though the groups in this party network may disagree at times on candidates or preferred tactics.

Because the American parties' activities center on electing candidates, the party in government dominates the party to a degree unusual among Western democracies. In parties more strongly committed to educating citizens about the party's ideology—European Marxist parties, for instance—party organizations are better able to dictate to their legislative parties, telling them what to emphasize and holding them accountable for their votes.

The Effects of Party Activity

How do these party activities affect American politics? Parties help people make sense of the complexities of politics. Most of us don't pay much attention to government. Parties simplify issues and elections for us; thus, people can make sensible choices in politics even when they don't have a lot of political information, by using their party attachment as a shortcut for evaluating candidates and issues. By making it easier for citizens to form political judgments, parties ease the way for people to become politically active. They educate Americans by transmitting political information and values to large numbers of current and future voters.

The American parties also help aggregate and organize political power. They put together individuals and groups into blocs that are powerful enough to govern. So in the political world as well as within the individual, parties help to focus political loyalties on a small number of alternatives and then to build support for them. Parties also provide an organized opposition. That is not a popular role to play; the behavior of a constant adversary may seem like that of a sore loser, but an organized opposition is vital to a democracy because it has a natural incentive—its own ambition—to serve as a watchdog over a powerful government. Few of us would be willing to devote the time and effort to play this important role on our own.

Because they are so focused on contesting elections, the parties dominate the recruitment of political leaders. Large numbers of legislators, political executives, and even judges entered public service through party activity. Because they are constants in the election process, parties help to make changes in government leadership more routine and orderly. In nations where parties are not stable from one election to the next, leadership changes can be much more disruptive.

Finally, the parties can bridge the separation of powers to get things done (though they may not always choose to do so). The U.S. government was designed to fragment political power, so that no single group could gain enough of it to become a tyrant. The division between the national government and the states, multiplied by the separation of powers at each level, does an impressive job of fragmenting power. The challenge is to make these fragmented units work together to solve problems. Democrats in Congress have a motive to work with a Democratic president—their shared desire for their party to win, to achieve their shared goals—to pass legislation that their party favors. So do Republicans. Thus, the two major national parties can provide a basis for cooperation within a government marked by decentralization and division. For example, we saw Republicans in the U.S. Senate and House (and, arguably, even Republican-leaning judges) working with the Republican executive branch in 2019 and 2020 to cut entitlement programs and the Affordable Care Act ("Obamacare"), halt Democratic initiatives on gun control and climate change, and try to prevent President Trump's impeachment.

How Do Parties Differ from Other Political Groups?

We have seen that parties have a lot of competition as intermediaries between citizens and the government. *All* political organizations, not just parties, try to educate at least some citizens and mobilize their supporters either to win public office or to influence those who do win. Both parties maintain close working relationships with a variety of organized interests, research groups, and media outlets with shared concerns. How do parties differ from these other political organizations?

Parties Are Paramount in Elections

Above all, a party can be distinguished from other political organizations by its role in structuring elections. In most elections, candidates are listed on the ballot as "Democrat" or "Republican"; they are not listed as "NRA member" or "LGBTQ rights activist." It is the major parties that normally recruit the election clerks and the poll watchers, not the AARP. Hence, parties are paramount among political groups in contesting elections.

Parties Have a Full-Time Commitment to Political Activity

The major American parties are fully committed to political activity; it is their sole reason for existing. Interest groups and other political organizations, in contrast, move frequently from political to nonpolitical activities and back again. A teachers' union, for example, exists mainly for the purpose of collective bargaining for better pay and working conditions. It may turn to political action to oppose unfriendly candidates or to lobby Congress against antiunion legislation, but its interests are rooted in the workplace. Parties live entirely in the political world.

Parties Mobilize Large Numbers

An interest group, such as an organization that wants people to be able to carry concealed weapons on college campuses, does not need millions of supporters to persuade Congress to pass a bill; it may be able to succeed with only a few strategists and a well-mobilized clientele. However, because winning elections is so vital to parties' goals, parties must mobilize an enormous range of supporters to win large numbers of races. As a result, a major party in a system like that of the United States will have to address a wide range of issues; it cannot afford to represent only a narrow range of concerns. Both major parties take stands on questions ranging from health care to North Korean nuclear weapons. A single-issue group such as the National Right to Life Committee takes positions only on the issue that energizes it.

Parties Endure

The American parties are unusually stable and long-lived. Most business, environmental, and single-issue groups are mere juveniles by comparison. Both major American parties can trace their histories for more than 160 years, and many of the major parties in other Western democracies also have impressive life spans. This remarkable endurance adds to their value for voters. The parties are there as points of reference election after election and candidate after candidate, giving continuity to the choices Americans face and the issues they debate.

Parties Serve as Political Symbols

Finally, political parties differ from other political organizations in the extent to which they operate as symbols, or emotion-laden objects of loyalty. For tens of millions of Americans, the party label is a social identity, like that of an ethnic or religious group. It is the chief cue for their decisions about candidates or issues; it relates their values to the real choices made in American politics. It may help guide their choice of media outlets and even their choice of friends.[21]

Remember that the differences between parties and other political organizations are differences of degree. Interest groups do become involved in elections, and the larger organized interests serve as political symbols, too. Groups such as the Sierra Club can recruit candidates, promote their endorsed candidates to their members and friends, and get their supporters to the polls on Election Day. Other groups may do the same (see box "Factions: A Party within a Party" on page 15). Interest groups also promote issue positions, try to influence officeholders, and give money to campaigns. But parties dominate the choices in elections; candidates are listed on the ballot as representatives of a party, not of an interest group.

In some respects, the major parties have more in common with some of the larger interest groups, such as the NRA and AARP, than they do with minor or third parties. Most minor parties are electoral organizations in name only. Their candidates are in no danger of needing a victory speech on election night. They may have few or no local organizations. Their membership base may be just as narrow as that of most interest groups. However, minor parties may qualify to be listed on the ballot, and their candidates can receive public funding where it is available and where they can meet the criteria for it. In these ways (and sometimes *only* in these ways), they can be more like the major parties than the large interest groups.

Factions: A Party within a Party

Some of President Trump's strongest supporters in Congress have been affiliated with the Tea Party, known in Congress as the House Freedom Caucus. The Tea Party formed a decade ago as a protest against taxes (named after the Boston Tea Party, when American colonists threw highly taxed British tea into Boston Harbor just before the revolutionary war). Others participated in Tea Party protests to demand stronger border security and higher military spending as well as the repeal of Obamacare (the Affordable Care Act), which they considered a benefit to "undeserving" people.

By 2011, polls showed that about one in five Americans—mainly older, white, Republican conservatives—supported the Tea Party movement. The 2010 elections were especially exciting for Tea Partyers; candidates they supported defeated several mainstream Republican incumbents in that year's primaries, and the wave of general election victories put conservative Republicans in control of most state legislative houses in time to redraw congressional and state legislative districts after the 2010 Census. By 2020, public approval of the Tea Party had dropped, but the House Freedom Caucus still claimed about 35 members.

The Tea Party is a good example of a party *faction*. Occasionally, groups within a political party (in this case, the Republicans) want something they aren't getting from the current party leadership. Their goal—for the current Tea Party, major crackdowns on undocumented immigration and reductions in government-provided social services—is so important to them that they are willing to shake up the party, and even risk the party's defeat, if it doesn't meet their needs. A faction, then, is a party within a party. It isn't a hostile takeover of the organization from the outside; factions are groups of party regulars who try to reorient their party's priorities from within. They do so by contesting a party's nomination or winning control of its leadership positions, especially at the local and state levels. Tea Party activists have been working to make the Republican Party more strongly conservative.

The party, then, is both the faction's home and its target. Factions work to dominate nominations and party organizational offices, in the hope of refocusing the party's stands and priorities. So the Tea Party's success will be judged by its effectiveness in pushing the Republican Party and its candidates further to the right. Factions tend to be rare; as the two major parties have polarized, the groups within each party have come to agree more with one another on most issues. But the influence of the Tea Party has endured for over a decade, while that of the party's moderates has declined.

Sources: See Rachel M. Blum, *How the Tea Party Captured the GOP* (Chicago: University of Chicago Press, 2020; and Pew Research Center, "Trump's Staunch GOP Supporters Have Roots in the Tea Party," May 16, 2019, https://www.people-press.org/2019/05/16/trumps-staunch-gop-supporters-have-roots-in-the-tea-party

How the American Parties Developed

The world's first political parties were created in the U.S. For more than 200 years, the development of the American parties has been closely interrelated with the expansion of popular democracy. At times historically, the party in government, then party organizations, and then both the parties in government and in the electorate have taken the dominant role within the parties.[22]

The Founding of American Parties

Although the founders of the American government hated the thought of factions or parties, they nevertheless began taking sides soon after the new government was formed, because they disagreed on big issues. The dominant group, led by the ambitious young treasury secretary Alexander Hamilton, believed that the nation's economic survival required centralized (federal government) control over the economy, especially by the executive branch. These **Federalists** pushed for a central banking system and high tariffs (taxes on imported goods) to protect newly developing American industries and to help fund the federal government (see box "The American Major Parties" on page 17).

Thomas Jefferson, James Madison, and others objected. They felt that Hamilton's proposals made the federal government too powerful and threatened states' rights. Each group gathered in meetings, called "caucuses," to plan how to get their ideas adopted. During the 1790s, these alignments took a more enduring form. Their differences, as is the case now, were both principled and personal; as historian David McCullough reports, the animosity between Hamilton and Jefferson "had reached the point where they could hardly bear to be in the same room. Each was certain the other was a dangerous man intent on dominating the government."[23]

These early parties, then, were formed largely "from the top" by the people who comprised the government. They focused at first on issues that concerned the national leaders who formed them—not surprisingly at a time when most Americans played only an indirect role in politics. At this time, in almost every state, the vote was restricted to free men who could meet property-owning or taxpaying requirements. Even the relatively smaller number of voters had limited power, as the writers of the Constitution intended. The president was chosen not directly by the voters, but indirectly by the Electoral College. U.S. senators were selected not by the voters, but by the state legislatures. Only members of the House of Representatives were selected by direct popular vote. This cautious start for a democratic self-government produced very limited political parties.

Because Jefferson's supporters were in the minority in Congress, their main hope of passing legislation was to elect more Jeffersonians. They collaborated with like-minded "discussion clubs" formed in local communities to oppose Federalist officeholders. Sympathizers at the grassroots level joined in "committees of correspondence" between national and local leaders. Each side established one or more newspapers to propagandize for its cause. As early as the middle of the 1790s, less than ten years after the Constitution was adopted, almost all national

The American Major Parties

There have been only five major political parties in almost two-and-a-half centuries of American history:

1. **The Federalist Party, 1788–1816.** The champion of the new Constitution and strong national (federal) government, it was the first American political institution to resemble a political party, although it was not a fully developed party. Its strength was rooted in New England and the Atlantic Seaboard, where it attracted the support of bankers, shopkeepers, manufacturers, landowners, and other established families of wealth and status. Limited by its narrow electoral base, compared with that of the Democratic–Republicans, it soon faded.

2. **The Democratic–Republican (Jeffersonian) Party, 1800–1832.** Many of its leaders had been strong proponents of the Constitution but opposed the extreme nationalism of the Federalists. It was a party of small farmers, workers, and less-privileged citizens, plus southern planters, who felt that the state governments would protect their way of life better than the national government would. Like its leader, Thomas Jefferson, it shared many of the ideals of the French Revolution, especially the extension of the right to vote and the notion of direct popular self-government.

3. **The Democratic Party, 1832–Present.** Growing out of the Andrew Jackson wing of the Democratic–Republicans, it was the first truly broad-based, popular party in the U.S. On behalf of a coalition of less-privileged voters, it opposed such business-friendly policies as national banking and high tariffs. It also welcomed new immigrants (and sought their votes) and opposed nativist (anti-immigrant) sentiment.

4. **The Whig Party, 1834–1856.** This party, too, had roots in the old Democratic–Republican Party, but in a faction that opposed the Jacksonians. Its greatest leaders, Henry Clay and Daniel Webster, stood for legislative supremacy and protested the strong presidency of Andrew Jackson. For its short life, the Whig Party was an unstable coalition of many interests, among them, nativism, property, and business and commerce.

5. **The Republican Party, 1854–Present.** The Republicans first formed to oppose slavery. As the Civil War approached, the new party came to stand for the Union, the North, Lincoln, the freeing of slaves, victory in the Civil War, and the imposition of Reconstruction on the South. It also inherited from the Whigs a commitment to promote business and industrial expansion.

politicians had aligned with either the Jeffersonian **Democratic–Republicans** (often called just Republicans) or Hamilton's Federalists, and these incipient parties had taken sides on the major issues facing the new government.[24]

The more elitist Federalists could not keep up, however, either in grassroots organizing or in winning elections. The Federalist candidate for president, John Adams, was defeated by Jefferson in 1800, and the Federalists faded into history during the next two decades. In short, the pressures for democratization were already powerful enough by the early 1800s to cripple an infant party whose leaders in the government could not adapt to the need to organize a mass electorate. Yet the Federalists gave a historic gift to American democracy. They accepted Adams's defeat in 1800 and handed control of the presidency to their Jeffersonian rivals.[25]

The Democratic–Republicans, who were the party of farming interests, the less-privileged, the South (including its wealthy landowners), and the frontier, then held a one-party monopoly for almost 20 years. They dominated American politics so thoroughly by the time of James Monroe's election in 1816 that the absence of party conflict was called the "Era of Good Feelings." Despite the decline of one party and the rise of another, however, the nature of party politics did not change much during this period. It was a time when government and politics were the business of an elite group of well-known, well-established men, and the parties reflected the politics of the time. Without party competition, leaders felt no need to organize more fully at the grassroots, so the parties' further development was stalled.

American politics began to change markedly in the 1820s. By then, most states had eliminated the requirement that only landowners could vote. The suffrage was extended to all white males, at least in state and federal elections. The growing push for democratization also led state and local governments to make more and more public officials popularly elected rather than appointed.[26]

Another big change at this time affected the election of a president. The framers of the Constitution had crafted an unusual selection process; they specified that each state, in a manner selected by its legislature, would choose a number of presidential voters (electors) equal to the size of its congressional delegation. Collectively called the Electoral College, these electors would meet in the state to cast their votes for president. The candidate who received a majority of the states' electoral votes became president. If no candidate won a majority, the president was to be selected by the House of Representatives, with each state casting one vote.

This Electoral College was an ingenious invention. By leaving the choice of electors to the state legislatures, the framers avoided having to set uniform election methods and voting requirements. Even if the framers themselves had agreed on these rules, some states might have objected to federal control over them. (The most explosive question was, of course, whether and how to count slaves in a state's population.) Requiring electors to meet simultaneously in their respective states helped prevent a conspiracy among electors from different states to put forward their own choice for president. At first, states used a variety of methods for choosing presidential electors. By the 1820s, popular election had become the most common method.[27] Ironically, this democratization of the Electoral College was seen very differently 200 years later, when majorities in the Electoral College elected two candidates to the presidency who lost the popular vote: George W. Bush and Donald Trump.

This growing enthusiasm for popular control also raised doubts about whether the party's congressional caucus should have the power to *nominate* presidential candidates for the Electoral College to consider. Some criticized caucus nominations as the actions of a small and self-appointed elite. The congressional party caucus was losing its role as the major force within the parties as the nation entered a new phase of party politics.

A National Two-Party System Emerges

The Era of Good Feelings gave way to a two-party system that has prevailed ever since. The Democratic–Republicans had developed factions that chose divorce rather than reconciliation. Andrew Jackson led the frontier and agrarian wing of the Democratic–Republicans, the inheritors of the Jeffersonian tradition, into what is now called the **Democratic Party**. Another faction of the old Democratic–Republicans who had promoted John Quincy Adams for president in 1824 and 1828 later merged with the **Whigs** (an old English term referring to those who opposed the dominance of the king, by whom they meant Jackson). That created two-party politics in the U.S.

Just as important, the parties developed a much bigger nationwide grassroots (citizen) base. Larger numbers of citizens were now eligible to vote, so the presidential campaigns became more concerned with reaching out to the public. New campaign organizations and tactics brought the contest to many more people. As the opposition to the Jacksonians formed, presidential elections became more competitive, and voter turnout increased. Party organizations in the states and localities also expanded with the help of improved roads and means of communication. Candidates for state and local office were increasingly nominated by conventions of state and local leaders, rather than by the narrower legislative caucuses. By 1840, the Whigs and the Democrats were established in the first truly national party system and were competitive in all the states.

During the 1840s and 1850s, both parties worked to keep the bitter issue of slavery off the political agenda because it threatened to break apart both parties' supporting coalitions. Finally, the Whigs fractured on the issue and then collapsed. Antislavery activists created the **Republican Party** to demand that slavery be abolished. The Republicans then adopted the Whigs' commitment to protect American businesses with high tariffs and taxes to subsidize industrial development: roads, railroads, and settlement of the frontier. The party organized widely, except in the South and the border states, which were Democratic strongholds, and won the presidency in 1860. That led southern states to secede from the union, and the party system and the nation broke into North and South in the bloody Civil War.

In short, modern political parties similar to those we know today, with their characteristic organizational structures, bases of loyal voters, and lasting alliances among governmental leaders, had developed by the mid-1800s.[28] The American parties grew hand in hand with the early expansion of voting rights in the U.S. Comparable parties did not develop in Great Britain until the 1870s, after laws were passed to give more adult males the right to vote.

The Golden Age of the Parties

As the parties were developing, they received another massive infusion of voters from a new source: European immigrants. Hundreds of thousands of Europeans immigrated to the U.S. before the Civil War. The newcomers were welcomed by the Democratic Party, which sought their votes. But others worried about this influx of new ethnicities and customs, and an anti-immigrant minor party, the American Party (also called the Know-Nothing Party), sprang up in response in the 1850s.

The tide of immigration was halted only temporarily by the Civil War. After the war ended, new nationalities came in an almost constant flow from 1870 until Congress closed the door to mass immigration in the 1920s. More than five million immigrants arrived in the 1880s (equal to one-tenth of the 1880 resident population). Ten million more came between 1905 and 1914 (one-eighth of the 1900 resident population).

The political parties played an important role in assimilating these huge waves of immigrants. The newcomers gravitated toward big cities where industrial jobs were available. A new kind of party organization developed in these cities, called the urban "machine," to respond to the immigrants' needs. These party machines were like social service systems that helped the new arrivals cope with the challenges of an urban industrial society. They softened the hard edge of poverty by helping needy families with food and funds, smoothed any necessary transactions with government and the police, and taught immigrants the customs of their new home—all in exchange for the immigrants' votes for the party's candidates at election time. With those votes, a party machine could gain and keep control over the city's government. The machines were the means by which the new urban working class won control of the cities from the largely Anglo-Saxon, Protestant elites who had governed for so long.

The period of the late 1800s and early 1900s was the "golden age" of the American parties: the high point of their power. Party organizations, now the dominant segment of the party, existed in all the states and localities and flourished in the industrial cities. Party discipline reached a record high in Congress and most state legislatures. Parties ran the candidates' campaigns for public office; they held rallies and torchlight parades, canvassed door to door, and brought voters to the polls. They controlled access to many government jobs ranging from sewer inspectors to members of the U.S. Senate. They were an important source of information and guidance for a largely uneducated and often illiterate electorate. As a result, the highest voter turnouts in American presidential history were recorded during the latter half of the 1800s. The parties suited the needs and limitations of the new voters and met the need for creating majorities in the rapidly industrializing nation.[29]

Progressive Reforms and Beyond

The drive to democratize American politics continued into the 1900s. With passage of the Seventeenth Amendment, voters, rather than state legislatures, were given the right to elect U.S. senators. Women and then blacks finally gained the right to vote. As popular democracy expanded, a movement arose that would impose major changes on the parties.

The period that parties saw as their "golden age" did not seem so golden to groups of reformers. To Progressive crusaders, party control of politics had led to rampant corruption and inefficient government. Because many Progressives saw party power as the culprit, they tried to weaken the control that the parties, and especially the party organizations, had achieved by the late 1800s. The reformers attacked party "boss rule" by pressing for primary elections (see Chapters 9 and 10), which gave party voters rather than party leaders the power to choose the parties' candidates. Presidential nominations were made more open to the public by establishing presidential primaries in many states. State legislatures wrote laws to regulate party organizations.

The reforms did weaken the party organizations and their power in elections. When the party in the electorate gained the right to nominate the parties' candidates, the party organizations and leaders lost their most important function. Candidates could now appeal directly to primary voters rather than having to depend on the party organizations. The effect of the Progressive reforms, then, was to undercut the dominance of the party organization within the party as a whole. Therefore, the expectations of a democratic society, which first made the parties more public and more active at the grassroots level, later turned on the party organization, leaving it less capable of the important role that it once played in American politics.[30]

More recently, however, the party organizations and their leaders have created new sources of power for themselves. Beginning in the 1970s, first the Republicans and then the Democrats expanded the fund-raising capacity of their national party organizations. They used this new money to provide more services to candidates and to increase the capabilities of state party organizations. In the past five decades, the Democratic Party, through its national committee and convention, has created rules for state Democratic Parties to follow in nominating a presidential candidate. Both of these changes have strengthened the national party organizations. In fact, the national organizations probably have more of a presence now within the two major parties, relative to the state and local party organizations, than at any other time in American history. (Chapters 3 and 4 say more about these changes.)

In short, the parties have changed dramatically and continue to change. Yet they remain the leading organizations of popular democracy. They grew with the expansion of the right to vote and the increasing role of citizens in electoral politics. They are the channel through which voters come together to choose representatives and ambitious people gain positions of power. They help to clarify the alternatives on such challenging issues as abortion, taxes, and terrorism. They amplify the voices of some groups in making demands on public policy and dampen the voices of others.

What Do the Parties Stand For?

Parties have changed their stands on many issues over time, including major ones.[31] The national Democratic and Republican parties, for example, have shifted their positions significantly over the years on the question of civil rights for black Americans and equal rights for women. The traditional decentralization of the American parties (discussed in Chapter 2) has meant that party organizations in some states or local communities have taken stands different from those of organizations of the same party in other areas.

Yet there have been times when the major parties offered clear alternatives on big policy questions. The current period is one such time. Although some would argue that the parties' stands on issues are simply a means to attract votes, the ongoing competition between the Democrats and Republicans has always been more than just a story of raw ambition. Ever since the parties began, they have organized to gain power to achieve particular policy goals. Changes in the electorate and the growing strength of the national party organizations in the past four decades have encouraged **party polarization:** greater agreement on policy stands *within* each party and sharper policy differences *between* the Democrats and Republicans.

If you explore the Republican National Committee's website, the party platform, or the votes of Republicans in Congress, you will find that the Republican Party has long believed in a strong business sector. It warns that a government powerful enough to remedy individual inequalities, by creating welfare programs or guaranteeing civil rights to minorities, is a government that can take away other people's rights and property. The party's platform has long criticized the existence of a Washington "governing elite" (sometimes called the "deep state") that prevents individuals from building up their own wealth. Especially since the 1980s, it has heavily emphasized the value of religion and faith in public life.

These principles can be seen in the party's stands on many current issues (see Table 1.1). Tax cuts for individuals and businesses rank high on the party's agenda. Lower taxes shrink the government's revenue and, therefore, its ability to create new programs—a strategy that some conservatives call "starving the beast" (government).[32] The tax cuts should favor those who are wealthy, Republicans argue, because that helps them create jobs. The party stresses the importance of protecting property rights, which also limits government's ability to interfere in citizens' economic decisions.

Republican positions on other issues also demonstrate these commitments to private rather than governmental solutions to problems and to state and local rather than national and international authority. With regard to the environment, for example, the party feels that many environmental laws keep businesses

---

TABLE 1.1 Party Differences in the 2020s: Issues and Core Supporters

Democrats	Republicans
Core belief	
A strong government provides needed services and remedies inequalities	A strong government interferes with business and threatens freedom
Biggest exception	
Government should stay out of people's decisions on such issues as abortion and LGBTQ rights	Government should regulate people's behavior in such matters as abortion, transgender, and gay rights
Issue agenda	
Social services, health, education	Less government spending on social services
Taxes on high incomes permit government to provide services to the needy	Tax cuts for the wealthy can grow the economy
International negotiations	Strong military
Environmental protection	Property rights
Emphasizes	
Fairness, especially for disadvantaged groups	Individual success, not group rights
Relations with labor unions	
Close and supportive	Distant and hostile
Core supporters	
Northeast, West Coast	South
Minority groups	Caucasians
Secular individuals	Conservative Christians
Teachers, trial lawyers	Business people

Source: Compiled by the author from materials including the 2020 party platforms.

from growing. The Republican tradition defines a strong national defense as requiring a powerful military, with equipment built by private contractors, rather than as giving priority to international arms control agreements.

Over time, Republicans have been more likely than Democrats to draw their party leaders and candidates from the business community. The party has long favored restricting labor unions' power because unions, they feel, interfere with the working of the free market. The relationship between labor unions and the Republican Party is somewhere between strained and nonexistent, as evident in state legislative battles over the rights of public employee unions in the 2010s. Recent polls report that although Americans' attitudes toward labor unions are growing more positive, only 45 percent of Republicans hold a favorable view of unions, compared with 80 percent of Democratic identifiers.[33] Core groups of Republican supporters include conservatives (conservative

Christians in particular), white southerners, and people living in rural and ex-urban areas.

The Democratic Party represents a different tradition. To Democratic activists, government is a valuable means of redressing the inequalities that the marketplace can cause. These activists believe that needed social services should be provided by government rather than be privatized. Tax cuts limit the ability of the government to provide these services. Any tax cuts, they say, should be directed toward helping the needy rather than those who are more affluent. Whereas Republicans believe that the purpose of government is to promote greater individual economic achievement, even at the cost of economic inequality, Democrats feel that fairness requires reducing economic inequality, and that it is the government's job to offer a safety net to those who need it.

During the past half-century, the national Democratic Party has favored the enforcement of civil rights for black Americans. In the past 40 years, it has been the party of abortion rights, women's and LGBTQ rights, and environmental action. If property rights get in the way of environmental protection, Democratic activists contend, then property rights must usually give way. The party's stand on education, similarly, stresses the need to invest in public schools and aim for equality of opportunity. That is one reason why the Democrats are more likely to draw their candidates and activists from among teachers and trial lawyers. The core of Democratic support comes from liberals, lower-income people, those living in the Northeast and West Coasts, minorities, and labor unions.

These party differences were crystal clear in the 2019–2020 Congress. Characteristically, the House Democratic majority proposed protecting the health services granted to individuals by Obamacare, acting on climate change, allowing some undocumented immigrants to apply for U.S. citizenship, and expanding voting rights. House Republican leaders, just as characteristically, argued for spending cuts in Medicaid and other federal health programs, reducing the federal government's role in environmental issues, stopping undocumented immigration, and protecting gun rights. Party identifiers in the public were similarly divided; on President Trump's policy of using harsh treatment to keep undocumented immigrants from entering the U.S., for example, a typical poll showed 93 percent of Democrats opposed compared with just 28 percent of Republicans.[34]

Yet, even today, neither party is perfectly consistent on issues. As Table 1.1 shows, the parties seem to switch core beliefs on some issues related to "values." The Republican Party, which usually opposes government interference, asks for government action to ban abortions and same-sex marriage and to support conservative family values. And the Democrats, the party that sees government as an ally for the needy, want the government to stay out of individuals' lives on issues such as abortion and homosexuality. Perhaps because issues related to "values" affect people in a different manner than economic issues, individuals' attitudes toward abortion and homosexuality do not always align with their preferences for a strong or a weak government on taxes and regulation of business.[35]

These inconsistencies often appear when the parties try to gain support from new groups. In the case of traditional values, for example, conservative Republicans in the 1970s realized that the stands of the Christian Right on pro-life and antigay rights were much more engaging to groups of swing voters (including, at that time, many conservative white southerners) than were many of the party's economic stances. Republican candidates increasingly began to appeal to conservative Christian values. And as more Christian conservatives became enthusiastic Republican converts, their concerns rose to the top of the party's agenda.

Donald Trump's presidency encouraged another coalitional shift. Trump's nativist, anti-immigrant stance appealed to the fears of many non-college-educated whites, especially among older voters. That appeal, in turn, repelled many big business leaders who depended on international trade (and, occasionally, on undocumented immigrant labor). Trump's positions differed from a number of traditional Republican stands. Rather than promote smaller government, he claimed to strongly support extensive government involvement in enforcing immigration laws and levying tariffs on imported goods. So the main difference between Trump Republicans and Democrats was not whether government should be small or large, but who should control the apparatus of a very powerful federal government.[36] Just as the Democratic New Deal coalition included both conservative southern whites and liberal northern blacks for decades, a Republican coalition that combined bigger government spending with nativist appeals and business tax cuts could hold for some time.

These changes also grew out of the powerful impact of their environment on the parties' development. The Republican Party could begin life as a party of both business interests *and* big government because the expanding businesses of the 1800s needed government help. Building roads and other means of transporting products, large-scale communications networks, and high tariffs to protect American-made goods could be done much more efficiently by the national government than by the states or businesses themselves. Once American businesses became well established and the needed infrastructure was in place, however, a strong national government could become a threat to businesses—as it did in responding to the Depression of the 1930s—because it could regulate their operations, raise their taxes to help fund social programs, and make it easier to unionize their workers.

Parties Are Shaped by Their Environment

Throughout their history, parties' activities, their positions on various issues, and their organizations have been influenced by their environment, and vice versa. A major task of this book is to explain those impacts. One of the most important of these forces has been the nature of the electorate: Who has the right to vote?

Voters and Elections

As we have seen, the expansion of the right to vote has helped shape the parties' development. Each new group of voters entering the electorate challenges the parties to readjust their appeals as they vie for the group's support. The biggest challenge for the parties now falls mainly on the Republicans. The U.S. is rapidly becoming a multi-ethnic nation. Demographers predict that by the mid-2000s, non-Latino whites will be a minority, particularly because of the growth of the Hispanic-American and Latino-American population. Some Republican strategists have warned that to remain competitive, their party needs to appeal to this growing segment of the electorate, but the harsh anti-immigrant, anti-minority rhetoric of the Trump presidency pushed the party in the opposite direction. Can the party adapt to a changing electorate without losing its base of older whites?[37]

The parties' fortunes are also bound up with the *nature* of American elections. If you were thinking about running for office in a state that had just adopted primary elections, attracting party leaders' support would become less vital than raising money for TV ads to persuade large numbers of primary voters or earning free media coverage. These electoral institutions set the rules within which the parties compete for votes and thus affect parties' efforts and organization.

Political Institutions

The two main "rules" of American politics, federalism and the separation of powers, profoundly affect the parties. Because of the separation of powers, American legislators and executives are elected independently of one another. That makes it possible and, in recent decades likely, for the legislature and the governorship or presidency to be controlled by different parties. Many other democracies, in contrast, have parliamentary systems in which the legislative majority chooses the officials of the executive branch from among its own members. When that parliamentary majority can no longer hold, a new government must be formed. In contrast, in the American system, legislators can vote against a president or governor of their party on key issues without fearing that they will bring down the government and force new elections. As a result, American legislative parties find it hard to achieve the degree of party discipline that is common in parliamentary systems.

The federal system, in which states have a number of independent powers (rather than being "branch offices" of the national government), has also left an imprint on the American parties. It has permitted the survival of local political loyalties and traditions. It has spawned a tremendous range of public offices to fill, creating a system of elections dwarfing that of all other democracies in size and diversity. These local traditions and loyalties have nurtured a large set of semi-independent local parties within the two national parties.

Laws Governing Parties

No other parties among the world's democracies are as regulated by laws as are the American parties. It was not always this way. Before the Progressive reforms a century ago, American parties were self-governing organizations, almost unrestrained by state or federal law. For most of the 1800s, for example, the parties made their own rules for nominating candidates and also printed, distributed, and often—with a wary eye on one another—even counted the ballots. Since then, the "Australian" (secret) ballot has given the government the responsibility of running elections. The arrival of the direct primary in the early 1900s and more recent reforms of the presidential nominating process have also severely limited the parties' freedom to govern themselves.

The existence of 50 different sets of state laws governing the parties has produced 50 different varieties of political parties. Most states try to govern their party organizations by regulating their fund-raising. State laws even define which groups will be considered parties in the sense of having the right to place candidates on the ballot. The federal government has a more limited set of rules for party fund-raising.

Political Culture

A nation's political culture is the set of political values and expectations held by its people. This chapter began by noting that the American political culture has long regarded party politics as underhanded and corrupt. Recent public opinion polls show near-record-low public approval ratings of the Democratic and Republican parties and the institutions they control; in fact, one memorable poll found that a sample of Americans held higher opinions of cockroaches, head lice, and Brussels sprouts than of the U.S. Congress.[38]

These and other elements of the political culture help shape the parties' behavior. Public distrust of parties leads many candidates to downplay mentions of their party when they campaign. Cultural values affect people's judgment as to whether a method of fund-raising is acceptable or improper. Whether a strongly worded campaign ad—for instance, "Congressman X has taken thousands in pay raises for himself while refusing to support our veterans"—is seen as "mudslinging" or as "hard-hitting and informative" depends on the political values held by large numbers of Americans at a particular time, not on some set of universal standards.

The Broader Environment

Parties are conditioned by other forces as well. Dramatic changes in media technology have greatly influenced the parties' behavior.[39] A few decades ago, the media world was dominated by network television, which required party and candidate ads to appeal to a broad, undifferentiated national audience. Today, candidates and parties can use Twitter, Facebook, YouTube, Instagram, and a wide range of other platforms to reach particular types of voters. Huge databases of political and consumer information allow parties to micro-target their communications to rural, conservative Christians over 65 who favor gun rights and Social Security or to high-income, suburban, agnostic professionals between 30 and 40 with an interest in alternative energy and an aversion to high taxes. Strong liberals tend to rely on different news sources from strong conservatives, in which they can hear their own views consistently reinforced.

Economic trends in the nation as a whole can greatly affect the parties. Income inequality—the income gap between the wealthy and the poor—has increased in recent decades.[40] That increases the ability of wealthy people to contribute to parties and campaigns. Income inequality is also affected by the core beliefs of the two major parties. When the Democrats hold power, the party is likely to respond to this inequality with government-funded social services for people in need. When power moves to the Republicans, we are more likely to see tax cuts for the wealthy, with the intention of putting more money into the hands of people who can create jobs.

In this chapter, we have explored the nature of parties, what they do, and how they have developed in and been shaped by their environment. These themes will continue to guide us throughout the book. The next chapter tackles one of the biggest puzzles that students of parties face when comparing the American parties with those in other nations: Why does the U.S. have two major parties, but most democracies have many more?

Notes

1 Gary C. Jacobson, *Presidents and Parties in the Public Mind* (Chicago, IL: University of Chicago Press, 2019), p. 206.

2 See, for example, "Republicans, Democrats Move Even Further Apart in Coronavirus Concerns," Pew Research Center, June 25, 2020, https://www.people-press.org/2020/06/25/republicans-democrats-move-even-further-apart-in-coronavirus-concerns (accessed August 12, 2020).

3 Data from Pew Research Center, "Partisanship and Political Animosity in 2016," June 23, 2016, at www.people-press.org/2016/06/22/partisanship-and-political-animosity-in-2016/ (accessed August 12, 2020).

4 Marc Hetherington and Thomas J. Rudolph, *Why Washington Won't Work* (Chicago, IL: University of Chicago Press, 2015).

5 See the data at https://voteviewblog.com/.

6 Alan I. Abramowitz, *The Disappearing Center* (New Haven, CT: Yale University Press, 2010), p. 112.

7 Lilliana Mason, *Uncivil Agreement* (Chicago, IL: University of Chicago Press, 2018).

8 Jacob Hacker and Paul Pierson, "No Cost for Extremism," *American Prospect* (Spring 2015) at http://prospect.org/article/no-cost-extremism (accessed August 12, 2020).

9 In September 2019, only 4 percent of respondents expressed "a great deal" of confidence in Congress; see Gallup's "Congress and the Public," https://news.gallup.com/poll/1600/congress-public.aspx (accessed August 12, 2020).

10 See the discussion of the costs and benefits of polarization in Nolan McCarty, *Polarization* (New York: Oxford University Press, 2019).

11 Anthony Downs, *An Economic Theory of Democracy* (New York: Harper & Row, 1957), p. 24.

12 John H. Aldrich, *Why Parties? A Second Look* (Chicago, IL: University of Chicago Press, 2011), p. 297.

13 See Marty Cohen, David Karol, Hans Noel, and John Zaller, *The Party Decides* (Chicago, IL: University of Chicago Press, 2008).

14 Among those who regard the party in the electorate as central to the political parties are William Nisbet Chambers, "Party Development and the American Mainstream," in Chambers and Walter Dean Burnham, eds., *The American Party Systems* (New York: Oxford University Press, 1967), p. 5; and V. O. Key, Jr., *Politics, Parties, and Pressure Groups* (New York: Crowell, 1958), pp. 180–182.

15 V. O. Key, Jr., used this "tripartite" conception to organize his classic text, *Politics, Parties, and Pressure Groups*. Key attributed the concept of party in the electorate to Ralph M. Goldman, *Party Chairmen and Party Factions, 1789–1900* (Ph.D. diss., University of Chicago, IL, 1951).

16 See Denise L. Baer and David A. Bositis, *Elite Cadres and Party Coalitions* (Westport, CT: Greenwood Press, 1988), pp. 21–50.

17 See, for example, Bruce E. Altschuler, *Running in Place* (Chicago, IL: Nelson-Hall, 1996), p. 107.

18 See Joseph A. Schlesinger, "The Primary Goals of Political Parties," *American Political Science Review* 69 (1975): 840–849.

19 See Joseph A. Schlesinger, "The New American Political Party," *American Political Science Review* 79 (1985): 1152–1169.

20 State legislative elections in Nebraska are nonpartisan, although the candidates' partisan ties are obvious to many voters, and statewide officials (such as the governor and attorney general) are elected on a partisan ballot.

21 See Shanto Iyengar, Gaurav Sood, and Yphtach Lelkes, "Affect, Not Ideology," *Public Opinion Quarterly* 76 (2012): 405–431.

22 See William N. Chambers, *Political Parties in a New Nation* (New York: Oxford University Press, 1963), and John Kenneth White and Matthew Kerbel, *Party On!* 2nd ed. (New York: Routledge, 2017), Chapter 2.

23 David McCullough, *John Adams* (New York: Simon & Schuster, 2001), p. 436.

24 Kathleen Bawn, Martin Cohen, David Karol, Seth Masket, Hans Noel, and John Zaller, "A Theory of Political Parties," *Perspectives on Politics* 10 (2012): 591–597.

25 See John H. Aldrich and Ruth W. Grant, "The Antifederalists, the First Congress, and the First Parties," *Journal of Politics* 55 (1993): 295–326.

26 Chilton Williamson, *American Suffrage* (Princeton, NJ: Princeton University Press, 1960).

27 Neal R. Peirce and Lawrence D. Longley, *The People's President* (New Haven, CT: Yale University Press, 1981).

28 See Aldrich, *Why Parties?* Chapter 4; and A. James Reichley, *The Life of the Parties* (Lanham, MD: Rowman & Littlefield, 1992), Chapter 5.

29 See Reichley, *The Life of the Parties*, Chapters 6–11.

30 On party reform, see Austin Ranney, *Curing the Mischiefs of Faction* (Berkeley: University of California Press, 1975).

31 See David Karol, *Party Position Change in American Politics* (Cambridge: Cambridge University Press, 2009).

32 See Mark A. Smith, *The Right Talk* (Princeton, NJ: Princeton University Press, 2000).

33 Lydia Saad, "Labor Union Approval Steady at 15-Year High," Gallup, August 30, 2018, at https://news.gallup.com/poll/241679/labor-union-approval-steady-year-high.aspx (accessed August 12, 2020).

34 CNN poll conducted June 28–30, 2019, by SSRS.

35 Thanks to Charles Prysby for emphasizing this point.

36 See Nicholas F. Jacobs, Desmond King, and Sidney M. Milkis, "Building a Conservative State," *Perspectives on Politics* 17 (June 2019): 453–469.

37 Some researchers argue that the low turnout rates of Hispanic- and African-Americans will prevent their growing numbers from being translated into a proportionate percentage of voters; see Bernard L. Fraga, *The Turnout Gap* (New York: Cambridge University Press, 2018).

38 Public Policy Polling, "Congress Less Popular than Cockroaches, Traffic Jams," January 8, 2013, at www.publicpolicypolling.com/main/2013/01/congress-less-popular-than-cockroaches-traffic-jams.html (accessed August 12, 2020). Distrust of parties is common in other nations as well; see Ingrid van Biezen and Michael Saward, "Democratic Theorists and Party Scholars," *Perspectives on Politics* 6 (2008): 21–35.

39 See Markus Prior, *Post-Broadcast Democracy* (Cambridge: Cambridge University Press, 2007).

40 See Larry M. Bartels, *Unequal Democracy* (Princeton, NJ: Princeton University Press, 2008).

CHAPTER 2

The American
Two-Party System

A two-party system seems natural to most Americans. In fact, minor parties in American politics are commonly called "third parties," on the assumption that only two political parties will take up the bulk of the space in elections, in legislatures, and in party activism. So it is easy to expect that all democracies work this way.

Except that they don't. Most democracies have more than two parties—and some have fewer. Some democratic nations, such as Mexico and Japan, have had extended periods of one-party rule. Many more democracies, including most European nations, support multiparty systems with three, four, or even more parties. Six political parties regularly win seats in the United Kingdom's Parliament. In these multiparty systems, when one single party fails to win a majority of the votes, then two or more parties come together in a coalition to govern.[1]

In the U.S. as well, some states and cities have a long tradition of one-party rule. In other areas, several parties have flourished at times. Minor parties and independent candidates occasionally affect elections. Green Party candidate Ralph Nader took just enough votes in key states from the Democrats in 2000 to tip the presidential election to Republican George W. Bush.[2] As an independent presidential candidate in 1992, Ross Perot actually ran ahead of both major parties' candidates in polls early in the race. At the state level, comic country singer Kinky Friedman ran for governor of Texas as an independent candidate in 2006 with the campaign slogan "Kinky: Why the Hell Not?" (He got a lot of media coverage but only 13 percent of the vote.)

These campaigns are fun to watch; Friedman, for instance, may have been the only candidate to support both school prayer and legalizing marijuana and had written a book titled *Kill Two Birds and Get Stoned*. Minor party and independent candidacies are rarely successful, however. For most of American history, since the Era of Good Feelings ended in the 1820s, only two parties have had a realistic chance of winning any given national election. Even the rapid rise of the most successful third party in American history, the Republican Party, shows the power of two-party politics in the U.S. The party was founded in 1854, but instead of competing with the existing Democrats and Whigs, it soon replaced the Whig Party.

What protects a two-party system in American politics, when most other democracies have more than two competitive national parties? In this chapter, we look at the level of competition between the parties, the major theories as to what sustains two-party politics, and the efforts by minor parties and independent candidates to break the two-party pattern.

The National Party System

Over this remarkably long period of two-party politics, the two major American parties have been close competitors, at least at the national level. Since 1868, the great majority of presidential elections have been decided by less than 10 percent of the vote. It has been decades since a presidential candidate—Ronald Reagan in 1984—won the popular vote by more than 10 percentage points. Some of the closest presidential contests in American history have taken place in the past 20 years.

Congress was a different story from 1932 to 1980, when Democrats controlled both houses most of the time. However, since 1980, the parties have exchanged control frequently. In the Senate alone, party control has switched seven times since then—a pace unprecedented in U.S. history.[3] If we average election results by decade during the past 70 years, we find that the percentage of the two-party vote cast for all Democratic candidates has not differed much from the percentage cast for Republicans (see Table 2.1).

TABLE 2.1   Percentage of the Two-Party Vote Won by Republican Candidates for President and House of Representatives, 1940–2020

Decade Average	Presidential Elections		House Elections	
	Republican Share of Two-Party Vote (%)	Difference between Republican and Democratic Vote (%)	Republican Share of Two-Party Vote (%)	Difference between Republican and Democratic Vote (%)
1940s	46.3	7.5	49.8	5.9
1950s	56.6	13.0	48.1	3.9
1960s	46.3	7.9	46.6	6.7
1970s	55.4	12.8	44.6	10.9
1980s	56.1	12.3	46.3	6.7
1990s	45.9	8.1	49.5	4.4
2000s	49.1	3.4	49.0	5.2
2010s	49.0	2.0	50.4	4.8
2020s	48.2	3.7	48.8	2.4

Sources: Calculated and updated from Norman J. Ornstein, Thomas E. Mann, Michael J. Malbin, Andrew Rugg, and Raffaela Wakeman, *Vital Statistics on Congress* (Washington, DC: Brookings Institution, 2014), Table 2.2, for House elections; and calculated from Dave Leip's "Atlas of U.S. Presidential Elections," at www.uselectionatlas.org for presidential elections (accessed August 13, 2020).

Note: Data for 2020 as of November 19.

Both major parties, then, have shown a great deal of resilience over time. Media coverage may suggest otherwise because it focuses on the events of the moment. But whenever one party has had a string of big wins, the other party has been able to restore the balance. For example, big Democratic gains in the House and Senate in 2006 and 2008 led one expert analyst to title a blog post, "Are the Republicans Still a National Party?" Just two years later, however, in the 2010 midterm elections, Republicans won a remarkable net gain of 63 House seats, bringing the party totals in Congress nearly back to what they were in 2004. Democrats recovered in 2012, only to face decisive congressional losses in 2014, when Republicans increased their House majority to nearly a hundred-year high. Then, in the 2018 congressional elections, a wave of opposition to President Trump produced big Democratic gains. The Democrats won control of the House, while Republicans kept their majority in the Senate. Washington observers have grown accustomed to regular bouts of whiplash.

The 50 State Party Systems

Yet close party competition is limited to the national level. Increasingly, we find one-party dominance within states and localities. Most states have voted for the same party's presidential candidate in almost every election since 2000—the longest such run since the late 1800s. Only about ten states are true battlegrounds between the parties. The presidential election remains competitive nationally because the one-party states are fairly balanced by party: A little less than half have consistently supported Democratic presidential candidates, and a little more than half have consistently been safe for Republicans. Even though governors' races can still supply a lot of drama due to changing economic conditions and other short-term events, most states and local governments have become relatively safe for one party or the other.

Measuring State Party Competition

How can we measure the competitiveness of the 50 state party systems? Political scientists often use an index created by Austin Ranney.[4] This index averages three indicators of party success during a particular time period: the percentage of the popular vote for the parties' gubernatorial candidates, the percentage of seats held by the parties in each house of the legislature, and the length of time plus the percentage of the time that the parties held both the governorship and a majority in the state legislature. Like any other summary measure, the Ranney index picks up some trends more fully than others, but it gives us useful information about states' partisan lean.

As you can see in Figure 2.1, showing the Ranney index for 2012–2016, states vary a lot in their competitiveness and their partisan lean. In comparison with previous four-year periods, two trends are clear. First, a number of states took a sharp right turn after Republican victories in the 2010 elections and the subsequent round of redistricting; the Ranney index leans much more

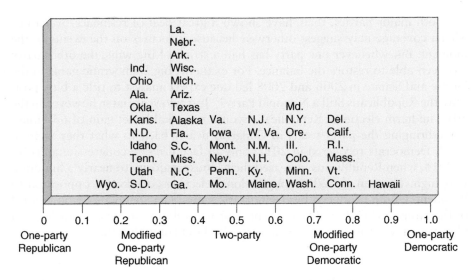

FIGURE 2.1 Interparty Competition in the States, 2012–2016

Source: Thomas M. Holbrook and Raymond J. La Raja, "Parties and Elections," in Virginia Gray, Russell L. Hanson, and Thad Kousser, eds., *Politics in the American States,* 11th. ed. (Washington, DC: CQ Press, 2017), Chapter 3.

Republican now than it did in 2007–2011. And second, the states have become more politically polarized: There has been an ongoing movement from one pattern of regional party strength to a different, but just as noncompetitive, pattern. Party change in the South and New England has driven this transition. For years a solid Democratic region, southern states have become dominantly Republican in recent decades. The tipping point occurred in 1994 (see Chapter 7). Since then, states such as Alabama have moved from "competitive" to "modified one-party Republican." The New England region has shifted dramatically in the opposite direction. Although moderate Republicans won most congressional elections in these states in the late 1900s, by 2020, only one Republican represented a New England state in Congress. The last time a Democrat won a statewide race in Texas was in 1994. A Republican last won statewide in California in 2006.[5]

Races below the statewide level, such as U.S. House races, are often even less competitive. In 2016, more than half of U.S. House primaries listed only one candidate on the ballot; that was true of more than two-thirds of the races where an incumbent was running for reelection.[6] In the 2020 elections, the great majority of U.S. House seats were regarded as safe for one party; fewer than 10 percent of House races were seen as competitive. Even in the Republican sweeps of 2010 and 2014, the great majority of House seats remained safe for the incumbent (or the incumbent's party). Competition at the state legislative level is so rare that in recent years only about 60 percent of the races had both a Democratic and a Republican candidate. In the remaining races, nothing but an occasional (and usually poorly funded) minor party contender stood between the sole major party candidate and victory.[7] And in city elections, a study of mayoral races in six states found that half the contests had only one candidate on the ballot—a decline from earlier times.[8]

The partisan tilt of the safe seats in state legislatures has shifted during the past two decades, reflecting the partisan swings in congressional elections. After big Democratic gains in 2006 and 2008 state legislative contests, Democrats lost more than 900 state legislative seats during President Obama's administration. After the 2016 elections, just as in Congress, Republicans held more governors' offices and state legislative seats than they had in almost 100 years.[9] But Democrats built on dissatisfaction with the national Republican administration in 2018 to recruit a greatly increased number of candidates, especially among women. As a result, the proportion of uncontested U.S. House and state legislative seats in the 2018 midterm contests dropped to its lowest level in half a century. These partisan swings, or "insecure majorities" in Frances Lee's term,[10] have profoundly affected state legislative actions and productivity.

Limits on Competitiveness: Incumbency

We've seen that a party's success in state-level races tracks closely with its strength in national elections, yet presidential elections are highly competitive but most congressional and state-level elections are not. What keeps the relatively close party competition at the presidential level from infiltrating congressional districts to a greater extent? One brake on competition in these districts has been the electoral value of incumbency. Although there was a lot of party turnover during the 1800s, members of Congress gained much greater electoral security between the 1960s and the early 1980s. During that time, well over 90 percent of U.S. House incumbents seeking reelection were returned to office, along with more than 80 percent of U.S. Senators. These rates were somewhat inflated by the fact that incumbents who think they might lose the next election may choose not to run again, but they are impressive indeed. Incumbents in most state legislatures were just as likely to keep their jobs.[11] In fact, the incumbency advantage increased in elections for all types of legislative and executive offices.[12]

Why were incumbents so safe? The temporary weakening of party identification during that time led some voters to look for other signals to guide their choices.[13] Incumbents' advantage in name recognition filled that void, along with other advantages of incumbency: the attention they receive in media coverage, the services they can provide to constituents, their advantage in raising campaign money, as well as their experience in having run previous winning campaigns.

The result was that between the 1960s and early 1980s, even those incumbents who represented districts favoring the other party could typically keep their jobs. But as levels of party identification rebounded and straight-ticket voting returned, these incumbents have had greater reason to watch their backs. Some observers calculate that the incumbency advantage dropped by more than half in the two decades preceding 2020.[14] The greater nationalization of voting behavior means that in an election year when national conditions heavily favor one party, the "wave" will carry into office candidates who win in districts that normally support the other party. These "exposed" candidates will then be at risk in the next election. Most of the elections since 2006 have been wave elections. The Republican sweep in the 2010 midterms cut the House reelection rate to a 40-year low of 85 percent. The losing incumbents were disproportionately those from districts dominated by the opposite party. Many of these losers were the moderate voices in both parties, as has been the case in more recent elections as well.[15] So the incumbency advantage now—in 2018, 91 percent of House incumbents running for reelection were returned to office, as were 84 percent of Senate incumbents—is more conditioned by party.

... And Other Reasons for Limited Competitiveness

Partisan redistricting, otherwise known as gerrymandering, also helps to limit party competition at the state level. In most states, the legislature redraws congressional and state legislative districts after the decennial Census. The big recent increase in single-party control of state governments has enabled the dominant party—in most states, the Republicans—to reduce the number of competitive legislative districts and increase those likely to elect a representative of the dominant party. Republican victories in the 2010 midterm elections permitted Republican state legislative majorities to control redistricting after the 2010 Census. The result was that in the latter 2010s, Democrats held fewer state legislative seats than they had since the 1920s. Another reason why gerrymandering could be seen as the culprit is that elections are more competitive in the few states where redistricting is done by independent commissions instead of partisan state legislatures.[16]

Redistricting can't be the only reason why competition has declined, because there is also less party competition for offices that are not redistricted, such as local and statewide offices. But it does give the dominant party in a state legislature a real advantage in holding and expanding its majority, as well as in improving the party's chances in the state's congressional elections. In 2016, for instance, Republicans won 49 percent of the total votes cast in congressional races, but partly because of their edge in redistricting, Republicans captured 55 percent of all House seats.

Stronger National Party Loyalties   A second culprit in the decline of party competition below the presidential level is the nationalization of congressional elections. The strong pull of the presidential race and national party loyalties makes it very difficult for a Democratic challenger to win in a mostly Republican area, and the same is true of Republican challengers in Democratic enclaves. This makes competitive U.S. House and state legislative elections more rare and states more inclined toward one-party rule. So in 2018, for instance, every state but one (Minnesota) had a single party in control of both legislative houses: 30 controlled by Republicans, 18 by Democrats.

Geographic "Sorting" along Party and Ideological Lines   Bruce Oppenheimer and others have suggested another alternative: New patterns of residential mobility can reduce party competition. As people have become more mobile, they are more able, and more inclined, to move to areas where like-minded people live. They may be motivated mainly by qualities such as an area's hip vibe or its concentration of churches, but these qualities, of course, have partisan relevance. As a result, areas become more homogeneous—and, thus, congressional districts are more likely to be dominated by one party.[17] This "sorting" (see Chapter 15) has added to the growing geographic divergence in party loyalties. An analyst found that although the 2000 and 1976 presidential elections were both won by narrow margins, almost twice as many of the voters in 2000 lived in counties where one candidate or the other won by a landslide. This suggests, he argues, that there has been a "voluntary political segregation" in the U.S.[18] It's easy to overstate the extent of this "segregation"; Americans are more likely to hold party loyalties than to actually move into partisan enclaves.[19] But the effects of sorting have made it easier for the dominant party to win elections in an area.

Figure 2.2 demonstrates the extent of this decline in party competition in House elections. A little more than two decades ago, almost four in ten House members were elected from "swing" districts—those in which both parties commanded enough voter support to stand a realistic chance of winning. Since then, competition has declined so dramatically that in the 2016 elections, a record-low number of House districts were classified as swing seats: only about one in six House districts were within a range of five points more Democratic

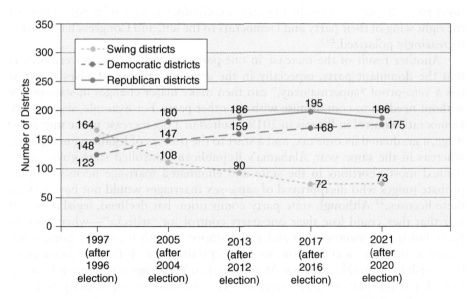

FIGURE 2.2 The Declining Number of "Swing" Districts in the U.S. House, 1997–2021

Note: A swing district is defined as a U.S. House district in which its winning candidate performed no more than 5 percentage points more Democratic to 5 points more Republican than the nation as a whole.

Source: Data compiled by the Cook Political Report in the Partisan Voter Index; see https://cookpolitical.com/pvi-0 (accessed August 13, 2020). 2020 data calculated by the author.

to five points more Republican than the nation as a whole. So in recent decades, when we have seen lively party competition in the nation as a whole, it has not been built on a lot of highly competitive House districts. Instead, it reflects a very large proportion of districts that vote consistently Democratic or consistently Republican, but in which the large number of fairly safe Democratic districts has been closely matched by the number of fairly safe Republican districts.

What difference does this make? Political competition is vital in a democracy. When an officeholder expects to win reelection easily, he or she has less incentive to pay close attention to voters' needs. In particular, the needs of disadvantaged citizens are more likely to be ignored (because advantaged citizens have other means to make their voices heard in government, in addition to voting). Further, the decline of swing districts is linked to the polarization of American political life. Because swing districts are closely divided by party, they tend to be diverse in population, so they are often inclined to elect moderate officeholders, who can appeal to both parties. The steady disappearance of these districts has eliminated most of the moderate Congress members who used to be elected in them—southern "Blue Dog" Democrats and moderate northeastern Republicans. When House members now represent districts in which their party wins by a comfortable margin, they are more likely to worry about a threat in their party's primary, where those who donate the most time and money are more likely to hold extreme views, than they are about a challenge from the other party. Republican candidates and elected officials have been pulled toward the right wing of their party and Democrats to the left, and Congress has become increasingly polarized.[20]

Another result of the increase in one-party control of state government is that the dominant party, especially in the growing number of cases where it has a veto-proof "supermajority," can then make major changes in state policy without needing to compromise with the other party. For example, single-party Democratic control in Illinois in 2019 resulted in a big increase in the minimum wage, a graduated income tax, and a start to the process of legalizing marijuana, whereas in the same year, Alabama's Republican-controlled state government banned most abortions in the state and eliminated marriage licenses so that probate judges who disapproved of same-sex marriages would not have to sign these licenses.[21] Although state party competition has declined, legislators still fear that they could lose their one-party control (or "trifecta"—when a single party holds the governorship and the majority in both legislative houses; see Figure 2.3) in the next election, so they typically waste little time in enacting their wish list of public policies. At a time when Washington is frequently deadlocked, parties and organized interests see states as the opportunity to enact major policy change.

Keep in mind, however, that because of the more competitive presidential contests, as well as frequent elections and long ballots, most Americans do experience at least one close race regularly.[22] That provides one clue as to why the U.S. has sustained a two-party system.

FIGURE 2.3 Change in Single-Party Control of State Governments, 2000–2019

Note: Lines are the number of states in which a single party controls the governorship and both state legislative houses, also known as a "trifecta," and the number with split party control. The numbers exclude Nebraska, where members of the single house of the state legislature are elected on a nonpartisan ballot.

Source: National Conference of State Legislatures, https://www.ncsl.org/research/about-state-legislatures/ (accessed August 13, 2020).

What Causes a Two-Party System?

We have seen that the American parties are durable and that, at least at the presidential level, when one party has had a run of dominance, the other party has been able to bounce back. Why have we had a two-party system for so long, when most other democracies do not? There are several possible explanations.

Institutional Forces

The most frequent explanation of the two-party system ties it to the nature of American electoral institutions. Called **Duverger's law,**[23] it argues that plurality elections in single-member districts (with no runoff elections) tend to produce two-party systems. **A single-member district** means simply that one candidate is elected to each office,[24] and a **plurality election** is one in which the candidate with the largest number of votes wins, even if not a majority. Finishing a close second, or third or fourth, brings no rewards. The American election system is, for most offices, a plurality election system with single-member districts; it offers the reward of winning an office only to the single candidate who gets the most votes. Thus, the theory suggests that minor parties will see no point in running candidates if they don't have a shot at winning.

The flip side of Duverger's law is that proportional representation in multi-member constituencies results in multiparty systems. A system with multimember constituencies is one in which a particular legislative district will be represented by, say, three or four elected legislators rather than one.[25] In proportional representation (PR), each party prepares a slate of candidates for these positions, and the number of party candidates who win is proportional to the overall percentage of the vote won by the party slate (see box "Plurality versus Proportional Representation: How It Works in Practice" on page 41). Because a party may be able to elect a candidate with only 15 or even 5 percent of the votes, depending on the system's rules, smaller parties have reason to keep competing.

However, a puzzle remains. Single-member district systems with plurality elections exist in some other democracies that support more than two parties. Shouldn't the U.S., with its great diversity, do the same? To some analysts, the nature of the American presidency helps to sustain Duverger's law. The presidency is the most visible single-member district in the U.S. It is the main prize of American politics, and only one person is elected to that office at a time. Many other democracies, which use a parliamentary system, have a governing "cabinet" as the executive authority. This cabinet is made up of a number of officeholders (for instance, a minister of defense, a minister of education, and so on), so it can be a coalition that includes representatives of several parties, including smaller parties.

In a system with a single executive such as the U.S., minor parties will be weakened because they do not have a realistic chance of competing for the presidency. That denies a minor party the national attention that major parties get. Add to that the uniquely American institution of the Electoral College. To win, a presidential candidate must get an absolute majority of electoral votes—so far, at least, an impossible task for a minor-party candidate. Because the presidency is so prominent in American politics, the argument goes, it shapes the politics of the system as a whole. Because minor parties have no chance of winning the presidency, they may survive for a time, but they will not thrive.[26]

Some minor parties try for the presidency anyway. In 1996, the Reform Party focused primarily on the presidential race. But its leader, Ross Perot, a billionaire willing to spend tens of millions on his presidential campaign, was clearly not typical of most minor parties' candidates, who can only dream of such an opportunity. In 2016, some Republican leaders and activists who opposed their party's nominee, Donald Trump, tried to recruit a conservative candidate to run in the general election against both Trump and Democratic nominee Hillary Clinton. They failed, largely because likely Republican supporters of an alternative to Trump realized that they would have divided Republican votes and assured Clinton's election. Thus, the importance of the single, indivisible executive office in the American system strengthens the tendency toward two-party politics.

Political scientist Leon Epstein has identified another institutional factor, the direct primary, as a force that prevented the development of minor parties in areas dominated by one party.[27] Primaries, which allow voters to choose the parties' nominees, have become the main method of selecting party candidates in the U.S. (see Chapter 9). When disgruntled groups have the opportunity to make their voices heard within the dominant party through a primary and may even succeed in getting a candidate nominated, the resulting taste of power will

Plurality Versus Proportional Representation: How It Works in Practice

Does it matter whether an election uses plurality or proportional representation (PR) rules to count the votes? To find out, let us compare the results of one type of American election in which both rules are used. In presidential primaries—the elections in which party voters choose delegates to the national parties' presidential conventions—Democratic state parties use PR to select delegates (with at least 15 percent of the vote needed for a candidate to win delegates) and Republican state parties can use some form of plurality election (also called "winner take all").

Imagine a congressional district that will send four delegates to the national convention, in which candidates A, B, C, and D get the following percentages of the vote. The candidates would win the following numbers of delegates, depending on whether the plurality or PR rule was used:

		Delegates Won	
	Vote %	Plurality	PR
Candidate A	40	4	2
Candidate B	30	0	1
Candidate C	20	0	1
Candidate D	10	0	0

With the **plurality** (winner take all) rule, candidate A, who received the most votes, wins all the delegates at stake in that district. So in the Republican primaries using the plurality rule, only the leading candidate will emerge with delegates; the other candidates win nothing. Under most circumstances, the less successful candidates will find it hard to stay in the race very long when they are not winning any delegates in return for their efforts. Under **PR** rules, in contrast, three candidates win delegates in rough proportion to their popular support. Therefore, in a typical Democratic primary, the less successful candidates are encouraged to stay in the race longer because the PR rules permit them to keep winning at least a few delegates.

We can see the effects of this rule difference even more clearly by looking at other nations' elections. Parliamentary elections in the Netherlands use PR, but with a much lower threshold than that of the U.S. Democrats: any party that wins as little as two-thirds of 1 percent of the national vote gets a seat in parliament. As a result, there were 28 political parties on the ballot in the 2017 Dutch parliamentary elections, and 13 parties won seats. One of them was the Party for the Animals (composed of animal welfare advocates), which won 3.2 percent of the general election vote and thus five of the 150 seats in the Dutch House of Representatives. (Note too that the voter turnout in that election was 82 percent; systems with PR rules typically prompt higher turnout than do plurality systems such as the U.S.)

probably discourage them from breaking away to form a third party. Thus, in the one-party Democratic South of an earlier era, where residual hatred kept most people from voting Republican, factional disputes that otherwise would have produced one or more minor parties were contained within the Democratic Party by the use of primary elections.

Manipulating the Rules

Once a two-party system has developed, the two dominant parties will do their best to protect it. The major parties will support election systems (such as plurality elections and single-member districts) that make it hard for minor parties to do well. Through their control of Congress and state legislatures, the Democrats and Republicans have manipulated the rules to keep minor parties from qualifying for the ballot. The major parties have no interest in leveling the playing field so that their minor-party competitors can take a shot at replacing them.[28] Further, after the two-party system was launched, it created loyalties within the American public to one party or the other (see Chapter 6).

Another challenge to the development of strong minor parties is that the major parties have been very open to absorbing new groups and adapting to changing conditions. Just when a minor party rides the crest of a new issue to the point where it can challenge the two-party monopoly, one or both of the major parties is likely to try to absorb the new movement.[29] Since the Tea Party movement began in 2009, for instance, Republicans have worked hard to keep its supporters within Republican ranks rather than breaking away to form another party.

The most important of these explanations for a two-party system is the institutional arrangement of American electoral politics. Without plurality elections, single-member districts, the Electoral College, and an indivisible executive, it would have been much easier for minor parties to break the duopoly enjoyed by the Republicans and Democrats. Other Anglo-American democracies such as Canada, which share many of the American institutional arrangements, also tend to be dominated by two parties, although minor parties are clearly more successful in these nations than in the U.S.

Exceptions to the Two-Party Pattern

As we have seen, the American two-party system contains many states and localities where one party dominates. Some areas have even developed a uniquely American brand of no-party (nonpartisan) politics. Minor parties or independent candidates have occasionally gotten media coverage. Where do we find these exceptions to two-party politics? Have they made a difference?

Nonpartisan Elections

One of the most treasured achievements of the Progressive movement was to restrict the role of parties by removing party labels from many ballots, mostly in local elections. About three-quarters of American cities and towns, including Los Angeles, Chicago, Miami, and Atlanta, run their local elections on a nonpartisan basis. Many states elect judges using a nonpartisan ballot. Nonpartisanship adds to the parties' burdens; even the strongest local parties have to work much harder to let voters know which candidates are affiliated with their party.

Removing party labels from the ballot has not usually removed partisan influences where parties are already strong. A resourceful party organization can still select its candidates and persuade voters when party labels are not on the ballot. Even where local elections are nonpartisan, local voters are still affected by the partisan content of state and national elections. Typically, however, the reform took root in cities and towns that already had weak parties and for offices, such as judgeships and school boards, where the traditional American dislike of party politics is most deeply felt. Most northeastern cities, where strong party machines were the main targets of the Progressives, were able to resist the reforms and to continue holding partisan local elections.

Beyond adding to the difficulties faced by party organizations, what difference does it make if an election is nonpartisan? Researchers had long believed that nonpartisan elections gave an advantage to Republican candidates, who were more likely to have the financial resources to attract voter attention in the absence of party labels. More recent research suggests, however, that it is the minority party in an area that benefits, because the nonpartisan ballot takes away the party cue that would remind the majority's voters to choose the majority party's candidates.[30] Nonpartisan elections also reduce voter turnout. Most voters use the party label as a helpful shortcut for making choices in elections. When this shortcut is not listed on the ballot, fewer people make the effort to vote.[31]

In an ingenious experiment, one group of researchers compared the behavior of state legislators in Nebraska, who are selected in nonpartisan elections, with those in partisan Kansas. The legislators in both states took clear stands on major policy issues, but legislators' votes on bills were not as clearly structured in Nebraska as they were in Kansas. That made it harder for Nebraskans to predict how their representatives would behave and to hold them accountable.[32] Therefore, nonpartisan elections can weaken the policy links between voters and their legislators—a result that would have greatly disappointed the Progressives.

Areas of One-Party Monopoly

In thousands of counties, cities, and towns, one party dominates public life so thoroughly that the other party might not even be able to field candidates. Where do we find these one-party areas? For most of their history, the major parties, especially in national elections, have divided the American voters roughly along social-demographic lines. (More about this can be found in Chapter 7.) A local constituency may be too small to contain the social diversity that supports both Democratic and Republican politics. Thus, we can find "safe" Democratic congressional districts in the poorer, older, and black neighborhoods of large cities and "safe" Republican districts in small town and rural, heavily white, Christian and southern areas. The less diverse its people are, at least in terms of the demographic characteristics that typically divide Republican from Democratic voters, the more likely the district is to foster one-party politics.

Alternatively, some forces may be so powerful in an area that they override the relationship between socioeconomic status and partisanship. In the classic one-party politics of the American South for many decades, racial fears, white hatred of Republicans as the party of abolition and Reconstruction, and laws and practices preventing blacks from voting long outweighed the factors that were dividing Americans into two parties in most of the other parts of the country.

Once one party has established dominance in an area, the weaker party will face an uphill climb. The winning party is likely to have the loyalty of most voters in the district. Voters do not easily change their partisan attachments, even when the reasons for the original attachment have faded. A party trying to become competitive may find itself caught in a vicious circle. Its inability to win elections limits its ability to raise money and recruit attractive candidates because, as a chronic loser, it offers so little chance of achieving political goals. For much of the 1900s, for example, the Republican Party in the South found that the Democrats had recruited the region's most promising politicians and claimed its most powerful appeals. Now, in many parts of the South, it is the Democrats who face this same disadvantage.

The weaker party's ability to attract voters locally is also affected by media coverage of its national party's stands. If the Democratic Party is identified nationally with the hopes of the poor and minority groups, its appeal in a largely white small town may be limited, no matter how attractive its candidates are. Thus, a nationalized politics may rob the local party organization of the chance to develop strength based on its own issues and candidates. To the extent that party loyalties grow out of national politics, as Democrats in the South have learned, competitiveness may be beyond the reach of some local party organizations.

And as noted earlier in this chapter, redistricting can make it harder for the weaker party to bounce back. Majority parties have found effective ways to redraw legislative district lines that preserve their advantage, so the minority party in an area must compete in districts drawn by the stronger party. This is why parties are especially concerned with winning state legislative majorities in years ending in zero, when district lines must be redrawn. The 2020 state legislative elections, then, were a do-or-die time for both major parties.

Minor Parties

In one of the many ironies of American politics, most people claim that we need a third major party,[33] but few people ever vote for candidates other than Democrats or Republicans. Only seven minor parties in all of American history have carried even a single state in a presidential election. The recent high point of minor-party strength was Ross Perot's run as the Reform Party candidate for president in 1996, when he won just over 8 million votes. Analysts speculated in 2016 that the Libertarian Party's candidate, Gary Johnson, might have a real shot in 2016 with Republican voters who couldn't stomach Republican nominee Donald Trump, but Johnson got only 3 percent of the general election vote and failed to win a single Electoral College vote.

Minor parties rarely succeed at the state and local level either. Of more than a thousand governors elected since 1875, fewer than 20 ran solely on a minor-party ticket and another handful ran as independents.[34] One of the best known was former professional wrestler Jesse "The Body" Ventura's election as governor of Minnesota in 1998. Ventura's Reform Party candidacy got enormous media attention precisely because it was so unusual, but Ventura stepped down from the governorship in 2002 after having been largely ignored by the state legislature, and the next candidate of his party attracted only 16 percent of the vote.[35] Nationally, minor-party and independent candidates for governor rarely win more than 5 percent of the vote. In 2018, the minor party and independent vote for the top office on the ballot in each state was the lowest in any midterm election in 35 years—not much encouragement for candidates to run on a minor party label.

The Libertarian Party has been the strongest vote getter of any minor party in the past quarter century. In addition to Gary Johnson's 4.5 million votes for president in 2016, Libertarian House candidates attracted 1.7 million votes. In 2020 the party's presidential candidate ran less well. The party runs candidates in many congressional races, but it has yet to elect a member of Congress. And among the more than 7,300 state legislators in the U.S., only about two dozen claim affiliation with a minor party. More Libertarian and other minor party candidates hold local offices, though most of these are elected on nonpartisan ballots, so it is not clear that their voters recognize their party affiliation.

More significantly, a minor party has sometimes shifted the balance in an important race. In 2008, the Minnesota Senate race was so close that a lengthy recount was required. The Democrat, Al Franken, finally won. The stakes were high: Franken's win gave the Senate Democrats 60 seats—in theory, enough to quash a Republican filibuster. An Independence Party candidate took 15 percent of the vote in the Minnesota Senate election; if only a tiny proportion of minor-party voters had chosen the Republican candidate instead, the Minnesota seat would have gone to Franken's Republican opponent, and the Senate Republicans would then have been assured of enough votes to block almost any Democratic legislation. However, for every example of minor-party success, there are thousands of races with no minor-party candidate. The two major parties have monopolized elections even more fully in the states and cities than at the national level. (See box "A Day in the Life: Competing Against the "Big Guys" on page 46.)

Minor parties in the U.S. vary greatly in their purposes, origins, and levels of activity.[36]

Differences in Ideology Most minor parties are driven by issues and ideologies, but they differ in the nature and scope of that commitment. The American Freedom Party and the Christian Liberty Party are very specific and targeted: the former in promoting white supremacy and the latter in favoring

A DAY IN THE LIFE
Competing Against the "Big Guys"

The Democrats and the Republicans, Brad Warren says, have a "death grip" on the American political process. Warren, a tax attorney in Indianapolis, is a Libertarian Party activist who ran for the U.S. Senate under that party's banner. "If I need a new pair of socks," he points out,

> I can go to dozens of stores and pick from several different brands and dozens of colors—for something as insignificant as socks. But when it comes to politics, which has a monopoly on the lawful use of force in our society, we have only two choices. That is tremendously scary! How do you hold them accountable? If you get angry with the incumbents, you can throw them out, only to reelect the nasty incumbents you had thrown out in the previous election. Four years from now, you'll be throwing out the incumbents you elected today. There's no choice.

Minor-party activists such as Warren must compete against the "big guys"—the two major parties—on an uneven playing field. A major problem for a minor party is simply to get its candidates' names on the ballot. The Arkansas state legislature used to permit any organized party to list its candidates on the state ballot. The American Party candidate for governor of Arkansas won 6 percent of the vote in 1970. The result? The legislature raised the hurdle the following year—to 7 percent. Ballot access requirements differ from state to state, making it difficult for a minor party to appear on the ballot in all 50 states.

"Even once you have ballot access," Warren argues,

> you will still be excluded from any meaningful participation in the election. In practice, we run elections on money, not on votes, and in presidential elections, the Republicans and Democrats divide up hundreds of millions of federal dollars among themselves.

The worst problem for minor parties, Warren feels, is getting noticed after the major parties hold primary elections.

> I got pretty good media coverage up to the primary election. After the primary, I was nobody. Even though the primary doesn't elect anybody to any office, it seems to. Primaries are a government-funded means of anointing the two major parties' candidates as the 'real' candidates and delegitimizing all the others. The media say we have no chance to win, so they won't cover any candidates except the [major] party-anointed ones. The debates typically don't include third-party candidates. Why? Because the commissions that decide who's going to be allowed to participate in debates are 'bipartisan' commissions, made up entirely of Republicans and Democrats, just like the legislatures that write the ballot access laws

and the judges who interpret them. A party that has gotten on the ballot in all 50 states, like the Libertarians, deserves to be heard.

"The two major parties won't give you any choice," Warren contends, and "if you continually vote for the lesser of two evils, what you get is evil." So what is the role of a minor party? To Warren, "It's like that of a bee: You rise up, you sting, and then you die."

Christian principles in politics. At the other extreme are socialist parties whose programs demand sweeping changes, including an end to capitalism and class privilege. The Libertarian Party wants government to involve itself mainly in national defense and criminal law and to turn over all other programs, from Social Security to education, to private efforts over time.[37] In sharp contrast, Green Parties argue for extensive government programs on behalf of the environment, peace, and social justice.

Difference of Origins   Minor parties differ in their origin. Some were literally imported into the U.S. Much of the early Socialist Party strength in the U.S. came from the freethinkers and radicals who fled Europe after the failed revolutions of 1848. Socialist candidates did well in cities such as Milwaukee, New York, and Cincinnati because of the concentrations of liberal German immigrants there. Other parties, especially the Granger and Populist Parties, were homegrown channels of social protest, born of social inequality and economic hardship in the marginal farmlands of America.

Some minor parties began as splinters or factions of one of the major parties. For example, the Progressives (the Bull Moose Party) of 1912 and the Dixiecrats of 1948 objected so strenuously to the platforms and candidates of their parent parties that they ran their own slates and presented their own programs in presidential elections. In fact, the Dixiecrats, an anticivil rights faction within the Democratic Party, substituted their own candidate for the one chosen by the party's national convention as the official Democratic presidential candidate in several southern states. If Tea Party activists were to nominate their own candidates for office, rather than try to influence Republican primaries, then they, too, could become a minor party.

Differing Purposes   Finally, minor parties differ in their intentions. Some of these parties aim to educate citizens about their issues; getting votes is merely a sideline. They run candidates because their presence on the ballot brings media attention that they could not otherwise hope to get. Many of these parties serenely accept their election losses because they have chosen not to compromise their principles to win office. The Prohibition Party, for example, has run candidates in most presidential elections since 1872 with unflagging devotion to the cause of banning the sale of alcoholic beverages even though its highest proportion of the popular vote was 2 percent, and that came in 1892. Other minor parties are serious about trying to win office. Often, their goal is local, although today they find it difficult to control an American city, as the Socialists once did, or an entire state, like the Progressives.

What Difference Do They Make?   Some argue that minor parties deserve the credit for a number of public policies—programs that were first suggested by a minor party and then adopted by a major party when they became politically popular. The minimum wage, for example, was advocated by the Socialist Party for more than two decades before a Democratic Congress passed the minimum wage law in the 1930s. Did the Democrats steal the Socialist Party's idea, or would they have proposed a minimum wage for workers even if there had been no Socialist Party? There is no way to be sure. Major parties usually propose a new policy once a lot of Americans have accepted the idea, so the party can gain votes. However, the major party might have picked up the new proposal from any of a number of sources in addition to the Socialists.

If minor parties have such limited impact, then how do they survive? To Steven Rosenstone and colleagues, minor parties result from the failure of major parties "to do what the electorate expects of them—reflect the issue preferences of voters, manage the economy, select attractive and acceptable candidates, and build voter loyalty to the parties and the political system."[38] Thus, minor parties gain support when they promote attractive ideas that the major parties have ignored, or because of public dissatisfaction with the major party candidates, rather than because many voters believe in a multiparty system as a matter of principle. And on occasion, they are helped by a major party trying to undercut an opponent, as in 2020 when some Republican organizers encouraged the presidential candidacy of rapper Kanye West, who they hoped would draw black voters away from Democrat Joe Biden.

The Rise of Independent Candidates

In some recent elections, dissatisfaction with the major parties has led several candidates to run as independents, unconnected with any party organization. The most successful was Ross Perot, who mounted a well-funded independent candidacy for president in 1992 before running as the Reform Party candidate in 1996. The story of Perot's two candidacies, one as an independent and the other as a minor-party candidate, helps us understand some of the advantages and disadvantages of each choice.

In his independent candidacy in 1992, Perot and his supporters built a remarkably strong national organization. Through its efforts, Perot got on the ballot in all 50 states. He ended the race with 19.7 million votes—a larger share of the popular vote than any "third" candidate in U.S. history who was not a former president. In fact, he outdrew the combined total of all his minor-party opponents in that race by more than 19 million ballots. The key ingredient in his success was money; Perot invested more than $65 million of his own funds in his campaign. That financed organizational efforts at the grassroots level and bought large blocks of expensive television time. Even so, Perot failed to win a single state, and much of his support came from voters who were more dissatisfied with the major-party candidates than they were attracted to a long-lasting commitment to another party or candidate.[39]

Three years later, Perot organized the new Reform Party and sought to qualify it for the ballot in all 50 states. That was harder than qualifying to run as an independent candidate. In California, his toughest challenge, Perot had to get at least 890,000 signatures on a petition by October 1995 to win a place on the state's ballot 13 months later. He failed. Using a different mechanism, Perot finally qualified in California and in all other states but found it difficult to recruit acceptable Reform candidates for other offices. On Election Day, Perot got less than half as many votes as a Reform Party candidate than he had four years earlier as an independent.

Why was his minor-party effort less successful? Many factors were at work. One reason may have been simple familiarity; some candidates do not benefit from letting voters get to know them better. Perot spent much less of his own money in 1996 than he had four years earlier. In addition, it is harder for an organization to support many candidates rather than just one. In 2000, for example, conflicts among Reform Party activists became so intense that the party's national convention disintegrated into a fistfight and the party split. (See box "Want to Run for Office as an Independent? Good Luck!" on page 50.)

Ralph Nader's experience as a presidential candidate in 2000 and 2004 was very different from Perot's because Nader ran as a candidate of the Green Party, which had already qualified for ballot access in 14 states. But when Nader tried to get on those same states' ballots as an independent candidate in 2004, he struggled. Democratic activists filed lawsuits to try to keep Nader off state ballots, because his candidacy was expected to hurt Democrat John Kerry more than Republican George W. Bush. The lesson for candidates? It's much easier to get on the ballot if you run on the ticket of a party that already has ballot access than if you try to start a new party.

Even when a minor party meets the difficult challenge of getting and keeping its line on the ballot, it will still face the enormous hurdle of recruiting candidates for thousands of state legislative seats and county offices as well as for president. The Greens and the Libertarians have made real effort since 2000 to establish themselves as organizations that contest offices from the top to the bottom of the ballot. If history is any guide, however, that is a battle they will lose. The result is that when voters consider alternatives to the major parties, independent candidates (especially if they happen to be billionaires) will continue to have advantages over those who try to form fully elaborated minor parties.

Will the Two-Party System Continue?

We can draw two main conclusions from this look at two-party politics and its alternatives. First, the two-party system is secure in the U.S. Minor parties are

Want to Run for Office as an Independent? Good Luck!

If you want to run for the U.S. House of Representatives as an independent (nonparty) candidate in Georgia, Montana, or South Carolina, you will have to get more than 10,000 people to sign a petition for you. (As a result, no independent candidate for the House has ever appeared on a government-printed ballot in South Carolina.)

If you'd prefer to run as an independent candidate for president, then you must get a total of almost a million valid signatures on petitions. Each state has its own requirements, which you will have to research and follow. In Texas alone, you'd need to get about 83,000 signatures from registered voters during a 75-day period, which ends in May of an election year, and none of the signers could have voted in the most recent party primaries. In Florida, you must have almost 135,000 signatures from registered voters by July 15 of the election year. (You'll actually need about twice as many signatures, because

Democratic and Republican election clerks can disallow any signatures they don't regard as valid.) And you'll need to counter major party efforts to thwart you; in 2014, for instance, the Ohio Republican Party's records show that it paid a law firm $300,000 to help keep the Libertarian gubernatorial candidate off the ballot.

Paid signature gatherers usually earn about $2 for each signature collected, so unless you are able to recruit a small army of volunteers, you'd pay several million dollars just to get the petitions signed and much more for the lawyers in each state who will be needed to defend your petitions against legal challenges from other candidates or parties. These are examples of ways in which state legislatures, made up almost entirely of Democrats and Republicans, have protected the two major parties by passing laws making it much tougher for minor party and independent candidates to get on the ballot.

Source: See Richard L. Winger, *Ballot Access News*, August 1, 2020, http://ballot-access.org/ (accessed August 13, 2020).

not gaining ground. Minor-party members of Congress, common in the early decades of the two-party system, have been rare in the past century and especially in recent years. Since 1952, only three members of Congress have been elected on a minor-party ticket. And minor-party and independent presidential candidates have not attracted a big following.

Some of the barriers to ballot access for minor-party and independent candidates have been lowered. And quirks in some states' election laws continue to support a few minor parties. New York is a good example; several minor parties, notably the Conservatives and the Working Families Party, have survived because state law has allowed them to nominate candidates of a major party to run under their own parties' labels as well.[40] But in most cases, candidates other than Republicans and Democrats must still jump substantial hurdles to get on state ballots and satisfy a patchwork of differing state laws to qualify for the ballot nationwide. Even when courts have overturned laws that discriminate against these candidates, the decisions have been limited, requiring petitioners to mount a challenge in each state.[41]

In addition, independent and minor-party candidates still face huge financial disadvantages. Although candidates don't need to be Democrats or Republicans to reach voters throughout the U.S. with television and the Internet, the enormous cost of modern campaigns probably restricts this opportunity to only a few highly visible or personally wealthy individuals. Minor-party presidential candidates can receive public funding for their campaign (as they do in other democracies, such as Canada and Australia) if they win at least 5 percent of the popular vote. However, in more than 30 years, the only campaign to qualify was that of Perot's Reform Party in 1996. That assured the Reform Party's 2000 presidential candidate of receiving $12 million in federal funds for his campaign. The money no doubt increased the attractiveness of the party's presidential nomination. Yet the eventual nominee, Patrick Buchanan, earned less than half of 1 percent of the popular vote.

Independent candidates for president and governor have made some elections less predictable. But running by themselves, with no other candidates on their "tickets," they are not likely to create a lasting challenge to the Democrats and Republicans. To make a sustained challenge that could fundamentally transform the American parties, these independents would need to organize to confront the major parties from the top to the bottom of the ballot. Those who try soon realize that the two-party system may not be greatly loved, but it is very well entrenched.

How would a multiparty system change American politics? Proponents could cite a number of benefits. Voters would have more choices. A greater variety of views would be able to find expression through a party platform. Smaller parties, speaking for identifiable segments of society, might give citizens in these groups more confidence that their voices are being heard. That could increase voter turnout closer to the levels seen in most other Western democracies.

On the other hand, when the threshold for ballot access is lowered, extremist parties are better able to compete. In a system where the government will probably be a coalition of several parties, voters need to anticipate the compromises that their preferred party will make to form a government. To influence that compromise, voters may cast their ballot strategically for a party whose views are more extreme than their own.[42] In contrast, votes are more directly translated into leadership in a majoritarian two-party system, though American politics, with its separation of powers, limits that direct translation now. Coalition governments can be unstable. And a multiparty system would likely require major changes in American electoral institutions, such as the single-member presidency and plurality elections. But these advantages and disadvantages are a moot point because American two-party politics remains durable.

The second major trend we have seen in this chapter is an especially intriguing one. The Democratic and Republican Parties are highly competitive at the national level. Presidential elections are won by relatively small margins, and both parties have had recent runs of dominance in Congress. When we look beneath this level at individual House and state legislative districts, however, much of the close competition disappears. The intense party competition at the national level reflects the existence of fairly equal numbers of safe Democratic and safe Republican congressional and lower-level seats.[43]

Officeholders elected in districts that are relatively safe for their party may not feel as great a need to appeal to independents and voters of the other party—and even moderates in their own party—as they would if the district were more competitive. Incumbents in safe districts face more of a threat from within their own party, in the primary election, than from the other party. These primary threats usually come from the ideological extremes of their party. As Chapter 13 shows, then, safe incumbents can take more partisan stands to ward off a primary challenger, knowing that they are not likely to suffer for it in the general election. Party polarization in Congress, state legislatures, and among politically involved citizens has accompanied this process. Even in a relatively stable two-party system such as that in the U.S., moderation in political debate can be in short supply.

Notes

1 Arend Lijphart, *Electoral Systems and Party Systems* (New York: Oxford University Press, 1994).
2 See John F. Bibby and L. Sandy Maisel, *Two Parties—Or More?* 2nd ed. (Boulder, CO: Westview, 2003), p. 46.
3 My thanks to Frances Lee for this point.
4 *Inter*party competition refers to competition between the parties, as opposed to competition within a particular party ("*intra*party"). The index was first presented in Austin Ranney, "Parties in State Politics," in Herbert Jacob and Kenneth Vines, eds., *Politics in the American States* (Boston, MA: Little, Brown, 1965), p. 65. For alternative indices, see Thomas M. Holbrook and Emily Van Dunk, "Electoral Competition in the American States," *American Political Science Review* 87 (1993): 955–962 and James W. Ceaser and Robert P. Saldin, "A New Measure of Party Strength," *Political Research Quarterly* 58 (2005): 245–256.
5 David A. Hopkins, *Red Fighting Blue* (Cambridge: Cambridge University Press, 2017), p. 217.
6 John Sides, Daron Shaw, Matt Grossman, and Keena Lipsitz, *Campaigns and Elections*, 3rd ed. (New York: W.W. Norton, 2018), p. 422.
7 See Adam S. Myers, "Explaining Increased Contestation in the 2018 State Legislative Elections," *PS: Political Science & Politics* 53 (2020): 429–434.
8 Eli Watkins, "US Mayoral Races Becoming Less Competitive, Study Indicates," CNN Politics, May 25, 2017, http://cnn.com/2017/05/25/politics/mayoral-race-competitiveness/index.html (accessed August 13, 2020).
9 Marc Hetherington, "The Election," in Michael Nelson, ed., *The Elections of 2016* (Los Angeles, CA: Sage, 2018), p. 83.
10 Frances E. Lee, *Insecure Majorities* (Chicago, IL: University of Chicago Press, 2016).

11 John M. Carey, Richard G. Niemi, and Lynda W. Powell, "Incumbency and the Probability of Reelection in State Legislative Elections," *Journal of Politics* 62 (2000): 671–700.

12 Stephen Ansolabehere and James M. Snyder Jr., "The Incumbency Advantage in U.S. Elections," *Election Law Journal* 1 (2002): 315–338. See also David W. Romero, "What They Do Does Matter," *Political Behavior* 28 (2006): 241–258.

13 Gary C. Jacobson, "It's Nothing Personal: The Decline of the Incumbency Advantage in US House Elections," *Journal of Politics* 77 (2015): 861–873.

14 Calculations from FiveThirtyEight.com.

15 Bradley Jones, "House Republicans Who Lost Re-Election Bids Were More Moderate than Those Who Won," Pew Research Center news release, December 7, 2018.

16 Jamie L. Carson, Michael H. Crespin, and Ryan Williamson, "Reevaluating the Effects of Redistricting on Electoral Competition," *State Politics and Policy Quarterly* 14 (2014): 165–177.

17 Bruce I. Oppenheimer, "Deep Red and Blue Congressional Districts," in Lawrence C. Dodd and Bruce I. Oppenheimer, eds., *Congress Reconsidered*, 8th ed. (Washington, DC: CQ Press, 2005), pp. 135–157. But see Phillip Klinkner, "Red and Blue Scare," *The Forum* 2 (2004).

18 Bill Bishop with Robert G. Cushing, *The Big Sort* (New York: Houghton Mifflin, 2008). See also Torben Lutjen and Robert Matschoss, "Ideological Migration in Partisan Strongholds," *The Forum* 13 (2015): 311–346.

19 Jonathan Mummolo and Clayton Nall, "Why Partisans Do Not Sort," *Journal of Politics* 79 (2017): 45–59.

20 Marjorie Randon Hershey, Nathaniel Birkhead, and Beth C. Easter, "Party Activists, Ideological Extremism, and Party Polarization," in Mark D. Brewer and L. Sandy Maisel, eds., *The Parties Respond*, 5th ed. (Boulder, CO: Westview Press, 2013), pp. 75–102.

21 See Perry Bacon, Jr., "What Republicans and Democrats Are Doing in the States Where They Have Total Power," May 28, 2019, https://fivethirtyeight.com/features/what-republicans-and-democrats-are-doing-in-the-states-where-they-have-total-power (accessed August 13, 2020).

22 Bernard L. Fraga and Eitan D. Hersh, "Are Americans Stuck in Uncompetitive Enclaves?" *Quarterly Journal of Political Science* 13 (3): 291–311.

23 Maurice Duverger, *Political Parties* (New York: Wiley, 1954). See also Octavio Amorim Neto and Gary W. Cox, "Electoral Institutions, Cleavage Structures, and the Number of Parties," *American Journal of Political Science* 41 (1997): 149–174.

24 On single-member districts, see Jay K. Dow, *Electing the House* (Lawrence, KS: University Press of Kansas, 2017).

25 In 1955, 58 percent of all American state legislative districts were multimember; this number had declined to 10 percent by the 1980s. See Richard Niemi, Simon Jackman, and Laura Winsky, "Candidates and Competitiveness in Multimember Districts," *Legislative Studies Quarterly* 16 (1991): 91–109.

26 See A. James Reichley, *The Life of the Parties* (Lanham, MD: Rowman & Littlefield, 2002), p. 4.

27 Leon Epstein, *Political Parties in the American Mold* (Madison, WI: University of Wisconsin Press, 1986), pp. 129–132.

28 Marjorie Randon Hershey, "How American Election Law and Institutions Cripple Third Parties," in Matthew J. Streb, ed., *Law and Election Politics* (New York: Routledge, 2012).

29 See Ronald B. Rapoport and Walter J. Stone, *Three's a Crowd* (Ann Arbor, MI: University of Michigan Press, 2005) on Republican successes in appealing to Ross

Perot supporters in 1994 and 1996; and Shigeo Hirano and James M. Snyder, Jr., "The Decline of Third Party Voting in the U.S.," *Journal of Politics* 69 (2007): 1–16.

30 Brian Schaffner, Matthew J. Streb, and Gerald C. Wright, "A New Look at the Republican Advantage in Nonpartisan Elections," *Political Research Quarterly* 60 (2007): 240–249.

31 Brian F. Schaffner, Matthew J. Streb, and Gerald C. Wright, "Teams without Uniforms," *Political Research Quarterly* 54 (2001): 7–30.

32 Gerald C. Wright and Brian F. Schaffner, "The Influence of Party," *American Political Science Review* 96 (2002): 367–379.

33 In a 2018 Gallup Poll, for instance, 57 percent said a third major party is needed because the Republicans and Democrats "do such a poor job" of representing the American people." See R.J. Reinhart, "Majority in the U.S. Still Say a Third Party Is Needed," Gallup Poll, October 26, 2018, https://news.gallup.com/poll/244094/-majority-say-third-party-needed.aspx (accessed August 13, 2020).

34 J. David Gillespie, *Politics at the Periphery* (Columbia, S.C.: University of South Carolina Press, 1993).

35 Holly A. Heyser, "Minnesota Governor," in Larry J. Sabato, ed., *Midterm Madness* (Lanham, MD: Rowman & Littlefield, 2003), pp. 233–245.

36 Among the best books on American third parties are Steven J. Rosenstone, Roy L. Behr, and Edward H. Lazarus, *Third Parties in America*, 2nd ed. (Princeton, NJ: Princeton University Press, 1996); Paul S. Herrnson and John C. Green, *Multiparty Politics in America*, 2nd ed. (Lanham, MD: Rowman & Littlefield, 2002); Bibby and Maisel, *Two Parties—Or More?*; Scot Schraufnagel, *Third Party Blues* (New York: Routledge, 2011); and Rapoport and Stone, *Three's a Crowd*.

37 Most minor parties' websites can be found at www.politics1.com/parties.htm (accessed August 13, 2020).

38 Rosenstone, Behr, and Lazarus, *Third Parties in America*, p. 162.

39 See Paul R. Abramson, John H. Aldrich, and David W. Rohde, *Change and Continuity in the 1992 Elections* (Washington, DC: CQ Press, 1994).

40 This is called "fusion." See Howard A. Scarrow, *Parties, Elections, and Representation in the State of New York* (New York: New York University Press, 1983). However, a commission set up by the New York state legislature voted to ban fusion; that would hurt these minor parties.

41 See *Ballot Access News* at www.ballot-access.org, and issues of the *Election Law Journal*.

42 Orit Kedar, "When Moderate Voters Prefer Extreme Parties," *American Political Science Review* 99 (2005): 185–199.

43 James E. Campbell, "The 2002 Midterm Election," *PS* 36 (2003): 203–207.

PART TWO

The Political Party as an Organization

The next three chapters examine the formal **party organization**—the set of party committees and volunteers who work at all the levels at which Americans elect public officials: precincts, townships, wards, cities, counties, congressional districts, states, and the federal government—and the groups of activists who give life to these organizations. How do the party organizations work, and how have they changed over time? What kinds of people become party activists? The nature of its organization influences the party's ability to act effectively in the larger political system.

American party organizations vary tremendously, from powerful and elaborate structures to empty shells. Compared with those of other Western democracies, however, most American party organizations would be considered fairly weak. Constrained by state laws, the party organizations have rarely been able to exercise much influence over the party's candidates and officeholders (the party in government) and the party in the electorate.

The three parts of a party differ in their goals. In an election, for instance, the party organization and party activists hope to support as many of the party's candidates as possible. In contrast, each individual candidate wants as much of the party's money as he or she can get, while party voters are concerned instead with taxes or immigration or cheaper college tuition. Each seeks control of the party to achieve its own ends. In the American system, party organizations find it difficult to hold their own in this competition and to get the resources they need to affect elections and promote policies. American party organizations cannot translate their platform planks into law. They must depend on the members of their party in government to do that. Party organizations must work hard to court and mobilize the party electorate, who may support some party candidates but not others.

This lack of integration among the party's component parts is typical of **cadre parties**—one of two terms that can describe the nature of party organizations. Imagine that party organizations are arranged along a continuum. At one end is the cadre party, in which the organization is run by a few leaders and activists with little or no broader public participation. These officials and activists make the organization's decisions, choose its candidates, and select the strategies they think will appeal to voters. They focus largely on electing party candidates rather than on issues. Thus the party becomes active mainly during campaigns, when candidates need their party organization's help the most. The cadre party, then, is a coalition of people and interests brought together temporarily to win elections, only to shrink to a smaller core once the election is over.

At the other end of this scale is the **mass-membership party**, a highly participatory organization in which all three parts of the party are closely linked. In this type of party, large numbers of voters become dues-paying members of the party organization and participate in its activities year-round, not just during campaigns. A mass-membership party concentrates on promoting an ideology and educating the public as well as on winning elections. Its voter-members decide what the party's policies should be and choose its organizational leaders. Members of the party in the electorate are so essential to the party organization that the party may even provide them with such nonpolitical benefits as insurance and leisure-time activities. Because the membership-based party organization has great power over candidate selection—it does not need to give less involved voters the right to choose party candidates in a primary election—it can also exercise much greater control over the party in government.

In important ways, the major American parties are cadre parties. The great majority of local and state party leaders and activists are not paid professionals but volunteers, whose party activities increase at election time. These organizational leaders do not try hard to control the party's candidates and elected officials, nor are they likely to succeed. Most party identifiers in the U.S. have no involvement in the party organization.

They do not fit the cadre mold perfectly; in practice, parties have a tendency to slip out of precise definitions.[1] For example, U.S. party leaders contact their supporters in the electorate more often now than they did a few decades ago, and the state and national party organizations are active year-round. Nevertheless, these changes have not made the major American parties into mass-membership organizations. The major parties concentrate on electing candidates more than on educating voters on issues.

Why does it matter whether party organizations are strong or weak, cadre or mass membership? Because party organizations are the backbone of the political parties. They are the sector of the parties that provides continuity, while the party's candidates, elected officials, and identifiers come and go. A strong party organization can hunt for the resources needed for long-term election success. It can provide voters with choices and candidates with expertise. When the organization is weak, a power vacuum develops that may be filled by interest groups, ambitious individuals, or unending conflict.

As the American party organizations have become more robust in recent years, they have altered our politics in ways ranging from campaign fundraising to the nature of political debate. Chapter 3 begins by exploring the party organizations closest to you: state and local parties.

Note

1 See Alan Ware, ed., *Political Parties* (New York: Basil Blackwell, 1987).

CHAPTER 3

State and Local Party Organizations

Statistically speaking, you are more likely to become an elected official in the U.S. than you are to become a school principal, a chief executive officer, a veterinarian, or a career firefighter. Americans elect more than 500,000 public offices in the U.S., and all but 537 are in state and local governments. State and local party organizations help to raise funds, attract volunteers, and publicize their candidates for all these state legislative, city council, county treasurer, and other elected posts. Even candidates for national office, such as Joe Biden and Donald Trump in 2020, must pay special attention to the health of the state and local parties' field organizations. Why? These are the organizations where much of the voter mobilization takes place. The stronger these party organizations, the more effectively they can mobilize support.

Yet in recent decades, battles between mainstream groups and insurgents have riddled many of these party organizations. In particular, evangelical groups and business-oriented factions have struggled for control over many state Republican parties. These splits worry national Republican leaders and presidential candidates, whose hopes for the future direction of their party are at stake. They also suggest that the state and local parties are important enough to party activists to be worth fighting for.

State and local party organizational power has shifted markedly over time. In the late 1800s, many urban party organizations functioned as political "machines," which controlled city governments by bringing lots of new immigrants to the polls to vote for their party. Just a few decades later, a variety of forces had drained the strength of these party machines, and most party organizations had become weak or inactive. Since that time, and coinciding with the national parties' growing strength, party organizations have revived at all levels and become a major presence on the Internet. State and local parties, in short, have been on a wild ride during the past century—demonstrating their ability to adapt even to major changes in the American political environment.

In turn, these changes in party strength have profoundly affected American politics. As noted in the introduction to Part II, the party organization is the foundation of a political party. It gives the party a way to endure, despite a changing cast of candidates and elected officeholders. More than the party in government or party identifiers, party organizations are the keepers of the parties' brands—the unifying labels and ideas that give candidates a shortcut in identifying themselves to voters and that give voters a means to choose among candidates. Without this organization, a party becomes only an unstable alliance of convenience among candidates, and between candidates and groups of voters—too changeable to accomplish the important work that parties can perform in a democracy.

This chapter will trace these tumultuous changes in the state and local party organizations. After considering how to measure "party strength," we will begin by exploring the evolution of local party organizations from the fabled political machines that dominated a number of eastern and Midwestern cities beginning in the late 1800s and early 1900s to the fall and rise of local parties more recently. Finally, we will see how state parties grew from weakness to greater strength in the past four decades.

What Is a "Strong" Party?

How can a "strong" party be defined? Many researchers measure a party's vigor by examining its organizational features. Stronger parties would have larger budgets and more full-time, paid staff members, which can be termed **party organizational strength.**

There are other ways to measure party strength. A strong party would work effectively to register voters, tell them about party candidates, and get them to the polls on Election Day. It would be successful in filling its ticket with attractive candidates. Its candidates would win more races than they lose. We could even measure whether the party is able to get its platform enacted into law (as we will in Chapter 15). But for a party to do these things—and especially to register voters, canvass, and get out the vote (GOTV)—it needs money, staff, and other forms of organizational strength. We will look at most of these measures of party strength in this chapter but focus mainly on party organizational strength.

How States Regulate Parties

Most states reflect the traditional American suspicion of political parties by extensively regulating their party organizations. State laws often tell parties how they must choose their candidates, who can sign a party's petition to get on the ballot, even the types of public buildings in which parties must hold their conventions. Party committees are regulated "lightly" in only about a third of the states, most of them in the South, Plains, and the upper Midwest.[1] At the other extreme, in 15 states—including California, New Jersey, and Ohio—lawmakers have chosen to control almost every detail of the parties' activities.

Even the most picky state restrictions have not necessarily weakened the parties. Some of the strongest party organizations in the nation are also the most tightly regulated. In fact, all these state laws help protect the Democratic and Republican parties against competition from minor parties. However, they do give state governments a set of tools for keeping an eye on their parties. They indicate as well that state law does not view the parties simply as private groups. As Leon Epstein argued, the major parties are seen as public utilities that can be subject to a great deal of state direction.[2] Congress, too, has passed several laws since the 1970s regulating national party organizations' campaign fund-raising.

States don't have complete freedom to make rules for their party organizations. Federal courts have frequently stepped in to protect citizens' voting rights (see Chapter 8), to keep the states from unreasonably limiting minor-party and independent candidates' ballot access (see Chapter 2), and to acknowledge the parties' right to control their internal affairs. In the 1980s, for example, the Supreme Court ruled that the state of Connecticut could not prevent the Republican Party from opening up its primary to independents if it wanted to. Soon after, the Court threw out a California law saying, among other things, that parties could not endorse candidates in primary elections. A 2000 Supreme Court decision overturned a California state initiative setting up a "blanket primary" on the ground that it violated the party organization's First Amendment right to decide who votes in its primaries.[3] Nevertheless, American party organizations are more heavily regulated than are parties in other democracies.

Levels of Party Organization

Americans elect officeholders at different levels: county, state, national. Party organizations follow the same pattern. This structure is often pictured as a pyramid based in the grassroots and stretching up to the statewide organization. A pyramid, however, gives the misleading impression that the layer at the top can give orders to the layers below. So picture these party organizations, instead, as they fit into a geographic map (Figure 3.1).

Local Party Committees

The county is the main unit of local party organization in most states, because so many important local officials are elected at the county level, and usually in partisan elections: sheriffs, prosecutors, clerks, judges, council members, treasurers, assessors, surveyors, coroners, and more. These officials control vital functions ranging from policing the area to assessing and collecting property taxes. Party organizations at the county level, which support candidates for these offices, are the parties' "grassroots," where most of the activity of party volunteers takes place. In a few states, local parties are organized at the town, state legislative, or congressional district level.

In most areas, counties are divided into smaller units called precincts. Each precinct (or town, township, or ward, in some areas) in theory has a party leader—a committeeman and/or committeewoman—to conduct the party's activities in that area. Because there are about 193,000 precincts in the U.S., it would be easy to imagine a vibrant party base made up of at least 200,000 committed men and women. However, this exists only in the dreams of party

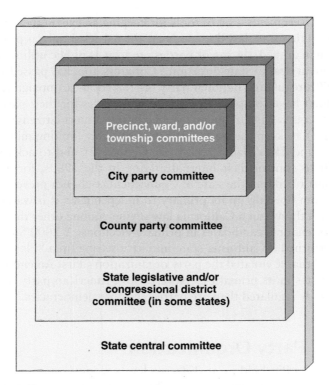

FIGURE 3.1 The Party Organization in a Typical State

leaders; in reality, up to half of these (unpaid) local committee positions are vacant because nobody volunteers to serve in them.

Most precinct committeemen and women are chosen at local party caucuses or in primary elections. Party caucuses are meetings in the precincts and wards that are open to any voters in the area who consider themselves affiliated with the party. These local party supporters elect the precinct committee leaders and often elect delegates to county and/or state conventions as well. In states that choose precinct committeemen and women in primaries, any voter may nominate him- or herself for the job by filing a petition signed by a handful of local voters. If, as often happens, there are no nominees, the committeeman or woman may be elected by an even smaller handful of write-in votes. These local committee positions, in short, are not normally in great demand, especially in the weaker party in an area. So the local parties are far from being exclusive clubs; their "front doors" are open to anyone who chooses to walk in.

What do these precinct and county party leaders do? Their three most important jobs are *registering new voters, going door-to-door (called "canvassing" or "D2D") to talk to potential supporters about the party's candidates, and getting voters to the polls (known as "GOTV," or "get out the vote")*. They need to recruit volunteers to help with these labor-intensive tasks. County party leaders may also try to raise money to support local candidates, and when there are vacancies on the party ticket—offices for which nobody wanted to run in the primary election—then the local party committees may be responsible for appointing someone to run. In the less active local parties, these tasks may not get done. The precinct committeemen and women usually come together to make up the next level of local party organization, or they elect the delegates who do.

State Central Committees

At the state level, the party organization is usually called the state central committee. The state parties typically help to recruit candidates for statewide offices (for instance, state treasurer and attorney general) and state legislative seats, help in training them, and raise money to support their campaigns. They may also work with local parties on the crucial tasks of voter registration, canvassing, and GOTV.

State law usually gives party central committees a number of other important powers: the responsibility for organizing party conventions, drafting party platforms, supervising the spending of party campaign funds, and selecting the party's presidential electors, representatives to the national committee, and some of the national convention delegates. In some states, the party's statewide convention has these powers instead. In a few states, such as Indiana, the party's state convention actually nominates candidates for some statewide offices, a reminder of the power that party conventions held in the days before primary elections.

We can draw four important conclusions from these organizational patterns. First, the levels of party organization have been set up to correspond to the voting districts in which citizens choose public officials in that state (for example, county and congressional districts), and the main responsibility of these organizations under state law is to contest elections. State laws, then, see party organizations as helpers in the state's task of holding nominations and elections—tasks that before the twentieth century belonged almost entirely to the parties alone.

Second, the laws indicate that state legislators are ambivalent about what constitutes a party organization. Many of these laws treat parties as cadre organizations (see page 55) run by a small number of party officials. Yet when they specify that the party's own officials, including local committeemen and women, must be chosen in a primary election, this gives party voters—and potentially, any voters—a vital, quasi-membership role in the party organization. Therefore, state laws help to create a party that is semipublic, rather than a genuinely private group whose active members choose its leaders and set its direction.

Third, party organizations in one state or locality can behave differently from party organizations in another area. One state's Democratic Party may use a primary election to choose a presidential nominee; another state's Democratic organization might choose a caucus instead. One state's Republican Party may use a winner-take-all system (see Chapter 2) to make that choice; another state's Republican organization might use a more proportional system.

Finally, one reason for these differences among state parties is that the American party organizations are not a hierarchy, in which the lower levels take their orders from the higher levels. Instead, through much of their history, the parties were best described as "a system of layers of organization,"[4] or as a "stratarchy,"[5] in which each level has some independent power. In fact, power traditionally flowed from the bottom to the top in the local and state parties.[6] Thus, party organizations remain fairly decentralized and rooted in local politics, even in the face of recent trends toward stronger state and national committees.

The Legendary Party Machines

In the U.S., local party organizational strength peaked in the late 1800s and early 1900s, when the urban political "machine" reached the height of its power. By some accounts, most American cities were governed by machines at this time.[7] The party machine was a disciplined organization that controlled the nominations to elective office. It had the hierarchical structure that today's local parties lack. It relied on material incentives—giving out jobs and favors—to build support among voters. Above all, it controlled the government in a city or county.

Yet, for all their power in shaping how we think of party organizations, the great urban machines were not found in all cities, and they gradually disappeared. The decline began in the 1930s, and almost all were gone by the 1960s and 1970s. These "traditional party organizations"[8] were brought down by a number of forces. Some party machines, such as those in Pittsburgh and New York, never recovered from election upsets by middle-class reformers. Others, including those in Philadelphia and Gary, Indiana, lost power when racial tensions overshadowed the old ethnic politics.[9]

How the Party Machines Developed

In the late 1800s, large numbers of immigrants arriving in major American cities had urgent economic and social needs. These newcomers were poor, often spoke no English, and faced a difficult adjustment to their new urban environment. Party leaders in many of these cities—usually Democrats, reflecting the party's history of openness to immigrants—saw the opportunity for a mutually profitable exchange. The immigrants needed jobs, social services, and other benefits that a city government could provide.

The party leaders needed a large number of votes to gain control of city government. If the party could register these new arrivals to vote, their votes could put the party in power. In return, the party would then control the many resources that were available to the government and could give the new voters the help they needed so desperately.

Jobs ranked high among the newcomers' needs. So the most visible benefits offered by party machines were **patronage** jobs in the city government—those awarded on the basis of party loyalty rather than other qualifications. During the glory days of the machine, thousands of these patronage positions were at the machines' disposal. By giving patronage jobs to party supporters, the party's leaders could be assured that city workers would remain loyal to the machine and work to help it win elections by delivering not only their own votes but those of their family, friends, and neighbors as well. After all, if the party lost the election, then these patronage workers would lose their jobs.

In its prime, many decades ago, the Chicago Democratic machine controlled an estimated 35,000 patronage government jobs and influenced hiring for another 10,000 jobs in the private economy. Adding the families and friends of these jobholders, the party machine could deliver 350,000 motivated voters at election time. Local party workers also won voter loyalties by finding social welfare agencies for the troubled or providing deliveries of coal to the poor. Machine leaders, called "bosses," attended weddings and wakes, listened to job seekers and business executives, bailed out drunks, and helped the hungry and homeless.

The machine had favors to offer local businesses as well. Governments purchase many goods and services from the private sector. If a bank wanted to win the city's deposits, it could expect to compete more effectively for the city's business if it were willing to contribute to the party machine. Insurance agents and lawyers who wanted city contracts, newspapers that printed city notices, even suppliers of soap to city bathrooms were motivated to donate money or services to the party machine. In addition, city governments regularly make decisions that affect individuals' and businesses' economic standing, such as issuing building permits and conducting health inspections. If you were helped by one of these decisions, you could expect the machine to ask for your thanks in the form of contributions. These so-called **preferments** could be used effectively to build political power.

How Machines Held on to Power

The classic urban machine, then, was not just a party organization but also an "informal government," a social service agency, and a ladder for upward social and economic mobility. In some ways, it looked like the local organization of a European mass-membership party, except that the American machine had little or no concern for ideology. Its world was the city; it focused on the immediate needs of its constituents, and its politics were almost completely divorced from the issues that animated national politics.

An important source of the machines' strength was their ability to appeal to ethnic loyalties. Although there were party machines in cities without large immigrant populations, the rise and fall of the American political machine is closely linked to changes in ethnic-group migration to big cities. The machine was a method by which ethnic groups, especially the Irish, gained a foothold in American politics.[10]

Machines could create a "designer electorate" by using force and intimidation to keep their opponents from voting. Because the party machines controlled the election process, it was possible, in a pinch, to change the election rules and even to count the votes in a creative manner. One of the indispensable tools of rival party workers in Indianapolis, for example, was a flashlight—to locate bal-lots that did not support the dominant party's candidates and happened to fly out of the window at vote-counting headquarters in the dark of night.

Machine politics was most likely to flourish in the big cities, but American party machines took root in other areas as well. The conditions that led to the development of machines, especially a large, parochially oriented population with immediate economic needs, were also found in small southern and one-company towns. Even some well-to-do suburbs have spawned strong machine-style party organizations. In the affluent Long Island suburbs of New York City, for example, a Republican Nassau County political machine dominated by Italian Americans controlled local government for generations before losing its power in the 1990s.[11]

We cannot be certain how powerful party machines really were, even at their strongest. A Chicago study found, for example, that the party machine distributed public services mainly on the basis of historical traditions and bu-reaucratic decision rules rather than to reward its political supporters.[12] In New Haven, researchers reported that the party machine was more concerned about ethnic loyalties than its own survival. The machine, led by Italian Americans, distributed summer jobs disproportionately to Italian kids from nonmachine wards, who rarely took part in later political work, and not to kids from strong machine areas.[13]

During the 1900s, however, the conditions that helped sustain party ma-chines waned. Political reforms took away most of the patronage jobs that used to reward the party faithful. People get government jobs now by scoring well on civil service exams, not by supporting party candidates. Federal entitlement pro-grams, such as food stamps and Social Security, reduced the need for the favors that party machines could provide. Economic growth has boosted many Amer-icans' income levels and reduced the attractiveness of the remaining patronage jobs; the chance to work as a sewer inspector just isn't as alluring as it once may have been. Higher education levels have increased people's ability to fend for themselves in a complex bureaucratic society, and in many areas, racial divisions have overwhelmed the machine's ability to balance competing ethnic groups. (Yet machines have maintained their power over Americans' *perceptions* of pol-itics; see box, "Political Machines and Dinosaurs: Extinct But Ever-Present," on page 65.)

Local Party Organizations Declined and Then Rebuilt

After the machines failed, local party organizations weakened. By the mid-1900s, many city and county parties were starved for leadership, money, and volunteers. Then, local organizations began to rebuild, but the new local parties were no longer as capable of *running* campaigns as the traditional machines had been. Instead, they focused on providing services to candidates.

Political Machines and Dinosaurs:
Extinct But Ever-Present

If the urban party machines and their political "bosses" are gone now, why do so many people still believe they exist? The notion of an all-powerful party boss making deals in a smoke-filled room has become part of American political legend. From TV dramas such as *House of Cards* to classic movies such as *All the King's Men*, writers have elevated the urban party leaders of the late 1800s and early 1900s into icons of ruthless power.

There's just one problem. The conditions that produced the party machines are gone, and with them, the dominance of urban (or state or national) political "bosses." In those earlier times, when waves of western and eastern European immigrants flooded big American cities, party machines arose to meet those immigrants' needs—for guaranteed jobs, financial help, and adaptation to their unfamiliar surroundings—in exchange for the new residents' votes on Election Day. Enter the Progressive reformers: Patronage jobs were largely replaced by civil

service exams, machine help gave way to government social service programs, and the absorption of new residents has become complicated by racial politics. Local party leaders no longer choose candidates for office; voters in primary elections do. And in national politics, if party leaders actually had the power of bosses, then Donald Trump, who was not endorsed by a single Republican Party leader or elected official until he had won a lot of state primaries, would not have become the Republican presidential candidate in 2016. (Republican party leaders did develop fervent support for Trump, of course, but only *after* he had become the favorite of a plurality of grassroots Republican identifiers.)

Local (and national) party leaders would probably love to have the authority and resources that they are commonly assumed to possess. Like the dinosaurs, the niche once held by party bosses and machines is gone, but they seem to live forever in popular culture.

Local Parties in the 1970s

We got the first comprehensive look at the nature of local party organizations in a 1979–1980 survey of several thousand county leaders (see Table 3.1).[14] The results showed the distinctive fingerprints of cadre parties, and fairly weak ones at that. The researchers found that most county organizations were headed by a volunteer party chair and executive committee; almost none were paid for their efforts. Not many of these local party leaders had even the most basic forms of organizational support, such as a regular budget, a paid staff, a year-round office, or a listed telephone number. Most did meet regularly and tried to recruit and raise money for candidates. Their activity peaked during campaigns and then dropped off.

TABLE 3.1 **Changes in Local Parties' Organizational Strength**

The local party organization has (in %)	Democrats		Republicans	
	1980	2019	1980	2019
A complete or nearly complete set of officers	90	85	81	88
A year-round office	12	22	14	16
A website	–	67	–	59
Some paid staff members				
Full-time	3	2	4	2
Part-time	5	4	6	3
A regular annual budget	20	29	31	26
A campaign headquarters	55	41	60	38
Campaign activities				
Door-to-door canvassing	49	77	48	55
Arranged fund-raising events	71	70	68	63
Contributed money to candidates	62	56	70	57
Distributed posters or lawn signs	59	82	62	82
Used public opinion polls	11	5	16	9
Conducted voter registration drives	56	54	45	33
Used social media	–	74	–	67
Helped candidates raise money online	–	21	–	14

Note: 1979–1980 figures are based on responses from 2,021 Democratic and 1,980 Republican organizations to a mail survey; 2019 data are from an Internet survey of local party chairs in 49 states, with responses from 349 Republicans and 711 Democrats. 2019 data were generously provided by Douglas D. Roscoe and Shannon Jenkins as an update to their book, *Local Party Organizations in the Twenty-First Century* (Albany, NY: SUNY Press, 2016).

Sources: John Frendreis and Alan R. Gitelson, "Local Parties in the 1990s," in John C. Green and Daniel M. Shea, The State of the Parties, 3rd ed. (Lanham, MD: Rowman & Littlefield, 1999), pp. 138–139 (for 1980), and Roscoe and Jenkins (for 2019).

Democratic local parties didn't differ much from Republican local parties in the overall strength of their organizations during the 1970s, but states differed a great deal in the organizational strength of their local parties. Some states in the East and Midwest had relatively strong local organizations in both parties, while others—Louisiana, Georgia, Alabama, Kentucky, Texas, and Nebraska— had weak parties at the county level. In a few states, such as Arizona and Florida, one party was much stronger than the other party at the local level, but most often, strong organizations of one party were matched with strong organizations in the other party.[15]

There is persuasive evidence, however, that county party organizations in 1980 were in the middle of a growth spurt. In a 1984 survey, researchers found that most local parties had become much more involved in the nuts-and-bolts activities of registering voters, raising money, and publicizing candidates. A national survey in 1988 indicated even higher levels of local party activity.[16] This was happening as national party politics was becoming more polarized (see Chapter 7), which may have motivated local activists to re-energize their party organizations.

Local Parties Today: More Active, Especially Online

Local party organizations continue to develop, though they are still not very highly structured. Typically, they function only during the campaign season, and they rely on unpaid volunteers; paid staff members are rare. Fewer than half the local parties have so much as a campaign headquarters, though their online presence is growing, but their organizational effort has increased somewhat in the past few decades. Especially in urban areas, more county parties in the 2020s had the basic ingredients for a viable party organization (such as a permanent office) than in 1980.[17]

What do they do? Most county parties report that they concentrate on labor-intensive grassroots activities: canvassing, voter contact by email, and distributing lawn signs and literature; and again, more local parties report conducting these activities now than they did in 1980. In particular, county parties are increasing their use of the Internet, including social media such as Twitter and Facebook. Websites, which can be more accessible to prospective volunteers than are local headquarters, especially during the corona virus pandemic, are a boon to local parties, but their use of the more costly activities—giving money to candidates, running ads, using polling data—has declined.

Recently, many county party leaders have stepped up their efforts to promote absentee and early voting. By 2008, most states had relaxed their requirements for casting an absentee ballot. Large numbers of people can now vote by mail or in person before Election Day (see Chapter 8). To take advantage of these changes, many local parties now mail absentee ballot requests to all known party voters. By working to "bank" as many loyalists' votes as possible, the party organization can protect itself against last-minute shocks or Election Day thunderstorms that might depress the party vote. Local parties can spread their GOTV efforts over several weeks and then focus their Election Day activities on mobilizing less involved voters. This became especially important – and controversial—when the pandemic in 2020 led many voters to avoid crowded polling places. As a result, voting by mail expanded tremendously, and President Trump, worried about a Democratic surge in mail ballots, endorsed new rules that slowed mail delivery (see Chapter 8).

Local parties have also expanded their efforts to recruit candidates.[18] One study found that congressional candidates are more likely to stay in the nomination race if they have the backing of party leaders.[19] In another study, more than a third of people regarded as potentially strong candidates for Congress had in fact been contacted by local party leaders, and those contacted were more likely to run.[20]

Not many local party organizations put a priority on mobilizing young voters,[21] in part because people under 30 usually have low voter turnout rates.

And some local party activities have declined in recent decades. The main decline has been in activities that require funding; local parties often have limited success in raising money on their own, and since BCRA (see Chapter 12), national and state party organizations find it much harder to transfer money to local parties. State parties are more likely to provide assistance such as campaign training and legal advice than cash.[22] But more local parties have been energized and communicate with voters.

Michigan's Democratic Party provides an example of these changes in party organizational strength. Michigan Democrats, long the minority party, were in sorry shape for the first half of the 1900s, after machine politics had faded. By the end of the 1940s, more than half of the state's counties had no Democratic county committees. Then, labor unions, led by the United Auto Workers, stepped in to bring volunteer and financial support to the Democrats. Within two years, there was a Democratic Party organization in almost every county in the state. After internal conflicts took their toll in both parties during the 1960s and 1970s, organized labor moved again to rebuild the Democratic organization. By the late 1990s, the great majority of local Democratic Party organizations were raising money and contributing to candidates, buying ads, and distributing literature.[23] Their resurgence has continued, though they face an uphill fight against Michigan's Republican organizations.

In sum, county party organizations are somewhat stronger and more active now than they were a generation ago, though their activity tends to ramp up mainly around elections. Local parties are especially active in urban, better-educated communities where residents have stronger social connections and canvassing is more convenient.[24] It is harder to determine whether county parties today are as effective organizationally as were the old city machines, because there are so few reliable records prior to the 1960s, but it is possible that some counties now have more robust party organizations than they have ever had, especially due to the availability of online communications.

At the same time, however, the nature of the local parties has changed. From organizations that once were at the very center of election activity, county parties have become service providers to candidates who often have several other sources of help. Parties provide labor in the form of volunteers, but they are no longer a major source of campaign funds. So the challenge for the local parties is this: In an age of largely candidate-centered campaigns, does this county organizational presence matter as much as it would have a few decades ago?[25]

State Parties: Gaining Money and Services

Throughout the parties' history, the state committees rarely had significant power within party organizations. There have been exceptions: Some powerful, patronage-rich state party organizations developed in the industrial heartland in the late 1800s.[26] But in most states, most of the time, the state committee was the weak link in the party organization. Yet in recent years, state parties have grown in importance. They are richer, more professional, and more active now, though they face major challenges from non-party groups and restrictive campaign finance laws. Let us start the story in the years before these changes began.

Traditional Weakness

State party organizations were traditionally weak for several reasons. They began as loose federations of semi-independent local party chairs. If one of these factions gained control over the state party organization, the others would be seriously threatened. Therefore, this threat was often avoided in the past by keeping most of the party's resources out of the hands of state organization. Power was decentralized, collecting in the most effective of the local organizations.

Progressive reforms in the early 1900s kept state party organizations weak. In particular, the introduction of the direct primary (see Chapters 9 and 10) limited the influence of state parties on campaigns for state offices. Candidates could win party nominations in primary elections, raise money for their own campaigns, and run them without party organizational help. Even today, relatively weak state party organizations are still found in the states where the Progressives and Populists had the greatest strength—the more rural, western states.[27]

Beginning in the late 1960s, the national Democratic Party adopted reforms that greatly increased the use of primaries in nominating a presidential candidate. That reduced the state party's role in presidential nominations. The voters, rather than the state party organization, choose most convention delegates now, and state party leaders no longer control delegates' votes. Extensions of civil service protections and unionization eroded the patronage base for many state parties. In fact, some courts have even prevented the firing of patronage workers when the governing party changes.

To add to state party organizations' burden, one-party dominance in several states during the first half of the 1900s left several state parties weak and conflict-ridden. Southern Democratic Parties were a notable example. When a single party dominates a state's politics, the diverse forces within the state are likely to compete as factions within that party. The state party organization lacks the incentive and the ability to unify, as it would be inclined to do if it faced a viable opposition party. For all these reasons, many state party organizations had become "empty shells" in the 1940s and 1950s.[28]

Increasing Strength in Recent Decades

Since the 1960s, however, state party organizations have become more active and organizationally complex. The number of state parties with a permanent headquarters and a full-time, paid executive director, which is perhaps the most crucial position in a state party organization, has greatly increased; currently, almost every state party has both. These resources—full-time leaders and a stable location—are vital to the development of parties as organizations.[29] Almost every state party does fund-raising and voter mobilization and recruits a full slate of statewide candidates; these parties also use and share the voter databases given by national party organizations.[30] In addition to their field staff members, many state parties have created internship programs for college students.

The problem is that state party organizations face much stronger competition now from outside groups—super PACs (political action committees that spend money only on independent advertising, not on contributions to candidates) and other non-party groups that can raise and spend unlimited sums, whereas party spending and receiving are regulated by law.

Fund-Raising   In the 1990s, the national party committees played a vital role in building the state parties' fund-raising by transferring increasing amounts to the state parties and candidates. The transfers peaked in 2000, when the national party organizations gave a whopping $430 million to parties and candidates at the state level, many times the amounts that the national parties had infused into state organizations just a few years earlier.[31]

But the 2000s have not been kind to state parties. Beginning in 2002, the Bipartisan Campaign Reform Act (BCRA, discussed in Chapter 12) took away national parties' ability to transfer soft money to state parties. That was a blow to state parties' finances. BCRA did allow state parties to spend federally regulated money (which the national parties could transfer to states without limits) on *federal* campaign activities and to raise a certain amount of soft money themselves (up to $10,000 per donor) for grassroots mobilization and party-building. States worked to become more efficient fund-raisers, spurred by the high stakes of polarized politics. Now, candidates for governor and state legislature receive at least some contributions from the majority of state party organizations. Most state parties recruit candidates for the state legislature, and almost half try to recruit congressional and gubernatorial candidates as well.[32]

Nevertheless, state parties' fund-raising has not been able to make up for the loss of national parties' subsidy. Meanwhile, other groups have far surpassed state parties in raising money. Changes in national campaign finance law, such as the SpeechNow.org ruling in 2010, allowed super PACs to raise unlimited sums from individuals, corporations, and unions, as well as to spend unlimited sums on their independent ads. (These and other recent changes in campaign finance are discussed in Chapter 12.) With more dollars than volunteers, super PACs have focused on costly broadcast and cable advertising. Their fund-raising has skyrocketed, allowing them to dominate the airwaves in some campaigns. State party organizations' advertising is minimal by comparison.

Congress has shown little interest in state party-building; although in 2014, it greatly increased the amount that national party organizations could accept from a single donor, the provision did not apply to state parties. As a result, state parties, like their local brethren, focus on providing labor to candidates rather than money.

Campaign Services   State parties have used their volunteer labor to focus on grassroots mobilization and targeting. To run a competitive campaign, state legislative and statewide candidates need field workers and voter lists, and they often turn to state party organizations for these services. State parties whose budgets are better suited to field activity than to big media buys have been able to comply. Almost all state parties now run GOTV drives and use online communications, especially social media, to motivate their strong supporters and offer information about candidates and issues.

Parity in Organizational Strength Up until 2000, state Republican parties had bigger budgets and larger and more specialized staff than did their Democratic counterparts. Because they were bigger and richer, they could provide more services to their candidates, such as polling, field staff, and researchers.

But Democratic state parties have now caught up.[33] Howard Dean was elected Democratic National Chairman in 2005 by promising state party chairs that he would give every state, not just the closely fought "battleground states," enough resources to hire at least three or four field organizers and access to a party database of voters. The effort was costly and controversial, but after Democrats made major gains in the 2006 and 2008 elections, Dean's work to build strong state parties was termed "visionary."[34] (For more on this program, see Chapter 4.) The national Democrats again put substantial sums into some state parties beginning in 2017, especially for outreach to voters of color. Although parties' strength may vary depending on the partisan environment in a given election year, both parties are now capable of field organizing in states and congressional districts, and the strongest state parties are those with the technological capabilities to function in an online world.[35]

Allied Groups A variety of groups such as labor unions, especially teachers' and government employees' unions, have worked closely with their state Democratic Party organizations to provide money, volunteers, and other services to party candidates. On the Republican side, small business groups, manufacturing associations, pro-life groups, and Christian conservative organizations often provide services to Republican candidates. As the state parties gain strength, these constituency groups often try to increase their influence on, or even take over, state party organizations. Christian Right and Tea Party groups, in particular, came to dominate or substantially influence a majority of state Republican Parties in the 2010s (see box "What's the Matter with Kansas Republicans?" on page 72).[36]

Because of the close association between parties and activists from these allied groups, it is possible to think of the parties as networks of organizations, which include the interest groups, consulting firms, and "think tanks" (research groups) that offer their resources and expertise to a party.[37] For party leaders, these allied groups can be a mixed blessing, of course; super PACs, labor unions, and religious groups have their own agendas, and at times they are as likely to try to push the party into locally unpopular stands as to help elect party candidates.

It is not easy to build a powerful state party organization. It requires having to overcome the localism of American politics, widespread hostility toward party discipline, and conflicts among party supporters. Strong and skillful personal leadership by a governor, a senator, or a state chairman helps. So does a state tradition that accepts the notion of a unified and effective party. State law

What's the Matter with Kansas Republicans?

Conflicts between more moderate and very conservative activists have plagued the Kansas Republican Party for decades. The conservatives won in 2010; Sam Brownback, a very conservative former U.S. senator, was elected governor with an impressive 63 percent of the vote. He then pushed a highly conservative agenda through the state legislature: deep tax cuts (intended to produce economic growth), and cuts in social programs and education so severe that several Kansas schools eventually had to end their school year early for lack of funds. To seal their victory, Brownback supporters tried to purge the state party of Republican moderates; they challenged and defeated several moderate officeholders in the 2012 party primary.

But the conservative Brownback program did not produce the results his backers hoped for. The big tax cuts created a drop in revenue so severe that the state's bond rating took a hit. Brownback's approval ratings tanked. When he ran for reelection in 2014, the long-standing internal party dispute erupted again; more than 100 moderate Republicans declared their intention to vote Democratic for governor.

Brownback was trailing in pre-election polls until he got an 11th-hour boost from outside groups. In an extraordinarily well-funded race, supported by funds from the highly conservative Koch brothers as well as almost $5 million from the Republican Governors Association, Brownback eked out a narrow victory. Then, the tide turned yet again in 2016 when candidates beat several Brownback allies in Republican state legislative primaries, and energized Republican activists rejected a far-right Republican candidate for governor in 2018, electing a moderate Democrat to succeed Brownback. The far right took another hit in 2020 when firebrand conservative Kris Kobach lost a Senate primary to a less incendiary conservative but gained in other races.

These sharp changes in direction demonstrate that the state and local party organizations are *permeable*. Party organization officials are usually elected by party activists and the volunteers they recruit. So groups within (or even outside of) the party structure can take over the party organization if they can gather enough supporters to win party elections. Conservative Christian, pro-life, and other groups have made serious efforts to do this in recent years, just as labor unions have been a vital part of the revival and vibrancy of the Democratic Party in many states. The result is that the direction and even the policies of a state party organization can change, depending on which group(s) control or influence its leadership at the time.

Sources: Seth McKee, Ian Ostrander, and M.V. Hood III, "Out of Step and Out of Touch," *The Forum* 15 (July 2017); Chris McGreal, "Could a Trump Cheerleader and Republicans' 'Worst Possible Nominee' Be The Best for Democrats?" *The Guardian*, August 8, 2019, https://www.theguardian.com/us-news/2019/aug/08/kris-kobach-why-democrats-hope-the-gop-wont-stop-his-run-for-us-senate (accessed August 14, 2020).

makes a difference as well. More centralized party organization has flourished in states that make less use of primary elections, so the party organization has more control over who the statewide and congressional candidates will be.

The Special Case of the South   Party organizational strength has grown most dramatically in the formerly one-party Democratic South. As the national Democratic Party showed greater concern for the rights of African Americans in the 1960s and 1970s, and particularly as the Voting Rights Acts increased the proportion of African American voters in southern states, conservative southern Democrats became increasingly estranged from their national party. Southern whites' support for Republican candidates grew, first in presidential elections and later in statewide and U.S. Senate races (as you will see in Chapter 7).

In the 1980s, state legislative candidates could sense the opportunity to run and win as Republicans. By 1994, Republicans were contesting as many as one-third of the state legislative seats in the South and winning two-thirds of the seats they contested. Since 1994, Republicans have overwhelmed Democratic candidates in state elections—this in a region where, just a few decades before, it was often more socially acceptable to admit to having an alcoholic than a Republican in the family.[38]

As their popularity with voters increased, southern Republican Parties strengthened their organizations. North Carolina's state Republican Party, for example, was only minimally organized in the early 1970s. It started in earnest to recruit state legislative candidates during the mid-1980s. By the 1990s, with a much expanded budget and staff, the party focused on attracting experienced candidates for targeted districts, producing direct mail and radio ads, and helping candidates with training and research.[39] Democrats have had to respond, so both parties' organizations have grown stronger since the 1990s.[40] Southern parties, long among the weakest and most faction-ridden in the nation, have become some of the strongest state party organizations in the past three decades.[41]

Summing Up: The Changing State and Local Party Organizations

Party organizational strength has changed dramatically over time at the state and local levels. The high point of *local* party organizations may have been reached a hundred years ago, when some parties could be described as "armies drawn up for combat" with an "elaborate, well-staffed, and strongly motivated organizational structure."[42] Although this description did not apply to all local parties even then, it would be hard to find a local party organization that could be described in these terms today.

Local parties have been buffeted by a variety of forces since then. Progressive reforms adopted in the early 1900s undermined party organizations by limiting their control over nominations and general elections as well as their patronage resources. Federal social service programs, economic growth, a more educated electorate, and even racial conflict also undercut the effectiveness of the local parties.[43]

However, local parties have tried to adapt to these changes. County parties have moved to fill at least some of the void created by the decline of the urban machines. New technologies such as websites and social networking are enabling county parties to expand their activities. Local party organizations, in short, are demonstrating again their ability to meet the new challenges posed by a changing environment—a resilience that has kept them alive throughout most of American history.

The state party organizations have followed a different route. Traditionally weak in all but a handful of states, the state parties have grown much more robust and professional in recent years. They are providing campaign and organizational services to candidates who, in earlier years, would not have dreamed of looking to their state headquarters for help. In fact, the flow of money, resources, and leadership from the national party to the state parties in the 1990s, and in turn from the state to the local parties, helped to modify the traditional flow of party power. Through most of their lives, the American parties have been highly decentralized, with power and influence lodged at the grassroots. The parties were hollow at the top, depending on the base for whatever influence and resources they had. Because of the death of urban machines and the birth of vigorous state and national party organizations, we no longer see this extreme decentralization. The nationalization of American society and politics has affected party organizations, leading to a greater balance of power among party organizations at different levels.

Ironically, although they are stronger now, state and local party organizations probably have less impact on politics than they once did. They have much more competition for the attention of voters, candidates, and the media. The campaign communications from the parties merge into a flood of Internet, television, and direct mail fund-raising and advertising by super PACs and nonprofit groups, who all try to influence voters' choices. These non-party groups can raise money much more easily than state party organizations can, because contributions to the state parties are limited by law, whereas super PACs and nonprofits can raise and spend unlimited funds. This unlimited spending can drown out the voices of party organizations, and at times even those of the candidates themselves.

The challenge is that many of these super PACs are funded by a handful of wealthy contributors whose commitment to politics may vary from year to year. They might advertise heavily in one election but not in the next. Party organizations, in contrast, are the "repeat players"—the stewards of the party's brand, who can serve as stable cues for voters over time. The parties must try to win majorities, so they may be more wary of extremist candidates and ideas than are the wealthy donors who drop in and out of elections. As repeat players, state and local party organizations can more easily be held responsible by voters than a super PAC that jumps into a race with a massive ad buy and then disappears.[44]

The increasing organizational strength of the state and some local parties has helped them adopt modern campaign skills and recapture a role in candidates' campaigns. But it is not a *dominant* role—not in the way it could have been if party organizations, rather than voters in primaries, selected party candidates. Party organizations rarely *run* campaigns; instead, their new resources give them more of a chance to compete for the attention of those who do—the candidates—at a time when other competitors (organized interests, consultants) have become more effective as well. And as the impact of national party images and activities on votes for Congress and governor has grown, and as national issues dominate state party platforms, "today's major parties are thoroughly nationalized brands," offering similar choices from state to state.[45]

Does this mean that the increases in state and local party organizational strength are unimportant? Not at all. In a very competitive political environment, clearly it is better to have a strong organization and many resources. In the end, however, despite all the changes in party organization during the past few decades, their basic structural features have not changed. The American state and local parties remain cadre organizations run by a small number of activists; they involve the bulk of their supporters mainly at election time. By the standards of parties in other democratic nations, American state and local party organizations are relatively weak—more limited in their activities and authority and more easily dominated by a handful of activists and elected officials. But by the standards of American politics, the state and local organizations are more visible and active than they have been in some time.

Notes

1 Andrew M. Appleton and Daniel S. Ward, *State Party Profiles* (Washington, DC: CQ Press, 1997), Appendix. See also the National Conference of State Legislatures at www.ncsl.org.

2 A public utility is a government-regulated provider of services, such as a gas or a water company. Leon Epstein, *Political Parties in the American Mold* (Madison, WI: University of Wisconsin Press, 1986), pp. 155–199.

3 The cases are *Tashjian v. Republican Party of Connecticut* (1986), *Eu v. San Francisco County Democratic Central Committee et al.* (1989), and *California Democratic Party v. Jones* (2000).

4 V. O. Key, Jr., *Politics, Parties and Pressure Groups* (New York: Crowell, 1964), p. 316.

5 Samuel J. Eldersveld, *Political Parties: A Behavioral Analysis* (Chicago, IL: Rand McNally, 1964).

6 The organization of American political parties differs from what Robert Michels calls the "iron law of oligarchy"—that organizations are inevitably controlled from the top. See Robert Michels, *Political Parties* (Glencoe, IL: Free Press, 1949).

7 M. Craig Brown and Charles N. Halaby, "Machine Politics in America, 1870–1945," *Journal of Interdisciplinary History* 17 (1987): 587–612.

8 See David Mayhew, *Placing Parties in American Politics* (Princeton, NJ: Princeton University Press, 1986), pp. 19–21.

9 See Kenneth Finegold, *Experts and Politicians* (Princeton, NJ: Princeton University Press, 1995).

10 Steven P. Erie, *Rainbow's End* (Berkeley, CA: University of California Press, 1988); but see John F. Bibby, "Party Organizations 1946–1996," in Byron E. Shafer, ed., *Partisan Approaches to Postwar American Politics* (New York: Chatham House, 1998), pp. 142–185.

11 Richard Perez-Pena, "The 1999 Elections," *New York Times*, Nov. 4, 1999, https://www.nytimes.com/1999/11/04/nyregion/1999-elections-republicans-fall-mighty-suburban-party-machine-nassau-county.html (accessed August 14, 2020).

12 Kenneth R. Mladenka, "The Urban Bureaucracy and the Chicago Political Machine," *American Political Science Review* 74 (1980): 991–998.

13 Michael Johnston, "Patrons and Clients, Jobs and Machines," *American Political Science Review* 73 (1979): 385–398. On the impact of patronage on party success, see Olle Folke, Shigeo Hirano, and James M. Snyder, Jr., "Patronage and Elections in U.S. States," *American Political Science Review* 105 (2011): 567–585.

14 James L. Gibson, Cornelius P. Cotter, John F. Bibby, and Robert J. Huckshorn, "Whither the Local Parties?" *American Journal of Political Science* 29 (1985): 139–160.

15 Cornelius P. Cotter, James L. Gibson, John F. Bibby, and Robert J. Huckshorn, *Party Organization in American Politics* (New York: Praeger, 1984), pp. 49–53.

16 See ibid., p. 54, for 1964–1980, and Charles E. Smith, Jr., "Changes in Party Organizational Strength and Activity 1979–1988," unpublished manuscript, Ohio State University, 1989.

17 Douglas D. Roscoe and Shannon Jenkins, *Local Party Organizations in the Twenty-First Century* (Albany, NY: SUNY Press, 2016), pp. 50–61.

18 Melody Crowder-Meyer, "The Party's Still Going," in John H. Green and Daniel J. Coffey, eds., *The State of the Parties*, 6th ed. (Lanham, MD: Rowman & Littlefield, 2010), p. 120.

19 Hans J. G. Hassell, *The Party's Primary* (New York: Cambridge University Press, 2017).

20 L. Sandy Maisel, "American Political Parties." in Jeffrey E. Cohen, Richard Fleisher, and Paul Kantor, eds., *American Political Parties: Decline or Resurgence?* (Washington, DC: CQ Press, 2001), pp. 112–114.

21 Daniel M. Shea and John C. Green, "Local Parties and Mobilizing the Vote," in John C. Green and Daniel J. Coffey, *The State of the Parties*, 5th ed. (Lanham, MD: Rowman & Littlefield, 2007), pp. 222 and 224.

22 Roscoe and Jenkins, *Local Party Organizations*, pp. 29–37.

23 Carol S. Weissert, "Michigan," in Appleton and Ward, *State Party Profiles*, pp. 153–160.

24 Roscoe and Jenkins, *Local Party Organizations*, p. 69.

25 John J. Coleman, "The Resurgence of Party Organization?" in Daniel M. Shea and John C. Green, eds., *The State of the Parties* (Lanham, MD: Rowman & Littlefield, 1994), pp. 282–298.

26 A. James Reichley, *The Life of the Parties* (Lanham, MD: Rowman & Littlefield, 2000), pp. 129–130.

27 Malcolm E. Jewell and Sarah M. Morehouse, *Political Parties and Elections in American States*, 4th ed. (Washington, DC: CQ Press, 2001), p. 4.

28 Ibid., p. 1.

29 See James L. Gibson, Cornelius P. Cotter, John F. Bibby, and Robert J. Huckshorn, "Assessing Party Organizational Strength," *American Journal of Political Science* 27 (1983): 193–222.

30 See Rebecca S. Hatch, "Party Organizational Strength and Technological Capacity," *Party Politics* 22 (2016): 195, 197.

31 Raymond J. La Raja, "State Parties and Soft Money," in John C. Green and Rick Farmer, eds., *The State of the Parties*, 4th ed. (Lanham, MD: Rowman & Littlefield, 2003), pp. 132–150.

32 Raymond J. La Raja and Jonathan Rauch, "The State of State Parties," Brookings Institution, 2016, at www.brookings.edu/~/media/research/files/papers/2016/03/08-state-parties-la-raja-rauch/states.pdf (accessed October 29, 2019).

33 Hatch, "Party Organizational Strength," 195.

34 See Ari Berman, "The Prophet," *The Nation*, January 5, 2009, at www.thenation.com/article/prophet (accessed October 29, 2019).

35 See Hatch, "Party Organizational Strength," 191–202.

36 Kimberly H. Conger, *The Christian Right and Republican State Politics* (New York: Palgrave Macmillan, 2009).

37 See Marty Cohen, David Karol, Hans Noel, and John Zaller, *The Party Decides* (Chicago, IL: University of Chicago Press, 2008), and Seth Masket, *No Middle Ground* (Ann Arbor, MI: University of Michigan Press, 2011).

38 See Edward G. Carmines and James A. Stimson, *Issue Evolution* (Princeton, NJ: Princeton University Press, 1989).

39 Charles Prysby, "North Carolina," in Appleton and Ward, *State Party Profiles*, pp. 234–243.

40 See the articles in John A. Clark and Charles Prysby, eds., "Grassroots Party Activists in Southern Politics, 1991–2001," *American Review of Politics* 24 (Spring and Summer, 2001), pp. 1–223.

41 Aldrich, "Southern Parties," p. 655.

42 Walter Dean Burnham, *Critical Elections and the Mainsprings of American Politics* (New York: Norton, 1970), p. 72.

43 Alan Ware, *The Breakdown of the Democratic Party Organization 1940–80* (Oxford: Oxford University Press, 1985).

44 LaRaja and Rauch, "The State of State Parties," p. 3.

45 Daniel J. Hopkins, *The Increasingly United States* (Chicago, IL: University of Chicago Press, 2018), p. 143.

CHAPTER 4

The Parties' National Organizations

The national Democratic and Republican parties are among America's billionaires. In the 2020 election cycle, the two national party organizations raised and spent more than $2 billion to support federal (and some state) candidates and to beef up their outreach to voters. Even with the explosive growth of nonparty super PACs and other big spenders, the parties' national committees have a larger profile in many federal candidates' campaigns and in state parties' activities than ever before.

It may sound odd, then, that the national party organizations had relatively little power throughout most of American history. But before the 1970s, the two major parties were relatively *decentralized*: the bulk of party organizational strength collected in the local parties. As you saw in Chapter 3, almost all American public officials are chosen in local and state elections. In years past, most of the incentives parties had to offer, such as patronage jobs, were available at the local and state levels. Because the population of Orlando is not the same as the population of Salt Lake City, it made sense for different local organizations of, say, the Republican Party to emphasize different issues and choose different candidates depending on the preferences of their local voters. Until recent decades, as a result, local and state party organizations were largely independent of the national party committees, which had little power.[1] The national parties lived like many college students: chronically short of cash and often searching for new housing.

So what changed? Both parties reacted to a series of challenges in the 1970s—Watergate for the Republicans and internal battles over civil rights and the war in Vietnam for the Democrats—by moving toward more energized national committees. Although the local pull remains strong, the distribution of power among the national, state, and local parties is now more balanced than ever before.

The National Parties

What is the national party? Officially, each major party's supreme national authority is the **national convention** it holds every four years to nominate a presidential candidate. However, the convention rarely does more than select the presidential and vice-presidential nominees and approve the party's platform and rules. Between conventions, the two parties' main governing bodies are their national committees.

The National Committees

Each party's **national committee** consists of representatives from all its state parties; its leaders run the national party on a daily basis. Their main focus is to help elect the party's presidential candidate. They also distribute polls and policy information, work with state parties, and assist in other races by recruiting and training candidates and helping them raise money.

Both national committees have a long history: the Democrats created theirs in 1848 and the Republicans in 1856. For years, every state was represented equally on both national committees, regardless of the size of its population or the extent of its party support. California and Wyoming, then, had equal-sized delegations to the national party committees, just as they do in the U.S. Senate, even though Wyoming's population is only 1/67th that of California's. That system overrepresented the smaller states and also gave roughly equal weight in the national committees to the winning and the losing parts of the party. In practice, this strengthened the southern and western segments of each party, which tended to be more conservative.

Since 1972, when the Democrats revised the makeup of their national committee, the parties have structured their committees differently. After briefly experimenting with unequal state representation in the 1950s, the Republicans give each of the state and territorial parties three seats on the RNC. In contrast, the DNC, now almost twice the size of its Republican counterpart, gives weight to party support as well as to population in representing the states. California, for example, has 19 seats on the DNC, and Wyoming has 4. This change reduced the influence of conservatives and moderates within the DNC.

The two national committees also differ in that the Democrats give national committee seats to representatives of groups especially likely to support Democratic candidates, such as blacks, women, and labor unions—a decision that shows the importance of these groups to the party—as well as to associations of elected officials, such as the National Conference of Democratic Mayors. National committee members in both parties are chosen by the state parties and, for the Democrats, by these other groups as well.

National Party Chairs

The national committee's chair and the staff he or she chooses are the heart of the national party organization. Members of the full national committees come together only two or three times a year, mainly to call media attention to the party and its candidates. The national committees have the power to select their own leaders. By tradition, however, the incumbent president normally chooses the national chair of his or her party. Thus, in practice, only the "out" party's national committee actually selects its own chair.[2] In both parties, the chair's most important job is to raise money for the party, as well as to support candidates and tamp down squabbles among important segments of the national party (see box "National Party Chairs: It's Not Easy"" below).

National Party Chairs: It's Not Easy

Donald Trump ran for president as a Republican, but his relationship with the Republican National Committee (RNC) started with suspicion on both sides. The previous Republican presidential nominee, Mitt Romney, had called Trump "a phony and a fraud." After Trump appointed RNC chair Reince Priebus to be Trump's Chief of Staff in 2017, Priebus was replaced at the RNC by Romney's niece, Ronna Romney McDaniel—who was pressed by Trump to drop the "Romney" from her official name. Strains arose; Trump's staff complained that the RNC wasn't doing enough to defend the president and needed to hire more Trump loyalists. The RNC complained that Trump's frequent position changes left the national party holding the bag too often. But McDaniel, a Trump loyalist, soon made it clear that the RNC was now Trump's political arm, even tweeting criticism of her uncle when, after he was elected U.S. senator from Utah, Romney sought to establish his independence from Trump.

Leadership of the Democratic National Committee (DNC) also became conflict-filled when the two major candidates for the 2016 Democratic presidential nomination supported different contenders in 2017. Former Secretary of State Hillary Clinton backed former Labor Secretary Tom Perez, and Clinton's rival, Senator Bernie Sanders, supported Minnesota Rep. Keith Ellison. Each would have been a "first" for DNC chair: Perez, the son of immigrants, is a Latino, and Ellison, an African-American, was one of two Muslims then in Congress. Perez won narrowly and soon became involved in a skirmish with Democratic state chairs as to how the party's voter data ought to be collected and made available.

Though McDaniel and Perez reflected very different political orientations, they faced similar challenges. To succeed, every national party chair must raise eye-popping amounts of money for the upcoming campaign, persuade the most electable political figures to run for office under their party's label, and promote the party's interests to the media and the public. Then, although neither leader has as much power as many voters assume, the national chair of the party that loses the presidency will be widely blamed for the election outcome, and the national chair of the winning party will have to give all the credit for the victory to the party's presidential candidate.

Sources: See, for example, Noah Bierman, "Ronna McDaniel Is Stuck Between Her Romney Roots and Trump's Republican Party," *Los Angeles Times*, May 6, 2019, https://www.latimes.com/politics/la-na-pol-ronna-romney-mcdaniel-trump-republican-party-20190506-story.html (accessed August 15, 2020), and David Weigel, "Thomas Perez Elected First Latino Leader of the Democratic Party," *Washington Post*, February 25, 2017, p. A1.

Serving as the party's national chair does not guarantee great authority. Reince Priebus, the Republican National Chair during Donald Trump's first presidential run, demonstrated this when he unsuccessfully tried to persuade Trump to tone down his rhetoric. Trump paid no attention to Priebus's request and still won the Republican nomination. National party chairs gain strength through their fund-raising and persuasive skills, not because their institutional positions have many formal powers.

Presidents and Their National Parties

Presidents came to dominate their national committees early in the twentieth century and especially since the 1960s. Thus, in the president's party, the national committee's role is whatever the president wants it to be. James W. Ceaser cites the classic example of Robert Dole, RNC chair from 1971 to 1973, who was quickly fired by the president when Dole tried to put a little distance between the party and the president's involvement in the Watergate scandal: "I had a nice chat with the President ... while the other fellows went out to get the rope."[3] Some presidents have turned their national committees into little more than managers of the president's campaigns and builders of the president's political support between elections. Other presidents, such as George W. Bush, worked to build up the national committee to achieve party, not just presidential, goals.

When their party does not hold the presidency, the national party chair and committee can play a more independent role in national politics. At these times, the "out" party's national chair becomes one of several people (including congressional leaders and past presidential nominees) who may speak for the party and its policies. He or she will also need to energize the party organization around the country and offer a vision for regaining the White House. After the 2012 losses of the "Grand Old Party" (GOP, a long-standing nickname for the Republicans), for instance, RNC Chair Priebus appointed a self-study task force (Democrats referred to it instead as an "autopsy"), which produced recommendations to "grow the party and improve Republican campaigns."[4] Above all, the chair must help repay any debts from the losing presidential campaign and raise new money for the party.

Because of changes in campaign finance rules (see Chapter 12), the national committee must work separately from the presidential candidate's own campaign organization in presidential elections. To play this more autonomous role, national chairs have recruited staffers with extensive experience in raising money, dealing with databases, and mobilizing organizers and grassroots supporters.

Other National Party Groups

Several other party organizations are normally included in the term "the national party." Note, however, that these organizations of the same party usually work independently of one another and often compete for donors and resources.[5]

Congressional Campaign ("Hill") Committees

The most important of these related groups are each party's **House and Senate campaign committees,** called the **Hill committees** (because Congress is located on Capitol Hill) or the CCCs (Congressional Campaign Committees). The House committees were founded in the immediate aftermath of the Civil War; the Senate committees came into being when senators began to be popularly elected in 1913. The Democratic Congressional Campaign Committee (DCCC) and the National Republican Congressional Committee (NRCC) are concerned entirely with House elections, and the Democratic Senatorial Campaign Committee (DSCC) and the National Republican Senatorial Committee (NRSC) put money into Senate races.

Incumbent House and Senate members control these committees, so it is not surprising that they face pressures to support incumbents' campaigns; the DCCC, for instance, refused to work in 2020 with consultants who support challengers to Democratic incumbent House members in primaries.[6] But they also support their party's candidates for open seats and challengers with a good chance of winning. In short, they concentrate their money where they think they can get the biggest payoff in increasing their party's representation in Congress. During the past four decades, the Hill committees have developed major fundraising and service functions, independent of the DNC and RNC. They provide party candidates with a wide range of campaign help, from get-out-the-vote (GOTV) efforts to hard cash and connections with important donors (see box "How the Hill Committees Help Targeted Campaigns" on page 83). For House and Senate candidates, the Hill committees are more influential than their parties' national committees; their help is highly valued, especially by the campaigns they target for special attention, even in comparison with that provided by interest groups and super PACs.[7]

Governors' Associations and Other Groups

Because of the recent gridlock in Congress, organized interests have increasingly turned to state governments to achieve their aims. This is feasible especially in the large number of state governments controlled by one single party. Several associations have formed to take advantage of this opportunity by targeting state-level campaigns. For instance, the two parties' governors' associations have become major-league fund-raisers since the early 2000s (see Chapter 12). The Republican Governors Association regularly raises between $50 and $100 million for governors' campaigns, funded largely by major corporations, and the Democratic Governors Association slightly less, with contributions from corporations and labor unions.[8]

Another set of major fund-raisers are the Republican Attorneys General Association and the Democratic Attorneys General Association. Because state attorneys general can sue the federal government and other entities directly (and have, on such issues as immigration and pollution), both parties have come to see the importance of controlling these state positions and raise hundreds of

How the Hill Committees Help Targeted Campaigns

The parties' Hill committees try to maximize their impact by targeting races they think they have a chance of winning and, in lean years, protecting their vulnerable incumbents. The most important criteria for choosing which campaigns to target are the competitiveness of the district and candidate quality, as measured mainly by the candidate's own fund-raising. Candidates, then, raise money not only to run their campaigns but also to leverage even more money by impressing party operatives. In giving money directly to candidates, Hill committee targeters also ask: Is the candidate's organization capable of spending the money effectively? Has he or she effectively generated media coverage? In making independent expenditures, they ask: How expensive are the district's media? Are other groups funding ads in the race? Targeting decisions can change daily as the election approaches, depending on movement in the candidates' poll numbers and on the parties' finances.

The Hill committees can offer these services to targeted campaigns:

- efforts to recruit attractive candidates

- research and "talking points" on issues
- "boot camps" especially for first-time candidates on strategy, polling, advertising, fund-raising, staffing, and hiring consultants
- monitoring or video tracking of opponents' campaigns
- help with voter contact, using micro-targeting and huge databases
- participating in coordinated grass-roots activities with the state and local party organizations
- collecting contributions from party members in Congress, holding fund-raising events, and party leaders' visits to candidate events
- "hard-money" direct contributions to campaigns*
- "coordinated spending" to buy polls, media ads, or other services for a candidate*
- independent spending by the party's IE (independent expenditure) group on ads in the candidate's district*
- help, contributor lists, and facilities for raising money from individuals, political action committees (PACs), and other groups

Sources: Paul S. Herrnson, Costas Panagopoulos, and Kendall L. Bailey, *Congressional Elections*, 8th ed. (Los Angeles, CA: Sage/CQ Press, 2020), chapter 4; Marian Currinder, *Money in the House* (Boulder, CO: Westview Press, 2009).

Note: * Explained in Chapter 12.

millions of dollars to do so. The Democratic association raises its funds mainly from labor unions, and both groups seek contributions from corporations. Their donors want a voice in state actions that benefit or regulate their corporations or unions, and state attorneys general play a vital role in these actions.[9] Party leaders have also formed the Republican State Leadership Committee (RSLC) and the Democratic Legislative Campaign Committee (DLCC), which provide money and field organizers to state legislative and statewide campaigns. The two groups budgeted a combined $80 million for 2018 state legislative races—twice as much as in 2016. And the National Democratic Redistricting Committee was created in 2017 to raise funds for state legislative and governor races, to reverse Republican gerrymanders in a number of states.

Women's and Youth Groups

For a long time, both the Democrats and Republicans have had women's divisions associated with their national committees.[10] These women's groups play different roles now that women have entered regular leadership positions in both parties.

On campuses, the College Republican National Committee (the CRs) and the College Democrats (whose weblog or "blog" is named Smart Ass, in honor of the party's donkey mascot) have grown substantially in the 2000s. Both groups train field representatives to recruit volunteers for campaigns at all levels. The CRs have been closely associated with a number of conservative nonparty groups. The Young Democrats of America and the Young Republicans National Federation also work actively among students and other young adults.

Party Networks

The national party committees work closely with a network of allied groups, just as state and local parties do. For the Democrats, these include labor unions, environmental, women's rights, civil rights, and other liberal organizations. Organized labor in particular has supplied many of the volunteer canvassers so vital to Democratic campaigns. The national Republican network includes small business groups, the National Rifle Association, and groups of conservative Christians. Although these groups are not formally a part of the party organizations, they communicate extensively with party organization leaders and play a big role in party campaigns. Hundreds of these groups typically run campaign ads attacking the candidates of the other party. In competitive races, allied groups often run parallel campaigns to those of the candidates—as do the parties themselves—featuring canvassing and other forms of electioneering.[11] Among the biggest advertisers are Americans for Prosperity, supporting conservative Republican candidates, and NextGen Climate Action, supporting Democrats. More rarely, they advertise in the opposition party's primaries to weaken that party's strongest candidate.

Several other groups outside of the formal party structure act as "idea factories" for the party in government. For the Democrats, the leftist Center for American Progress and the more moderate Progressive Policy Institute serve this function. On the Republican side, groups such as the conservative Heritage Foundation and the more libertarian Cato Institute try to affect party policy.

The national party organizations differ from the other parts of their party network—the interest groups, PACs, and other policy demanders that ally with the party—in that they each answer to different groups of contributors and constituents. The contributors to a Republican super PAC, for instance, are a narrower and often more homogeneous group than those who give funds to the RNC and Republican Hill committees.[12] So the national party committees are distinct organizations with their own rules and challenges, not just an undifferentiated part of a larger party network.

Two Paths to Power

The national parties have traveled two different roads to reach these new levels of effectiveness. The Republicans followed a service path by building a muscular fund-raising operation that pays for needed services to their candidates and state parties. The Democrats, in contrast, first followed a procedural path, strengthening their national party's authority over the state parties in nominating a presidential candidate.

The central element in both national parties' continued development, at least until recently, was their ability to attract thousands of small contributions through mass mailings to likely party supporters. This gave the national parties, which formerly depended on funding from the state parties, an independent financial base. Ironically, then, at a time when some were warning that the parties were in decline, the national party organizations were reaching unprecedented levels of strength in American politics.

The Service Party Path

A party organization that supports candidates' campaigns with money and other resources, as opposed to running the campaigns itself, can be termed a **service party**. The Republicans pioneered the notion of a service party in response to their electoral defeats during the New Deal. Then, during the 1960s, RNC Chair Ray Bliss expanded the committee's efforts to improve state and local parties' organizational capacity.[13] Chair William Brock continued this work in the mid- to late 1970s to revive the party's election prospects after the devastating losses caused by the Watergate scandals. Under Brock, the RNC helped provide salaries for the executive directors of all 50 state Republican Parties; offered expert assistance to the state parties in organizing, strategizing, and fund-raising; and contributed to more than 4,000 state legislative candidates. Bliss and Brock fashioned a new role for the RNC by making it an exceptionally effective service organization for the state and local parties.[14]

Money and campaign technologies were the key elements in fulfilling this service role. Using a marketing innovation of that time, computer-generated mailing lists, the Republicans began a program of direct-mail appeals that brought in ever-higher levels of income. The RNC's fund-raising jumped from $29 million in 1975–1976 to $106 million in "hard money" (contributions regulated by federal law)[15] in 1983–1984 (see Table A.1 in the Online Appendix). The RNC used the money, as Bliss and Brock had, to offer a broad array of services to candidates and state and local party organizations. These services included candidate recruitment and training, research, public opinion polling, data processing, computer networking and software development, production of radio and television ads, direct mailing, and legal advice. State party leaders were glad to accept the help; as the party more closely identified with the business community, Republicans felt comfortable with these marketing techniques.

The Democrats' Procedural-Reform Path

At about the same time, Democrats expanded the power of their national party organization for other reasons. Reformers supporting the civil rights movement and opposing American involvement in the Vietnam War pressed for change in the Democratic Party's positions on these issues. The reformers focused on the rules for selecting presidential candidates. Their aim was to make the nominating process more open and democratic and, in particular, more representative of the concerns of people like themselves: young people, blacks, and women.

The reforms started in the mid-1960s with efforts to tell southern Democratic Parties that they could no longer exclude blacks from party participation and send all-white delegations to the national convention. After the 1968 election, the first of a series of reform commissions, the McGovern–Fraser Commission, overhauled the party's presidential nominating process. (This story is told in more detail in Chapter 10.) The Democrats limited the autonomy of the state parties and the authority of state law in determining how convention delegates were to be selected. That gave the national party the authority over the rules for nominating a presidential candidate.[16] Key court decisions upheld these actions, further solidifying the newfound power of the national party.

This change was limited to the Democrats, however. Republican leaders, consistent with their party's commitment to states' rights, did not want to centralize power in their own party organization.[17] Yet the GOP was still affected by the tide of Democratic Party reform because the bills passed by state legislatures to implement the reforms, including a big increase in the use of primary elections to select a party's presidential candidate, usually applied to both parties.

In the early 1980s, the Democrats took stock of the reforms and did not like what they saw. The newly centralized authority for nominating a presidential candidate and increased grassroots participation in the nominating process had done little to win elections. Further, it had divided the party and alienated much of the Democratic Party in government, many of whom stayed home from party conventions in the 1970s. Therefore, the national Democrats decided to soft-pedal procedural reforms and move toward the Republican service model. Long dependent on the organizational help provided by labor unions, the DNC responded to big Democratic defeats in 1980 by working seriously to broaden its fund-raising base, help recruit candidates, and revitalize state and local party organizations. When the dust from all this effort settled, authority over party rules had become more nationalized, and what had been two models for strengthening the national party were rapidly converging into one.[18]

Both Parties Take the Service Path

The good news for the Democrats in the 1980s was that they were dramatically improving their fund-raising, reducing their long-standing debt, and increasing their activities in the states and localities. The bad news was that the Republicans were far ahead of them and continuing to break new ground. The national Democrats made no secret of their effort to imitate the Republican success in raising money and using it to buy services. Slowly, they began to catch up; what began as a three-to-one and even five-to-one financial advantage for the Republicans was reduced over time (see Figure 4.1).

One reason was the Democratic Party's increasing reliance on "soft money" (see Chapter 12)—funds donated to party organizations in unlimited amounts, most often by labor unions, businesses, and wealthy individuals, and exempted from federal campaign finance rules. Big contributions from labor unions made it easier for the Democrats to compete with Republicans in soft money than they could in raising federally regulated donations. Both national parties' committees began major efforts to solicit soft money in the early 1990s. By 2000, almost half of the national parties' fund-raising came in the form of soft money.

Some of the money went into building up the state and even the local parties. A much larger portion of the national parties' money was devoted to races for the U.S. House and Senate. Since the mid-1980s, both parties provided increasing amounts of aid to selected candidates. The Republican committees opened an early lead; the stunning success of GOP candidates in the 1994 congressional elections, for example, was due in part to aggressive fund-raising as well as candidate recruitment by their Hill committees.

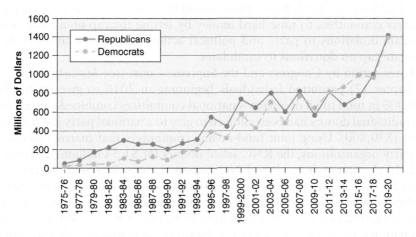

FIGURE 4.1 Democratic and Republican Fund-Raising, 1975–1976 to 2019–2020

Note: The data points are total party receipts (including state/local, House, Senate, and national committees) in millions of dollars. Soft money is not included, nor is money (after 1987) transferred among committees. Table A.1 in the Online Appendix provides a breakdown of these totals by type of party committee within each party.

Source: Federal Election Commission data at www.opensecrets.org/parties/ (accessed November 28, 2020). Data for 2020 are as of November 28, 2020.

Campaign finance reform adopted in 2002 (the Bipartisan Campaign Reform Act, or BCRA, discussed in Chapter 12) barred the national committees from collecting soft money after the 2002 elections. The Democrats saw the coming ban on national party soft money as a particular threat because their soft-money collections had been flourishing—the Democratic Hill committees outdid their Republican counterparts in raising soft money by $151 million to $136 million in 2002—but their federally regulated contributions had expanded only gradually.

Rising to the Challenge of New Campaign Finance Rules

Once the BCRA rules came into effect in 2004, many observers felt that the loss of soft money would seriously weaken the national parties. Transfers of money from national party committees to state and local parties dropped markedly in most states, because BCRA allowed the transfer of federally regulated money only. But as they have so often in their history, the parties adapted to the new rules.

Both national parties tried to make up for the lost soft money by striving to attract hard-money donations from individuals. The DNC greatly expanded its direct mail fund-raising program, which had been minimal during the 1990s, and reaped millions of new donors. In all, the DNC collected more than four times as much federally regulated money in 2004 as it had in 2002—$404 million compared with $93 million—and raised more than 40 percent of its total fund-raising in small contributions of less than $200. The DCCC and the RNC both doubled their hard-money fund-raising in 2004. BCRA made it easier for the party committees to raise hard money by setting the cap on an individual's aggregate donations to party and political action committees higher than the aggregate cap on donations to candidates.

Later action by Congress and the Supreme Court (see *McCutcheon v. FEC* in Chapter 12) permitted individuals beginning in 2016 to give up to about $800,000 in total to all of a party's national committees combined—much more than individual donors had been allowed to give to a national party just four years earlier ($30,800). Using joint fund-raising committees that married candidates and party organizations, the RNC asked donors for $1.34 million per couple in the 2016 election cycle, and the DNC requested about $1.6 million. The givers got a variety of perks in return. Both parties encouraged big hard-money donors to solicit similar contributions from their friends and colleagues and to "bundle" these donations, in return for recognition from the party. In addition, by 2019, both national parties had set up online fund-raising platforms—ActBlue for the Democrats, WinRed for the Republicans—to serve as national clearinghouses through which donors can give to House and Senate races throughout the country. Through ActBlue, Democratic small donors put more than $700 million into the 2018 midterm campaigns and raised $1 billion in 2019.

Thus, even after the 2010 *Citizens United* decision (see Chapter 12), which was expected to cut into the parties' appeal as fund-raisers, the two parties' committees came up with a monumental total of over $1.7 billion during 2015–2016—money raised by party committees at all levels that could be spent on federal elections, and over $2 billion in 2019–2020. Although the Democrats surpassed the Republican Party's fund-raising during the 2010 election cycle for the first time in at least 30 years, and did so again in 2014 and 2016, President Trump's energetic pursuit of contributions, beginning the day he was inaugurated, brought back the more usual Republican funding edge in 2018 and 2020.

Party Money and Activism in the 2020s

Although the biggest portion of party fund-raising comes from individual citizens, an increasing proportion of party committees' money comes from members of Congress. In the early 1990s, some Republican House leaders, fed up with their long-time minority status, pressed party colleagues to donate some of their campaign war chests to Republicans in more competitive races. The aim was to redirect campaign money from those who could most easily raise it to those who most needed it, to increase the number of House Republicans. Winning a majority of seats would give all House Republicans the power to achieve their policy goals, because the majority party controls the flow of legislation in the House. Republicans did capture control of both the House and Senate in 1994, and soon after, the new minority Democrats also saw the value of spreading the wealth to help vulnerable incumbents and promising challengers.

Since then, both parties' Hill committees have urged—and House committees have required—their members to channel money to the party committee, not just to particular candidates. This gives the party the opportunity to target the races it considers the most winnable, rather than leaving the decisions to individual incumbent donors. House members can donate funds from their personal campaign committees and their "leadership PACs" (see Chapter 12), set up joint fund-raising operations with party committees, and also ask their own contributors to give to the party's Hill committee.

In the late 2010s, both House Hill committees asked their top party leaders for about $1 million each. Those who want to get or keep these leadership positions find this fund-raising vital to their success; then-Speaker Paul Ryan donated millions to the NRCC in 2018 to try to ward off (what would become successful) threats to his leadership from Tea Party-aligned House members. Lesser amounts were requested from key committee chairs and lower-level party leaders, and rank-and-file members were each assessed "only" $125,000. In all, current members of Congress contributed a total of $78 million to congressional candidates in 2018.[19]

Each member's contributions were tracked by party leaders, just as party whips track legislative votes.[20] The Senate committees follow a less formal system of raising funds from their party colleagues. The parties' success in getting incumbents to hand over impressive sums and to put their fund-raising skill in the service of other party candidates demonstrates the extent to which the congressional parties have become important instruments of collective power for their members.

The Hill committees doled out the money carefully. Before an incumbent or a targeted challenger could get funds from the NRCC or DCCC, he or she had to meet a series of benchmarks for fund-raising, media visibility, and numbers of voter contacts. Incumbents were advised to start raising money for their 2020 campaigns immediately after they won in 2018. In fact, the DCCC welcomed newly elected Democratic House members to Washington after the 2012 elections with a slide show recommending that in a typical ten-hour workday, they should spend four hours on the phone with potential donors and another hour on "strategic outreach," which includes fund-raisers.

Even on home visits to their district, they were told, they should devote three hours to donor "call time" and an hour to outreach—a schedule that cuts deeply into their legislative work and constituent service. An observer commented, "It is considered poor form in Congress—borderline self-indulgent—for a freshman to sit at length in congressional hearings when the time could instead be spent raising money." Although one member responded, "You might as well be putting bamboo shoots under my fingernails,"[21] these expectations continue.

The increased fund-raising from Congress members and other sources gave the Democratic committees the money to take a page or two from the Republicans' playbook. Starting in 2000, the national GOP had created a massive databank of voter information gleaned from party canvassers and commercial databases—individuals' past voting records and their opinions and consumer preferences—so that, just as corporate market researchers do, party strategists could make predictions as to how particular types of people were likely to behave. This "micro-targeting" helped the Republicans focus their persuasive efforts and get-out-the-vote activities on the individuals most likely to support Republican candidates. The resulting database, called Voter Vault, required funding and computer facilities on a scale that the national Republicans could afford. It was widely heralded as a major reason for the Republican victories in 2002 and 2004.

Democrats were slow to respond but later created two separate national databases. VoteBuilder, the DNC's 50-state voter file, is managed by the data systems vendor NGP VAN. The master list is rented to national and state campaigns and some super PACs, which then add the data they've gathered from their own field work. The other, a huge data set with information on 240 million voting-age Americans, managed by the group Catalist with funds from unions, nonprofits, and individuals, was used extensively by the Barack Obama campaign and liberal groups supporting Obama.

Voter contact programs based on these data sets were field-tested in some congressional special elections in 2008, all of which resulted in Democratic wins. The DCCC and DSCC first applied these programs nationally in the 2012 elections. (This story is told more fully in Chapter 11.) By then, the Republicans were the ones who were lagging technologically. In 2011 they outsourced their list-building to a party-related group, Data Trust, which collects personal, demographic, and consumer information from state parties and data brokers. In 2014, oil billionaires Charles and David Koch agreed to share the voter files gathered by their political groups, such as Freedom Partners, with Data Trust. Other Republican-leaning groups such as the Congressional Leadership Fund super PAC and Deep Root Analytics began their own data-collection efforts. By 2020, Republicans had regained the technological advantage.

In addition to campaign contributions, the Hill committees have also used their increased fund-raising to mount lavish independent spending drives in targeted races. As you'll see in Chapter 12, court cases have allowed party organizations to run unlimited amounts of advertising in House and Senate campaigns as long as the party spends its money independently of the candidate it intends to help ("independent spending"). This produces the odd picture of two groups of partisans from the same party—those helping the candidate and those doing independent spending—working to elect the same candidate but officially ignorant of one another's activities. The great majority of party funds in recent House and Senate races now take the form of independent spending (see Figures 4.2 and 4.3), because it is not limited by law, whereas party direct contributions to candidates and coordinated spending are limited. The two parties spent a total of over $250 million on independent expenditures in 2016 and more than $600 million in 2020—an impressive increase over earlier election cycles.

So since the mid-1980s, both national parties have become institutionalized as active, well-staffed service parties working to support party candidates and state and local party organizations.[22] Their focus has changed from prospecting for soft money to soliciting federally regulated contributions. They have shifted from investing in computerized direct mail to integrating fund-raising

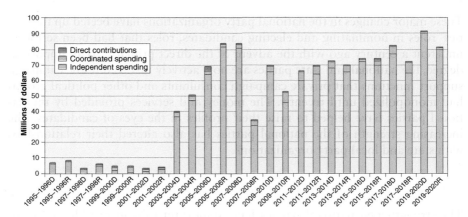

FIGURE 4.2 National Party Money in House Races, 1995–1996 to 2019–2020

Source: Federal Election Commission data from the Center for Responsive Politics (www.opensecrets.org) as of October 23, 2020.

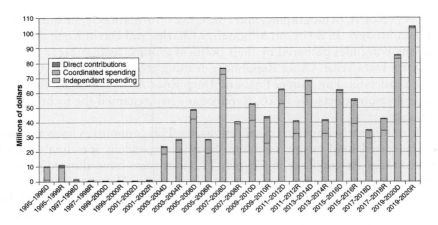

FIGURE 4.3 National Party Money in Senate Races, 1995–1996 to 2019–2020

Source: Federal Election Commission data from the Center for Responsive Politics (www.opensecrets.org) as of October 23, 2020.

databases with e-mail databases, social media, and other data. They also coordinate their activities quietly with non-party spenders such as super PACs, as we will see in Chapter 12. In particular, Donald Trump proved to be an unparalleled fund-raiser, both for the Republican committees supporting him and for the Democratic groups opposing him. As campaign finance rules change and new technologies develop, the committees adapt.

What Is the Impact of These Stronger National Parties?

These major changes in the national party organizations have beefed up the parties' roles in nominating and electing candidates, roles that had been seriously undercut a century ago with the advent of the direct primary. To an important degree, the national and state parties are now actively involved in the campaign support functions that private campaign consultants and other political groups had monopolized until recently. The money and services provided by the national parties have helped to raise their profiles in the eyes of candidates. The increasing strength of the national parties has also altered their relationships with state and local party organizations.

Effects on Candidates' Campaigns

The strengthened national parties have important jobs in presidential campaigns. As we have seen, both national committees research issues, study the opponent's record and background, and search for their own candidate's weak points and ways to thwart attacks. They train state party staff and field directors and maintain relationships with important groups in the party's network.

In Senate and House campaigns, however, there have been some marked changes in the national parties' decisions as to where to deploy their newfound strength. In the 1980s and 1990s, the national party committees had supported a wide range of viable candidates. The committees tended to protect their incumbents when they expected a lean election year and to invest in challengers and open seats when a big victory looked likely. But by the early 2000s, the House and Senate were so closely divided by party and the number of truly competitive seats had shrunk so much that both parties' congressional committees were pouring the great majority of their money and help into those competitive races.[23]

So much party money and field staff flooded these competitive campaigns that at least in those targeted races, party money at times outweighed candidate spending. The national party committees' money and other resources have given them real power over the targeted campaigns. For instance, early in the 2000s, the national parties spent more in a closely fought Colorado congressional race than the candidates' own campaigns did, and the national party committees specified exactly what the campaigns had to do with the party money. The Democratic candidate's campaign manager probably spoke for both candidates in his exasperation at the national party's micromanaging: "They crawl up our ass on a daily basis."[24]

The party committee normally agrees to provide funding only if the campaign accepts certain party mandates: that the campaign hire or fire particular staffers, use a particular consultant, or adopt a given campaign technique. Sometimes, party influence on targeted campaigns can backfire. For instance, party-funded ads are much more likely to attack the opposition than are the candidates' own ads. Because most voters do not distinguish between candidate and party ads, a candidate can be tarred with a negative image that he or she has worked hard to avoid. Thus, conflicts can develop between the party committee and the campaign.

In some recent "wave" elections such as 2018, the playing field of targeted campaigns has expanded. But because most congressional races are not competitive, their candidates do not have the luxury of worrying about the strings attached to the party money. In elections where the outcome is predictable, there is no reason for national party committees to invest much of their scarce resources. The lack of party investment can become a self-fulfilling prophecy, because non-party donors often use the party's targeting decisions to guide their own contributions. As one campaign staffer noted, "That is such a death blow to a campaign, when the national party pulls out their money."[25] But the party committee's goal is to place its resources strategically and win enough campaigns to gain control of the House or Senate, so party staffers must make hard choices based on analytics, not compassion.

Effects on State and Local Parties

More generally, have the increasing visibility and resources of the national parties led to a transfer of power from the state and local to the national party organizations—to centralization rather than decentralization of the parties? Probably not. The forces that encourage a state and local party focus remain strong, but it is clear that the national parties' new strength has lessened the *de*centralization of the party organizations. When the national parties have a lot of money and services to give, their power and influence grow. The result can be more of a national imprint on the nature of state and even local campaigns, the kinds of candidates recruited, and the ways in which the parties are organized.

At times, state parties have welcomed this national involvement. One of the more successful examples of national and state party cooperation was former DNC Chair Howard Dean's **50-state strategy** in the 2006 and 2008 elections. As mentioned in Chapter 3, Dean used DNC money to pay field organizers to work with each of the state parties. Colorado, for instance, had been a Republican state for several decades but had experienced an influx of younger, more liberal voters in the early 2000s. Therefore, starting in 2005, the DNC provided money for the state party to fund field directors in rural areas and to purchase a new database of voter information. The DNC investment invigorated several other state parties in areas that the national Democrats had previously written off as Republican-dominated. One study found that these DNC staffers improved the candidates' vote totals in these races, even beyond the other advantages that Democrats had in 2006.[26]

President Obama's administration was less enthusiastic about the DNC's involvement in the Obama campaigns. They felt that their victories reflected their own efforts, not those of the DNC.[27] So Obama kept his campaign organization, renamed Organizing for Action (OFA), active after the 2012 election and used its e-mail list and grassroots organization to promote the president's agenda. Although OFA claimed strong ties to the Democratic Party, it remained independent of the party organization, even competing with the DNC and state parties in raising money.[28] But after Obama left office, the DNC again pumped money into each of the state parties and gave them access to an online canvassing app to rebuild the state and local groups' organizational strength.

This increased national influence can strain the relationships among party organizations at different levels, just as it has produced strains between the parties and some candidates. One of the areas of greatest conflict between the national parties and their state and local brethren centers on national party involvement in primaries. National party officials are always tempted to try to select and groom the candidate they think will have the best odds of winning in a district. The House and Senate campaign committees, whose chance for a majority in Congress depends on the effectiveness of candidates in competitive races, dread the possibility that a less-capable candidate will win their party's primary and go on to run a lackluster campaign for the seat. But the risk of becoming involved is that if the national party backs a candidate who later loses the primary, then the party might alienate the winning candidate, make itself look weak, and even split the state party and lose the election.

Republican national leaders took the risk in 2010, anticipating a Republican wave election. National Republican campaign committees endorsed several Republican primary candidates who seemed very electable. In some cases, Tea Party supporters and other strongly conservative voters ignored the party establishment's advice. One notable example was the Delaware Senate race, where Republican primary voters rejected the national and state parties' preferred candidate in favor of a colorful, Tea Party-endorsed challenger. Unfortunately, her first general election campaign ad had to explain her earlier admission that she had dabbled in witchcraft, and she was soundly defeated by a Democrat who was previously seen as the underdog in the race.

In response, the NRSC chair vowed to stay out of Republican primaries in 2012. But when some far-right candidates who won their party's nomination stumbled in the general election campaign, state and national party leaders were drawn in anyway. The NRSC and other Republican groups felt the need to step in again prior to the state primaries beginning in 2014, at least to the extent of encouraging more electable Republican primary candidates and helping them deal with missteps in their campaigns. Similarly, the DCCC endorsed several moderate Democratic House candidates in 2018 primaries who were opposed by a progressive Democrat in the Bernie Sanders tradition.[29] These interventions often come at a cost (see box "When Should the National Party Intervene in State or Local Races?" on page 96).

In short, when national party committees use their money to affect the choice of candidates or the direction of a campaign, there will probably be ruffled feathers within the state party and the campaign, who feel that they are better judges of what works in the district. Yet it is difficult for national party committees to stay on the sidelines. As long as primaries can be dominated by activists more extreme in their views than the average voter (see Chapter 5), party organizations will miss chances to capitalize on winnable races.

Effects on the Presidency

Is a stronger national party likely to compete with the president's power or to add to it? Clearly, the national committees' increasing resources enable them to take a more independent political role. Federal funding of presidential campaigns, which strictly limited party spending for presidential races, freed the national committees from limiting their focus to presidential elections and allowed them to dedicate some of their resources to state and local party-building. At the same time, the party committees carved out new roles in raising money for federal campaigns.

On the other hand, these new capabilities make the national committee an even more attractive resource for presidents. Naturally, presidents want the new party power to be at their service, and every president in recent memory has kept his party's national committee on a short leash. President Trump's staffers moved to gain control of the RNC's database operations and fund-raising beginning in 2017, giving him substantial power over the party's actions and financial investments.[30] Presidents certainly expect the party committees to mobilize all

When Should the National Party Intervene in State or Local Races?

Imagine that you are a state party chair at a time when your national party organization publicly attacks one of your state's party candidates. In 2018, for instance, the Democratic Congressional Campaign Committee (DCCC), which raises money for Democrats running for the U.S. House, attacked a Democratic candidate in a Texas congressional race. The DCCC judged that the incumbent Republican was vulnerable but that Democratic candidate Laura Moser was "unelectable." Other Democrats in that race blasted the DCCC's intervention and boasted that they were not the party establishment's candidates. One claimed, "We're Texans .... We don't need partisan hacks up in D.C. meddling in this race."

Similarly, in 2020, the National Republican Senatorial Committee (NRSC) warned GOP senators to boycott a fundraiser for Doug Collins, a Republican challenging the Republican incumbent in a 2020 Georgia primary. The NRSC's tactic backfired; Collins used its opposition as a fund-raising device.

In other areas, national party intervention can cause confusion. In the 2018 California midterm elections, both the DCCC and the state Democratic Party organization recruited candidates in what they regarded as winnable races. The problem was that they weren't recruiting the same candidates. The result: too many Democratic candidates. A worried DCCC then feared that all those Democrats running in U.S. House primaries would divide the Democratic vote in California's top-two primary (see Chapter 9), where the two top vote-getters regardless of party move on to the general

election, and lead to Republican wins. So the DCCC changed approaches and tried to winnow some candidates from the race.

National party organizations hope to win a majority for their party in Congress; they hate to lose a winnable seat because the congressional candidate is a poor campaigner or because local party activists prefer a candidate whose views are more extreme than those of most general election voters. On the other hand, many state and local party activists resent the national party's "meddling" and feel it's a waste to send a representative to Washington who doesn't reflect their core beliefs. "It makes me feel a bit insulted and betrayed," said one liberal activist who resented the DCCC's backing of a Democratic congressional candidate who opposed same-sex marriage and got an A rating from the National Rifle Association.

Democratic activist Elaine Kamarck favors the national party's argument. She writes that national party leaders should intervene in state and local primaries to try to clear the field for the candidate they think is most likely to win the general election. "That's what party leadership is all about," she states; national party leaders should often press for candidates who match the ideology of the districts they're running in, because they are "painfully aware that not all congressional districts are Berkeley, California.... No other political parties in democracies in the world have abdicated their leadership role as much as America's have, weakening themselves and their ability to govern in the process."

Sources: David Weigel and Sean Sullivan, "Texas Kicks Off Crowded Democratic Primary with Enthusiasm and Meddling," *Washington Post*, March 6, 2018, https://www.washingtonpost.com/powerpost/texas-kicks-off-crowded-democratic-primary-with-enthusiasm-and-meddling/2018/03/05/fe107d82-200a-11e8-badd-7c9f29a55815_story.html (from which the Texas quote is drawn; accessed August 15, 2020), and Elaine Kamarck, "Parties Should Meddle in Primaries," *New York Times*, May 3, 2018, p. A23.

those members of Congress whom they recruited, trained, and financed to support the president's program. Presidents in their first term will want to draw on the national party's assets for their reelection campaigns, as much as campaign finance rules permit. Thus, there is considerable pressure on these stronger national parties to put their capabilities at the service of presidential goals.

Effects on Congress

At around the time that the Hill committees have become much more active in recruiting and supporting party candidates, Congress members have been more likely to cast legislative votes with the majority of their party (as Chapter 13 shows). Did these new campaign resources help convince Congress members to vote for their party's positions on bills? To this point, the party committees have not made their allocations of campaign money and services contingent on candidates' support for the party's program. The Hill committees want as many as possible of their party's candidates to win, so that their party gains or keeps a majority in Congress. So they put money into close races, even when their candidate has bucked the party leadership, rather than give only to candidates who are ideologically "pure."[31]

Yet the committees have not been bashful in reminding members, especially newly elected members, that the party played a role in their election success. Party campaign help is only one part of the story of party support in Congress, but the remarkable cohesion of the House Republicans since 1995 was surely bolstered by the party leadership's financial and other support for Republican candidates. Constituency pressures will always come first in Congress. However, the more that senators and representatives can count on campaign help from the congressional party, the more open they will be to party-based appeals.

Relationships within the National Party

The three national committees of each party—the DNC or RNC and the party's Hill committees—have many shared goals. When the party's presidential candidate does well, most of the voters he or she attracts will also vote for the party's Senate and House candidates. Similarly, an effectively run Senate campaign can bring out voters for party colleagues running for president and House seats.

But the party's resources are limited, and each of the party's national committees wants the biggest share. In 2020, for instance, the NRCC complained that the RNC wasn't sharing the money it was raising, even though House

Republican candidates were being outspent by their Democratic opponents.[32] The party committees have long competed with one another in raising money from the same contributors (and jealously guard their contributor lists), and they recruit political talent from the same limited pool.

The Limits of Party Organization

The national party organizations have recently generated remarkable amounts of new money and other resources. They have used these resources and expertise to become major players relative to the state and local parties and major influences on the lives of many federal and even state-level candidates. Organizations capable of raising and spending more than a billion dollars during a two-year period are not easily ignored. The rise of super PACs (see Chapter 12) probably cut into the parties' fund-raising capability in 2016 and beyond, but the national party organizations are stronger now than they have been through most of their history.

This impressive increase in strength has not come at the expense of the state and local parties. In fact, the national parties have used at least some of their resources to build the capabilities of state party organizations. Nor has the national parties' new strength made the local and state party organizations into branch offices of their national parties, following their orders in developing campaign strategy and taking stands on issues. Too many forces in American politics encourage independence, especially in the local parties, to permit the two major parties to centralize their organization and power. The federal system, in which most public officials are elected at the local level, the separation of powers, variations among states and local areas in public attitudes and regulation of the parties, and the BCRA rules that discourage cooperative campaigns between federal and nonfederal candidates all work against a centralized party system.

Thus, as resource rich as they have become, the American party organizations remain fairly decentralized by international standards. At a time when Americans can be assured of getting the same Big Mac in Cincinnati as they can in San Diego, the American parties lack the top-down control and efficiency, the unified setting of priorities, and the central responsibility that we often find in other nations' parties. Where the party organizations of many other Western democracies have had highly professional leadership and large party bureaucracies, most American party organizations, especially at the local level, are still in the hands of part-time activists.[33]

The parties have increased their emphasis on grassroots campaigning through canvassing and phone banks and have used the information to develop micro-targeting, aiming specific messages at individuals known to be receptive to those messages. Yet even this greater reach into the grassroots may not be enough to make the party organizations more prominent in the public's mind. The parties' messages focus on the candidates rather than on the party itself. Service-oriented parties may be better at helping candidates run for office than in expanding the role of the party organization in citizens' political thinking.[34]

American political values do not welcome stronger and more centralized party organizations with more power in American political life.

The American party organizations are fundamentally flexible and election oriented. Their purpose is to support candidates for office and to make the adjustments needed to do well in a pragmatic political system. As a result, they have long been led by candidates and officeholders, not by career party bureaucrats. As the political system grows more polarized, the party organizations have taken the opportunity to expand their roles and add to the polarization. However, at least to this point, even though the national party committees now have unprecedented levels of funding and activity, their impact is felt mainly through the candidates they support.

Notes

1 Cornelius P. Cotter and Bernard C. Hennessy, *Politics without Power: The National Party Committees* (New York: Atherton, 1964).

2 See Philip A. Klinkner, *The Losing Parties* (New Haven, CT: Yale University Press, 1994).

3 James W. Ceaser, "Political Parties—Declining, Stabilizing, or Resurging," in Anthony King, ed., *The New American Political System* (Washington, DC: American Enterprise Institute, 1990), p. 115. See also Sidney M. Milkis, *The President and the Parties* (New York: Oxford University Press, 1993).

4 See the RNC's "Growth and Opportunity Project," March 18, 2013, https://online.wsj.com/public/resources/documents/RNCreport03182013.pdf (accessed August 15, 2020, no longer on the RNC's website).

5 David Karol, "Parties and Leadership in American Politics," in Jeffery A. Jenkins and Craig Volden, eds., *Leadership in American Politics* (Lawrence, KS: University Press of Kansas, 2017), pp. 141-166.

6 Kayla Epstein, "Ocasio-Cortez Creates PAC to Push Back on Democratic Party's 'Blacklisting' Rule," *Washington Post*, January 12, 2020, https://www.washingtonpost.com/politics/2020/01/12/alexandria-ocasio-cortez-pac-dccc-dues/ (accessed August 15, 2020).

7 Paul S. Herrnson, Costas Panagopoulos, and Kendall L. Bailey, *Congressional Elections*, 8th ed. (Los Angeles, CA: Sage/CQ Press, 2020), Chapter 4.

8 See their websites at https://democraticgovernors.org/ and https://www.rga.org/.

9 Jonathan Weisman, "G.O.P. Error Reveals Donors and the Price of Access," *New York Times*, September 24, 2014, p. A13.

10 These now include the (Democratic) Women's Leadership Forum, the Democratic Women's Network, the Democratic Women's Caucus, and RNC Women.

11 David B. Magleby, "Electoral Politics as Team Sport," in John C. Green and Daniel J. Coffey, eds., *The State of the Parties*, 6th ed. (Lanham, MD: Rowman & Littlefield, 2010), pp. 81–100.

12 Raymond J. LaRaja, "Richer Parties, Better Politics?" *The Forum* 11 (2013): 313-338.

13 See Brian Conley "Route to '66," *American Review of Politics* 31 (2010): 67-89.

14 See Daniel J. Galvin, "The Transformation of the National Party Committees," in Marjorie Randon Hershey, ed., *Guide to U.S. Political Parties* (Los Angeles, CA: Sage, 2014), Chapter 15.

15 The terms *hard money* and *soft money* are explained in Chapter 12.

16 See Austin Ranney, *Curing the Mischiefs of Faction* (Berkeley, CA: University of California Press, 1975); William J. Crotty, *Decisions for the Democrats* (Baltimore, MD: Johns Hopkins University Press, 1978); and John S. Jackson, *The American Political Party System* (Washington, DC: Brookings Institution, 2015), Chapters 3 and 4.

17 John F. Bibby, "Party Renewal in the Republican National Party," in Gerald M. Pomper, ed., *Party Renewal in America* (New York: Praeger, 1981), pp. 102–115.

18 See Paul S. Herrnson, "The Revitalization of National Party Organizations," in L. Sandy Maisel, ed., *The Parties Respond*, 2nd ed. (Boulder, CO: Westview, 1994), pp. 45–68.

19 Herrnson et al., *Congressional Elections*, 8th ed., p. 106.

20 See Marian Currinder, *Money in the House* (Boulder, CO: Westview, 2009), pp. 34–39.

21 Ryan Grim and Sabrina Siddiqui, "Call Time for Congress Shows How Fundraising Dominates Bleak Work Life," *Huffington Post*, January 8, 2013, https://www.huffpost.com/entry/call-time-congressional-fundraising_n_2427291 (accessed August 15, 2020).

22 See Paul S. Herrnson, *Party Campaigning in the 1980s* (Cambridge, MA: Harvard University Press, 1988), p. 47.

23 See David B. Magleby and J. Quin Monson, eds., *The Last Hurrah?* (Provo, UT: Center for the Study of Elections and Democracy, 2003).

24 Daniel A. Smith, "Strings Attached," in Magleby and Monson, eds., *The Last Hurrah?* p. 194.

25 Quoted in Jonathan Weisman, "Democrats' Hopes to Gain in House Fade," *New York Times*, October 15, 2014, p. A25.

26 Elaine C. Kamarck, "Assessing Howard Dean's Fifty State Strategy and the 2006 Midterm Elections," *The Forum* 4 (2006), issue 3, article 5.

27 Adam Nagourney, "Dean Seeks Some Respect (and Credit) for Obama's Victory," *New York Times*, November 11, 2008, https://www.nytimes.com/2008/11/12/us/politics/12web-nagourney.html (accessed August 15, 2020).

28 See Sidney M. Milkis and John W. York, "If the Obama Presidency Is Winding Down, Why Is His Group Organizing for Action Ramping Up?" "The Monkey Cage," *Washington Post*, July 29, 2015, https://www.washingtonpost.com/news/monkey-cage/wp/2015/07/29/if-the-obama-presidency-is-winding-down-why-is-his-group-organizing-for-action-ramping-up/ (accessed August 15, 2020).

29 "The Fight for the Soul of the Democratic Party," *CQ Magazine*, May 21, 2018, p. 1.

30 Danny Hakim and Glenn Thrush, "How the Trump Campaign Took Control of the G.O.P.," *New York Times*, March 9, 2020, p. A1.

31 Timothy P. Nokken, "Ideological Congruence Versus Electoral Success," *American Politics Research* 31 (2003): 3–26.

32 Rachael Bade, Josh Dawsey, and Michelle Ye Hee Lee, "Cash-Rich Trump Campaign Leaving House GOP High and Dry, Officials Say," *Washington Post*, July 26, 2020, p. A6.

33 Leon D. Epstein, *Political Parties in the American Mold* (Madison: University of Wisconsin Press, 1986), p. 200.

34 John J. Coleman, "The Resurgence of Party Organization?" in Daniel M. Shea and John C. Green, eds., *The State of the Parties* (Lanham, MD: Rowman & Littlefield, 1994), pp. 311–328.

CHAPTER 5

Party Activists

Most people who work on behalf of the U.S. parties are volunteers. The only "pay" they receive is the satisfaction they get in championing an issue, watching their candidate win, or making a like-minded friend. Volunteers, including a lot of college students, do most of the parties' work of registering people to vote, canvassing door-to-door, bringing voters to the polls, and updating a party organization's Facebook and Instagram accounts and Twitter feed.

But the parties pay a price for all that free labor. People who volunteer time and money to a party organization or candidate are often motivated by strong political views. These party activists tend to be more extreme in their attitudes toward issues than most other voters are; Democratic activists are more consistently liberal, and Republican activists more conservative, than their own party's less-active supporters. And they would like their party's candidates to share their intensity.

In the run-up to the 2020 election, liberal Democratic activists claimed that some potential Democratic presidential nominees were not fervent enough in supporting universal health care and higher taxes on the rich, and conservative Republican activists called for the scalps of Republicans who dared to speak of compromise with Democrats on immigration or trade.

Party organizations must keep their volunteer activists engaged and enthusiastic. At the same time, the parties want to avoid sounding extreme; that could turn off less-partisan voters. How party organizations achieve this difficult balance, and whether they do, is determined by the ways they attract and keep volunteers.

What Draws People into Party Activity?

People become involved in organizations of all kinds, from party organizations to dance marathons, for three types of reasons. **Purposive incentives** refer to the sense of satisfaction people feel when promoting an issue or cause that matters to them. **Solidary incentives** are intangible as well: the social benefits that people can gain from associating with others, networking, and being part of a group. **Material incentives**, which are no longer common, are tangible rewards for activity—cash payments or other concrete rewards for one's work.[1]

Purposive (Issue-Based) Incentives

To an increasing extent, people are led to party activism by their commitment to particular issues. Someone dedicated to abortion rights, for example, might begin by working for a pro-choice Democratic candidate and then come to view the candidate's party as a vehicle for keeping abortion legal. A very conservative Christian who believes that life begins at conception might be drawn to the Republican Party as a means of stopping abortion.

Since the parties have polarized on so many issues in recent years, most of those who volunteer for party work have been motivated to use the party to achieve policy goals.[2] Although we do not have comparable data on earlier times, there is reason to believe that this was less true of party workers in other periods of the nation's history.[3] The energy and passion in party organizations come increasingly from issue-driven activists—those on the right in the Republican Party and those on the left for the Democrats.

Issue-driven party activism has shaped politics at all levels. In the 2020 state and local elections, many Democrats were propelled into activism by reports that police officers had violated black Americans' rights, and many Republicans urged others to vote to restore law and order in cities experiencing protests against racial injustice. Some issues have had enough power to lead activists to switch parties. The abortion and race issues, for example, induced many formerly Democratic pro-lifers and southern conservatives to join the Republican Party beginning in the 1970s, and they soon cemented a set of favored issue positions into the platform of their new party.[4]

A large proportion of these issue-based activists are convinced that their activity has made a difference. In one survey, three-quarters of campaign volunteers believed that their involvement had affected at least some votes.[5] So although it might seem irrational to spend a lot of time on party activity in support of an issue that could be termed a "collective good"—one that, if achieved, will benefit the whole society rather than only the activists who worked hard to achieve it—many people become active in a party to do just that. Others become party activists out of a more general sense that citizen participation is essential in a democracy. (See box "A Day in the Life: An Activist Runs for Congress: Alexandria Ocasio-Cortez," on page 103).

Solidary (Social) Incentives

Many people are drawn to party work by the social contact that it provides. In an age when some people's closest relationship is with their tablet or their smartphone, the face-to-face contact at a party headquarters or in a campaign offers a chance to meet like-minded people and to be part of an active group. Family traditions may lead some young adults to go to party activities looking for social life, just as others may look to a softball league or a bar. Party activism is a form of networking—a standard means of looking for a job. Some find it exciting to meet local officials or others who appear on the news and to feel that they are helping to create a small part of history. Researchers find

A DAY IN THE LIFE

An Activist Runs for Congress:
Alexandria Ocasio-Cortez

She was a third-generation New Yorker with family roots in Puerto Rico. She graduated from Boston University with majors in economics and international relations and returned home to the Bronx to work as a community organizer. But her father's death and the Great Recession of the late 2000s shook her family's economic foundation, and Alexandria Ocasio-Cortez (known as AOC) took jobs as a waitress and bartender to help out.

Her work experiences deepened her conviction that working-class Americans were getting the shaft from public policy. Her commitment to such remedies as universal health care, tuition-free college, and criminal justice reform led her to become active in Democratic Socialists of America and then in Sen. Bernie Sanders' campaign for the 2016 Democratic presidential nomination. Her activism left her disappointed about party politics:

> What I see is that the Democratic Party takes working class communities for granted, they take people of color for granted and they just assume that we're going to turn out no matter how bland or half-stepping these proposals are.

So she agreed to offer an alternative. In 2018 AOC ran against the older, white Democrat who represented her majority–minority district in the U.S. House. The incumbent, a powerful member of the House Democratic leadership, had not faced a primary challenge in more than a decade, and he outraised her by ten to one. She countered with an aggressive social media campaign as well as personal contact: knocking on the doors of people she felt her party had long ignored, such as young people, working-class people, and those who spoke English as a second language. To the surprise of many, she won the primary handily and then the general election, becoming the youngest woman ever elected to Congress. She had just turned 29.

After becoming an incumbent herself, she tweeted that her insurance premium as a member of Congress was less than half the premium she paid as a waitress: "It's frustrating that Congressmembers would deny other people affordability that they themselves enjoy. Time for #MedicareForAll."

Her outspoken stands attracted a lot of media coverage as well as a public invitation from President Trump to, along with other progressive Congresswomen, "go back and help fix the totally broken and crime infested places from which they came." Her passion for progressive issues—renewable energy, universal health care, minority rights—illustrates the importance of *purposive* (issue-based) incentives in attracting people to party activism.

Sources: Shane Goldmacher and Jonathan Martin, "Democratic Power Broker, Once a Possible House Leader, Loses New York Primary," *New York Times,* June 27, 2018, p. A1; and Max Benwell, "How Alexandria Ocasio-Cortez Beat Everyone at Twitter in Nine Tweets," *The Guardian*, February 12, 2019, https://www.theguardian.com/us-news/2019/feb/12/alexandria-ocasio-cortez-twitter-social-media (from which quotes are drawn; accessed August 16, 2020).

that a large number of party activists cite the social life of party politics as a valuable reward for their efforts.[6]

Material Incentives

The American parties once offered a lot of material incentives for party work. Even before the age of the party "machine," people got involved in party activity mainly to share in the "spoils" gained when a party controlled the government. These "spoils" came in the form of patronage and preferments. **Patronage** means appointing an individual to a government job as a reward for party work. Although patronage is very limited today, the party can still provide loyal workers with a base of support if they seek elected office. **Preferments** are other favors a governing party can grant to party supporters, such as contracts or preferred treatment in enforcing laws. Patronage, access to elected office, and preferments have all played important roles in building and sustaining American party organizations.

Patronage   Early in the life of the American republic and for more than a century afterward, people were attracted to party work by the prospect of being rewarded with government jobs if the party won. Patronage has been used in other nations as well, but no other party system relied on patronage as much and as long as the American system. When party machines controlled many cities, city governments were staffed almost entirely by loyalists of the party in power.[7] In return for their jobs, patronage appointees traditionally "volunteered" their time, energy, and often even a part of their salary to the party organization. They were especially active during campaigns; American party politics is rich with tales of the entire staff of certain government departments being put to work in support of their boss's reelection. Even now, when such practices are usually frowned on and sometimes illegal, some types of government employees can still face pressure to contribute time or money to their party.

As the number of government jobs grew, however, the number of patronage jobs available to the parties dropped dramatically. Most government employees are now hired under civil service and merit systems, in which applicants get jobs based on their scores on competitive exams and have certain employment protections. The number of full-time federal positions filled by political appointees has dwindled over the years to a few thousand today, many of them high-level policy-making positions. States and cities have followed the same path, though more slowly.

The Supreme Court has helped dismantle patronage at the state and local levels. In 1976 and 1980, the Court ruled that some county political employees could not be fired simply because the party in power changed. The Court went further in a 1990 Illinois case, determining that politically based hiring and promotion violated the First Amendment freedoms of speech and association. In each case, the Court agreed that party affiliation might be a relevant qualification in filling policy-making positions but not in lower-level offices.[8] Even where patronage jobs remain, they are usually under the control of elected executives—mayors, governors, and others—who want to use patronage to build their own political followings rather than to reward loyal service to the party organization.

Some patronage jobs still exist. Mayors, governors, and presidents continue to reserve top policy-making positions for their trusted supporters. Legislatures often resist bringing their staff members under the protection of civil service systems. In 2013, the governor of Kansas convinced the state legislature to limit the coverage of civil service hiring for state jobs. Civil service rules for governmental employees can be bypassed by hiring politically loyal, "temporary" workers outside of the civil service system or by channeling party loyalists into jobs in private firms that depend on government contracts. A few big campaign contributors will continue to be named ambassadors to small and peaceful nations. Whenever political leaders have some discretion in hiring people, in short, they will find a way to award jobs to their supporters, who usually share their party affiliation, so these opportunities will attract at least some people to party activity.

Keep in mind that some observers are sorry to lose the practice of patronage. President Andrew Jackson promoted its use as a way of encouraging a more democratic and less elitist government.[9] When government jobs are filled (and then protected) only by civil service procedures, it becomes almost impossible for reform-minded leaders to replace a sluggish or ineffective bureaucrat with a more efficient worker. Patronage was also thought to keep party organizations strong as instruments of democracy. Material incentives can be very effective in attracting workers. Patronage employees usually share the party organization's main goal: winning elections. That gave the party organization the flexibility to take the issue stands and appeal to the groups that would produce a victory. Patronage, then, helped the American parties behave pragmatically and inclusively.

Patronage jobs in government are not the only employment opportunities a party can offer. State and national party organizations now hire thousands of professional campaign workers, as do consulting firms associated with the parties. To provide services to their candidates, party organizations need pollsters, field organizers, researchers, fund-raisers, strategists, webmasters, database managers, and others. Some activists are drawn to party work by the chance of landing these jobs, but *in general, patronage is no longer an important force in motivating activists.*

Elected Office   Some women and men become party activists because they see party work as a first step toward running for office. This has been true for a long time; about 40 percent of the county chairs interviewed in a 1979–1980 national survey hoped to hold public office, and an earlier study found that one-third of all state party chairs became candidates for elective office after serving the party.[10] Because of primary elections, of course, very few party organizations can just "give" nominations to public office to loyal party activists. It is far more common for candidates to see the party as one of the bases of support for winning votes and, in some areas, as the most important one. Candidates need money, advice, and people (staff and volunteers), and the party remains a likely source of all of these. So the lure of party support in a later campaign for elected office may bring some people into party work.

Preferments   Party activity can bring tangible rewards for some people, other than elective or appointive office. Because public officials can use some discretion in distributing government services and granting government contracts, there is the potential for political favoritism. Some people contribute money or time to their party in the hope of attracting these favors. The head of a construction company might give a big campaign contribution to win a government contract to build a new school or highway. It is no accident that leaders of the construction and real estate industries are so active politically in states and cities that spend millions every year on roads and public buildings.

There are other forms of preference as well. People may hope that in return for activism on behalf of the party, they will get special treatment such as tolerant inspection of their pizzeria by the health department or prompt snow removal in front of their place of business. Or they may provide political support in the hope of receiving a scarce resource, such as a liquor license for a local restaurant.

Reformers have promoted a number of safeguards to limit government's discretion in giving out benefits and buying goods and services from private firms. Examples are competitive and sealed bidding, conflict of interest laws, and even affirmative action. Yet, because the potential benefits are so great for both sides, there always seem to be ways of evading even the tightest controls. In addition, many reformers don't want to eliminate *all* government discretion in the awarding of contracts just to stamp out *partisan* discretion. The result is that preferments may have taken the place of patronage as the main material incentive for political activity. Unfortunately for party organization leaders, however, they don't grant the preferments now; it is the elected officials who do.

Mixed Incentives

Most party organizations rely on a variety of incentives to attract activists. Those hoping to build support for a later run for office work together with those motivated by a particular issue and with those who come to party activities for social contact. That can produce strains among party volunteers motivated by different incentives. Someone who became a Democratic activist to work for abortion rights, for instance, is not likely to be satisfied with a party that supports a pro-life Democratic candidate, whereas others who participate in the party for social reasons may feel that the party needs to be a "big tent" to win elections, including people who differ in their attitudes toward abortion.

The incentive that attracts people to party work may not be the incentive that keeps them there. Several studies suggest that those who become active in the party to fight for certain issues are more likely to remain in the party if they come to value the social contact it gives them. The motive that sustains their party work, in short, often shifts to solidary incentives: friendships, identification with the party itself, and other social rewards.[11] It may be that committed issue activists simply burn out, or that the American parties, which try to remain flexible enough to win elections, do not always provide the level of ideological dedication needed to sustain party workers whose lives are devoted to a set of uncompromising ideals.

Pragmatists (Professionals) and Purists (Amateurs)

Drawing on research on these incentives, scholars have classified party activists into two types. One type of party activist is the **pragmatist** (sometimes known as "professional")—the party worker whose first loyalty is to the party itself. These are the party "regulars" who support their party in good times and bad, when it nominates candidates they approve of and even when it doesn't. A different type is the **purist** (or "amateur")—the issue-oriented activist, motivated by purposive incentives, who sees party activity as only one means of achieving important political goals.[12] (On the differences between these two types, see Table 5.1.)

A party organization populated by purists may behave very differently from a party dominated by pragmatists. Above all, purists are drawn into the party to further some issues or principles; their goal is the issue, and the party is a means of achieving it. If the party or its candidates pull back on its commitment to their issue, they may pull back on their commitment to the party. So they tend to be less willing to compromise their positions to win elections. Policy-driven activists want a candidate "they can trust to safeguard their most intense concerns."[13] When they lead party organizations, they often bring a strong push for reform in both the party's internal business and the larger political system, as Bernie Sanders Democrats did in 2016 and 2020.

TABLE 5.1 Comparing Pragmatists and Purists

	Pragmatists	Purists
Political style	Practical	Ideological
What do they want?	Success for the party	Success for particular issues, candidates
Their loyalty is to	Party organization	Officeholders, other political groups
They want the party to focus on	Candidates, elections	Issues, ideology
The party should choose candidates on the basis of	Their electability	Their principles
Their support of party candidates is	Automatic	Conditional on candidates' principles
They were recruited into politics through	Party work	Issue or candidate organizations
Their socio-economic level is	Average to above average	Well above average

For pragmatists, on the other hand, the goal is for the party to win elections. Issues and candidates are the means of achieving that goal. If they believe that their party is most likely to win by downplaying an issue, moderating a position, or nominating a candidate who is popular but not in lockstep with their views, then that is the course they are likely to favor. Some Republican Party leaders and elected officials, for instance, swallowed their objections to President Trump's stand on trade and his inflammatory style because they thought his fervent base support was the Republicans' best chance of winning the White House. And many Democrats of different ideological stripes moved quickly to back Joe Biden in 2020 on the assumption that Biden was more electable than Sanders. Party leaders, then, must find a balance between the demands of the growing numbers of issue-oriented, purist activists and those of their more pragmatic colleagues. It is a common dilemma: whether to remain loyal to the group (or the nation) to keep it strong and vibrant or to give priority to the principles for which the group was formed.

Many activists fall between these two extremes. In practice, even most dedicated purists often come to realize that they can't achieve their policy goals unless their candidates win office. Among county party chairs in 1972, a time when purists were thought to hold the upper hand in the Democratic Party, the purists did not differ from pragmatists in their effort to run effective campaigns, maintain party morale, or communicate within the party.[14] But these two types of party activism don't always get along well together. When pragmatists note that candidates can't accomplish anything unless they first win office, purists reply that there's little point in working hard to elect a candidate who does not share your policy priorities.

Where Do Activists Come From?

Like almost all other community groups, party organizations have a hard time attracting volunteers. Except at the national level and in some states where there has been an increase in paid positions and exciting professional opportunities, parties often have few effective means of enlisting new activists. To add to the challenge, state laws often take at least part of the recruitment process out of the party's hands. Rules requiring open party caucuses and the election of party officials in primaries limit the party's control over its personnel. This can lead to the takeover of a local (or even a state) party organization by an intense group of issue activists. At the least, it leaves a party vulnerable to shifts in its direction as some leaders and activists move on and new, self-recruited leaders take their place, as Chapter 3 showed.

Finding Volunteers: Is Anybody Home?

In a much discussed set of writings, political scientist Robert Putnam showed that Americans' participation in community activities has declined in recent years. Groups ranging from churches to bowling leagues have been starved of participants. Many culprits have been identified, from the number of hours Americans spend surfing the Internet and watching television to the increasing numbers of dual-career families. The consequences, Putnam argues, are profound: a reduction in "social capital"—the social connections, values, and trust that enable communities to solve their problems more easily.[15]

The party organizations have not been spared. Fewer people are involving themselves in the face-to-face activities of politics—attending a political speech or a meeting—while the long-distance activities of Internet surfing and tweeting about politics are on the increase. One well-designed survey found that only 8 percent of its national sample reported working on a campaign and just 5 percent said they were involved in a party organization, among the smallest percentages reporting activity in any type of civic organization.[16] Similarly grim conclusions come from the American National Election Studies, in which, in each year since 1994, only about 5 percent have reported going to any political meetings and only about 3 percent said they worked for a party[17]—even in elections such as 2020, when political passions ran high. Granted, even these small percentages represent a lot of people; 3 percent of the adult population would be about 6 million party and campaign activists. But although some of these activists spend a lot of time on political work, mainly at the local level, others are "checkbook participants" who mail in their contributions but do not volunteer their time and energy.

Party organizations need a constant supply of activists of all kinds, so when volunteers are in short supply, the parties are glad to accept whatever help is available. The nature of that help often varies from one political period to another, depending on events in the political world at that time. Thus, activists' political outlooks may differ considerably, depending on the time when they became active.[18] The nature and direction of the Democratic Party were heavily influenced by the influx of liberals activated by the Vietnam War and the Civil Rights Movement in the 1960s and 1970s. Tax revolts and the appeal of Ronald Reagan in the 1980s brought new blood into Republican Party organizations. In recent years, activists from evangelical Christian groups and Tea Party supporters have brought their issues and styles of partisanship into state and local Republican Parties. Because this recruitment process often depends on the presence of magnetic personalities and powerful issues, it usually takes place in spurts rather than continuously.

The parties' recruitment system, then, is not very systematic, and it is closely linked to the movements and passions in the larger society at the time. Yet, although the parties have only limited control over their own recruitment, it clearly affects the parties' ability to achieve their goals. A local Democratic Party whose activists come mainly from labor unions will have different concerns from a local Democratic Party dominated by environmental activists, and a Republican organization run by local business leaders can differ from one controlled by conservative Christians. Depending on the nature of the community that these parties are trying to persuade, these local parties will probably have different levels of election success as well.

What Kinds of People Become Party Activists?

People are most likely to become involved in party politics if they have the resources to take part, the attitudes that support involvement, and if somebody has encouraged them to do so.[19] The resources needed to become a party activist include time, money, and civic skills such as the ability to organize and communicate. It takes free time to help plan a party's activities, canvass or call people, and attend other party events. People need money if they plan to contribute to the party organization or its candidates or go to party conventions. Their educational level helps to determine how much money and time they have available to spend.

Their attitudes toward politics also propel them toward party activism or steer them away from it. People are more likely to take part if they are interested in what happens in campaigns and concerned about the workings of government, if they feel attached to a party, and if they believe that their involvement could make a difference. Most of these attitudes are related to one's income and education levels and thus add to their impact.

The third important question is simply: Has anybody asked them? The parties now have a large arsenal of tools to contact potential activists: texts, e-mail, postal mail, various social media, websites, phone calls, rallies, and in-person canvassing (see box "How Social Media Have Changed Political Activism" on page 111). However, most appeals to take part in campaign work—and especially most *successful* appeals—come from friends or acquaintances of the potential activist. Over the years, most activists have reported that they first became involved with the party as a result of these informal, personal requests for help.[20] Being urged to participate is a powerful motivator; in a major study, almost half of those who were asked to do campaign work said yes. But most people are never asked; only about 12 percent of the respondents in that study reported that anyone had ever invited them to work on a campaign.[21] This helps to explain why the proportion of party activists is so small.

Who are these people who are active in party affairs? How representative are they of the rest of the American population?

Better Educated and Wealthier Than Average

American party activists have several characteristics in common that set them apart from the general population. One of the most distinctive characteristic of party activists—and one of the most concerning—is that they tend to have higher incomes, more years of formal education, and higher-status occupations than does the average American. People with higher incomes are much more likely to contribute to campaigns and to do campaign work than are those with lower incomes. Those who are politically active online tend to be wealthier and more educated as well (see Figure 5.1). The only way that the Internet reduces inequalities in participation is that younger people are not as underrepresented in online political activity as they are offline.[22]

How Social Media Have Changed Political Activism

Twitter, Instagram, YouTube, Pinterest, Facebook, and other social media have given party organizations and their activists new ways to mobilize and inform prospective supporters. Donald Trump's 2020 reelection campaign is a good example; even though he collected unprecedented sums during a four-year fund-raising drive, Trump could reach an audience of more than 85 million people through his Twitter account, and many more through re-tweets, without spending a penny. Here's Trump on Twitter at a critical point in his first nomination campaign: "How do you fight millions of dollars of fraudulent commercials pushing for crooked politicians? I will be using Facebook & Twitter. Watch!" Previous presidential candidates might have sold their souls to the devil to achieve that kind of exposure for free.

Of course, very few candidates can attract 85 million followers online. But the national parties, many state party organizations and even a lot of local parties now use social media to energize volunteers, ask for contributions, and post photos and other images for supporters to use as their profile pictures. Facebook likers or Twitter followers can be directed to a party or campaign website, asked to sign a petition, or provided with information that the party feels is being ignored or distorted by the traditional media. After Democratic campaigns used a Facebook application in 2012 called Social Organizing, which connected their Facebook friends to voting records and let them know which friends had already voted or donated and which ones might still be open to persuasion, activating supporters with highly targeted ads on social media became standard procedure for any campaign that could afford the necessary research (see Chapter 11).

Keep in mind, however, that the ability to *reach* people does not necessarily include the ability to *persuade* them. An interesting recent study found that legislators who tweet about particular issues don't necessarily increase their followers' attention to those issues. Social media users are just as likely as other interested citizens to pay attention to information they already agree with, rather than to change their views in response to media exposure.

The ability to spread a message almost instantly to widely dispersed populations has affected much more than American campaigns. Social media have let new social movements, from Black Lives Matter to the Arab Spring, take form and gain recruits. They can give a voice to the underdog (if the underdog knows how to tweet or tag people) and help elected leaders learn more about public sentiment. But social media can also be used to enable governments to market their appeals more effectively to citizens, to monitor protest movements, and even to spread disinformation for the purpose of disrupting elections. As with most technologies, social media can enhance and also threaten a democratic system.

Sources: Ludwig Siegele, "The Signal and the Noise," *The Economist*, March 26, 2016, https://www.economist.com/special-report/2016/03/23/the-signal-and-the-noise (accessed August 16, 2020), and Pablo Barbera, Andreu Casas, Jonathan Nagler, Patrick J. Egan, Richard Bonneau, John T. Jost, and Joshua A. Tucker, "Who Leads?" *American Political Science Review* 113 (November 2019): 883–901.

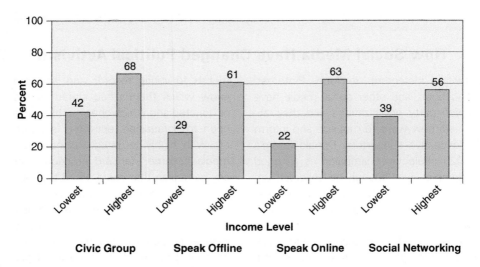

FIGURE 5.1 Wealthy People Are More Politically Active Online and Offline

Note: Bars show the percentage of respondents in each income group who took part in each political activity. *Lowest annual household Income:* less than $10,000; *Highest household Income:* $150,000 and above. *Civic group:* directly involved with a civic group; *Speak offline:* Communicate publicly about political issues offline. *Speak online:* Communicate publicly about political issues online. *Social Networking:* Politically active on social networking sites.

Source: Data from Aaron Smith, "Civic Engagement in the Digital Age," Pew Research Center Pew Internet and American Life Survey, April 25, 2013, www.pewinternet.org/2013/04/25/civic-engagement-in-the-digital-age/ (accessed August 16, 2020).

This tendency for party activists to be better educated and wealthier than the average citizen may seem perfectly natural; people with more money and higher education are more likely to have the means to participate in politics, the interest in political affairs, and the expectation that they would be successful at it. As a result, we might expect this pattern to hold in other democratic nations as well. But that is not the case. Most other democracies have a viable socialist party that recruits many of its activists from within labor unions. That dampens the relationship between party activism and higher education and wealth.

In fact, it was not always true of American politics either. The urban political machines of the 1800s and early 1900s recruited party activists who were more representative of the populations with which they worked. The machines' jobs and favors were the main reasons for political activism at this time. When patronage and other material incentives dwindled, the social character of these parties changed. A comparison of county committee members from both Pittsburgh parties in 1971, 1976, and 1983 shows that as machine control declined, the education levels of party workers increased.[23] As issue-based incentives become more common in the American parties, party activists become even better educated and wealthier than the average citizen.

The social characteristics of Democratic activists differ from those of Republicans, just as the social bases of the parties' voters do. Democratic activists are more likely than their Republican counterparts to be female, black, unmarried, and union members. But differences in education, income, and occupation between the two parties' activists have declined in recent years. Although they may come from different backgrounds and certainly hold different political views, the leaders of both parties come disproportionately from higher-status groups in American society, even more now than in decades past.[24] As a result, party activism and other forms of political participation amplify the voices of privileged groups even more in the U.S. than in many other democracies.

People from "Political Families"

Party activists often come from families with a history of party activity. Many party activists had an adult party activist in their immediate family when they were growing up. Consider the case of Joe Kennedy III. When he was elected to Congress from Massachusetts in 2012, he became the fourth member of the Kennedy family to serve in the U.S. House, after his great-uncle John; his father, Joe Kennedy II; and his cousin Patrick. In 2020 he joined the list of three family members who had run for the U.S. Senate (grandfather Bobby and great-uncles John and Ted). Great-uncle John had been President of the U.S. from 1960 to 1963. The family's history also included a lieutenant governor of Maryland (aunt Kathleen Kennedy Townsend), a Maryland state legislator (cousin Mark Kennedy Shriver), and a California mayor and city councilor (cousin Bobby Shriver). With such a background, politics becomes the family business, just as the daughter of a small business owner might grow up to manage the family store.

Different Agendas

In addition to these differences in income, education, and family background, party activists also differ from other Americans in the types of issues that they regard as important. A large study of political activists found that they were concerned especially about education, abortion, the economy, and human needs (including Social Security and Medicare, jobs, health care, and housing). In particular, abortion mattered more to party activists—it was mentioned by almost one in five activists—than to citizens as a whole, as did education.[25]

The activists' issue agendas varied according to their income and education levels. Higher-income activists expressed greater concern about abortion and the environment, whereas lower-income activists' involvement was more likely to be prompted by a concern about basic human needs.[26] To the extent that higher-income activists are better represented in the parties, issues such as abortion may get more attention in party politics, even though health care, housing, and other types of human needs are obviously critical to lower-income Americans.

The types of issues that most clearly divide Democratic from Republican activists have changed over time. In the early 1970s, one of the primary distinctions between the two major parties' activists was the question of social welfare—how big a role government should play in issues such as welfare and other social services. At that time, there was a lot of variation among both parties' activists in their views about abortion. Today, in contrast, Democratic activists differ greatly from Republican activists on abortion, though the issue is more important to Republican activists than it has been to Democrats.[27]

More Consistent (and Intense) Views

Most significantly, party activists (and activists in other areas of politics as well) tend to hold more consistent views on issues than does the average American, and those views have come more closely in line with their party's positions. During the past 20 years, consistent liberals have become a larger proportion of Democratic activists, and consistent, strong conservatives have dominated the ranks of Republican activists. This polarization is especially pronounced on health-care reform and other redistributionist economic policies as well as on issues of traditional values.[28] Activists are more likely to hold deeply negative views of the other party and its leaders; in fact, these activists are often driven more by their hostility toward the other party than by their attachment to their own. This "negative partisanship" has become much more common during the past two decades, as you'll see in Chapter 6.[29]

These polarized liberals and conservatives are more likely to talk with people who share their strong views, to contact politically like-minded people on social media (especially true of liberal Democrats[30]), and, among the strong and consistent conservatives, to restrict their news sources to a few that share their views, such as Fox News.[31] Those who vote in primary elections—a major source of influence among activists—think of themselves as being more liberal (among Democrats) or more conservative (among Republicans) than are most general election voters in their area.[32] Because party activists are so important to campaigns, party candidates and elected officials tend to listen when activists urge them to take more consistent and intense stands on issues. That produces increasingly bitter political debate and gridlock.[33]

The main reason for this widening gap has been the increasing conservatism of Republican activists.[34] As you can see in Figure 5.2, most Democratic primary voters consider themselves liberals. But not nearly as many call themselves "*very* liberal" as the proportion of Republicans who call themselves "very

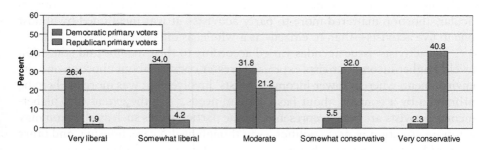

FIGURE 5.2 Republican Primary Voters Are More Likely to Call Themselves "Very Conservative" Than Democrats Are to Call Themselves "Very Liberal"

Note: Bars show the percentage of self-reported Democratic and Republican primary voters who describe themselves as liberals, moderates, and conservatives.

Source: Data from Elaine Kamarck and Alexander R. Podcul, "The 2018 Primaries Project," Brookings Institution, October 23, 2018, https://www.brookings.edu/research/the-2018-primaries-project-the-ideology-of-primary-voters/ (accessed August 16, 2020).

conservative." We also find more self-described "moderates" among Democratic than among Republican primary voters.

This helps us understand the strong rightward trend of the Republican Party in recent years. Especially since 1994, when Republicans won a majority in both houses of Congress, Republican activists have been motivated by issues and principles to an even greater extent than Democratic activists have, and their dedication to conservative principles has become more intense. So now, on most issues, those active in the Republican Party stand even further to the right of the average voter than Democratic activists are to the left of the average voter.

Party Activists and Democracy

In short, American party activists differ a lot from other citizens—the very people these activists aim to persuade—and the gulf has been growing.[35] Research tells us that the major parties attract men and women with the time and financial resources to afford political activity, the attitudes that make politics a priority to them, and the connections with others who are similarly engaged. These activists also tend to be motivated by controversial issues, hold more extreme attitudes than other citizens do, and are more polarized by party than was the case in the mid-1900s. These findings raise some important questions: Does it matter if party activists are not very representative of other Americans? What has been the impact of the increase in issue-oriented, "purist" activists? More generally, how do the characteristics of Republican and Democratic activists affect the workings of party organizations?

The Problem of Representation

When party activists give the appearance of being "true believers" on contentious issues and do not share the concerns of less involved voters, then it is not surprising that many Americans think of party organizations as alien places. A party system needs to strike the delicate balance between offering clear and consistent alternatives to voters and straying too far from the average voter's political perspective. When the two parties sound too much alike on issues, citizens may feel that there's no reason for them to vote. Democracy can be well served when the major parties take easily distinguished stands on major policy questions. However, when Republican and Democratic activists take polarized, "us vs. them" positions, especially on questions that are not central to most Americans' daily lives, and try to marginalize anyone who disagrees, then the parties expose themselves to public distrust, an old problem in American politics. The challenge increases when these activists recruit and support extremists as party candidates for public office. Recent research finds that extremist candidates tend to drive down their party's voter turnout, increasing the chance that the other party will win the race.[36]

Further, when both parties' activists come from more privileged backgrounds than most other citizens do, we have to ask whether they are truly able to understand the forces that affect most Americans' lives. It is possible, of course, for wealthy and educated individuals to speak for others who are disadvantaged. But we have seen indications that party activists' issue *priorities* differ from those of many other citizens in ways consistent with the economic differences that separate them.[37]

Purists and Pressure for Internal Party Democracy

Larger numbers of issue-oriented, purist activists increase the demands on the party organization. In the past five decades, these activists have insisted on a much louder voice in the party's organization, and their demands have been met. Because volunteer activists are so essential to the party's success, party leaders are often willing to accept greater levels of internal party democracy to retain their volunteers' loyalty.

An internally democratic party organization might result in a stronger party, better able to fulfill its responsibilities in a democracy. Rank-and-file activists who contribute their time and effort in the service of a strongly held principle and who feel sure that their views are taken seriously by party leaders may work even harder on the party's behalf. They might also press the party to remain consistent in its issue stands and strive to hold the party's leaders accountable, at least to the activists themselves.

On the other hand, pragmatic parties, dedicated to the party's success above all else, have a long tradition in American politics. Much of the discipline in the classic party machine resulted from the willingness and ability of party leaders to give or withhold material rewards. A disobedient or inefficient party worker sacrificed a patronage job or the hope of one. The newer incentives cannot be given or taken away so easily. A local Republican organization is not likely to punish an errant, ideologically motivated activist by ending the party's opposition to same-sex marriage. Besides, the activist could find many other organizations that may be more effective at pursuing that goal, such as religious lobbies or other organized interests.

Activists, Party Strength, and Democracy

Strong party organizations have often been considered a threat to American politics. Since the beginning, American political culture has been dominated by a fear that a few "bosses," responsible to no one but themselves, control the selection of public officials and the choice of policies. Supporters of candidates as diverse as Donald Trump and Bernie Sanders made this claim in 2020. That has produced anti-party efforts: reforms limiting the role of parties in the lives of candidates, elected officials, and voters.

Those efforts have often succeeded. The shortage of volunteers means that party organizations have to pay attention to their activists' concerns. This prevents a centralization of party power (unless, of course, the party activists push for greater centralization, as they sometimes have). The demand by many activists for internally democratic parties restrains the authority of party leaders at the top. And, in turn, because power in the American parties is diffused through the various levels of party organization, precinct committee members, city leaders, county officials, and activists at all levels are free to define their own political roles and to nourish their separate bases of party power.

The traditional worry about the excesses of party power, then, is probably misplaced. There have been few occasions in American history when parties have been able to corral the kinds of incentives and resources that they would need to develop a fully staffed, vibrant organization at all levels of government. Although the national, state, and local party organizations have raised more money and mastered new campaign skills in the past few decades (as Chapters 3 and 4 show), the continuing need to put "boots on the ground"—to attract volunteers able to relate to the people they are trying to persuade—remains one of the biggest challenges faced by American parties.

Notes

1 For the original formulation, see Peter B. Clark and James Q. Wilson, "Incentive Systems: A Theory of Organizations," *Administrative Science Quarterly* 6 (1961): 129–166.
2 John H. Aldrich, *Why Parties? A Second Look* (Chicago, IL: University of Chicago Press, 2011), p. 188.
3 Samuel J. Eldersveld, "The Party Activist in Detroit and Los Angeles," in William Crotty, ed., *Political Parties in Local Areas* (Knoxville, TN: University of Tennessee Press, 1986), Chapter 4.
4 John A. Clark, John M. Bruce, John H. Kessel, and William Jacoby, "I'd Rather Switch than Fight," *American Journal of Political Science* 35 (1991): 577–597; and Dorothy Davidson Nesbit, "Changing Partisanship among Southern Party Activists," *Journal of Politics* 50 (1988): 322–334.
5 Sidney Verba, Kay Lehman Schlozman, and Henry E. Brady, *Voice and Equality* (Cambridge, MA: Harvard University Press, 1995), p. 121.
6 See ibid., pp. 112–121.
7 See Martin Shefter, *Political Parties and the State* (Princeton, NJ: Princeton University Press, 1994).
8 The 1976 case is *Elrod v. Burns*; the 1980 case is *Branti v. Finkel*, and the 1990 case is *Rutan v. Republican Party of Illinois*.
9 On the case for patronage, see the dissenting opinions to the Supreme Court's *Elrod, Branti*, and *Rutan* decisions. The case against patronage is well put in Anne Freedman, *Patronage: An American Tradition* (Chicago, IL: Nelson-Hall, 1994), Chapter 5.
10 Cornelius P. Cotter, James L. Gibson, John F. Bibby, and Robert J. Huckshorn, *Party Organizations in American Politics* (New York: Praeger, 1984), p. 42; and Robert J. Huckshorn, *Party Leadership in the States* (Amherst, MA: University of Massachusetts Press, 1976), p. 37.
11 See M. Margaret Conway, *Political Participation in the United States*, 3rd ed. (Washington, DC: CQ Press, 2000).
12 See Clark and Wilson, "Incentive Systems." Note that the term "professional," as used here, does not necessarily refer to someone who is paid for party work, and the term "amateur" is not meant to be derogatory. See Byron E. Shafer and Regina L. Wagner, *The Long War over Party Structure* (Cambridge: Cambridge University Press, 2019) for a discussion of party structural change from "organized" (professional) to "volunteer" (purist or amateur) party organizations.

13 See Marty Cohen, David Karol, Hans Noel, and John Zaller, *The Party Decides* (Chicago, IL: University of Chicago Press, 2008), pp. 88–91, 178 (quote on p. 89).

14 Michael A. Maggiotto and Ronald E. Weber, "The Impact of Organizational Incentives on County Party Chairpersons," *American Politics Quarterly* 14 (1986): 201–218.

15 Robert D. Putnam, *Bowling Alone* (New York: Simon & Schuster, 2000).

16 Verba et al., *Voice and Equality*, Chapter 3. This seems to be true in other democracies as well; see Paul F. Whiteley, "Is the Party Over?" *Party Politics* 17 (2011): 21–44.

17 American National Election Studies, University of Michigan; data made available by the Inter-University Consortium for Political and Social Research.

18 See Paul Allen Beck and M. Kent Jennings, "Updating Political Periods and Political Participation," *American Political Science Review* 78 (1984): 198–201; and Steven E. Finkel and Gregory Trevor, "Reassessing Ideological Bias in Campaign Participation," *Political Behavior* 8 (1986): 374–390.

19 See Verba, Schlozman, and Brady, *Voice and Equality*, pp. 15–16 and Chapters 9–14.

20 Henry E. Brady, Kay Lehman Schlozman, and Sidney Verba, "Prospecting for Participants," *American Political Science Review* 93 (1999): 153–168.

21 Verba et al., *Voice and Equality*, pp. 135 and 139–144.

22 See Kay Lehman Schlozman, Sidney Verba, and Henry E. Brady, *The Unheavenly Chorus* (Princeton, NJ: Princeton University Press, 2012), especially Chapter 16.

23 See Michael Margolis and Raymond E. Owen, "From Organization to Personalism," *Polity* 18 (1985): 313–328.

24 Marjorie Randon Hershey, Nathaniel Birkhead, and Beth C. Easter, "Party Activists and Political Polarization," in Mark D. Brewer and L. Sandy Maisel, eds., *The Parties Respond*, 5th ed. (Boulder, CO: Westview Press, 2012).

25 Verba *et al.*, *Voice and Equality*, pp. 84–91.

26 Ibid., pp. 220–225.

27 Edward G. Carmines and James Woods, "The Role of Party Activists in the Evolution of the Abortion Issue," *Political Behavior* 24 (2002): 361–377.

28 Alan I. Abramowitz, *The Disappearing Center* (New Haven, CT: Yale University Press, 2010), pp. 47–48; Alan I. Abramowitz, *The Polarized Public?* (Boston, MA: Pearson, 2013), pp. 10 and 73.

29 Pew Center for the People and the Press, "Political Polarization in the American Public," June 12, 2014, www.people-press.org/2014/06/12/political-polarization-in-the-american-public (accessed August 16, 2020).

30 Monica Anderson and Jing Jing Jiang, "Liberal Democrats More Likely Than Other Groups to be Active on Social Media," Pew Research Center Fact Tank, November 5, 2018, https://www.pewresearch.org/fact-tank/2018/11/05/liberal-democrats-more-likely-than-other-groups-to-be-politically-active-on-social-media/ (accessed August 16, 2020).

31 Amy Mitchell, Jeffrey Gottfried, Jocelyn Kiley, and Katerina Eva Matsa, "Political Polarization and Media Habits," Pew Research Journalism Project, October 21, 2014, www.journalism.org/2014/10/21/political-polarization-media-habits/ (accessed August 16, 2020).

32 Elaine Kamarck and Alexander R. Podcul, "The 2018 Primaries Project," Brookings Institution, October 18, 2018, https://www.brookings.edu/research/the-2018-primaries-project-the-ideology-of-primary-voters/ (accessed August 16, 2020).

33 Geoffrey C. Layman, Thomas M. Carsey, John C. Green, Richard Herrera, and Rosalyn Cooperman, "Activists and Conflict Extension in American Party Politics," *American Political Science Review* 104 (2010): 324–346. See also Schlozman et al., *The Unheavenly Chorus*, Chapter 9.

34 Kyle L. Saunders and Alan I. Abramowitz, "Ideological Realignment and Active Partisans in the American Electorate," *American Politics Research* 32 (2004): 285–309.

35 Ryan D. Enos and Eitan D. Hersh, "Party Activists as Campaign Advertisers," *American Political Science Review* 109 (2015): 252–278.

36 Andrew B. Hall and Daniel M. Thompson, "Who Punishes Extremist Nominees?" *American Political Science Review* 112 (August 2018): 509–524.

37 See Schlozman et al., *The Unheavenly Chorus*, especially Chapter 9.

PART THREE

The Political Party in the Electorate

If there were a Pollsters' Hall of Fame, surely the first question in it would be: Generally speaking, do you usually think of yourself as a Republican, a Democrat, an independent, or what? The question is meant to classify **party identifiers**—people who feel a sense of psychological attachment to a particular party. If you respond that you do usually think of yourself as a Democrat or a Republican, then you are categorized as belonging to the **party in the electorate**—the third major sector of the American parties. Party identifiers (also called **partisans**) make up the core of the party's support: the people who normally vote for a party's candidates and who see politics through a partisan's eyes. They are more apt to vote in their party's primary elections and to volunteer for party candidates than are other citizens. In short, they are the party organization's and its candidates' closest friends in the public.

Survey researchers have measured Americans' partisanship since the 1940s. The dominant measure, just cited, has been used in polls conducted by the University of Michigan, now under the auspices of the American National Election Studies (ANES). After asking whether you consider yourself a Republican or a Democrat, the question continues:

[If Republican or Democrat] Would you call yourself a strong [Republican or Democrat] or a not very strong [Republican or Democrat]? [If independent, no preference, or other party:] Do you think of yourself as closer to the Republican Party or to the Democratic Party?

Using these answers, researchers classify people into seven categories of party identification: strong party identifiers (Democrats or Republicans), weak identifiers (Democrats or Republicans), independent "leaners" (toward the Democrats or Republicans), and pure independents.[1]

Note that this definition is based on people's attitudes, not on their actual voting choices. Strong party identifiers usually vote for their party's candidates, but the essence of a party identification is an attachment to the idea of the party itself, distinct from feelings about particular candidates. Someone can remain a committed Republican, for example, while choosing to vote for the Democratic candidate in a specific race, as did a few anti-Trump Republicans in 2020. Because there are so many elective offices in the United States, and given the value American culture places on independence, party identifiers sometimes vote for a candidate or two of the other party. In the same sense, we do not define the party electorate by the official act of registering with a party. Almost half of the states do not require voters to register their party affiliation, and in states that do, some voters change their party attachments long before they change their official registration.[2]

The party electorate's relationship with the other two party sectors, the party organization and the party in government, is not necessarily close and cooperative. Party organizations and candidates ask their party identifiers for contributions and votes during campaigns but often don't keep in touch with partisans at other times. Party identifiers, in turn, seldom feel any obligation to the party organization other than to vote for its candidates, if they choose. Party identifiers are not party "members" in any real sense. In these ways, the American parties resemble cadre parties (see pages 55–56): top heavy in leaders and activists without any real membership, in contrast to the mass-membership parties that have been an important part of the European democratic experience.

Even so, party identifiers give the party organization and its candidates a continuing base of voter support. The parties, then, don't have to start from scratch in each campaign. The party in the electorate also determines almost all of the party's nominees for office by voting in primaries. It is a potential source of activists for the organization. Partisans help keep the party alive by transmitting party loyalties to their children. A party identification is usually the most significant landmark in an individual's mental map of the political world.

A party in the electorate is not just a collection of individuals; it is a coalition of social groups. Our images of the two parties often spring from the types of people the parties have attracted as identifiers. When people speak of the Democrats as the party of minorities or of the Republicans as the party of business, they are probably referring mainly to the party in the electorate. The groups in a party's coalition help shape its choice of nominees and stands on issues, and in turn, those candidates and appeals help to structure elections and political debate.

The three chapters in Part III explore the nature and importance of these parties in the electorate. Chapter 6 looks at the development of party identification and its impact on individuals' political behavior. Chapter 7 examines parties as coalitions of social groups and traces the meaning of changes in those coalitions over time. Chapter 8 focuses on parties' efforts to affect voter turnout, not only by mobilizing their supporters but also by trying to change the rules that govern who can vote.

Notes

1 See Angus Campbell, Philip E. Converse, Warren E. Miller, and Donald E. Stokes, *The American Voter* (New York: Wiley, 1960), Chapter 6.
2 Steven E. Finkel and Howard A. Scarrow, "Party Identification and Party Enrollment," *Journal of Politics* 47 (1985): 620–642.

CHAPTER 6

Party Identification

If you were to ask an average fourth-grader whether he or she is a Democrat, a Republican, or an independent, you'd probably get an answer. Most Americans develop a **party identification**, or **party ID**, in childhood, even before they have learned what the words mean.[1] A party ID is the psychological attachment that most Americans develop toward a political party.[2] By the time they get to be young adults, about one-third of Americans call themselves "strong" partisans, and almost as many express some party attachment, though not a strong one. Even most people who say they are independents admit to leaning toward one party and favoring that party in their voting.

Most researchers see party attachment as a kind of lasting "team loyalty" that helps people find their place in the group conflicts that characterize the political world.[3] It is an emotional as well as a social tie, which often grows out of other deeply rooted loyalties, such as family, religious, or ethnic identities. A college student might consider herself a Republican because her parents and relatives are Republicans or because she is an evangelical Christian. Many of these researchers view party ID as a perceptual screen, which filters out any conflicting information the student may receive.

Other researchers think party identification is more changeable. To them, it is a running tally of an individual's positive or negative experiences with the party's stands or its performance in office.[4] But no matter how we characterize it,[5] party identification is a vital link between citizens and the party organization as well as the party in government. People's party ID tells us more about their political attitudes and behavior than does any other single piece of information. For individuals, it is also a valuable decision-making shortcut. Politics is complicated, even for political junkies. Americans cope with more elections and longer ballots than do citizens of any other democracy. A party ID offers a useful means of cutting through the complexity. It can help people make efficient voting decisions without taking time to learn much about specific candidates.

How, then, do people—you, for example—develop a party ID?

How People Develop Party Identifications

Families are the most common source of our first party ID, as they are of so much else in our early lives. As children become aware of politics, they absorb their family's judgments about political parties and usually come to think of themselves as sharing their family's partisanship.

Childhood Influences

Parents are the main teachers of political attitudes, even though most do not consciously indoctrinate their children into partisanship. Their casual conversations about political events are enough to convey their party loyalties to their children, just as children learn where their family "belongs" in relation to other social groups. In fact, in these polarized times, you can even find children's books titled *Why Mommy Is a Democrat* (in which the narrator explains, "Democrats make sure we all share our toys") and *The Liberal Clause* (Christmas is threatened when elves unionize and make the North Pole into a socialist disaster).[6] Family and other early influences are often powerful enough to last into adulthood, even when young adults are pulled toward independence in other aspects of their lives.

This early party ID usually takes hold before children have much information about what the parties stand for. Only in middle school and high school do many students begin to associate the parties with economic interests—business or labor, the rich or the poor—and thus have some reasoning to support the party ID they have already developed. Note the importance of the sequence here. Party loyalty comes first, so it can have a long-lasting impact on political orientations. Only later do people learn about political issues and events, which they may then see through a partisan lens.[7]

Once developed, people's party loyalties are often sustained because we gravitate toward people like ourselves. People's friends, relatives, and coworkers typically share the same partisanship.[8] Some people do leave the party of their parents. Those whose early party loyalty is weak are more likely to change. So are people whose mother and father identified with different parties or who live in a community or work in a setting where the dominant party ID differs from their own. But when parents share the same party ID, they are more likely to produce strong party identifiers among their children.

Other sources of political learning tend to support a person's inherited party loyalty or at least do not challenge the family's influence. Schools typically avoid partisan politics; they are more inclined to teach political independence than partisanship. Many churches and other religious groups have become very engaged in politics recently, but they are not likely to lead young people away from their parents' partisan influence. And the American party organizations do much less outreach than some European parties, which sponsor party youth groups, social, and recreational activities.

Influences in Adulthood

The party ID most people develop in childhood and adolescence is more likely to be challenged in young adulthood, when we move into new environments: college, work, relationships, a new community, and the unexpected honor of paying taxes. At this time, young adults can test their childhood party loyalties against their own personal experience with government. They can get to know others with different party preferences. Their adult experiences may reinforce their early-learned loyalties or undermine those loyalties.[9] Or, at times, the old loyalties may exist peacefully alongside contradictory new information. People can learn more about candidates and issues, and even change their attitudes toward those political objects, without necessarily changing their party ID.[10]

The longer someone holds a party ID, the more stable it becomes.[11] Although about 15 percent of people aged 18–34 report that they identified with the other party at some point within the past decade, this is true of only about 5 percent of older adults.[12] Party ID tends to become a habit. Partisanship may grow stronger across the life cycle because it is so useful a shortcut for simplifying the political decision-making of older voters,[13] or because they surround themselves increasingly with others who share their party loyalties. In fact, researchers find that marriage partners and other mates are more likely to share a party ID than they are to share other social traits, perhaps because partisanship increasingly stands for a range of qualities that are important to us.[14]

At times, however, even the strongest partisans may rethink their attachments. During periods of major party change, when the issue bases of partisanship and the party coalitions themselves are being transformed, some voters drop or switch party loyalties. (We look more fully at the idea of party coalitional change or realignment in Chapter 7.) This happened in the South in the closing decades of the 1900s as conservative whites moved from Democratic partisanship to independence and then to Republican Party ID. Economic calamities and debates about strongly felt issues such as immigration can make someone rethink her partisanship, especially when party leaders' stands attract a lot of media coverage.[15] Older adults may be caught up in the excitement of the moment as well, but their partisanship, reinforced by years of consistent partisan behavior, resists change more effectively. Thus, when partisan turmoil begins, young adults are more likely than older adults to embrace the change.[16]

Patterns of Partisanship over Time

Large-scale change in party identifications is the exception, however, not the rule. Most Americans, once they have developed party loyalties, keep them. People who do change their party ID often change only its intensity (e.g., from strong to weak identification) rather than convert to the other party.

We can see this stability in Americans' responses to the poll question measuring party ID that has been asked in every presidential election year since 1952 by researchers for the American National Election Studies. The data are summarized by decade in Figure 6.1; the full data set can be found in Table A.2 in the Online Appendix.[17] The overall partisanship of Americans has changed somewhat: although most Americans have identified as Democrats throughout these years, the gap narrowed in each decade, and especially beginning in the

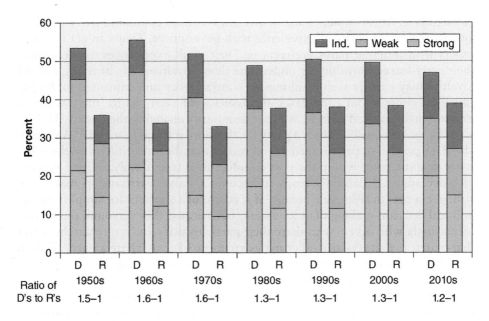

FIGURE 6.1 Party Identification by Decade, 1950–2020

Note: Based on surveys of the national electorate conducted immediately before each presidential and most congressional elections as part of the American National Election Studies program. For each party grouping in each decade, the segment at the base of the bar is the percentage of respondents calling themselves strong Democrats or Republicans; in the middle are weak Democrats or Republicans, and at the top is the percentage calling themselves independents who lean toward the Democratic or the Republican Party. For the full presentation of data for presidential election years, including the "pure" independents, see Table A.2 in the Appendix.

Source: American National Election Studies, University of Michigan; data made available by the Inter-University Consortium for Political and Social Research.

1980s. The increase in Republican support since that time, as we will see in Chapter 7, was propelled largely by the gradual movement of white southerners from Democratic to Republican identification. But the proportion of Americans who call themselves Republicans dropped a bit during the Trump administration.[18]

Changes in overall partisanship usually happen slowly. In Figure 6.1, look, for example, at the percentage who call themselves *strong* Republicans (represented by the segment at the bottom of each Republican column). From decade to decade, this proportion never rises above 14 percent nor drops below 9 percent. The full data set in the Online Appendix shows that during 70 years of history, at times when the Republican Party was triumphant and years when it seemed almost dead, the proportion of strong Republicans has stayed within a 7-percentage-point range, between 9 and 16 percent of those surveyed. The percentage of respondents in each category of partisanship changes very little from one election year to the next; the usual difference is just 2 percentage points. Election campaigns and other events can produce "bumps" in the pattern, but these are often short lived.[19]

This story of fairly stable partisanship has been interrupted only a few times. During an especially turbulent period—1972 through 1976, spanning President Richard Nixon's landslide reelection, the Watergate scandals that caused Nixon to resign, his subsequent pardon by President Gerald Ford, and Ford's own 1976 defeat—researchers interviewed the same set of individuals in three successive surveys. Almost two-thirds of the respondents remained in the same broad category of party ID (44 percent were stable strong/weak Democrats or Republicans, 20 percent stable independents) throughout all three surveys. Only 3 percent changed parties. Party identification was remarkably stable even during these agitated times.[20]

Yet a third of the respondents did move from a party ID to independence (or the reverse) during these three waves of surveys. At the national level (see Figure 6.2), the proportion of respondents calling themselves *strong* partisans (Democrats or Republicans) dropped during the 1960s and the percentage of independent "leaners" increased, especially among younger voters. Combined with other major changes at that time—the civil rights movement, protests against American involvement in the Vietnam War, the women's and LGBTQ movements, environmental activism—the growing number of independents suggested to many observers that partisanship was fading in the U.S.

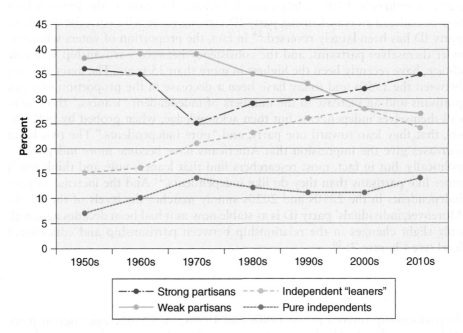

FIGURE 6.2 Change in Strength of Party ID, 1950s–2020

Note: This is a "folded" party ID scale in which Democrats and Republicans in each category are combined (i.e., the category "strong partisans" includes strong Democrats and strong Republicans).

Source: Calculated from American National Election Studies, University of Michigan; data made available through the Inter-University Consortium for Political and Social Research.

Was There a Decline in Partisanship?

Research in other democracies bolstered the argument that partisanship was declining in the 1960s and 1970s. Across the Western industrialized world, the percentage of self-reported independents rose, public confidence in political parties fell, and more people voted a **split ticket** (supported candidates of more than one party).[21] This "party decline" could have profoundly changed American democracy.[22] What could have caused it? Education levels were rising; perhaps better educated voters had so much other information available that they didn't need parties as a decision shortcut any more. Maybe media coverage of politics stressed nonpartisanship or ignored parties.

These explanations provoked even more questions, however. If Americans have more information available than ever before, wouldn't they need a device, like a party ID, to help them sift through it? Even though education levels are rising, we know that most Americans are not very interested in politics, do not know much about it, and therefore depend on shortcuts to make sense of it.[23] Party ID, then, should become even more helpful. And among people for whom partisanship is a strong group attachment, more information would probably not weaken their partisan feelings.

In fact, partisanship *has* rebounded since the 1970s. In particular, strong partisanship has made a comeback (see Figure 6.2). The proportion of strong party identifiers in 2020 slightly exceeded what it had been in the 1950s, which was considered an era of strong party ID. Among those who vote, the decline in party ID has been largely reversed.[24] In fact, the proportion of voters who consider themselves partisans, and the consistency between partisanship and vote choice, have recently been the highest in more than 25 years. The main changes between the 1950s and today have been a decrease in the proportion of weak partisans and an increase in the numbers of independent "leaners," those who call themselves independents but then acknowledge, when probed by poll takers, that they lean toward one party, and "pure independents." The two latter increases give the impression that Americans have become more independent politically. But in fact, most researchers find that leaners vote and think much more like partisans than they do like independents.[25] And the increase in pure independents in the 2010s and 2020s simply matches the levels of the 1970s. Moreover, individuals' party ID is as stable now as it had been decades ago, with only slight changes in the relationship between partisanship and educational level (see Chapter 7).[26]

Recent Changes in the Direction of Party ID

As partisanship revived in the 1980s and 1990s, the Democratic edge in party ID began to shrink. The increase in partisanship, then, seemed at first to benefit Republicans. But the parties' fortunes have varied a lot since then. Another measure of people's feelings toward the parties is the public approval ratings of the two parties. As you can see in Figure 6.3, there has been a lot of volatility recently in those ratings. The Republican Party's approval soared and then dropped during the presidency of Democrat Bill Clinton. After the September 11, 2001 terrorist attacks, Republican standing rose, only to sink dramatically during Republican president George W. Bush's second term. The decline continued during the presidency of Democrat Barack Obama. The Trump presidency hardened the loyalties of strong Republicans but frayed the attachment of weak and independent Republicans.

The Democratic Party has risen and fallen in public opinion as well. For instance, the Democrats' image took a major hit in 2009 and 2010 when economic recovery from the Great Recession moved at a snail's pace. Democratic approval ratings have improved only slightly since then, but Democrats have usually held more positive feelings toward their party and its leaders than Republicans do about theirs.[27] So the two parties' approval ratings are not always mirror images; sometimes both parties gain public support, but more often, both parties' approval ratings have declined.

What accounts for these shifts in the parties' fortunes? Because the parties now differ clearly in their stands on issues, (see Chapter 15) a change in the party in power can lead to big changes in policy. In the late 2010s, for instance, American trade and immigration policy changed a great deal when President Trump succeeded President Obama. Voters often recognize what they oppose more easily than what they favor.[28] When a Republican-led government cuts back on government services, many voters find that they miss the lost services.

FIGURE 6.3 Public (Dis)approval of the Parties since 1992

Note: Data points are the percentages who say that "your overall opinion of [the party] is very favorable [or] mostly favorable," as opposed to "mostly unfavorable," "very unfavorable," or "can't rate." Multiple data points in a given year are averaged.

Source: Pew Research Center for the People & the Press, www.pewresearch.org/data-trend/political-attitudes/democratic-party-favorability/andhttps://www.people-press.org/wp-content/uploads/sites/4/2019/01/PP_2019.01.24_political-priorities_FINAL.pdf (both accessed August 17, 2020).

When Democrats put new government programs in place, many voters are irritated by the greater reach of government into their lives. Big policy change produces a big backlash.[29] But overall, the steady diet of partisan gridlock and negativity has probably damaged both parties' approval ratings over time.[30]

Longer-term demographic trends seem to favor the Democrats.[31] The share of the electorate who are married, white Christians—the core supporters of the Republican Party—has declined in recent years. The fastest-growing groups in the adult population are Latino Americans and young people who came of age politically during the Obama years. Both groups leaned heavily Democratic in the 2010s and 2020. But their continued enthusiasm for the Democrats depends heavily on the two parties' candidates and issue stances. If Republicans were to recruit more Latino American candidates, that might increase their appeal to Latino and Hispanic voters. On the other hand, if major Republican figures continue to take stands on immigration and social services that are unpalatable to many Latinos and young people, the Democratic leanings of Latino and Hispanic American and young voters are likely to strengthen. No matter which party is favored at any given time, however, party remains an influential attachment, and the earlier discussion of party decline is at an end.

Negative Partisanship

The data you've seen so far paint a mixed picture. Partisanship has made a comeback, yet both parties' public approval ratings are clearly more negative now than they were two decades ago. Why would people become more attached to parties they like less? An important part of the answer involves partisans' growing hostility toward the *opposition* party.[32]

Recently, people's party ID has become more and more infused with anger, fear, and even hatred toward the other party and its supporters—powerful emotions that have come to dominate political debate. In many cases, party identifiers' disgust with the other party's policies is stronger than their agreement with their own party's stands. Not only do most partisans hold very unfavorable views of the opposition party, one poll found that a remarkable 45 percent of Republican identifiers saw the Democratic Party's policies as "so misguided that they threaten the nation's well-being," and 41 percent of Democrats felt the same about Republican policies. The figures were even higher among those who contributed money to campaigns—a level of animosity that has grown substantially in the past 20 years.[33]

Partisanship has always had an emotional component. But among many Americans, party ID is now driven more by negative feelings toward the other side than by positive feelings toward their own. This was especially obvious in 2016; although both parties' presidential candidates held the distinction of being the least popular presidential nominees in polling history,[34] about 90 percent of each party's identifiers nevertheless voted for their party's presidential candidate because "the idea of the other party occupying the White House was too painful to consider."[35]

TABLE 6.1 Partisans See the Other Party as Dishonest and Disrespectful, 2019	
	Percent
Republican identifiers see the Republican Party as:	
Governing in an honest and ethical way	83
Respectful and tolerant of others	82
Caring about the middle class	82
Republican identifiers see the *Democratic* Party as:	
Governing in an honest and ethical way	15
Respectful and tolerant of others	29
Caring about the middle class	23
More closed-minded than other Americans	64
More immoral than other Americans	55
More unpatriotic than other Americans	63
Democratic identifiers see the Democratic Party as:	
Governing in an honest and ethical way	85
Respectful and tolerant of others	92
Caring about the middle class	90
Democratic identifiers see the *Republican* Party as:	
Governing in an honest and ethical way	12
Respectful and tolerant of others	9
Caring about the middle class	11
More closed-minded than other Americans	75
More immoral than other Americans	47
More unpatriotic than other Americans	23

Source: Data from Pew Research Center, "Partisan Antipathy: More Intense, More Personal," October 10, 2019, https://www.people-press.org/2019/10/10/how-partisans-view-each-other/ (accessed August 17, 2020).

Table 6.1 shows that partisans have polar-opposite views of the other party's qualities. Most Democrats see Republicans as more closed-minded than other Americans, and near-majorities claim Republicans are more dishonest and immoral. Republicans' views of Democrats are just as hostile.[36] In fact, another poll found that 20 percent of partisans in their survey described the opposing party as "downright evil."[37] These negative feelings have increased on both sides in just the past three years. These are not happy thoughts in a system that depends on negotiation and compromise.

Yet negative partisanship (or "affective polarization") is not yet universal. Poll takers find that it declines when respondents are primed to think about events they hold in common with other Americans, such as the Olympics.[38] And for most party identifiers, it is still outweighed by their attraction to their own party's policies.[39]

Party Identification and Political Views

Party loyalties guide most Americans' feelings about policies and candidates,[40] even more than is the case in many other democracies.[41] The polarization of American politics (see Chapter 15) strengthens the impact of partisanship on people's attitudes.[42] Republicans, for example, are much more critical of big government than Democrats are. Republicans are a lot more likely than Democrats to say that blacks in society today face little or no discrimination, but that whites do.[43] Republicans are less inclined to feel that increasing racial and ethnic diversity makes the U.S. a better place to live,[44] and much more likely to believe that colleges and universities have a negative effect on the nation.[45] And Democrats are much more liberal than Republicans on issues such as abortion, the environment, gun control, civil rights, and government involvement in the economy and health care.[46]

Party ID is even powerful enough to lead some strong partisans to change their attitudes on a variety of issues. Consider Figure 6.4: at the very end of President Barack Obama's second term, almost half of Democratic identifiers rated the U.S. economy as "excellent" or "good," though fewer than one in five Republicans agreed. Just a few months after President Trump entered the White House in 2017, Republicans' views of the economy had grown much more positive, and during the next two years, the proportion of Republicans saying the economy was "excellent" or "good" jumped to about eight in ten. At the same time, the percentage of Democrats holding a rosy view of the economy dropped to 33 percent. They were, of course, looking at the same economy. And Democrats' attitudes differed from Republicans' even on whether they were concerned about the pandemic corona virus in spring 2020.[47]

These party differences on issues have grown much bigger in a fairly short time. Twenty-five years ago, the Pew Research Center found that the average gap between Republicans' and Democrats' views on such issues as race, immigration, and aid to the needy was just 15 percentage points on a 100-point scale. Currently, the difference has grown to 36 percentage points. In fact, the average party divide is now wider than the average difference in views between blacks and whites, between more and less educated people, and between those who attend religious observances frequently or not at all.[48] (Chapter 15 will examine reasons for this increase in party differences: party and ideological sorting and "conflict extension.")

Party Identification and Voting

The most important effect of party attachments is their influence on voting behavior. Even though partisans have to fight their way through long ballots and

FIGURE 6.4 Changing Feelings about the Economy, by Party ID, 2016–2019

Note: Data points are the percentages of Republican and Democratic identifiers (including leaners) in each year who rate the U.S. economy as "excellent" or "good."

Source: Pew Research Center, "Public's Views of Nation's Economy Remain Positive and Deeply Partisan," July 25, 2019, https://www.people-press.org/2019/07/25/publics-views-of-nations-economy-remain-positive-and-deeply-partisan/ (accessed August 17, 2020).

the culture's traditional distrust of strong parties, party identifiers tend to support their party fairly faithfully. Where partisanship is weak, as in new democracies where party ID is still developing, voting choices are more likely to be unstable and changeable.[49]

Party Voting

Party voting weakened along with party ID during the late 1960s and 1970s. But the impact of party ID on people's voting choices has been growing since the mid-1970s, and even more during the past two decades.[50] (The data can be found in Tables A.3 and A.4 and Figures A.1 and A.2 in the Online Appendix.) The greater differentiation between the two parties has helped some voters clarify their political attachments and heighten their sense of loyalty to a party and its candidates. The most faithful are the strong partisans. In the last four presidential elections, at least 94 percent of strong Democrats supported their party's candidate. Strong Republicans have been just as loyal; only once in 50 years has their support for the GOP presidential candidate dipped below 90 percent.

These patterns appear in congressional elections as well. A majority within each group of partisans has voted for their party's congressional candidates in each election, and strong partisans have been the most consistent party voters. In 2016 House races, more than 90 percent of partisans voted for the congressional candidate of their party.[51] We find similar results in voting at the state and local levels. **Straight-ticket voting**—voting for one party's candidates only—declined among all partisan groups during the 1960s and 1970s, but the stronger an individual's party ID, the more likely he or she was to vote a straight ticket.[52] And as with other indicators of party influence, the decline has reversed. The

2016 elections were the first time every state voting for a Democrat for Senate also voted Democratic for president, and the same consistency was true for Republicans: an impressive level of straight-ticket voting.

Party versus Candidates and Issues

The level of party voting varies over time because individuals' voting decisions are affected by the give-and-take of two sets of forces: the strength of their party ID (if they have one) and the power of the **short-term forces** operating in a given election, such as the attractiveness of the candidates and issues in that campaign. Usually these two sets of forces incline the voter in the same direction; as we have seen, a party ID encourages an individual to see the party's candidates and issue stands in a favorable light.

At times, however, an especially attractive candidate or a particularly compelling issue—an economic disaster, a pandemic, or the threat of terrorism— may lead a voter to desert one or more of his or her party's candidates. Although some voters split their tickets to ensure a moderate or divided government,[53] it is more common for voters to defect from their party ID because they are attracted to a well-known candidate running a well-funded campaign, most often an incumbent of the other party.[54] A well-known but unpopular incumbent can sometimes produce the opposite result; Democratic congressional candidates gained votes in 2018 from people who had supported Republicans in 2016, in part due to their opposition to the Trump presidency (see Chapter 14).[55] Typically, those with the weakest party ID or the most ambivalent attitudes about the parties—for example, those who have at least some positive feelings about both parties[56]—are most likely to defect.

Partisanship as a Two-Way Street

Which is more important in influencing people's votes: party ID, candidate characteristics, or current issues? One challenge for political scientists in answering this question is that these three forces are strongly interrelated.[57] The early studies of party ID in the 1950s assumed that party "came first" in the causal ordering—that it affected people's feelings about candidates and issues but was not in turn influenced by them. These early studies did not have good measures of how close the voter felt to the candidates on issues.

Since then, using better measures, researchers have shown that these three influences are reciprocally related. Just as an individual's party loyalty influences the way he or she views politics, feelings about candidates and issues can affect the individual's party ID. In particular, reactions to a president's management of the economy (so-called **retrospective evaluations**, in that they refer to past actions rather than hopes for the future) can feed back on party loyalties and weaken or change them. In this way, it is possible to see partisanship as a kind of running tally of party-related evaluations.[58] Even if party ID is usually stable enough to withstand an individual's disappointment in a particular party candidate or in the party's position on an issue or two, an accumulation of these negative experiences, especially on issues important to him or her, can weaken or change an individual's partisanship.[59] That is what happened over several decades to the long-standing Democratic loyalties of many conservative white southerners, when Democratic presidents and legislators became increasingly committed to civil rights for black Americans and liberal positions on social issues such as abortion.

People's attitudes toward presidents can also affect their party identification.[60] Enthusiasm for president Ronald Reagan drew many new voters into the Republican Party in the 1980s. Many analysts are watching to see whether the growing Republican lean of blue-collar white men and the declining Republican ID of college-educated women will continue after Donald Trump leaves public life, or whether these trends are closely tied to people's feelings about Trump.

In the short run, then, issues and the candidates in a particular election can have a major impact on the outcome. But party ID has continuing power to influence voters' choices and to affect their feelings about issues and candidates as well.[61] For instance, even though President Trump exerted a powerful pull on Americans' attention and political attitudes, the great majority of voters in 2020 supported the same party as they did in 2016, and the same was true between 2016 and 2012. So whether we want to explain the general trends of American voting behavior or voters' choices in a particular election, party ID gives us a lot of leverage.

Party Identification and Political Activity

People who consider themselves Democrats and Republicans are also more involved in political life than are those who call themselves independents. Partisanship is emotionally engaging; it gives partisans a stake in the outcome of political events. Therefore, the strongest partisans are the most likely to vote, pay attention to politics, and become politically active. In 2020, as in previous years, strong Democrats and Republicans were more likely than weak identifiers or independents to attend political meetings, discuss political questions with others, and to be registered to vote. And party identification can even guide less politically relevant behavior: Republicans have been less likely than Democrats to enroll in the insurance exchanges known as "Obamacare" (the Affordable Care Act[62]), in part because of its association with Democratic President Obama.

Party Identification and Party Differences

Two decades ago, only about 25 percent of poll respondents said there was a great deal of difference between the two parties' stands. That figure reached a majority (54 percent) for the first time in 2019.[63] The two parties' identifiers (excluding independent leaners) see greater party differences than the average American, and partisans who say they follow what's happening in government and politics most of the time—the most attentive identifiers—are even more likely to recognize these party differences (see Figure 6.5). So for those with

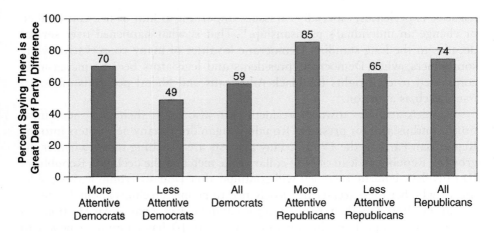

FIGURE 6.5 How Different Are the Parties? 2019

Note: Bars are the percentage of respondents in each category responding "There is a great deal of difference in what the Democratic and Republican Parties stand for." Partisans do not include independent leaners.

Source: Pew Research Center, "Partisan Antipathy: More Intense, More Personal," October 10, 2019, https://www.people-press.org/2019/10/10/the-partisan-landscape-and-views-of-the-parties/ accessed August 17, 2020).

stronger party ID and greater political awareness, the parties are more clearly defined and very different from one another on the important dimensions of politics.

A stronger party ID, by itself, is not enough to account for greater political activism and sharper party images. Other factors, such as higher socioeconomic status (SES), can also promote political activity. The relatively greater involvement of partisans (and, in most years, of Republicans) comes in part from their generally higher SES as well as from their more ideological commitment to politics.[64] Even so, party ID has a major impact on people's political attitudes.

The Myth of the Independent

Americans cherish independence in politics as well as in other areas of life. In contemporary elections, however, it has become increasingly rare. The age-old notion of the independent—the thoughtful citizen who votes for the candidate or the issues, not the party—has given way to the reality of almost universal partisanship, even among those who prefer to call themselves independent.

Attitudinal Independents

The definition of "independent" used so far in this chapter is someone who tells a poll taker that he or she does not identify with a political party. Studies show that these independents tend to split their tickets more often than other voters do and wait longer in the campaign to decide how to vote. In those ways, they would seem to fit the myth of the thoughtful, deliberative citizen. But they fall short of the mythical picture of the independent in most other ways. In 2020, independents stayed home from the polls at a higher rate than party identifiers did and scored lower than partisans on several other indicators of political involvement.

When pollsters ask these independents a follow-up question, however, they hear a different story. Those who say they do not consider themselves a Democrat or a Republican are then asked if they *lean toward* either major party. In fact, two-thirds of these "independents" report that they do. Evidence suggests that these independent leaners are often more politically involved and sometimes even more partisan in voting and in their policy attitudes than weak partisans are, though their attitudes toward candidates and parties tend to be more negative.[65] This suggests that independent leaners are really "closet partisans" who call themselves independents mainly because "independence" is an admired quality.[66] It is only in comparison with strong partisans that these leaners fall short.

The remaining respondents are classified as "pure" independents. But this highly valued independent vote turns out not to be so valuable. First, it's small; only about 10 percent of survey respondents are "pure" independents. Second, it's largely apolitical; pure independents are less informed, on average, than are other Americans.[67] And finally, most pure independents don't vote. Few campaigns can succeed, then, by putting major emphasis on mobilizing independents.

Behavioral Independents

We can also define independents in terms of their behavior. In his final work, the unparalleled researcher V. O. Key, Jr. explored various definitions of political independence.[68] Concerned about the picture of the American voter that was emerging from research in the 1950s and 1960s, showing an electorate much more driven by deeply ingrained party loyalties than by an understanding of major political issues, Key looked for evidence of rational behavior among voters. He focused in particular on "party switchers"—those who supported different parties in two consecutive presidential elections—rather than on the self-described independents. In practice, party switchers came much closer to the flattering myth of the independent than did the self-styled independents. These party switchers, Key found, expressed at least as much political interest as did the "stand-patters" (those who voted for the same party in both elections). Above all, the switchers showed an issue-related rationality that fit the mythical picture of the independent. They agreed on policy issues with the stand-patters toward whose party they had shifted, and they disagreed with the policies of the party from which they had defected.

It is harder to find true party switchers today. The percentage of voters choosing candidates of one party in one election and the other party in the next has never been lower; even among the pure independents who actually vote, most stick with the same party over time. During the 2000s, only an average of 6 percent of Americans voted for a different party's presidential candidate than they had in the previous election; younger people and those less engaged in politics were more likely to switch.[69] As the distinctions between the two major parties have clarified, the battle lines have hardened and become more emotionally fraught.

Are Independents a Likely Source of Support for Minor-Party Candidates?

One possible role remains for pure independents. Because they have the weakest ties to the two major parties, they could be more open to the charms of minor-party and independent candidates than other citizens are.[70] That has happened on occasion. One of the biggest stories of the 1992 presidential election was the unprecedented showing of independent candidate Ross Perot. A very rich man, Perot spent millions on a campaign criticizing the two major parties as irresponsible and corrupt. Unlike most independents, Perot flourished rather than faded as the campaign came to an end. He finished with almost 20 million votes, 19 percent of those cast.

On Election Day, Perot did draw many of his votes from pure independents and to a lesser extent from independent leaners.[71] Fully 37 percent of pure independents said they voted for Perot, compared with only 4 percent of strong Democrats and 11 percent of strong Republicans. The same was true of Perot's third-party candidacy in 1996, although the percentages decreased by more than half. In the end, however, there were not enough independents and disgruntled partisans to make a majority for Perot. It would be difficult for any independent or minor-party candidate to construct a winning coalition from a group as diverse as independent voters, who have little in common other than their dislike of the major parties, and who are much less likely to vote than partisans are. Such a candidate can serve as a "spoiler," however. Ralph Nader got enough votes as the Green Parties candidate in 2000, most of them from independents, to give the election to Bush, and some wondered in 2020 whether the small proportion of votes for the Libertarian presidential candidate would tip the election to Trump or Biden. In the close party competition that has characterized recent presidential elections, even a small percentage of voters have the power to determine the winner.

Change in the Impact of Party ID

Party ID, then, is a psychological commitment that is often strong enough to guide other political beliefs and behavior. Strong partisans tend to see issues and candidates through party-tinted glasses. They are more likely to vote for their party's candidates and to be politically active than other citizens are. Yet partisanship functions in a very different context now than it did a century ago.

A More Candidate-Centered Politics

Although the great majority of Americans still hold a party ID or "lean toward" the Democrats or Republicans, several major changes have affected the parties' influence on citizens. Early in the 1900s, states began adopting the direct primary, in which voters had to choose candidates without the useful guidance of a party label. Partisanship remains a helpful shortcut in general elections but does not distinguish one candidate from another in a party's primary. New campaign and fund-raising technologies developed that were harder for party organizations to monopolize. Candidates with enough money could use television, direct mail, and now social media and other online platforms to reach voters directly, over the parties' heads.

During the turbulent years of the 1960s and 1970s, the number of self-identified independents grew, and the impact of party ID on people's voting choices declined. Candidates found it helpful to downplay their party label, running instead as individual entrepreneurs. Now, even though party loyalties have regained much of their influence, candidates still tend to downplay their partisanship as a means of attracting voter support. In addition, other elements of American politics—new and traditional media, organized interests, campaign consultants, candidates' characteristics, issues, and current events—have important effects on campaigns. The consequence is that most elections have become less party centered and more candidate centered (see Chapter 11).[72]

The weakness of candidate-centered elections is that they make it more difficult for voters to hold government responsible. Voters may be able to hold a single candidate accountable for his or her campaign promises, but a typical election includes dozens of candidates. Most citizens are too busy to gather the information necessary to evaluate each candidate as an individual. When elections focus on individual candidates, rather than on teams of candidates in which each team stands for an identifiable set of policy proposals, elections may ask more of voters than they are willing to give.

The Continuing Significance of Party

Yet even in an era when candidates have so many resources to support their independence from their parties, party ID has gained strength as a force in American politics. More now than in the early days of survey research, when party ID was regarded as the "unmoved mover"[73] of voting behavior, voters see candidates, issues, and elections in partisan terms and vote accordingly. Partisanship has taken on a more emotional character for millions of Americans whose political interest and information are otherwise low. Elections since 2000 have mobilized strong partisans to an exceptional degree. Party-dominated contests are still very possible, even in a candidate-centered political world. The story continues in Chapter 7, where we look more closely at the changes in the two major parties' supporting coalitions over time.

Notes

1 Classics in this field are David Easton and Jack Dennis, *Children in the Political System* (New York: McGraw-Hill, 1969) and Fred I. Greenstein, *Children and Politics* (New Haven, CT: Yale University Press, 1965).

2 Party identification is developing in newer democracies such as Russia and the Ukraine as well, even in the face of overwhelmingly negative attitudes toward political parties. See Ted Brader and Joshua A. Tucker, "The Emergence of Mass Partisanship in Russia, 1993–1996," *American Journal of Political Science* 45 (2001): 69–83.

3 Donald Green, Bradley Palmquist, and Eric Schickler, *Partisan Hearts and Minds* (New Haven, CT: Yale University Press, 2002). See also Lilliana Mason, *Uncivil Agreement* (Chicago, IL: University of Chicago Press, 2018).

4 For a summary of these approaches, see Green, Palmquist, and Schickler, *Partisan Hearts and Minds*, Chapter 5 and Thomas M. Carsey and Geoffrey C. Layman, "Changing Sides or Changing Minds?" *American Journal of Political Science* 50 (2006): 464–477.

5 Alternative forms of measurement have been suggested by John R. Petrocik, "An Analysis of the Intransitivities in the Index of Party Identification," *Political Methodology* 1 (1974): 31–47; and Herbert F. Weisberg, "A Multidimensional Conceptualization of Party Identification," *Political Behavior* 2 (1980): 33–60. See also Green, Palmquist, and Schickler, *Partisan Hearts and Minds*, Chapter 2.

6 Jeremy Zilber, *Why Mommy Is a Democrat* (Madison, WI: Jeremy Zilber, 2006); and David W. Hedrick, *The Liberal Clause* (Camas, WA: Freedoms Answer, 2010).

7 Paul Allen Beck and M. Kent Jennings, "Family Traditions, Political Periods, and the Development of Partisan Orientations," *Journal of Politics* 53 (1991): 742–763.

8 Paul Allen Beck, Russell J. Dalton, Steven Greene, and Robert Huckfeldt, "The Social Calculus of Voting," *American Political Science Review* 96 (2002): 57–73.

9 Richard G. Niemi and M. Kent Jennings, "Issues and Inheritance in the Formation of Party Identification," *American Journal of Political Science* 35 (1991): 970–988.

10 Green, Palmquist, and Schickler, *Partisan Hearts and Minds*, pp. 7–8.

11 Duane F. Alwin and Jon A. Krosnick, "Aging, Cohorts, and the Stability of Sociopolitical Orientations Over the Life Cycle," *American Journal of Sociology* 97 (1991): 185–187.

12 Pew Research Center, "Partisanship and Political Animosity in 2016," June 22, 2016, www.people-press.org/2016/06/22/partisanship-and-political-animosity-in-2016/ (accessed August 17, 2020).

13 See William Clagett, "Partisan Acquisition vs. Partisan Intensity," *American Journal of Political Science* 25 (1981): 193–214.

14 John R. Alford, Peter K. Hatemi, John R. Hibbing, Nicholas G. Martin, and Lindon J. Eaves, "The Politics of Mate Choice," *Journal of Politics* 73 (2011): 362–379. See also David E. Broockman and Timothy J. Ryan, "Preaching to the Choir," *American Journal of Political Science* 60 (2016): 1093–1107.

15 Logan Dancey and Paul Goren, "Party Identification, Issue Attitudes, and the Dynamics of Political Debate," *American Journal of Political Science* 54 (2010): 686–699.

16 James E. Campbell, "Sources of the New Deal Realignment," *Western Political Quarterly* 38 (1985): 357–376; and Warren E. Miller, "Generational Changes and Party Identification," *Political Behavior* 14 (1992): 333–352.

17 The Online Appendix can be found at www.routledge.com/9781138683686. The seminal report of studies of partisanship is Angus Campbell, Philip E. Converse, Warren E. Miller, and Donald E. Stokes, *The American Voter* (New York: Wiley, 1960).

18 B. Pablo Montagnes, Zachary Peskowitz, and Joshua McCrain, "Bounding Partisan Approval Rates under Endogenous Partisanship," *Journal of Politics* 81 (January 2019): 321–326.

19 See Luke Keele and Jennifer Wolak, "Value Conflict and Volatility in Party Identification," *British Journal of Political Science* 36 (2006): 671–690.

20 Philip E. Converse and Gregory B. Markus, "Plus ça change …: The New CPS Election Study Panel," *American Political Science Review* 73 (1979): 32–49. See also Paul Goren, "Party Identification and Core Political Values," *American Journal of Political Science* 49 (2005): 881–896.

21 Russell Dalton, "The Decline of Party Identification," in Russell J. Dalton and Martin P. Wattenberg, eds., *Parties without Partisans* (Oxford: Oxford University Press, 2000), pp. 19–36. On split-ticket voting, see Barry C. Burden and David C. Kimball, *Why Americans Split Their Tickets* (Ann Arbor, MI: University of Michigan Press, 2002).

22 Martin P. Wattenberg, *The Decline of American Political Parties, 1952–1994* (Cambridge, MA.: Harvard University Press, 1996), p. ix.

23 See James H. Kuklinski, Paul J. Quirk, Jennifer Jerit, and Robert F. Rich, "The Political Environment and Citizen Competence," *American Journal of Political Science* 45 (2001): 410–424.

24 Jeffrey M. Stonecash, "Changing American Political Parties," in Stonecash, ed., *New Directions in American Political Parties* (New York: Routledge, 2010), pp. 4–5.

25 See John R. Petrocik, "Measuring Party Support: Leaners Are Not Independents," *Electoral Studies* 28 (2009): 562–572. Russell J. Dalton presents a differing view in *The Apartisan American* (Washington, DC: CQ Press, 2012) .

26 Pew Research Center, "Voters Rarely Switch Parties," August 4, 2020, https://www.pewresearch.org/politics/2020/08/04/voters-rarely-switch-parties-but-recent-shifts-further-educational-racial-divergence/ (accessed August 17, 2020).

27 Pew Research Center, "Partisanship and Political Animosity in 2016."

28 On negativity bias, see Tiffany A. Ito, Jeff T. Larsen, N. Kyle Smith, and John T. Cacioppo, "Negative Information Weighs More Heavily on the Brain," *Journal of Personality and Social Psychology*, 75 (#4 1998): 887–900.

29 See James A. Stimson, *Tides of Consent* (New York: Cambridge University Press, 2004), p. 81.

30 Hannah Hartig, "Democrats, Republicans Give Their Parties So-So Ratings for Standing up for 'Traditional' Positions," Pew Research Center, May 16, 2018, https://www.pewresearch.org/fact-tank/2018/05/16/democrats-republicans-give-their-parties-so-so-ratings-for-standing-up-for-traditional-positions/ (accessed August 17, 2020).

31 David Madland and Ruy Teixeira, "New Progressive America: The Millennial Generation," May 13, 2009, https://www.americanprogress.org/issues/democracy/reports/2009/05/13/6133/new-progressive-america-the-millennial-generation/ (accessed August 17, 2020).

32 See Leonie Huddy, Lilliana Mason, and Lene Aaroe, "Expressive Partisanship," *American Political Science Review* 109 (2015): 1–17, and Marc J. Hetherington and Thomas J. Rudolph, *Why Washington Won't Work* (Chicago, IL: University of Chicago Press, 2015).

33 Data from Pew Research Center, "Partisanship and Political Animosity in 2016."

34 Eliza Collins, "Poll: Clinton, Trump Most Unfavorable Candidates Ever," *USA Today*, August 31 2016, https://www.usatoday.com/story/news/politics/onpolitics/2016/08/31/poll-clinton-trump-most-unfavorable-candidates-ever/89644296/ (accessed August 17, 2020).

35 Marc J. Hetherington, "The Election," in Michael Nelson, ed., *The Elections of 2016* (Los Angeles, CA: Sage, 2018), p. 79.

36 Pew Research Center, "Partisan Antipathy: More Intense, More Personal," October 10, 2019, https://www.people-press.org/2019/10/10/partisan-antipathy-more-intense-more-personal/ (accessed August 17, 2020).

37 Lilliana Mason and Nathan Kalmoe, "Surprised by the Anger Toward McCain?" *Washington Post*, May 16, 2018, https://www.washingtonpost.com/news/monkey-cage/wp/2018/05/16/surprised-by-the-anger-toward-mccain-party-loyalists-can-hate-apostates-as-much-as-opponents/ (accessed August 17, 2020).

38 Matthew S. Levendusky, "Americans, Not Partisans," *Journal of Politics* 80 (January 2018): 59–70.

39 Hannah Fingerhut, "Why Do People Belong to a Party?" Pew Research Center, March 29, 2018, press release.

40 See, for example, Alan S. Gerber, Gregory A. Huber, and Ebonya Washington, "Party Affiliation, Partisanship, and Political Beliefs," *American Political Science Review* 104 (2010): 720–744, and Michael W. Wagner, "Think of It This Way," Ph.D. dissertation, Indiana University, 2006.

41 Caitlin Milazzo, James Adams, and Jane Green, "Are Voter Decision Rules Endogenous to Parties' Policy Strategies?" *Journal of Politics* 74 (2012): 262–276.

42 James N. Druckman, Erik Peterson, and Rune Slothuus, "How Elite Partisan Polarization Affects Public Opinion Formation," *American Political Science Review* 107 (2013): 57–79.

43 Bradley Jones, "Democrats Far More Likely Than Republicans to See Discrimination Against Blacks, Not Whites," Pew Research Center, November 1, 2019, news release.

44 Hannah Fingerhut, "Most Americans Express Positive Views of Country's Growing Racial and Ethnic Diversity," June 14, 2018, http://www.pewresearch.org/fact-tank/2018/06/14/most-americans-express-positive-views-of-countrys-growing-racial-and-ethnic-diversity (accessed August 17, 2020).

45 Kim Parker, "The Growing Partisan Divide in Views of Higher Education," August 19, 2019, https://www.pewsocialtrends.org/essay/the-growing-partisan-divide-in-views-of-higher-education/ accessed August 17, 2020).

46 See, for instance, Brian Kennedy and Courtney Johnson, "More Americans See Climate Change As a Priority, But Democrats Are Much More Concerned Than Republicans," Pew Research Center, February 28, 2020, https://www.pewresearch.org/fact-tank/2020/02/28/more-americans-see-climate-change-as-a-priority-but-democrats-are-much-more-concerned-than-republicans/ (accessed August 17, 2020).

47 Likhitha Butchireddygari, "How Concerned Are Americans About Coronavirus So Far?" March 13, 2020, https://fivethirtyeight.com/features/how-concerned-are-americans-about-coronavirus-so-far/ (accessed August 17, 2020). See also Cindy D. Kam, "And Why Is That a Partisan Issue?" *Journal of Politics* 82 (January 2020): 361–366.

48 Pew Research Center, "The Partisan Divide on Political Values Grows Even Wider," October 5, 2017, http://assets.pewresearch.org/wp-content/uploads/sites/5/2017/10/05162647/10-05-2017-Political-landscape-release.pdf (accessed August 17, 2020).

49 Andy Baker, Barry Ames, and Lucio R. Renno, "Social Context and Campaign Volatility in New Democracies," *American Journal of Political Science* 50 (2006): 382–399.

50 See, for example, Larry M. Bartels, "Partisanship and Voting Behavior, 1952–1996," *American Journal of Political Science* 44 (2000): 35–50.

51 2016 exit poll at www.cnn.com/election/results/exit-polls/national/house.

52 Paul Allen Beck, Lawrence Baum, Aage R. Clausen, and Charles E. Smith, Jr., "Patterns and Sources of Ticket Splitting in Subpresidential Voting," *American Political Science Review* 86 (1992): 916–928.

53 Kyle L. Saunders, Alan I. Abramowitz, and Jonathan Williamson, "A New Kind of Balancing Act," *Political Research Quarterly* 58 (2005): 69–78.

54 Barry C. Burden and David C. Kimball, "A New Approach to the Study of Ticket-Splitting," *American Political Science Review* 92 (1998): 533–544.

55 Ron Brownstein, "Rumblings from Trump's Base Could Shape Democrats' Choice for 2020," *CNN*, June 4, 2019.

56 Scott Basinger and Howard Lavine, "Ambivalence, Information, and Electoral Choice," *American Political Science Review* 99 (2005): 169–184.

57 Michael Barber and Jeremy C. Pope, "Does Party Trump Ideology?" *American Political Science Review* 113 (February 2019): 38–54.

58 See Morris P. Fiorina, *Retrospective Voting in American National Elections* (New Haven, CT: Yale University Press, 1981); and Michael B. MacKuen, Robert S. Erikson, and James A. Stimson, "Macropartisanship," *American Political Science Review* 83 (1989): 1125–1142.

59 And on which the individual sees differences between the parties; see Carsey and Layman, "Changing Sides or Changing Minds?"

60 Gary C. Jacobson, *Presidents and Parties in the Public Mind* (Chicago, IL: University of Chicago Press, 2019).

61 See Paul R. Abramson, John H. Aldrich, and David W. Rohde, *Change and Continuity in the 2008 and 2010 Elections* (Washington, DC: CQ Press, 2012), Chapter 8.

62 Amy E. Lerman, Meredith L. Sadin, and Samuel Trachtman, "Policy Uptake as Political Behavior," *American Political Science Review* 111 (November 2017): 755–770.

63 Pew Research Center, "Public's 2019 Priorities," January 24, 2019, https://www.people-press.org/2019/01/24/publics-2019-priorities-economy-health-care-education-and-security-all-near-top-of-list/ (accessed August 17, 2020).

64 Kay Lehman Schlozman, Sidney Verba, and Henry E. Brady, *The Unheavenly Chorus* (Princeton, NJ: Princeton University Press, 2012), Chapter 9.

65 John Laloggia, "6 Facts about U.S. Political Independents," Pew Research Center, May 15, 2019, https://www.pewresearch.org/fact-tank/2019/05/15/facts-about-us-political-independents/ (accessed August 17, 2020).

66 Samara Klar and Yanna Krupnikov. *Independent Politics* (Cambridge: Cambridge University Press, 2016).

67 David B. Magleby, Candice J. Nelson, and Mark C. Westlye, "The Myth of the Independent Voter Revisited," in Paul M. Sniderman and Benjamin Highton, eds., *Facing the Challenge of Democracy* (Princeton, NJ: Princeton University Press, 2011), pp. 238–263.

68 V. O. Key, Jr. (with Milton C. Cummings), *The Responsible Electorate* (Cambridge, MA: Harvard University Press, 1966).

69 Corwin D. Smidt, "Polarization and the Decline of the American Floating Voter," *American Journal of Political Science* 61 (April 2017: 365–381.

70 Todd Donovan, "A Goal for Reform," *PS: Political Science and Politics* 40 (2007): 683.

71 See Paul R. Abramson, John H. Aldrich, and David W. Rohde, *Change and Continuity in the 1992 Elections* (Washington, DC: CQ Press, 1995), p. 245.

72 See Martin P. Wattenberg, *The Rise of Candidate-Centered Politics* (Cambridge, MA: Harvard University Press, 1991).

73 This seems true of many other democracies as well; see Richard Johnston, "Party Identification: Unmoved Mover or Sum of Preferences?" *Annual Review of Political Science* 9 (2006): 329–351.

CHAPTER 7

Party Coalitions and
Party Change

An older couple in Wisconsin has managed their partisan differences for years. He is a retired business manager who loves Fox News. A retired teacher and a former labor union member, she sticks with CNN. (They cope by using ear buds to listen to their favorite political commentary and by placing their respective candidates' yard signs on different sides of their yard. They do admit, however, to occasionally hiding a remote from one another.)[1]

Can you tell which one of this couple is the Democrat and which is the Republican? It's not hard. Certain groups of people including business owners and managers, evangelical white Protestants, and Fox News viewers tend to vote Republican. Other groups such as women, union members, and black and Latino Americans are more likely to support Democrats. In fact, both parties are often stereotyped according to their group support; both Republicans and Democrats guess that more than a third of Republicans earn more than $250,000 a year (though the actual figure is 2 percent), and Republicans estimate that almost half of all Democrats are African-Americans (actually, 23 percent).[2]

The link between each party and certain social or demographic groups is central to understanding party politics. The groups most inclined to favor a party's candidates at a particular time make up what is called that party's *coalition*. Groups may align with a party for many reasons, but once a group has become part of a party's coalition, its interests affect the stands the party takes on at least some issues and the strategies it follows in campaigns.

The differences between the two parties' coalitions are also a helpful clue as to which issues dominate the nation's politics at that time. The facts that African-Americans have identified overwhelmingly as Democrats in recent decades and that southern whites are now largely Republican remind us that racial issues continue to be powerful in American elections.[3] At various points in U.S. history, regional conflicts, ethnic and religious divisions, disputes between agriculture and industry, and differences in social class have also helped distinguish the two parties' coalitions, as they have in other Western democracies.

Party change occurs in many forms, including shifts in party control of the federal government[4] and organizational changes producing "service parties"[5] (see Chapters 3 and 4) and more candidate-centered campaigns (see Chapter 11). Yet party researchers have lavished the most attention on coalitional changes. In

144

much of this literature, great and enduring changes in the parties' coalitions have been called **party realignments.**[6] The concept of realignment is controversial, as you'll see later in the chapter. But no matter how we characterize them, changes in patterns of group support for the Democrats and the Republicans have made a major difference in American politics and policies over time and make a fascinating story.

In this chapter, then, we will look at party change with special attention to the parties' supporting coalitions. We'll examine the development of the parties' current coalitions: from what races, regions, educational backgrounds, and other social groups these supporters come, what attracts them to one party rather than the other, and why that matters. Finally, we will consider how best to characterize the changes in the parties' coalitions since the New Deal.

The American Party Systems

The U.S. has experienced at least six different electoral eras or **party systems.** (See Table 7.1 for a summary of each party system.) Although some common themes run through all of these eras, each has had a distinctive pattern of group support for the parties. Each party system can also be distinguished by the kinds of issue concerns that dominated it and the types of public policies the government put into effect. In Chapter 1, we looked at party history to learn about the interrelationships among the three parts of the party. Now, let us get a different take on these events, from the perspective of changes in social group support for the parties.

The First Party System

The initial American party system (from about 1801 to 1828)[7] emerged out of a serious conflict between opposing groups in George Washington's administration: How much power should the national government exercise relative to that of the states? As Chapter 1 noted, the Federalists, led by Alexander Hamilton, wanted a strong national government that would work closely with business and industry to build the nation's economy. A national bank would centralize the states' banking systems. This plan would benefit business owners and wealthier citizens, who were concentrated in New England; these groups became the core support for the Federalists.

Farmers and the less well-off, living in the southern and mid-Atlantic states, suspected that the Federalists' proposals would hurt them financially; farmers would pay taxes but businesses and speculators would reap more of the benefits. So they supported Thomas Jefferson and James Madison's demand for states' rights, limits on the national government's power, and a more egalitarian vision of the new democracy. So did southern slave owners; states' rights would protect them against northern abolitionists. The less well-off may have had little in common with southern plantation owners other than their preference for states' rights, but that was enough; the Jeffersonian coalition expanded, and

TABLE 7.1 Years of Partisan Control of Congress and the Presidency, 1801–2020

	House		Senate		President	
	D-R	**Fed.**	**D-R**	**Fed.**	**D-R**	**Opp**
First party system						
(1801–1828)	26	2	26	2	28	0
	Dem.	**Opp.**	**Dem.**	**Opp.**	**Dem.**	**Opp.**
Second party system						
(1829–1860)	24	8	28	4	24	8
	Dem.	**Rep.**	**Dem.**	**Rep.**	**Dem.**	**Rep.**
Third party system						
(1861–1876)	2	14	0	16	0	16
(1877–1896)	14	6	4	16	8	12
Fourth party system						
(1897–1932)	10	26	6	30	8	28
Fifth party system						
(1933–1968)	32	4	32	4	28	8
Sixth party system						
(1969–1980)	12	0	12	0	4	8
(1981–2020)	20	20	17	23	16	24
(1969–2020)	32	20	29	23	20	32

Note: Entries for the first party system are Democratic–Republicans and their opponents (mainly Federalists); for the second party system, Democrats and their opponents (first Whigs and then Republicans); and for subsequent party systems, Democrats and Republicans. In 2001, Republicans were in the majority in the Senate for the first five months and Democrats for the last seven, so the Senate is counted as being under Democratic control.

the Democratic–Republicans, as they came to be called, gained the presidency in 1800. The Federalists slowly slipped into a fatal decline, and the supporters of Jefferson and Madison then dominated politics for more than two decades.

The Second Party System

The next party system (from approximately 1829–1860) developed when the one-party rule of the Democratic–Republicans could not contain all the conflicts generated by a rapidly changing nation. The party split into two factions on the major issues of the period: not just the national government's economic powers but also whether the newly admitted states should permit slavery. One faction continued the Jeffersonian tradition of opposition to a strong national government. It included the small farmers and slave owners of the South and the western frontier, as well as the addition of many urban workers and their political bosses. Led by Andrew Jackson, it would later call itself the Democratic Party or, at times, "the Democracy." The other, a more elitist and eastern commercial faction represented by John Quincy Adams, referred to itself as the National Republicans and was eventually absorbed into the Whig Party.[8]

This second party system was just as class based as the first. Wealthier voters (except those in the South) supported the Whigs, and the less privileged (and southerners) identified as Democrats. The Democrats dominated, growing as the franchise was extended to more and more Americans, and the party system became much more mass based. Democratic rule was interrupted only twice, both times by the election of Whig war heroes to the presidency. As the issues of this period grew more disruptive, however, the Whigs began to fracture, especially over the issue of slavery, and several minor parties were formed.

The Third Party System

One of these new parties, the antislavery Republicans, quickly gained support. Founded in 1854, it soon replaced the seriously divided Whigs as the main opposition to the Democrats. The bitter conflict of the Civil War ensured that the new third party system (1861–1896) would have the most clearly defined coalitions of any party system before or since.

In the first part of this party system, during the war and the relatively short period of Reconstruction that followed, the victorious federal government, led by Republicans, forced southern states to set aside their racially discriminatory policies.[9] But a political bargain ended Reconstruction in 1877 and, with it, southern blacks' brief access to the vote. The South again became a Democratic bastion, and the Northeast and Midwest were a fairly reliable base for Republicans. The party system remained divided roughly along geographic lines.

The regional division was so clear that the Democratic Party's only real strongholds in the North were in the cities controlled by Democratic machines (for example, New York City's Tammany Hall) and areas settled by southerners (such as Kentucky, Missouri, and the southern portions of Ohio, Indiana, and Illinois). In the South, GOP support came only from the few black Americans allowed to vote after Reconstruction ended and people from mountain areas originally opposed to the southern states' secession. By 1876, there was close party competition in presidential voting and in the House of Representatives as these regional forces balanced one another. Competition was so intense that this period contained two of the four elections in American history in which the winner of the popular vote for president lost the vote in the Electoral College.

American industries grew during this time, especially in the Northeast and then in the Midwest. Republicans dominated the areas where these new businesses were expanding, and the GOP leadership, which had long been identified with "moral Puritanism and emerging industrial capitalism,"[10] worked to support the new industries with protective tariffs (taxes) on imported goods, a railroad system that could haul products from coast to coast, efforts to develop the frontier, and high taxes to pay for these programs. In contrast, the Democrats represented groups that had been passed over by economic expansion and who were deeply suspicious of capitalism, such as farmers and the working class, as well as the white South. Economic issues, and especially attitudes toward the growth of huge industrial monopolies, were thus closely linked with the regional divisions between the parties.

The Fourth Party System

The powerful imprint of race and the Civil War continued to shape southern politics for the next century, while economic conflict dominated politics elsewhere. The national Democratic Party had become riven by conflict. After the economic panic of 1893 and a series of farm and rural protests, tensions within the party between poor whites and the more conservative party leaders erupted into a fight over the party's leadership. The less wealthy, more egalitarian wing won, nominated populist William Jennings Bryan as the Democratic presidential candidate in 1896, and reformed the party's issue stances. Bryan lost, and Republicans then dominated national politics until 1932, disrupted only by their own internal split in 1912.

This period (from approximately 1897–1932) thus reflected both regional and economic conflicts. It pitted the eastern business community, which was heavily Republican, against the Democratic-dominated South, with the Midwest in contention. The waves of immigrants into an increasingly urban America swelled the ranks of both parties, although Catholic immigrants, especially from Europe, tended to be mobilized by the Democratic Party.

The Fifth Party System

The shock of the Great Depression of 1929 and the resulting election of Democrat Franklin Roosevelt prompted the fifth, or New Deal, party system (from approximately 1932–1968). During the 1930s, as a means of pulling the nation out of economic ruin, Roosevelt pushed Congress to enact several large-scale social welfare programs. These Roosevelt "New Deal" programs—Social Security, wages and hours laws, and protection for labor unions—again strengthened the Democrats' image as the party of the disadvantaged. Even groups such as black Americans, long allied with the Republicans, were lured to the Democratic banner; their socioeconomic needs were powerful enough to keep both blacks and southern whites as wary allies in the Roosevelt coalition. So by 1936, the new Democratic majority party had become a grand **New Deal coalition** of the less privileged and minorities—lower-income people, industrial workers (especially union members), poor farmers, Catholics, Jews, blacks—plus the South, where Democratic loyalty was deeply ingrained among whites. The costs of the New Deal and the impact of its programs heightened the stakes of the conflict between higher- and lower-income groups and between business and labor.

The Sixth Party System

The New Deal's policies had a profound impact on the parties' supporting coalitions. Once World War II brought an end to the Depression, some groups that had benefited from government assistance under Roosevelt moved up into the growing middle class. In return for this economic gain, however, they found themselves paying higher taxes to support those who still needed assistance. That led many people to reevaluate the costs and benefits of the welfare state in their own lives. At the same time, the issue of race, which had been held in check by Roosevelt's deft maneuvering, was pushed to the top of both parties' agendas by activists hoping to change their parties' stands.

As black Americans migrated to the North in the late 1940s, liberal northern Democrats pressed their party to deliver on the long-delayed promise of civil rights for blacks.[11] When Democratic administrations responded and used federal power to end the racial segregation of schools and public accommodations such as restaurants and hotels, some conservative white southern Democrats— especially those holding conservative views about race[12]—felt betrayed by their national party. They found an alternative in 1964 when Republican presidential candidate Barry Goldwater proclaimed his opposition to the Civil Rights Act. Goldwater, the candidate of the party's newly triumphant conservative wing, believed that Republicans needed a new bloc of supporters to become the majority party. Rather than trying to regain blacks' votes, Goldwater contended, it made more sense to persuade the larger population of southern whites to switch parties by showing them that the Republican Party represented their views better than the Democrats did.[13]

Goldwater argued that the Republican commitment to smaller government and states' rights required it to oppose federal government efforts to force integration on reluctant state governments. Both national parties, then, had markedly changed their positions on civil rights, due to the combination of group pressure and the lure of new voter support. The Democrats moved from an acceptance of segregation in the South to a commitment to use government as the means to secure rights for black Americans. The Republicans reacted against the big-government programs of the New Deal with a stand in favor of states' rights, even at the cost of the party's traditional pro-civil rights stand.[14]

These changes in the parties' positions led to a steady reformation of their constituencies.[15] Southern whites responded by moving slowly in the direction of Republican partisanship. The same forces caused blacks to shift rapidly toward the Democrats. When the Voting Rights Act restored southern blacks' right to vote, their overwhelmingly Democratic voting patterns led the national Democratic Party to become even more liberal on race and related issues. A further push came from legislative redistricting in 1992, in which legislatures were asked to draw majority–minority districts (see Chapter 8), and which led to the defeat of a number of longtime conservative southern Democrats.[16]

Table 7.2 shows shifts between the 1950s and the most recent decade in the representation of various groups within the Democratic and Republican parties in the electorate. Look first at the dramatic changes with regard to race.

TABLE 7.2   Change in the Parties' Coalitions, from the 1950s to the 2020s

	Democratic Voters (%)			
	1952–1960	1996	2012	2019
Non-Hispanic Whites	93	76	61	59
Blacks, Latinos, Asian, Native	7	22	37	40
High school or less	81	51	35	28
Some college	NA	27	29	31
College degree	NA	13	20	22
Postgrad	NA	9	16	19
White Evangelical Protestants	NA	NA	9	6
Unaffiliated/not religious	2	NA	24	38

	Republican Voters (%)			
	1952–1960	1996	2012	2019
Non-Hispanic Whites	97	94	87	81
Blacks, Latino, Asian, Native	3	6	10	16
High School or less	70	41	34	35
Some college	NA	31	32	35
College degree	NA	17	21	19
Postgrad	NA	10	13	10
White Evangelical Protestant	NA	NA	34	32
Unaffiliated/not religious	2	NA	11	15

Note: Entries are the proportion of all Democratic or Republican Party identifiers, among those who say they voted, who belong to the group named in the first column.

Source: American National Election Studies data for 1952–1960, calculated by Alan Abramowitz and excerpted with kind permission from Abramowitz, *Voice of the People* (New York: McGraw-Hill, 2004), p. 87, and for 1996-2019, data from the Pew Research Center, https://www.pewresearch.org/fact-tank/2020/10/26/what-the-2020-electorate-looks-like-by-party-race-and-ethnicity-age-education-and-religion/ (accessed October 31, 2020). NA = not available. *Included with College degree.

Blacks were only 6 percent of the Democratic Party in the electorate, on average, between 1952 and 1960; at this time, of course, very few southern blacks were permitted to vote. By 2019, on average, blacks constituted 19 percent of all Democrats. Latinos, Asian Americans, and Native Americans added another 21 percent, totaling two-fifths of Democratic voters. The change was especially profound in the South; by 2000, blacks made up a majority (52 percent) of the Democratic voters in the Deep South states of Alabama, Georgia, Louisiana, Mississippi, and South Carolina.[17]

At the same time, surveys show that in 1956, 87 percent of white southerners called themselves Democrats, but in 2000 only 24 percent did so.[18] In the 2010s

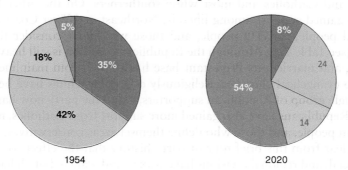

FIGURE 7.1 Democratic and Republican House Seats by Region, 1954 and 2020

Note: Percentages do not always add up to 100 percent due to rounding error.

Sources: CQ Weekly, April 20, 2009, for 1954 data; 2020 data calculated from www.house.gov and www. senate.gov. "South" includes border states.

Democrats regained strength in the coastal South, due in part to an increasing black population and in-migration to these states from other areas. But elsewhere in the South, few Democrats were elected to the U.S. House and Senate, and all represented majority-black districts. The Democratic Party's loss was the Republican Party's gain. Southern whites had increased from a mere 8 percent in the 1950s to a third of the current Republican Party in the electorate. Consistent with the change in the national parties' stands, it was the conservatives among these southern whites who moved first to a Republican identification.

This change was part of a larger shift in the parties' regional bases. In the mid-1950s, as you can see in the upper part of Figure 7.1, almost half of all Democrats in the U.S. House were southerners. By 2020, the drop in Democratic support among white southerners had left the party's House contingent much more regionally balanced.

Republicans in the House, on the other hand, have moved from one regional base to another. In 1954, the great majority of Republican House members were from the Midwest and Northeast, and a substantial number of northeastern Republicans were liberals and moderates. But the Republican platform changes that drew conservative southern support made it harder for the party to appeal to liberals and moderates in New England and the Midwest. So the Northeast is predominantly Democratic now, and almost half of all House Republicans now represent the South. As Seth Masket writes, emphasizing the profound shift in southern partisanship (at least in deep South states such as Alabama), "Today, southern states are largely off-limits to Democrats, and no amount of spending or strategizing is about to change that."[19]

In sum, the two parties' coalitions of group support are growing more unlike. The current Democratic Party in the electorate differs from the New Deal coalition in important ways. Although it continues to include black and Latino Americans and young people, the Democrats have lost a portion of white union members and Catholics and most white southerners. On the other hand, the party has gained support among liberals, Northeast and West Coast residents, unmarried people, LBGTQ people, and those who don't consider themselves religious (see Table 7.3). Although the Republican coalition is still heavily white, Christian, and married, its Protestant base has shifted from mainline denominations to evangelical churches. Religiously observant whites have become the largest single group of Republican supporters,[20] and the party now has a southern base. Republicans have also gained more support from Catholics, men, rural or exurban people, and those who define themselves as conservatives.

It is clear from this brief tour of party history that the effects of socioeconomic, racial, and regional divisions have waxed and waned, but all have played a major role in shaping the parties' coalitions over time. Let us take a closer look at these relationships, before asking how changes in these coalitions affect the nature of American political debate.

The Social Bases of Party Coalitions

Socioeconomic Status Divisions

James Madison noted, with characteristic perception, that economic differences are the most common source of factions.[21] The footprints of socioeconomic status (SES) conflict are scattered throughout American history, just as they are in most other democracies.[22] Social and economic status differences underlay the battle between the wealthy, aristocratic Federalists and the often less privileged Democratic–Republicans. These differences were even sharper between the Jacksonian Democrats and the Whigs a few decades later, and again during the fourth and fifth party systems. The connection between SES and partisanship weakened during the 1960s and 1970s but strengthened again beginning with the Reagan years in the 1980s.

SES is still closely related to people's partisanship, though the relationship has changed in some interesting ways. The lowest-income voters became more consistently Democratic in the late 1900s and early 2000s as income inequality

TABLE 7.3	The Current Democratic and Republican Party Coalitions		
	% Democratic/ Lean Democratic	**% Republican/ Lean Republican**	**Difference**
Democratic-Inclined Groups			
Black non-Hispanic	83	10	D+73
Asian-American	72	17	D+55
Hispanic Catholic	68	27	D+41
All Hispanic	63	29	D+34
Jewish	68	27	D+41
No religious affiliation	67	24	D+43
Urban	62	31	D+31
College grad or more education	57	37	D+20
Millennial	54	38	D+16
Millennial women	60	31	D+29
Millennial men	48	44	D+4
All women	56	38	D+18
Republican-Inclined Groups			
White evangelical Protestant	17	78	R+61
Mormon	21	74	R+53
White Catholic	38	57	R+19
Rural	35	58	R+23
Suburban	46	47	R+1
White, no college degree	35	59	R+24
All races, no college degree	45	47	R+2
All non-Hispanic white	42	53	R+11
All men	42	50	R+8

Note: Latino/Hispanics can include people of any race; whites and blacks are non-Latino/Hispanic only. Data include 12,044 registered voters surveyed during 2018-2019.

Source: Pew Research Center surveys, https://docs.google.com/spreadsheets/d/1v58Nt6SW83 2ZUq7xLI6N8qdDs3qN4qWoDU-2EyEOGZg/edit#gid=2104546316 (accessed August 18, 2020).

increased.[23] This reflects the parties' differing stands on issues of special concern to lower-income people (such as government-insured health care and social services) and also the very strong Democratic identification among blacks, who tend to be lower income.[24] In 2008 and 2012, Barack Obama won a greater percentage of low- and lower-middle-income voters (with incomes up to $50,000) than had other recent Democratic presidential candidates. Upper-income people traditionally voted Republican, but this group is less distinctively Republican now than it used to be.

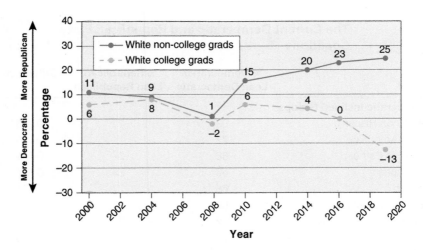

FIGURE 7.2 Whites' Party Identification by Education Level, 2000–2019

Note: Data points are the percentage of Republican identifiers (including leaners) minus the percentage of Democratic identifiers and leaners in each group.

Source: Adapted from Jeffrey M. Jones, "Non-College Whites Had Affinity for GOP Before Trump," April 12, 2019, https://news.gallup.com/poll/248525/non-college-whites-affinity-gop-trump.aspx (accessed August 18, 2020).

The effects of educational level tell a somewhat different story. Like lower-income people, those with very limited education (high school or less) used to be more Democratic than Republican, though not by a large margin. In the past two decades, this group has shrunk as a portion of the electorate, and especially as a portion of Democratic voters.

On the other hand, whites with moderate levels of education—perhaps some college, but no college degree—captured media attention in 2016, when many analysts called them the driving force behind President Trump's victory. To some observers, this was evidence that "working class whites" were now part of the Republican base. In fact, whites without college degrees had been moving toward Republican identification for more than two decades (see Figure 7.2).[25] This movement was in full flower by the summer of 2020, when 64 percent of white voters with no college degree expressed support for Trump, whereas 61 percent of white voters with at least a four-year college degree supported or leaned toward Biden.[26]

Why the shift? Some researchers suggest that this change has had less to do with people's economic concerns than with their attitudes toward race and cultural issues. Barack Obama's presidency and the heavy racial and anti-immigrant undertones in Trump's public statements may have helped moderately educated whites see the connection between Democrats and liberal racial policies.[27] Issues involving race and traditional morality often relate differently to people's partisanship than their economic views do.[28] Groups deeply concerned with these cultural issues may locate themselves in the "wrong" party from an SES point of view. For example, white fundamentalist Protestants have voted largely Republican in recent years even though their average income is closer to that of the typical Democrat than to the average Republican, and Asian Americans, with one of the highest average income levels of demographic groups, vote dominantly Democratic.

Perhaps the biggest change is that those with at least a college degree, who are a growing share of all voters, have become disproportionately Democratic. In earlier years, only the well-to-do were able to go to college, and their income levels led them to support Republicans. But as more Americans from more varied backgrounds have graduated from college, voters with at least a college degree have lost their Republican edge. This group now contains a larger proportion of professionals, such as teachers and health-care specialists, many of whom are concerned with quality-of-life issues such as the environment and women's rights. Democratic candidates now receive significant support from professionals such as teachers and trial lawyers.[29]

In short, wealthier and more educated Americans are no longer predictably Republican. Democrats have recently improved their standing at the upper end of the SES scale, and Republicans have gained support in the middle. But these changes have occurred only among whites; black Americans support Democrats regardless of income or educational level. Because of this complicated relationship, the American parties don't usually promote explicitly class-based appeals, especially in general elections.

Race

The most striking demographic impact on party ID—and the most dramatic change—involves race.[30] The Republican Party was founded in the 1850s to oppose slavery. For almost a century it remained associated with racial equality in the minds of both black and white Americans. But when the New Deal's social welfare programs began to help lift blacks and other disadvantaged groups out of poverty, the parties' images began to change. As noted earlier, blacks' increasing presence within the Democratic Party during the New Deal of the 1930s and 1940s encouraged civil rights groups to press for a national Democratic stance in favor of racial desegregation. Especially after Democratic Congresses and presidents passed civil rights laws in the 1960s and Republican leaders reversed the party's previous stands on race, black Americans became increasingly Democratic.

Since 1964, blacks have identified as Democrats in overwhelming numbers, regardless of their income, urban or rural residence, or other characteristics. Look at the stark difference in Table 7.3: Democratic identifiers outnumber Republicans by a full 73 percentage points among blacks. And although whites are not as dominantly Republican as blacks are Democratic, no Democratic presidential candidate has won a majority of whites' votes in almost 60 years. Racial differences in partisanship were especially clear during the two presidential elections in which Barack Obama was a candidate.

Interestingly, black Americans have remained staunchly Democratic even though blacks tend to be more conservative than non-black Democrats on issues such as same-sex marriage and abortion.[31] The vital importance of civil rights and the economy to black Americans has outweighed the impact of these other issues. There's good reason for this: Research shows that the economic position of racial and ethnic minorities improves when Democrats hold the White House and Congress.[32]

Attitudes toward race and race-based policies also correlated even more closely with partisanship beginning in the Obama presidency. Donald Trump's campaign in 2016, making more explicit appeals to racial resentment than previous Republican candidates (for instance, calling Mexican immigrants "criminals" and "rapists") primed racial attitudes among some voters. As a consequence, racial resentment better predicted Republicans' support for Trump in 2016 than did their economic concerns.[33] The remarkable gulf between the parties' racial attitudes continued in the 2020 election cycle: when asked about racial discrimination, 78 percent of Democrats and Democratic leaners said the bigger problem for the U.S. is people "not seeing discrimination where it really does exist," whereas 77 percent of Republicans/leaners responded, "seeing discrimination where it does *not* exist."[34]

Regional Divisions

Historically, where we live has divided Americans almost as much as SES. Different sections of the country have often had differing political interests. When a political party has championed these distinct interests, it has sometimes united large numbers of voters who may disagree about other issues. But the nationalization of American politics has recently dampened regional effects.[35]

The most enduring regional (more properly called "sectional") conflict in American party history was the one-party Democratic control of the South. Well before the Civil War, white southerners shared an interest in slavery and an agricultural system geared to export markets. The searing experience of that war and the Reconstruction that followed made the South into the "Solid South" and delivered it to the Democrats for most of the next century. The 11 states of the former Confederacy cast virtually all their electoral votes for Democratic presidential candidates in every election from 1880 through 1924. Although the party's nomination of a Catholic presidential candidate in 1928 worried many Protestant southerners, the New Deal economic programs and the South's relative poverty kept it allied with the Democratic Party from 1932 through 1944.

As we have seen, however, the civil rights movement was the opening wedge in the slow process that separated the South from its Democratic loyalties. The Democratic dominance of the South persisted to some degree as late as the 1990s, thanks to the overwhelming Democratic partisanship of southern blacks. But southern white voters are now predominantly Republican. In fact, in 2015, Republicans held every U.S. Senate seat, every governorship, and every state legislature in the former Confederacy except Virginia and Florida, and the last remaining white Democrat in the U.S. House from a Deep South state was defeated for reelection. All the remaining House Democrats from the Deep South were African-American.[36]

At times, the party system has also reflected the competition between the East, which used to dominate the nation's economy, and the South and West. In the first years of the American republic, the Federalists held on to an ever-narrowing base of eastern financial interests, while the Democratic–Republicans expanded westward with the new settlers. Northeasterners remained largely Republican—though moderate Republican—until recent decades, when the party's platform began to shift away from their policy stands.

Urban vs. Rural

For much of party history, Democrats won national elections by combining their strength in big cities with an overwhelming Democratic vote in both the urban and rural South. But as we've seen, white southern support for the Democrats was decimated after the national Democratic Party committed itself to action on civil rights for African-Americans. As a result, the Democrats became a predominantly urban party in the late 1900s. After the 2018 elections, not a single U.S. House district in an urban area was represented by a Republican.

The most recent change in this pattern is the increasing Democratic strength in suburban areas. In the 2018 elections, Democratic vote totals rose substantially in many suburban areas, especially the so-called "Whole Foods suburbs" populated by well-off and well-educated people.[37]

This diversification in Democratic support is welcome news to the party, but its dependence on urban votes has had a major downside. Because big cities are so overwhelmingly Democratic, big-city Democrats tend to win their elections by large, wasteful margins—as much as 85 percent of the vote—though they need only a little more than 50 percent. Because of these wasteful majorities in urban areas, it is not unusual for Democrats to get the most votes nationwide for the U.S. House of Representatives but to win a minority of the actual House seats. If the concentration of Democratic votes in large cities were spread more evenly across the country, then Democrats might win more House seats, rather than elect fewer Democrats by lopsided margins.[38] The Democratic Party's powerful urban base also leads the national party to take more straightforwardly cosmopolitan stands on issues such as LGBTQ people's rights. This can undercut the electoral chances of the more moderate Democrats who used to be elected from more rural districts. Republican supporters, in contrast, are more evenly distributed around the nation and outnumber Democrats in rural areas.

Population shifts in particular areas can make a big difference in partisanship. Hurricane Katrina destroyed large sections of New Orleans in 2005, dispersing large numbers of heavily Democratic New Orleanians into other states and contributing to subsequent Republican gains in Louisiana. The severe economic decline in Puerto Rico since 2010 and the devastating hurricane in 2017 led to the relocation of tens of thousands of largely Democratic Puerto Ricans to Florida, a swing state.

Age

Younger people have become even more Democratic in recent years, and the oldest voters have become more Republican (see Figure 7.3). Although the Democratic advantage in party ID appears in all but the oldest age groups, the party

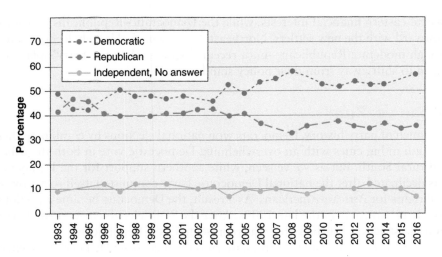

FIGURE 7.3 Young People's Partisanship since 1993

Note: Data points are the percentages of people aged 18–29 who identify themselves as Democrats, Republicans, and "pure" independents. Independent "leaners" are included with the party toward which they lean.

Source: Data derived from Gallup polls through 2013 and Pew Research Center since 2016.

now has its greatest advantage among those who are college-aged and the smallest among those over 50. The reason has less to do with age and more to do with race and ethnicity; younger Americans in the 2020s are more racially and ethnically diverse than older generations have been, as well as more liberal.[39]

These trends also reflect the state of the nation at the time when each generation moves into young adulthood. When the economy is strong and the incumbent president is popular, more young adults will come into the electorate favoring the president's party; this affiliation tends to stay with these people as they age. Those currently in their 60s reached adulthood at the time of the Ronald Reagan presidency, when Republican identification was on the rise.[40] The proportion of Democrats among millennials, as well as their turnout rate, shot up after the election of President Trump.[41]

Religion and Religious Commitment

White evangelical Protestants, who constitute one in five U.S. voters, are now among the strongest supporters of Republican candidates. In contrast, those who claim no religious affiliation are much more likely to be Democrats.

In the mid-1900s, religion had a different relationship with party politics. Then, Catholics and Jews both leaned Democratic, and most Protestant denominations leaned Republican. But as conservative white southerners began to move away from their earlier Democratic roots, Republican leaders moved to incorporate this group's commitment to social conservatism and traditional values into the party's appeals. In 1980, the Republican platform took a stand against abortion for the first time and ended its longtime commitment to the Equal Rights Amendment for women. Conservative Catholics and evangelical Protestants responded to these appeals by increasing their support for Republicans.

So although white evangelicals split their votes fairly evenly between the two parties until the late 1980s, about 80 percent have voted Republican in the past four presidential races. This link is now so strong that most Americans see evangelical Christians as a largely Republican constituency.[42] (Black Protestants are predominantly Democratic.) Republican state legislators have promoted bills called "religious freedom restoration acts," which would allow businesses and individuals to refuse to provide services that the provider feels violate his or her religious beliefs: for example, for health care workers to refuse to provide birth control or participate in abortions if their religion taught them to reject birth control and abortion.[43]

When this rightward turn among evangelicals began, only a small percentage of Americans told pollsters that they had no religious affiliation. Currently, almost one-fourth of Americans say so. Thus, the impact of religion on partisanship has changed; from Protestants vs. Catholics and Jews, the main split is now between evangelicals and other strong religious adherents, on one hand, and secularists on the other.[44]

Ethnicity

Hispanic or Latino Americans are growing in numbers much faster than other ethnic groups in the U.S., but their voting power is increasing less quickly.[45] A large proportion of Latino Americans are too young to vote yet, and even older Latinos turn out to vote less than non-Latino whites do. In 2012, for instance, 64 percent of non-Latino white eligible voters cast ballots, compared with only 48 percent of Latino Americans. The power of the Latino vote is limited further by the fact that about half of Latino Americans live in California and Texas, neither of which has been competitive in recent presidential elections. But because the Latino American population has increased by 15–20 percentage points in several swing states just since 2012, and Latinos have surpassed non-Latino blacks as the nation's largest minority group, both parties have worked to attract Latino voter support.

Most Latino voters lean Democratic. Earlier in the 2000s, national Republican leaders hoped to erode this Democratic edge. In 2004, President Bush's proposal to give temporary legal status to undocumented (largely Mexican and Central American) workers met with some success among Latinos, as did the party's advertising in Spanish-language media. In 2012, when Republicans won only 27 percent of the Latino vote, a Republican National Committee report strongly urged the party to expand its outreach to Latinos. But then came the 2016 nomination race, in which Republican presidential candidates, led by Donald Trump, vied with one another to be seen as the toughest opponents of illegal immigration and offended many Latino-Americans in the process.[46]

Gender

For more than three decades, women have supported Democrats to a greater extent than men have. The gender difference was especially clear in response to President Trump, whose approval ratings among women have been consistently 10–15 percentage points lower than men's.[47]

Why should gender be related to partisanship? Men's and women's attitudes differ on some major issues. On average, women express greater support for government social services and less support for military spending than men do. These differences correspond to the two parties' issue agendas; the Democratic Party emphasizes health care, education, and other social programs, whereas the Republicans put a priority on tax cuts and military strength. Interestingly, becoming the father of a daughter increases men's support for gender equality politics.[48] And people's attitudes toward gender equality and abortion, in particular, have become more closely correlated with their party identification during the past three decades. When these and other "women's issues" are stressed by candidates, a gender gap is more likely to appear.[49]

Although women's political preferences have shifted leftward in many Western democracies,[50] the gender gap in American politics has evolved differently. During the 1980s and 1990s, both men and women became more Republican, but men did so at a faster pace and to a greater degree.[51] After 2000, women returned to the Democratic Party more quickly than men did. Black women and single women have become particularly distinctive Democratic constituencies. While Democrats outnumber Republicans 1.4–1 among all women, the ratio rises to 2–1 among single women. According to the exit poll in 2016, 64 percent of single women (comprising more than one in five voters) supported Democratic House candidates, compared with only 49 percent of married women.[52] Single women, especially single mothers, are more economically insecure on average than married women are, and are probably more likely to see government social programs as an ally.[53]

The Central Role of Issues in the Group–Party Linkage

As this discussion of the gender gap suggests, there is a close relationship between groups' partisan leanings and the parties' stands on issues. A group's presence in a party coalition indicates that many of the group's members—white evangelical Christians, for instance—have some shared reactions to major issues and candidates, which have led them to one party rather than the other. To keep their support, the party is likely to express solidarity with the group's concerns, to speak its language, and to feature some of the group's leaders in its conventions and campaigns.

But demography isn't destiny. This relationship between social groups and parties' stands can change over time. As was the case with racial issues, a party may adapt its stands on issues to attract new sources of support, or a group may realize that the other party is becoming more sensitive to its concerns.[54]

Consider, for example, that until the 1980s, there was no relationship between the abortion issue and party ID; both Democrats and Republicans were split on the issue.[55] But as pro-choice activists gained strength in Democratic ranks and convinced party leaders to support abortion rights, many pro-life Democrats, including white evangelical Christians and southerners, felt alienated from their national party. Some pro-life Democrats saw an opportunity to be heard within the Republican Party and were welcomed as a new source of Republican support. As they became a larger proportion of the voters in Republican primaries, they encouraged their new party's candidates to take stronger pro-life stands. Republican Party leaders and activists responded to these new Republican voters by incorporating stands against abortion and same-sex marriage into their platform and faith-based initiatives into their rhetoric.

As a result, abortion is now a partisan issue; Republicans tend to be pro-life and Democrats pro-choice. So abortion is an example of an issue on which the party coalitions have evolved over time. On other issues, such as attitudes toward labor unions, both parties' stands and coalitions have been very stable for many decades.

Clearer Differences between the Two Parties' Coalitions on Issues

The two parties in the electorate now differ clearly from one another in their attitudes toward major issues. These party differences in attitudes closely track the issue preferences of key groups in the parties' coalitions. As you can see in Table 7.4, Democrats are much more likely than Republicans to see economic inequality as a big problem, to feel that government should provide more help to

TABLE 7.4   Issue Attitudes and Party Identification, 2020

% Who Agree That	Democrats/ Lean Democratic	Republicans/ Lean Republican
Economic inequality is a very big problem in the U.S. today	66	19
Government should provide more assistance to people in need	59	17
Our country has not gone far enough in giving black people equal rights with whites	67	15
Significant obstacles still make it harder for women to get ahead than men	77	33
Same-sex marriage now being legal in the U.S. is a very good thing for our society	54	15

Source: Pew Research Center, "In a Politically Polarized Era, Sharp Divides in Both Partisan Coalitions," December 17, 2019, https://www.people-press.org/2019/12/17/in-a-politically-polarized-era-sharp-divides-in-both-partisan-coalitions/ (accessed August 18, 2020).

needy people, and to agree that the U.S. hasn't gone far enough in giving blacks equal rights with whites. Recall that lower-income Americans and African-Americans are important groups in the Democratic coalition.

Republicans and Democrats also differ a lot on issues involving women's and LGBTQ rights. In recent years, Democrats have been much more likely than Republicans to support requiring businesses to pay women and men the same wage for doing the same job. Table 7.3 showed that most women—especially single women, who are often heads of families—identify as Democrats. The greater support for gay rights among Democratic identifiers and leaners reflects the greater support for Democrats among LGBTQ voters. As one pollster put it, "We have two massive, colliding forces ... One [the Republican coalition] is rural, Christian, religiously conservative, with guns at home. ... And we have a second America [the Democratic coalition] that is socially tolerant, pro-choice, secular, living in New England and the Pacific coast, and in affluent suburbs."[56] Party divisions have accurately been termed "culture wars."[57]

In short, there is a close but evolving relationship between the stands a party takes and the groups that form the party's core support. Parties take positions on issues to maintain the support of the groups in their existing coalition. Sometimes party leaders use issue positions to draw members of other social groups to the party, as Republicans did with white southerners since the 1960s. At times, it is the group that tries to put its concerns on the party's agenda, as was the case with the abortion issue. As these newer groups become a larger force within the party coalition, the party's leadership will try to firm up their support with additional commitments on their issues. In recent years, this process has led to a growing division on issues between the two parties' coalitions. The result is that even if most voters have not become more ideologically extreme, political debate has become more clearly divided by party, as voters have sorted themselves into the party that is closer to their views on issues (see Chapter 15).[58]

From Democratic Majority to Close Competition

The party system has changed in other important ways since the New Deal as well. The party organizations do not expect to select candidates now, run their campaigns, or hand out patronage jobs. Rather, party organizations work mainly to help fund and support campaigns that are run by candidates and their paid consultants. And the relationship between party ID and election results has changed. Until 1952, the elections of the New Deal party system had usually been **maintaining elections,** in which the presidential candidate of the majority party—the party with the most identifiers—normally won. Since 1952, most national elections have been **deviating elections**—those in which short-term forces such as candidate characteristics or issues are powerful enough to cause the defeat of the majority party's candidate. Racial issues have figured prominently in this change.

Another major change has been the gradual wearing away of Democratic dominance in party identification. In the 1950s and early 1960s, many more Americans called themselves Democrats than Republicans or independents. The

Democratic edge began to erode after 1964, but Republicans were not immediately able to capitalize on the Democrats' losses. The proportion of "independent leaners" increased, and there was a steady stream of independent and minor-party candidates.[59] These changes in partisanship struck many scholars as resembling a **dealignment,** or a decline in party loyalties.

Yet as we have seen, even as both parties were losing adherents nationally, signs of the coming change were apparent in the South. The movement toward Republican partisanship in southern states began to accelerate in the late 1960s, and Republican candidates reaped the fruits. In 1960, there had been no Republican candidate on the general election ballot in almost two-thirds of southern U.S. House districts. The only real competition was in the Democratic primary. By 1968, the number of these one-party House races had been cut by half.[60]

Party change speeded up again during the 1980s. For the first time in 50 years, young voters were more likely to call themselves Republicans than Democrats.[61] Two powerful reasons were President Reagan's popularity and the increased efforts of evangelical Christian groups to promote Republican affiliation. Republicans gained a majority in the U.S. Senate in 1980 that lasted six years, and in 1994, the GOP won control of both houses of Congress for the first time in 40 years. Republicans were now competing effectively with Democrats in statewide races in the South. In 1994, Republicans won a majority among the region's Congress members and governors for the first time since Reconstruction, over a century earlier. The George W. Bush administration later worked to reinforce this hoped-for Republican majority by attracting more Latino, Catholic, and black votes and by collaborating with evangelical preachers to promote voter turnout among conservative Christians.[62] But the Republican efforts were only partly successful; currently, the two parties are relatively balanced in strength, with Democrats most competitive for the presidency and Republicans dominating state governments (see Chapters 2 and 8).

How Can We Characterize These Changes: Realignment, Dealignment, or What?

A number of researchers have argued that these changes can best be called a **party realignment**—a significant and enduring change in the patterns of group support for the parties, usually (but not always) leading to a new majority party. We have certainly seen big changes in group support for the parties; the Republican coalition has become more southern, more evangelical, and more conservative, and a Democratic Party that used to draw much of its strength from the white South now depends to a much greater extent on the votes of blacks, liberals, and secularists.

These coalitional changes have affected the parties' policy stands. A Democratic Party that now draws a substantial minority of its followers from among blacks will surely take different stands from a Democratic Party that used to depend heavily on conservative white southerners. Southern whites have provided the critical mass for the Republicans to adopt more socially conservative positions today, not only on civil rights but also on health care, abortion, women's rights, aid for big cities, and support for private schools. Chapter 15 shows these changes in the two parties' platforms. Further, as the policy preferences of blacks, southern whites, and evangelical Christians have become more consistent with their partisanship, each party has become more homogeneous internally, and more distinct from the other party on issues, than had been the case in many decades; the Democratic Party's identifiers in 2020 are much more consistently liberal than was the Democratic Party in the electorate in the 1970s, and Republican identifiers are even more homogeneously conservative.

Issue Positions Can Combine and Then Re-Combine

This evolving relationship suggests that over time, different sets of issues will "go together" in a party's coalition. During the third party system, the Republican coalition was characterized by strong support for business as well as a powerful federal government, which could meet businesses' needs (see pages 147–148). By the fifth party system, as the Democratic-led federal government had become more inclined to tax and regulate business to provide social services, the Republican bundle of beliefs was shifting to a combination of pro-business and states' rights stands. Similarly, in the current party system, Donald Trump attracted support from many business people whose incomes depended on international trade as well as people without college degrees, who felt threatened by foreign trade and illegal immigration.[63] These combinations and re-combinations of beliefs and characteristics happen when a party seeks to gain new groups of supporters loosened from their traditional partisanship by environmental change or by a candidate who speaks the language of a group recently added to the party's coalition.

Problems with the Idea of Realignment

There are both practical and theoretical reasons why other scholars are reluctant to use the *R* word (realignment) to describe these changes. In practical terms, although Republican strength has increased, Democrats still hold the edge among party identifiers. And in a theoretical sense, the idea of realignment is difficult to apply with any precision. How much change has to occur in the parties' coalitions to call it a realignment? As political scientist David Mayhew points out, there are no clear standards for sorting elections into periods of realignment as opposed to nonrealigning periods.[64] Many prefer to use the concept of "issue evolutions" to discuss the variety of ways in which issues have affected partisanship over time.[65]

Although the changes in southern whites' and blacks' party ID are highly significant, the parties retain their New Deal character in several ways. The Democrats remain the party of minority racial and religious groups, though the minorities have changed. As Catholics have entered the mainstream of economic and political life, they have divided more evenly between the two parties, but the Democrats still represent the majority of black, Latino, Asian, LGBTQ, and nonreligious people. And even if the movement of blacks and white southerners has been dramatic enough to propel the U.S. into a new party system, when did that system begin? Was it during the 1960s, when southern blacks regained the right to vote and the civil rights movement shook the South? Was it in the 1980s, when southern partisan change accelerated and Ronald Reagan attracted many new voters to the Republicans? Was it in the early 1990s, when Congress finally came under Republican control? Or does it encompass all of these periods in a constantly evolving (so-called secular) change?

The debate will continue as to whether the concept of realignment is a valuable tool in understanding party system change. Perhaps a more useful approach is to recognize that there are many different kinds of party changes and we have seen all of them to some degree in the past 50 years. The evidence for party organizational change, as presented in Chapters 3 and 4, is convincing. There is little doubt that Democratic dominance of the New Deal party system gave way to a greater balance in national party strength. And whether we call it a realignment or not, there has been enough change in the two parties' coalitions to produce a palpable shift in campaign and congressional debate. When Democrats support same-sex marriage and Republicans agree with the pope on abortion, we know that there is a broader agenda in national politics than simply the economic conflicts of the 1930s and 1940s.

As we enter the third decade of the 2000s, then, the American electorate is composed of two groups of partisans of roughly comparable size. The group of Democrats includes liberals, some highly educated professionals, secularists, and racial and ethnic minorities. Although it has shrunk a bit in recent decades, the Democratic coalition has the potential for growth, especially among Latino or Hispanic Americans. The group of Republicans is dominated by conservatives, southerners, rural dwellers, and churchgoers. It is increasingly whiter and older. And there is a third group that could truly be termed "dealigned," in that it feels no lasting party loyalties and usually stays out of political activity.[66] Because of the demonstrated ability of both major parties to bounce back from defeat, it is also an electorate capable of producing mercurial election results. American politics, then, has the potential for rapid change.

Notes

1 Craig Gilbert, "Political Battle Lines Clear for Couple," *USA Today*, October 8, 2018, p. 4B.
2 Douglas J. Ahler, "The Group Theory of Parties," *The Forum* 16 (#1 2018).
3 See Edward G. Carmines and James A. Stimson, *Issue Evolution* (Princeton, NJ: Princeton University Press, 1989).
4 See, for example, Larry M. Bartels, *Unequal Democracy* (Princeton, NJ: Princeton University Press, 2008).
5 See John H. Aldrich, *Why Parties? A Second Look* (Chicago, IL: University of Chicago Press, 2011), pp. 281–287.

6 See V. O. Key, Jr., "A Theory of Critical Elections," *Journal of Politics* 17 (1955): 3–18; and Walter Dean Burnham, *Critical Elections and the Mainsprings of American Politics* (New York: Norton, 1970).

7 These events typically unfold over a period of time, but for convenience, the beginning of each party system is located in the year in which the new majority party coalition first took office.

8 Michael Holt, *The Rise and Fall of the American Whig Party* (New York: Oxford University Press, 2003).

9 On Reconstruction, see John Hope Franklin, *Reconstruction After the Civil War* (Chicago, IL: University of Chicago Press, 1995), and Eric Foner, *Reconstruction: America's Unfinished Revolution, 1863–1877* (New York: Harper, 2002).

10 A. James Reichley, *The Life of the Parties* (Lanham, MD: Rowman & Littlefield, 2000), p. 104.

11 See Hans Noel, "The Coalition Merchants," *Journal of Politics* 74 (2012): 156–173. For a more public opinion-driven argument, see Eric Schickler, "New Deal Liberalism and Racial Liberalism in the Mass Public, 1937–1968," *Perspectives on Politics* 11 (2013): 75–98.

12 Ilyana Kuziemko and Ebonya Washington, "Why Did the Democrats Lose the South?" *American Economic Review*, 108(#10 2018): 2830–2867.

13 See David Karol, *Party Position Change in American Politics* (Cambridge: Cambridge University Press, 2009), p. 112.

14 Nicholas A. Valentino and David O. Sears, "Old Times There Are Not Forgotten," *American Journal of Political Science* 49 (2005): 673.

15 Jeffrey M. Stonecash, *Political Parties Matter* (Boulder, CO: Lynne Rienner, 2006), Chapter 4.

16 Seth C. McKee, *Republican Ascendancy* (Boulder, CO: Westview Press, 2010).

17 Merle Black, "The Transformation of the Southern Democratic Party," *Journal of Politics* 66 (2004): 1001–1017.

18 Valentino and Sears, "Old Times There Are Not Forgotten," p. 676. See also Earl Black and Merle Black, *Divided America* (New York: Simon & Schuster, 2007), pp. 32–39 and 74–91.

19 Seth Masket, "How Doomed Are the Democrats?" *Pacific Standard blog*, May 3, 2017, https://psmag.com/news/how-doomed-are-the-democrats (accessed August 18, 2020).

20 John R. Petrocik, "Party Coalitions in the American Public," in John C. Green and Daniel J. Coffey, *The State of the Parties*, 5th ed. (Lanham, MD: Rowman & Littlefield, 2007), p. 285.

21 James Madison, *The Federalist No. 10*, November 22, 1787.

22 See Jeffrey M. Stonecash, "Class in American Politics," in Stonecash, ed., *New Directions in American Political Parties* (New York: Routledge, 2010), pp. 110–125.

23 See Jeffrey M. Stonecash, *Class and Party in American Politics* (Boulder, CO: Westview Press, 2000), pp. 13 and 139, and Chapter 4, and Jonathan Knuckey, "The Survival of the Democratic Party Outside the South," *Party Politics* 21 (2015): 539–552.

24 Paul R. Abramson, John H. Aldrich, and David W. Rohde, *Change and Continuity in the 2008 and 2010 Elections* (Washington, DC: CQ Press, 2011), pp. 203–204.

25 See Jeffrey M. Jones, "Non-College Whites Had Affinity for GOP Before Trump," *Gallup Poll*, April 12, 2019, https://news.gallup.com/poll/248525/non-college-whites-affinity-gop-trump.aspx (August 18, 2020).

26 Pew Research Center, "Election 2020," August 13, 2020, https://www.pewresearch.org/politics/2020/08/13/the-2020-trump-biden-matchup (accessed August 18, 2020).

27 See John Sides, Michael Tesler, and Lynn Vavreck, *Identity Crisis* (Princeton, NJ: Princeton University Press, 2018), pp. 25–27.

28 Gary Miller and Norman Schofield, "The Transformation of the Republican and Democratic Party Coalitions in the U.S.," *Perspectives on Politics* 6 (2008): 433–450.

29 On the change in upper-income people's attitudes toward the Republican Party, see Mark D. Brewer, *Party Images in the American Electorate* (New York: Routledge, 2009), pp. 25–26.

30 See John H. Aldrich, Jamie L. Carson, Brad T. Gomez, and David W. Rohde, *Change and Continuity in the 2016 and 2018 Elections* (Los Angeles, CA: Sage/CQ Press, 2020), p. 137.

31 Frank Newport, "Blacks as Conservative as Republicans on Some Moral Issues," *Gallup Poll*, December 3, 2008, https://news.gallup.com/poll/112807/Blacks-Conservative-Republicans-Some-Moral-Issues.aspx (accessed August 18, 2020).

32 Zoltan Hajnal and Jeremy D. Horowitz, "Racial Winners and Losers in American Party Politics," *Perspectives on Politics* 12 (2014): 100–118.

33 Jon Green and Sean McElwee, "The Differential Effects of Economic Conditions and Racial Attitudes in the Election of Donald Trump," *Perspectives on Politics* 17 (June 2019): 358–379.

34 Pew Research Center, "Race in America 2019," April 3, 2019, https://www.pewsocialtrends.org/2019/04/09/race-in-america-2019/psdt_04-09-19_race-00-06/ (accessed August 18, 2020). See also Christopher DeSante and Candis Watts, *Racial Stasis* (Chicago, IL: University of Chicago Press, 2020), Chapter 8.

35 Daniel J. Hopkins, *The Increasingly United States* (Chicago, IL: University of Chicago Press, 2018).

36 Campbell Robertson and Richard Fausset, "Swamped in a Red Surge, Southern Democrats Contemplate Their Rebuilding Plans," *New York Times*, November 6, 2014, p. A1. See also Ismail K. White, Cheryl N. Laird, and Troy D. Allen, "Selling Out?" *American Political Science Review* 108 (2014): 783–800.

37 Alan Greenblatt, "All or Nothing," *Governing* (January 2019), https://www.governing.com/topics/politics/gov-state-politics-governors-2019.html (accessed August 18, 2020).

38 See, for example, Nate Cohn, "Why Democrats Can't Win," *New York Times*, September 7, 2014, p. SR1.

39 Pew Research Center, "The Generation Gap in American Politics," March 1, 2018, https://www.people-press.org/2018/03/01/the-generation-gap-in-american-politics/ (accessed August 18, 2020).

40 See Frank Newport, "Party Identification Varies Widely Across the Age Spectrum," *Gallup Poll*, July 10, 2014, https://news.gallup.com/poll/172439/party-identification-varies-across-age-spectrum.aspx (accessed August 18, 2020).

41 Pew Research Center, "The Generation Gap in American Politics."

42 See David E. Campbell, John C. Green, and Geoffrey C. Layman, "The Party Faithful," *American Journal of Political Science* 55 (2011): 42–58.

43 On religion in American campaigns, see Christopher Weber and Matthew Thornton, "Courting Christians," *Journal of Politics* 74 (2012): 400–413.

44 Pew Research Center, "An Examination of the 2016 Electorate, Based on Validated Voters," August 9, 2018, https://www.people-press.org/2018/08/09/an-examination-of-the-2016-electorate-based-on-validated-voters/ (accessed August 18, 2020). See also David E. Campbell, Geoffrey C. Layman, John C. Green, and Nathanael G. Sumaktoyo, "Putting Politics First," *American Journal of Political Science* 62 (July 2018): 551–565.

45 Bernard L. Fraga, *The Turnout Gap* (New York: Cambridge University Press, 2018).

46 This was also the result of anti-immigrant ballot propositions sponsored by California Republicans in the 1990s and in other states since then; see Shaun Bowler, Stephen P. Nicholson, and Gary M. Segura, "Earthquakes and Aftershocks," *American Journal of Political Science* 50 (2006): 146–157.

47 Hannah Hartig, "Gender Gap Widens in View of Government's Role," Pew Research Center, April 11, 2019, https://www.pewresearch.org/fact-tank/2019/04/11/gender-gap-widens-in-views-of-governments-role-and-of-trump/ (accessed August 18, 2020).

48 Elizabeth A. Sharrow, Jesse H. Rhodes, Tatishe M. Nteta, and Jill S. Greenlee, "The First Daughter Effect," *Public Opinion Quarterly* 83 (September 2018): 493–523.

49 Kira Sanbonmatsu, *Democrats, Republicans, and the Politics of Women's Place* (Ann Arbor, MI: University of Michigan Press, 2002), Chapter 3; see also Christina Wolbrecht, *The Politics of Women's Rights* (Princeton, NJ: Princeton University Press, 2000); and Brian Schaffner, "Priming Gender," *American Journal of Political Science* 49 (2005): 803–817.

50 See Torben Iversen and Frances Rosenbluth, "The Political Economy of Gender," *American Journal of Political Science* 50 (2006): 1–19.

51 Janet M. Box-Steffensmeier, Suzanna De Boef, and Tse-Min Lin, "The Dynamics of the Partisan Gender Gap," *American Political Science Review* 98 (2004): 515–528; and Karen M. Kaufman and John R. Petrocik, "The Changing Politics of American Men," *American Journal of Political Science* 43 (1999): 864–887.

52 2016 exit poll at www.cnn.com/election/results/exit-polls/national/president (accessed November 10, 2016).

53 On marriage, parenthood, and political attitudes, see Laurel Elder and Steven Greene, *The Politics of Parenthood* (Albany, NY: SUNY Press, 2012).

54 Mark D. Brewer and Jeffrey M. Stonecash, *Dynamics of American Political Parties* (Cambridge: Cambridge University Press, 2009), Chapter 11.

55 Greg D. Adams, "Abortion: Evidence of an Issue Evolution," *American Journal of Political Science* 41 (1997): 718–737.

56 Quoted in Thomas B. Edsall, "Political Party Is No Longer Dictated By Class Status," *Washington Post,* November 9, 2000, p. A37.

57 See Geoffrey C. Layman, *The Great Divide* (New York: Columbia University Press, 2001).

58 Matthew Levendusky, *The Partisan Sort* (Chicago, IL: University of Chicago Press, 2009).

59 Martin P. Wattenberg, *The Decline of American Political Parties 1952–96* (Cambridge, MA: Harvard University Press, 1998).

60 Donald Green, Bradley Palmquist, and Eric Schickler, *Partisan Hearts and Minds* (New Haven, CT: Yale University Press, 2002), pp. 141 and 158.

61 Helmut Norpoth, "Under Way and Here to Stay: Party Realignment in the 1980s?" *Public Opinion Quarterly* 51 (1987): 376–391; and Warren E. Miller, "Party Identification, Realignment, and Party Voting," *American Political Science Review* 85 (1991): 557–570.

62 Alan Cooperman and Thomas B. Edsall, "Evangelicals Say They Led Charge for the GOP," *Washington Post,* November 8, 2004, p. A1.

63 Lilliana Mason and Nicholas Davis, "Trump Attracts Poor Voters with Multiple Republican Social Identities," *Vox,* March 10, 2016, https://www.vox.com/mischiefs-of-faction/2016/3/9/11186314/trump-voters-identities (accessed August 18, 2020). See also David Karol, *Party Position Change in American Politics* (Cambridge: Cambridge University Press, 2009).

64 David R. Mayhew, *Electoral Realignments* (New Haven, CT: Yale University Press, 2002); see also Carmines and Stimson, *Issue Evolution*; Byron E. Shafer, ed., *The End of Realignment?* (Madison, WI: University of Wisconsin Press, 1991); and Samuel Merrill III, Bernard Grofman, and Thomas L. Brunell, "Cycles in American National Electoral Politics, 1854–2006," *American Political Science Review* 102 (2008): 1–17.
65 Carmines and Stimson, *Issue Evolution.*
66 See Paul Allen Beck, "A Tale of Two Electorates," in John C. Green and Rick Farmer, eds., *The State of the Parties*, 4th ed. (Lanham, MD: Rowman & Littlefield, 2003), pp. 38–53.

CHAPTER 8

Parties and Voter Turnout

American elections are decided by those who *don't* vote as well as those who do. Unusually large voter turnouts among young people, blacks, and Latino Americans helped propel Barack Obama to victories in 2008 and 2012. When young people and blacks stayed home from the polls in larger numbers in 2016, Hillary Clinton and many other Democrats lost. So the Democratic and Republican Parties try not only to affect voters' preferences but also to mobilize those who favor their candidates and, if possible, discourage their opponents from going to the polls.

Parties try to shape voter turnout in three ways. First, each party has worked hard over time to get its likely supporters the *right* to vote. The early Jeffersonians and then the Democrats fought to expand voting rights to include renters and other non-property owners—groups that would naturally favor their candidates rather than the Federalists or Whigs.

Second, once its supporters have the right to vote, the party can promote policies that make voting *easier and more accessible* to them (and less accessible to its opponents). Parties have been doing this since the U.S. began.[1] Laws governing the ease of voting may seem nonpartisan, but they often have partisan effects. State laws requiring voters to show a photo ID, for instance, cause controversy because they may increase the burden on some types of people more than on others. Drivers' licenses are the most common form of photo ID, but people who can't afford a car or who are unable to drive because of physical disabilities—groups that tend to support Democratic candidates—have to make more effort to get the required ID. Similarly, local governments' decisions to site early voting centers in some parts of the community rather than others affect the ease with which different types of people can vote.

Finally, party organizations and candidates can strive to bring more of their supporters to the polls in a particular election. In these polarized times, this *voter mobilization* is key to winning competitive elections. The shifts in blacks' and Latinos' turnout between 2016 and 2020, for instance, resulted in part from differences in the effectiveness of the Republicans' and the Democrats' get-out-the-vote (GOTV) drives.

As we examine these party efforts, we need to consider their impact on American democracy. Voter turnout in the U.S. has been relatively low. Turnout in the intense 2016 presidential race was just 59 percent of eligible voters, well below the voting rates of almost every other industrialized democracy, though turnout increased in 2020. We need to ask why voter turnout in American elections is so limited, and what responsibility the parties bear for these low turnouts.

Elections: The Rules Affect the Results

The rules in politics, as in everything else, are never neutral. Each rule of the electoral process—such as who is eligible to vote or when elections can be held—affects different parties and candidates differently.[2] For example, if polling places close at 6:00 P.M. (as they do in Indiana and Kentucky), making it harder for office workers to get to the polls on time, then the Democratic Party may lose a disproportionate number of votes. If a state makes it easy to vote by mail, then any local party organized enough to distribute mail-in ballot applications to its supporters will benefit.

Because election rules have partisan consequences, there will be partisan debates about whether to adopt them. The U.S., unlike almost every other democracy, has no national list of eligible voters. The voter rolls are maintained by counties and towns and their partisan elected officials. For much of U.S. history, the debate leaned toward expanding voting rights to more Americans. Since 2000, at a time of very close national elections, state legislatures have considered a variety of ways to limit that expansion.

Expansion of the Right to Vote

White male citizens were given the right to vote earlier in the U.S. than in any other democracy. In the early 1800s, prompted by the Jeffersonians (who expected to benefit from the change), the states gradually repealed the property, income, and taxpaying qualifications for voting by which they had so severely constrained male suffrage.[3] By 1860, no states required property holding, and only four required substantial taxpaying as a condition for voting. But that didn't stop some northeastern patricians from trying to take voting rights away from workers and immigrants in the 1870s, to weaken support for the urban party "machines."[4]

Women did not win the right to vote in all states until much later. The Nineteenth Amendment, forbidding states to deny the right to vote based on gender, was finally approved in 1920 after a decades-long struggle. The most recent change, the constitutional amendment lowering the voting age to 18 for all elections, was ratified by the states in 1971.

The history of black Americans' voting rights is more complex—a story of both human rights and partisanship. Some New England states granted suffrage to blacks before the Civil War. The Fifteenth Amendment, adopted after that war with support from the Republican administration, declared that no state could abridge the right to vote on account of race. (Most blacks then supported Republicans, who had championed the emancipation of slaves.) But the federal government soon turned its attention to other matters, and Democratic-run southern states worked effectively to keep blacks from voting, as we will see. By the early 1900s, black turnout in the South had dropped to negligible levels. It remained that way in most southern states until the 1960s, when the Democratic Party, then the majority in Congress, changed its stance on civil rights, and federal authorities began to enforce new voting rights laws in the states.

Rules Affecting Access to Voting Rights

The Progressive movement in the late 1800s and early 1900s promoted several changes in election rules. Progressives claimed that these changes were intended to democratize American politics, but they were also designed to weaken the political party "machines" of the time.

The Secret Ballot

American elections did not always use secret ballots. In fact, not until the late 1800s was the secret ballot used throughout the nation. In the early 1800s, in many areas, voters simply told the election officials which candidates they preferred. Gradually, this "oral vote" was replaced by ballots printed by the parties or candidates. The voter brought the ballot of a particular party to the polling place and put it in the ballot box. The ballots of different parties differed in color and appearance, so observers could tell how an individual had voted. That was how the party machine wanted it; if party leaders had done a favor for someone in exchange for a vote, they wanted to be sure they had gotten their money's worth.

To discourage vote buying and weaken the party machines, Progressives pushed for a new secret ballot system, which came into widespread use in the 1880s and 1890s. These ballots were printed by the government and marked by the voter in private. Because the ballot is administered and paid for by the government, this reform involved the government in running elections, which opened the door to government regulation of the parties. Secret ballots also made it easier for voters to split their tickets—to vote for the candidates of more than one party on the same ballot.[5]

The Progressives did not succeed in doing away with the **long ballot,** however, in which each state's voters are asked to elect large numbers of state and local officials who would be appointed in other democracies. To cast a meaningful vote on each of 60 or 70 state and local offices, citizens would need to spend a lot of time gathering information, a task most citizens do not find fascinating. That drives down voter turnout. People who do vote may cast ballots for some offices but not others. This "roll-off" can reduce the vote for minor offices and referenda by 20 or 30 percent compared with offices at the top of the ballot.[6] Voter fatigue caused by the long ballot leads people to use various shortcuts to make their choices. Party identification is the most common shortcut—an outcome the Progressives would certainly have hated.

Citizenship

Prior to 1894 at least 12 states permitted noncitizens to vote,[7] although some required the individual to have applied for American citizenship. Since the 1920s, all states have required that voters be U.S. citizens. This is the biggest legal barrier to voting; millions of adults, most of them in California, Florida, Texas, and Illinois, work and may even pay taxes but cannot vote until they are "naturalized" as citizens, a process that can take years to complete. Given their average income levels and ethnicity, these noncitizen residents would be more likely to vote Democratic than Republican.

Residence

For most of American history, states could require citizens to live in a state and locality for a certain amount of time before being allowed to vote there. Southern states had the longest residence requirements (to keep migrant farm workers from voting). In 1970, Congress limited states' residence requirements to a maximum of 30 days for voting in presidential elections. Since then, almost half of the states have dropped residence requirements altogether. Even so, many Americans move frequently, and those who have moved recently are much less likely to vote.[8]

Registration

Another major obstacle to voting is the registration requirement—the rule in most states that citizens must register in advance to vote in an election. During much of the 1800s, voters needed only to show up on Election Day to cast a ballot. Progressive reformers in the late 1800s urged states to require advance registration to limit voter fraud by party bosses. That increased the motivation needed to vote because it doubled the effort involved: one trip to register and a second trip to vote. These registration requirements helped to reduce the high turnout levels of that time.[9] In many other democracies—and in several American states since 2015—voters are registered automatically when they get drivers' licenses or other state services, taking the burden of registering off the individual voter.

The Special Case of Voting Rights for Black Americans

Soon after blacks had been granted the right to vote by constitutional amendments in the 1860s, these new voters—one-third of the South's population—elected some African-American candidates to Congress and state legislatures. The newly elected black Republicans advocated for reforms such as state-funded public schools. (Remember that changing who has the right to vote can also result in changed government policies.) Southern Democrats, who had lost their hold on power, responded with violence and, eventually, laws and administrative rulings that kept blacks from voting. So just 15 years after the Confederacy lost the Civil War, white southerners had deprived black citizens of their newly achieved voice in elections.

The Long Struggle for Voting Rights

Blacks remained largely disenfranchised for almost a century after the 1880s. During this time, southern states would devise a way to disenfranchise blacks, the Supreme Court would strike it down as unconstitutional, and the states would find another. One example was the "white primary." The Republican Party barely existed in the South at this time, so the candidate who won the Democratic primary was assured of winning the general election. Faced with the threat of blacks voting in the Democratic primary, some states declared the party to be a private club, open only to whites, so blacks could not cast a primary ballot. It took 21 years of lawsuits and five Supreme Court cases to end this practice.[10]

In addition, most southern states required payment of a poll tax to vote—just one or two dollars, but often demanded well before an election, with the requirement that the taxpayer keep a receipt and present it weeks later at the polling place. And local election officials in some states used tests to decide who was "literate" enough to vote. These laws were intentionally directed at the poor and uneducated black population.

Southern lawmakers also designed endless delays and other technicalities to prevent blacks from registering to vote. Observers reported:

> Separate [registration] tables would be assigned to whites and Negroes [then the customary term for African Americans]. If a line of Negroes were waiting for the Negro table, a white might go ahead of them, use the empty white table, and leave. In Anniston, Alabama, a report said the white table was larger, and Negroes were not allowed in the room when a white was using it …. In one north Florida county, the registrar … simply sat with his legs stretched out across the doorway. Negroes didn't break through them.[11]

Those who kept trying were often faced with economic reprisal (the loss of a job or a home) and physical violence. It is not surprising, in this relentlessly hostile environment, that only 5 percent of voting-age blacks were registered in the 11 southern states as late as 1940, when the U.S. celebrated its 164th birthday.[12]

Because courts found it difficult to counter these extra-legal hurdles, reformers turned to Congress and the executive branch. The federal Voting Rights Act of 1965, extended in 1982 and 2006, authorized the U.S. Justice Department to seek injunctions against anyone who prevented blacks from voting. When the Justice Department could convince a federal court that a "pattern or practice" of discrimination existed in a district, the court could send federal registrars there to register voters. It could also supervise voting procedures in states and counties where less than 50 percent of potential voters had gone to the polls in the most recent presidential election.[13]

This unprecedented federal intervention in state elections, combined with the civil rights movement's efforts to mobilize black voters, enabled the black electorate to grow enormously in the South (see Figure 8.1). By the 1990s, black registration finally reached a level closer to that of white southerners. Today, blacks in the South are registered at about three-quarters of the rate of white southerners. In the process, the conflicts between these new black voters and southern whites ate away at the Democratic Party from within and caused dramatic changes in the two parties' supporting coalitions (see Chapter 7).

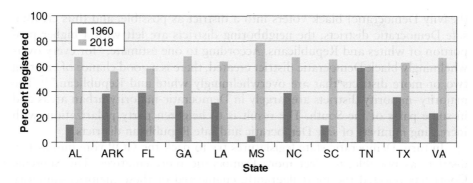

FIGURE 8.1 Black Voter Registration in the South, 1960 and 2018

Note: Bars show the proportion of blacks in each year who were registered to vote, based on the voting-age citizen population. Note that registration levels in 2020 will be higher than those for 2018, because 2020 is a presidential election year, as was 1960.

Source: For 2018, U.S. Census Bureau, Table 4b at https://www.census.gov/data/tables/time-series/demo/voting-and-registration/p20-583.html (accessed August 19, 2020).

From Voting Rights to Representation

Even after blacks gained voting rights, some states kept trying to dilute the impact of black votes. The federal government responded with a new twist on an old practice. Every ten years, after the U.S. Census, state legislatures must redraw the boundaries of congressional and state legislative districts so that these districts remain equal in population size. This **legislative redistricting**, ordered by the Supreme Court in the 1960s to stop state legislatures from overrepresenting rural areas and underrepresenting bigger cities,[14] has been used by resourceful politicians for short-term political gain. **Gerrymandering**—drawing district lines to maximize one's own party's strength and disadvantage the other party—is prevalent and is usually permitted by the courts.[15] For years, in the case of black Americans, it was common for legislators to draw legislative district lines that divided black voters among several districts ("cracking"), so as to weaken their voting strength, or to pack black voters into a few districts so that pro-civil rights candidates won these districts by large, wasteful majorities ("packing").

After the 1990 census, the first Bush administration pressed southern states to redraw congressional district lines to create some districts with a majority of black or Latino voters, called **"majority-minority" districts**. The argument was that these districts would usually elect minority legislators to Congress and thus improve the representation of minority citizens. Many of these districts were created by an interesting alliance of black and Latino Democrats with white Republicans. This did increase the number of congressional seats held by black Americans. And it appeared to increase turnout among registered blacks living in black-majority districts.[16]

Another effect of these majority-minority districts, however, was to elect more Republicans to Congress from the South—one reason why Republicans supported their creation. Because the districts are fashioned by packing as many (heavily Democratic) black voters into a district as possible, and thus creating safe Democratic districts, the neighboring districts are left with a higher proportion of whites and Republicans. According to one estimate, "for every overwhelmingly black Democratic district created, there is a good chance of creating two or more districts that are overwhelmingly white and Republican."[17] The majority–minority districts are largely in Democratic-majority urban areas and in some parts of the South. The result is to heighten party polarization, with increasing numbers of safe Democratic and safe Republican districts.

In turn, Democratic state legislatures try to pack the GOP vote into as few districts as possible, to elect more Democratic representatives. The Supreme Court has rejected the most flagrantly engineered of these majority–minority districts, but has ruled that race can be an element in redrawing district lines, as long as it is not the controlling factor.[18]

Getting Blacks' Votes Counted

Achieving fair representation for black Americans is limited by the fact that more than 15 percent of black males have lost voting rights because they have had felony convictions. Mandatory sentences for drug use appear to target drugs used more often by blacks, and almost all states deny felons the right to vote, at least while they are behind bars and, in most states, through the individual's parole. Almost 4 million Americans of all races are estimated to have lost their right to vote because of a felony conviction.[19] Predicting from their SES and race, most of these people would probably vote Democratic. Florida voters in 2018 ran counter to this trend by amending the state constitution to return voting rights to about 1.4 million people who served time for felonies—the biggest extension of the franchise since the Voting Rights Act.

In addition, several states have recently passed laws restricting the activities of groups that register new voters. These laws seemed to be aimed at minority voters, who are twice as likely to register through groups' registration drives as whites are. So, although black turnout rates are much higher now than they were in the mid-1900s, more subtle challenges to blacks' voting rights remain.

Efforts to Liberalize Voting Rules

Registration requirements and other "costs" imposed on voting are associated with lower turnout.[20] Yet reforms intended to reduce the costs of voting don't always increase turnout.

Election Day Registration

North Dakota does not require its citizens to register at all, and 20 other states allow citizens to register and vote on the same day, known as **Election Day Registration (EDR)** or **Same Day Registration**.[21] These states tend to have higher turnout rates,[22] because citizens can cast a ballot even if they do not get interested enough to take part until the last, most engaging days of the campaign. But these laws remain controversial, and in most states, prospective voters must still take the initiative to find out where and when to register, make the effort to do so, and then re-register whenever they move or fail to vote for a number of years. Experts have estimated that millions of eligible people, many of whom are less educated, lower income, or residentially mobile, tried but were unable to vote in recent elections because of registration problems.[23]

"Motor Voter" Laws and Automatic Voter Registration (AVR)

Another effort to ease restrictive registration rules was the so-called **Motor Voter law** (1993), which required that states let citizens register to vote at driver's license bureaus, by mail, and through agencies that give out federal benefits. Voter registration surged in many areas as a result.

In 2015–2016, Oregon, Alaska, and California became the first states to *automatically* register eligible residents when they get a new or renewed driver's license, unless the individual declines. Fifteen other states have since passed AVR laws as of July 2019. Most studies have shown, however, that although stricter registration rules are linked with lower voter turnout, reforms to ease these rules, including "motor voter" and AVR, do not always increase turnout. Those who register at these alternate sites are less likely to vote than are other registrants.[24]

Voting by Mail, Early, and No-Excuse Absentee Voting

The 2020 elections proved to be a perfect storm. Although the stakes in the election were unusually high—in one poll, 83 percent of voters said in August that "it really matters" who would win in November—many more voters said they expected to have difficulties casting their ballot than was the case in 2018.[25] The reason was the COVID-19 pandemic. Older people, who are the most consistent voters, feared catching the virus if they stood in long lines to vote in person, and long lines were guaranteed because most poll workers, typically retired people, couldn't risk their health to work at the polls. The obvious answer was to greatly expand voting by mail. Prior to 2020, five states were voting entirely by mail. But the huge increase in mail voting produced challenges for some states: in particular, not all who requested mail ballots received theirs in time.

Then, voting by mail became a partisan issue. Although studies indicate that neither party is advantaged by a move to voting by mail,[26] President Trump claimed that it increased voter fraud and that if mail voting were universal, "You'd never have a Republican elected in this country again."[27] His choice to head the U.S. Postal Service soon implemented reforms, ostensibly to cut spending, which slowed mail delivery just as requests for absentee and mail ballots multiplied.[28] Post offices across the nation struggled under the pressure of the increased work. All-mail elections had previously been found to increase turnout by 2–4 percentage points, especially among infrequent voters,[29] and even more when all registered voters are sent ballot applications. In fact, over 63 percent of voters cast their 2020 ballots either by mail or through early voting, an all-time high. The president insisted that as a result, the election would be fraudulent, especially if he were to lose.

The Backlash: Restricting Voting Rights

Laws removing obstacles to voting rights sound like a good thing in a democracy. But because changes in election rules can affect the turnout of Democratic-leaning groups differently from Republican-leaning groups, liberalizations of voting laws have provoked a powerful backlash. In 2013, the Supreme Court invalidated a key part of the Voting Rights Act; *Shelby County v. Holder* freed states with a history of racial discrimination in elections (mainly southern states) from having to get approval from the U.S. Attorney General or a federal district court before making any changes in their voting laws and practices. About 25 states responded by restricting voting rights.[30]

Voter ID Laws

Before 2006, not a single state required voters to show a photo ID. But in a remarkably short time, many states passed and most others are considering laws requiring voters to show a state or federal government-issued photo ID card at the polls.[31] As of January 2019, 35 states required voters to show some kind of ID at the polls. (A non-photo-ID alternative used by other states is to compare the voter's signature or other details with the signature or information already on file.[32])

These laws have been highly controversial. Proponents, usually Republicans,[33] contend that the laws are needed to limit vote fraud. Democratic opponents counter with evidence that vote fraud at the polls is extremely rare—in fact, one study showed that reports of voter impersonation are about as common as reports of alien abductions[34]—and that the slightly more common cases of fraudulent absentee ballots are not covered by most voter ID laws. In particular, these laws seem to target disadvantaged groups. For instance, researchers find that voter ID requirements are more likely to be passed in states where minority turnout increased since the previous presidential election.[35] Despite the widespread impression that IDs are required everywhere, opponents point out that disproportionate numbers of poor, minority, and disabled people—who vote predominantly Democratic—are less likely to have driver's licenses and passports and therefore might lose their chance to vote, though they are otherwise eligible.

Congress has heard evidence that these rules are often applied arbitrarily. Blacks are more likely to be asked by election officials to show identification than whites are, regardless of the state's voter ID laws.[36] And in several states whose legislatures gained Republican majorities in 2010 and 2014, bills were introduced to prevent college students from using university IDs to satisfy voter ID requirements or to make it harder for students to vote in their college towns at all.[37] Some recent federal court rulings have struck down voter ID laws in North Carolina and Texas on the ground that these laws are discriminatory.[38] They cite cases such as Alabama's which, after passing a stricter voter ID requirement in 2015, closed 31 driver's license offices, most of them in rural and black-majority areas,[39] thereby making it harder for their residents to apply for an alternative state ID.

Proof of Citizenship

Several states have debated laws requiring all voters to bring documents to the polls proving that they are American citizens (usually, an original birth certificate, naturalization papers, or a passport), though the U.S. Supreme Court has disallowed such requirements at the federal level. Supporters of these laws say they are needed to curb voting by non-citizens. Others claim that, as with voter ID laws, poor, disabled, and minority citizens have a harder time obtaining the required documents and could therefore have their access to the ballot taken away improperly. The Trump administration worked to include a question about the respondent's citizenship status in the 2020 Census, which might have reduced response rates in big cities and affected their representation in the U.S. House and state legislatures. But the effort met successful resistance.

State legislatures and counties often vote on other bills that would make it easier or harder to vote. These include laws allowing people to vote at malls and supermarkets, creating more or fewer precinct polling places,[40] and requiring or prohibiting the mailing of absentee ballot requests to all registered voters. In general, Democrats have been more favorable to liberalizing registration and turnout laws than Republicans, presumably because they feel their party would benefit, though little evidence supports this assumption.

Voter Suppression

In some instances, parties, candidates, and other groups have relied on the more straightforward techniques of voter intimidation that have stained American political history. One time-honored technique has been to station police cars near some polling places and warn prospective voters (falsely) that they could be arrested for unpaid parking tickets or child support if they cast a ballot. Another is for employers to pressure their employees to vote for certain candidates. Democrats were especially concerned about voter intimidation in 2016 and 2020 when Donald Trump urged his supporters to "patrol" urban polling places and challenge voters who looked ineligible to them. An uptick in these incidents has led both parties to recruit large numbers of lawyers as poll watchers in recent elections. Prior to the 2020 elections, several states purged large numbers of infrequent voters from their polling lists, including 300,000 in Georgia and 230,000 in Wisconsin. Although federal law requires purging to keep voter lists accurate, these purges are often used for partisan purposes, especially because Democratic-leaning groups—young people and minorities—are more likely to be infrequent voters than Republican supporters.[41]

Foreign Interference

Many Americans were startled to learn that hackers sponsored by the Russian government targeted every U.S. state in the 2016 elections and gained access to the voter database in at least two states.[42] They shouldn't have been; Russian interference in European elections had been documented at least as early as the 2000s. Former special counsel Robert S. Mueller III reported to Congress in 2019 that "They're doing it [again] while we sit here."[43] Much of the foreign sabotage involved using sham social media accounts to post election misinformation or to try to stir up racial or other conflicts among Americans.

Voting Systems: Are Votes Counted Fairly?

Once people have gotten to the polls, we assume that their choice of candidates will be registered accurately. That isn't always the case. Most Americans would probably be surprised to learn that U.S. elections are ranked lower than other industrialized democracies on a wide range of criteria, from the accuracy of voter lists to the clarity of voter ID requirements.[44] Some types of voting machines (such as punch card systems and electronic voting systems without a paper trail) are especially problematic.[45] Confusing ballot layouts can lead to trouble. Prospective voters in some areas—particularly large cities—continue to face lines at the polling place so long that would-be voters may give up in frustration.[46]

Why does this happen? Because elections are run by states and localities, voters in one county, even one polling place, may be treated differently from voters in another. Voters fill out mail ballots that differ from county to county. Poll workers are typically poorly paid, lightly trained, partisan volunteers, supervised by local election officials often elected on partisan ballots.[47] Voter registration systems are still usually paper-based, resulting in recording errors, out-of-date information, and other inaccuracies.

In particular, counties differ in their ability to pay for the most reliable (and costly) voting systems. The result is that error-prone systems are more likely to be found in poorer and minority-dominated counties, which tend to vote Democratic. The U.S. Commission on Civil Rights reported in 2001 that although it found no evidence of a systematic effort to disenfranchise blacks, they were ten times more likely than whites to have their ballots undercounted or rejected because they lived in districts with less reliable voting systems.[48] This has also been found to be true of mailed ballots.[49]

After media coverage of the problems with the 2000 vote, Congress passed the 2002 Help America Vote Act (HAVA) offering $3 billion to help states upgrade their voting systems, set minimum federal standards, and create computerized statewide voter registration rolls. Many counties used the money to

Democracy on the Cheap: Is Every Vote Counted?

After two decades of concern about voting systems, problems remain:

- The final results of the 2020 Iowa caucuses were reported as soon as they became available—two weeks after the event ended. The culprits: an untested app, an overcomplicated system, and phone lines clogged by dirty tricks.
- An 11-year-old boy at a DEFCON convention was able to hack into and change the voting results of the Florida state election website in 2018. It took him less than 10 minutes.
- Voters in the Texas primary in 2020 waited up to seven hours to cast a ballot. The paperless machines were prone to breakdown, and Texas is no longer covered by sections of the Voting Rights Act that require federal supervision.
- In 2016, almost a quarter of voting jurisdictions used electronic voting machines with no paper trail. With these machines, a "recount" consists of pressing the "total" button a second time and, presumably, getting the same result. That percentage dropped in 2020, but about 16 million voters still used such machines.
- Even when counties buy updated voting machines, they often don't keep the software up-to-date. Many counties bought new voting systems in 2019 using Windows 7 or older operating systems for which Microsoft stopped providing tech support in January 2020. Such systems are more vulnerable to hacking.

As one expert put it, "We'd never tolerate this level of errors with an ATM. The problem is that we continue to do democracy on the cheap."

Sources: Isaac Stanley-Becker, "Iowa Caucus Chaos Was Years in the Making," *Washington Post*, February 16, 2020, p. A1; Michael D. Regan, "An 11-year-old Changed Election Results on a Replica Florida State Website in Under 10 Minutes," *PBS NewsHour Weekend*, August 12, 2018; Elise Viebeck, "Lengthy Wait Times in Tx. Raise Questions of Equal Access," *Washington Post*, March 5, 2020, p. A8; Lulu Friesdat, "A Two-Tier Approach," *Electoral Integrity Project Workshop on Protecting Electoral Security and Voting Rights*, 2017; "Old Software Makes New Electoral Systems Ripe for Hacking," *Associated Press*, July 15, 2019.

buy electronic—touch-screen or direct-recording electronic (DRE)—voting machines. In 2006, over 80 percent of all voters used some form of e-voting, more than a third of them for the first time.

That produced new challenges. The e-voting systems raised issues familiar to anyone who has used a college computer lab: computer crashes, altered programming codes, and the possibility of hacking and rigged machines. The first cyber attack against an online election system was discovered in 2012, when a Miami-Dade County election website got 2,500 "phantom requests" for absentee ballots from a computer program.[50] If it had gone undetected, those votes could have been cast by the hacker. A Florida newspaper found that voters in counties using touch-screen machines were six times more likely to have their vote go unrecorded as were voters in counties using optical-scan devices, like those often used to grade multiple-choice exams.[51] Another issue was that HAVA granted the right to cast a "provisional" ballot to anyone whose eligibility to vote was challenged by an election official. But Congress set no uniform national standards as to which of these provisional ballots should be counted. That produced concerns about partisan and unequal treatment.

Studies show that at least a million registered voters have been prevented from casting their ballots in presidential elections because of administrative glitches: their names were accidentally purged from or not recorded properly on the registration rolls or they didn't bring the proper identification to the polls (see box "Democracy on the Cheap: Is Every Vote Counted?" on page 181). Solving many of these problems requires money. Even though accurate and reliable voting systems are vital to a democracy, cash-starved counties may decide not to devote the necessary resources to elections, which take place at most only once or twice a year, when they face daily demands to fund other crucial services, such as law enforcement, garbage collection, and road repair.

Turnout in American Elections: On the Rebound?

In addition to enfranchising their supporters and passing laws making it easier for them to get to the polls, parties can also try to shape the electorate by mobilizing voters in a particular election. Turnout in American elections has risen recently, but even at its highest, it trails that of most other Western democracies. Although turnout rates were higher in the late 1800s,[52] voter turnout in U.S. presidential elections never exceeded 62 percent between the 1970s and 2016[53] (see Figure 8.2).

Presidential turnout in 2020 topped recent benchmarks. Midterm election voting in the 2018 was the highest in a century.[54] But by contrast, voters in Belgium, Denmark, and Sweden regularly turn out at rates of 80 percent or more.

American voter turnout ought to have risen dramatically since the mid-1900s.[55] Educational levels have increased substantially, and higher education is linked with higher voter turnout. Liberalized registration, residence, and early voting rules have made it easier to cast a ballot. Of course, some types of people do vote at much higher rates than 60 percent, which gives their preferences greater weight in election results. After considering the reasons for the overall low turnout rates, this chapter will explore which groups are best represented at the polls and whether party efforts help make the electorate more representative of all citizens.

Social Group Differences in Turnout

We can think about the decision to vote in terms of its costs and benefits to the individual. Each of us pays some costs for voting, not in cash but in time, energy, and attention. What we get in return may seem minimal; the influence of a single vote in most elections is usually small. From that perspective, it may be remarkable that anyone votes at all.[56] A variety of economic and social forces,

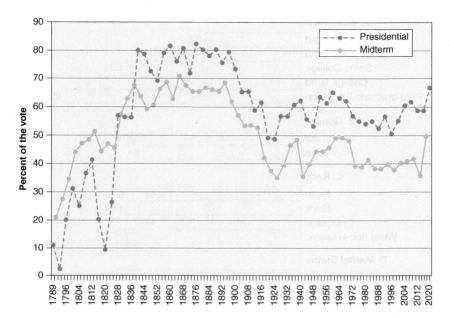

FIGURE 8.2 Turnout in American Elections, 1790–2020

Note: These are the percentages voting for president and for the office with the highest vote in midterm elections, calculated as described in Note 53 to this chapter. Data are from Walter Dean Burnham, "The Turnout Problem," in A. James Reichley, ed., *Elections American Style* (Washington, DC: Brookings Institution, 1987), pp. 113–114, updated for presidential elections since 1984 using https://infoguides.gmu.edu/USelections/president (accessed August 19, 2020). Midterm data since 1986 come from Curtis Gans, Director of the Center for the Study of the American Electorate, and Michael McDonald.

from citizens' levels of education to their social connectedness, affect the way individuals weigh the costs and benefits of voting.[57] That in turn affects the parties' ability to mobilize different types of people.

Education

The biggest difference between voters and nonvoters is their level of education. Less educated Americans are much less likely to vote[58] (see Figure 8.3, Section A). Financially insecure people, who tend to identify as Democrats, also vote in lower proportions. More education helps people understand the political system and find the information they need to make political choices. More educated people are more likely to feel that they ought to vote, to gain satisfaction from voting, and to have the experience with meeting deadlines and filling out forms that will be necessary to register and vote.[59]

This relationship between education and voting sounds so obvious that we would expect to see it everywhere. Yet the relationship is weaker in many other democracies, where labor parties and other groups work to bring less-educated and lower-income people to the polls. In some nations, then, party mobilization drives can compensate for the dampening effect of lower educational levels on voter turnout.[60]

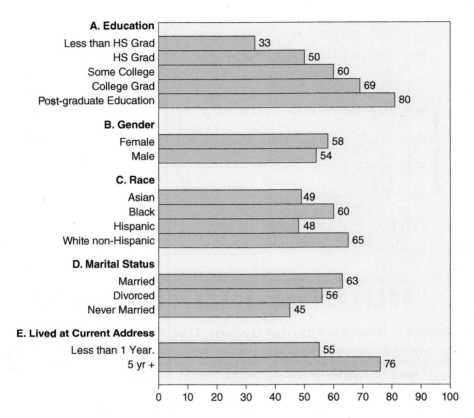

FIGURE 8.3 Group Differences in Voter Turnout, 2016

Note: Bars show the percentage of each group who reported having voted in the 2016 presidential election.

Source: Calculated from U.S. Census Bureau data by Michael McDonald, U.S. Elections Project, http://www. electproject.org/home/voter-turnout/demographics (accessed August 19, 2020). Voting turnout data for 2020 will not be available until late 2021, when they will be posted in the Online Appendix to this book.

Youth

Younger Americans, now disproportionately Democratic in their party ID, are much less likely to go to the polls than are older people (see Figure 8.4). Younger people are no less likely than their elders to take part in other community activities, such as volunteer work.[61] But their interest in service has not extended to include political service. In one survey, the only occupation young people (age 26 and under) rated less attractive than being an elected official was farming.[62] Headlines in 2018 stressed the big increase in voter turnout among younger people, and in fact turnout among those aged 18–29 rose substantially over the previous midterms. But turnout rose in all other age categories as well, so younger voters' participation still lagged behind voters 60 and over. In short, younger voters are voluntarily underrepresented in elections.

Why does the lower turnout of young adults matter? There are some notable differences between younger people's and older people's attitudes. Current

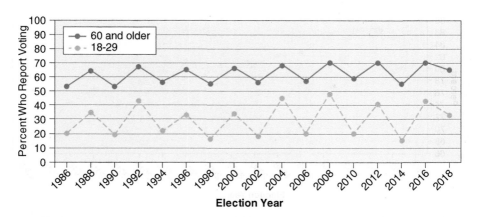

FIGURE 8.4 Voter Turnout of Younger and Older Americans, 1986–2018

Source: Calculated from U.S. Census Bureau data by Michael McDonald, U.S. Election Project, http://www. electproject.org/home/voter-turnout/demographics (accessed August 19, 2020). Turnout data for the 2020 election will not be available until late 2021, when they will be posted in the Online Appendix to this book.

young adults, on average, are much more ethnically and racially diverse, much more tolerant of interracial dating and same-sex marriage, and much less committed to traditional gender roles than their elders are.[63] When large numbers of young people don't vote, candidates pay greater attention to the issues that concern those who do vote. Social Security and Medicare rank high on the campaign agenda because older people, for whom these issues are important, have higher turnout rates than younger adults do.

Gender, Race, and Ethnicity

For many decades after getting the right to vote, women voted less often than men. Now, women's increasing education levels and changes in women's roles have eliminated or reversed this gender difference (see Figure 8.3, Section B).

Turnout among racial and ethnic minorities tells a different story (see Figure 8.3, Section C). Research shows that blacks have lower turnout rates than whites, and Latino or Hispanic and Asian Americans have a much lower turnout. The partisan implications are threatening to Democrats, because African-Americans are the single most pro-Democratic group in the U.S., and Latino and Asian Americans vote more Democratic than Republican.[64] In 2016, for instance, the 7 percent drop in black American turnout may have doomed Democrat Hillary Clinton's chances of winning the presidency.

The Census Bureau reports that because of the growing proportion of racial and ethnic minorities among American children, the population as a whole should be majority-minority within three decades.[65] But the lag in minority voting turnout will delay the political effects of this demographic change, as it did in 2016, when white turnout increased and black turnout dropped. Overall, however, non-Latino whites are steadily falling as a percentage of all voters (see Figure 8.5).

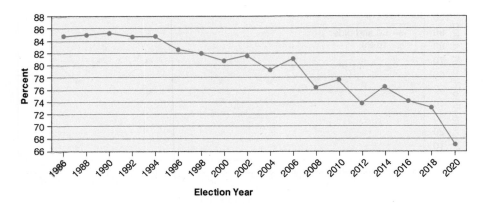

FIGURE 8.5 White (non-Hispanic) Voters as a Percentage of All Voters, 1986–2020

Source: Calculated from U.S. Census Bureau data by Michael McDonald, http://www.electproject.org/home/-voter-turnout/demographics (accessed August 19, 2020).

Social Connectedness

People who belong to several organizations and are closely connected with friends and family are much more likely to be mobilized to vote. Contact with politically knowledgeable people increases that likelihood.[66] Voting is also more common among those who are well integrated into the community through home ownership, long-time residence, church attendance, or a job outside the home. Even being married increases someone's likelihood of voting (see Figure 8.3, Sections D and E).[67]

Some forms of social connectedness have declined recently. Americans are less inclined to attend religious services now and less likely to be married. These declines may counteract the effects of rising educational levels and liberalized registration rules, by weakening the social networks that stimulate voter participation.

Political Attitudes

Some civic attitudes predispose individuals to vote: feelings that government is responsive to citizens (**external political efficacy**) and can be trusted to do what is right (**trust in government**), and a sense of responsibility to take part in elections (**citizen duty**).[68] These civic attitudes have faded in recent decades. Many relatively well-informed, well-educated young people have become cynical about government and politics. More education and easier access to the vote, then, do not tempt them to become politically involved.[69] The strength of people's partisanship also affects voting. When party ID weakened in the 1970s, turnout declined (see Chapter 6).

Why Didn't You Vote?

Here's why people registered to vote said they didn't cast a ballot in 2016:

Didn't like the candidates or campaign issues	25%
Not interested	15%
Too busy or conflicting schedule	14%
Illness or disability	12%
Out of town or away from home	8%
Registration problems (among registered citizens)	4%
Forgot to vote	3%
Transportation problems	3%
Inconvenient polling place	2%
Other	11%

(Excludes don't know, refused to answer, bad weather) .

Source: U.S. Census Bureau data, Current Population Survey, November supplement, 2016 at Table 10, https://www.census.gov/data/tables/time-series/demo/voting-and-registration/p20-580.html (accessed August 19, 2020).

The Impact of the Current Campaign

Voter participation is typically highest in presidential elections and lowest in local races.[70] Presidential races are highly publicized and usually exciting. Because of the publicity, it will not take much effort for people to get information about the candidates, and because of the excitement, they will probably pay more attention to the information they find. Both of these conditions reduce the costs of voting and increase its appeal.[71]

The lack of a presidential contest usually leads to a big drop in midterm congressional election turnout. The 2018 midterms were an exception; turnout in 2018 was almost as high as in the 2016 presidential race. Democrats usually suffer more than Republicans from the drop in midterm turnout, because their young and minority supporters are more likely to stay home when there is no presidential contest. In 2018, however, minority and youth turnout dropped less than usual, and first-time voters were especially likely to support Democratic candidates.

More generally, hotly contested races bring voters to the polls. In addition to their excitement, competitive elections give voters more assurance that their vote will matter.[72] In fact, seeing a competitive campaign has long-term effects: It makes voters more interested and better informed about politics a year later.[73]

Party Efforts to Mobilize Voters

Party organizations know that the most effective means of mobilization is person-to-person contact.[74] Personal canvassing is especially useful in mobilizing first-time voters; most new voters say that they came to the polls because "my family or friends encouraged me to vote."[75]

Face-to-face voter mobilization had become less common in the 1900s. But during the past two decades, the parties and several other groups have developed programs to increase turnout among their supporters. Civil rights groups have worked closely with the Democratic Party to bring more blacks to the polls. Organized labor mounts major GOTV drives built on union members' contacts with their friends and neighbors. Beginning in 2012, both party organizations have worked hard to inform voters about new state voter ID laws and limits on early voting. These mobilization drives have helped increase turnout, though they were limited by the pandemic in 2020.[76]

Conventional wisdom says that because nonvoters tend to come from groups usually inclined to vote Democratic, such as lower-income and less-educated people, voter mobilization drives should help Democratic candidates. That is why proposals to make registering and voting easier are often assumed to benefit Democrats. It explains why organized labor spends so much money and effort on registration and GOTV campaigns.

Conventional wisdom is not always correct, however. As we have seen, close contests, dramatic conflicts, and exciting candidates can bring more people to the polls, and these conditions are not always generated by Democratic candidates. In fact, Republican presidential candidates have won most of the large-turnout elections in the past five decades.[77] And one recent study showed that nonvoters are evenly divided between Democrats and Republicans. The one attitude they often share is a lack of interest in news or politics.[78]

Do Party Efforts Diversify the Electorate?

Have these party mobilization drives helped to create an American electorate that more closely reflects the diversity of the American people? Or have they simply increased the representation of those already likely to vote?

Researchers find that parties and party activists tend to contact higher-income and older people more than less wealthy and younger people, a tendency that has increased in recent elections.[79] College students change their addresses often, which makes it harder for party activists to find them. And both parties know that it is easier to activate those already predisposed to vote than it is to entice previous nonvoters to the polls.

As a result, most voter mobilization drives do relatively little to increase the turnout of groups whose voting rates have been low. The most recent exception was the Obama campaign in 2008 and 2012. Its organizers set out to increase turnout because many of Obama's most likely supporters were a part of groups with traditionally low turnout. In addition to minority racial and ethnic groups, the campaign especially targeted young people who had recently become eligible to vote. Their work paid off. One pollster estimated that Obama won the vote of people under age 30 by a margin of about 8.3 million votes in 2008; Obama's overall margin in the popular vote was about 8 million.[80]

The Challenge to the Parties

One argument in favor of democracy is that the best decisions are made when the responsibility for decision-making is widely shared. If so, then we ought to strive for the widest possible participation in elections (see box "Which Would You Choose? We Need Every Vote ..." below).[81] Yet we have seen that American voter participation lags behind that of most other democracies, and those whose voices are not heard at the polls tend to come from disadvantaged groups: young people, Latino and Asian Americans, and those with fewer economic resources and greater need for government help.

WHICH WOULD YOU CHOOSE?

We Need Every Vote...

Democracy is most vibrant when all views are heard. When as many people as possible take part in elections, governments are more likely to come up with the creative solutions needed to solve problems.

Politicians pay more attention to the needs of those who vote than to those who don't. So the views and interests of the nonvoters, though real, may go unrepresented.

The most committed voters tend to be older, more educated, and more affluent than other citizens are. These people will get more than their fair share of government benefits and attention from elected officials who are anxious to get their votes.

It is the alienated and dissatisfied people who stay away from the polls. They can become ripe for extremist appeals. It's better to bring them into the political system where they can voice their concerns in more productive ways.

Let Sleeping Dogs Lie...

Those who are least likely to vote are also the least well informed and the least interested in the ways a government functions. Why should we encourage them to take part in elections? If they don't care enough or know enough to vote, shouldn't we be grateful that they stay home?

If people have the right to vote and choose not to, maybe this means they are satisfied with things as they are. If they really wanted change, they could use their votes to obtain it.

If we relax registration and residence requirements to encourage more people to vote, we're encouraging voting by people who don't care enough to register at the proper time.

American democracy has been strong enough to survive impeachments, scandals, and candidates who lost the presidency even though they won the popular vote. If it ain't broke, why fix it?

What responsibility do the parties bear for these low turnouts? Party organizations are among the main sponsors of voter mobilization drives. They have the capacity to recruit large and diverse groups of people into politics. But parties, like individuals, are self-interested; they want to stimulate turnout only among their likely supporters and to limit turnout by their likely opponents. And they find it easier to locate people who have voted in previous elections. In practice, then, the parties usually preach to their choir. They don't often work hard to attract new voting groups, especially the disadvantaged. The success of the Obama campaigns and the growing number of Latino and Asian Americans may change this pattern, however.

The fact that the active electorate in the U.S. is not as diverse as the nation's population probably reduces the amount of conflict in American politics and the range of political interests to which the parties must respond. Understandably, candidates and elected officials think more about the needs of those who take part in elections than those who don't. For example, studies show that members of Congress are more likely to vote for the preferences of those constituents who go to the polls and who are active politically beyond voting than of those who don't vote.[82] The cost, however, is that the American parties have fallen short of fulfilling their capabilities in involving people in this single most accessible democratic activity.

Notes

1 See John H. Aldrich, "Did Hamilton, Jefferson, and Madison 'Cause' the U.S. Government Shutdown?" *Perspectives on Politics* 13 (2015): 7–23.

2 See Pippa Norris, *Electoral Engineering* (Cambridge: Cambridge University Press, 2004).

3 The term "suffrage" means the right to vote. See Alexander Keyssar, *The Right to Vote* (Boulder, CO: Basic Books, 2009).

4 James McGregor Burns and Susan Dunn, *The Three Roosevelts* (New York: Atlantic Monthly Press, 2001), p. 23.

5 Ticket splitting at the local level did occur prior to the secret ballot; see Alan Ware, *The Democratic Party Heads North, 1877–1962* (Cambridge: Cambridge University Press, 2006), p. 21.

6 Stephen M. Nichols and Gregory A. Strizek, "Electronic Voting Machines and Ballot Roll-off," *American Politics Quarterly* 23 (1995): 300–318.

7 Paul Kleppner, *Continuity and Change in Electoral Politics, 1893–1928* (Westport, CT: Greenwood, 1987), pp. 165–166.

8 Peverill Squire, Raymond E. Wolfinger, and David P. Glass, "Residential Mobility and Voter Turnout," *American Political Science Review* 81 (1987): 45–65.

9 Walter Dean Burnham, "Theory and Voting Research," *American Political Science Review* 68 (1974): 1002–1023.

10 The Supreme Court finally ended the white primary in *Smith v. Allwright* (1944).

11 Pat Watters and Reese Cleghorn, *Climbing Jacob's Ladder* (New York: Harcourt Brace Jovanovich, 1967), pp. 122–123.

12 See V. O. Key, Jr., *Southern Politics in State and Nation* (New York: Knopf, 1949).

13 Chandler Davidson and Bernard Grofman, eds., *Quiet Revolution in the South* (Princeton, NJ: Princeton University Press, 1994).

14 The landmark Supreme Court cases are *Baker v. Carr* (1962); *Reynolds v. Sims* (1964); and *Wesberry v. Sanders* (1964).

15 The most recent case was *Rucho et al. v. Common Cause et al.*, decided on a 5–4 vote in 2019. On gerrymandering, see Erik J. Engstrom, *Partisan Gerrymandering and the Construction of American Democracy* (Ann Arbor, MI: University of Michigan Press, 2016).

16 See Bernard L. Fraga, "Redistricting and the Causal Impact of Race on Voter Turnout," *Journal of Politics* 78 (2016): 19–34.

17 Thomas B. Edsall, "Parties Play Voting Rights Role Reversal," *Washington Post,* February 25, 2001, p. A1. See also Kevin A. Hill, "Does the Creation of Majority Black Districts Aid Republicans?" *Journal of Politics* 57 (1995): 384–401.

18 The cases are *Miller v. Johnson* (1995) and *Easley v. Cromartie* (2001), respectively. On majority-minority districts, see David T. Canon, *Race, Redistricting, and Representation* (Chicago: University of Chicago Press, 1999).

19 See Edward M. Burmila, "Voter Turnout, Felon Disenfranchisement and Partisan Outcomes in Presidential Elections, 1988–2012," *Social Justice Research* 30 (February 2017): 72–88.

20 See Robert L. Dudley and Alan R. Gitelson, *American Elections: The Rules Matter* (New York: Longman, 2002), pp. 7–15.

21 Data as of June 2019 from "Same Day Voter Registration," *National Conference of State Legislatures*, June 28, 2019, http://www.ncsl.org/research/elections-and-campaigns/same-day-registration.aspx (accessed August 19, 2020).

22 See Benjamin Highton and Raymond E. Wolfinger, "Estimating the Effects of the National Voter Registration Act of 1993," *Political Behavior* 20 (1998): 79–104.

23 Nathaniel Persily, testimony before the U.S. Senate Committee on Rules and Administration, March 11, 2009.

24 Raymond E. Wolfinger and Jonathan Hoffman, "Registering and Voting with Motor Voter," *PS: Political Science and Politics* 34 (2001): 85–92; and Michael D. Martinez and David Hill, "Did Motor Voter Work?" *American Politics Quarterly* 27 (1999): 296–315.

25 Pew Research Center, "Election 2020," August 13, 2020, https://www.pewresearch.org/politics/2020/08/13/election-2020-voters-are-highly-engaged-but-nearly-half-expect-to-have-difficulties-voting (accessed August 19, 2020).

26 See, for example, Reid J. Epstein and Stephanie Saul, "Does Vote-by-Mail Favor Democrats? No," *New York Times*, April 10, 2020, https://www.nytimes.com/2020/04/10/us/politics/vote-by-mail.html (accessed August 19, 2020).

27 Sam Levine, "Trump Says Republicans Would 'Never' Be Elected Again If It Was Easier to Vote," *The Guardian*, March 30, 2020, https://www.theguardian.com/us-news/2020/mar/30/trump-republican-party-voting-reform-coronavirus

28 Elise Viebeck, Annie Gowen, and Kayla Ruble, "In Bad Sign for Fall, Mail Delays Mar Voting," *Washington Post*, August 5, 2020, p. A1.

29 Alan S. Gerber, Gregory A. Huber, and Seth J. Hill, "Identifying the Effect of All-Mail Elections on Turnout," *Political Science Research & Methods* 1 (June 2013): 91–116.

30 Jesse Rhodes, *Ballot Blocked: The Political Erosion of the Voting Rights Act* (Palo Alto, CA: Stanford University Press, 2017).

31 Dan Hopkins, "What We Know about Voter ID Laws," August 21, 2018, https://fivethirtyeight.com/features/what-we-know-about-voter-id-laws/ (accessed August 19, 2020).

32 On states' voting requirements, see Wendy Underhill, "Voter Identification Requirements/Voter ID Laws," National Conference of State Legislatures, January 19, 2019,

http://www.ncsl.org/research/elections-and-campaigns/voter-id.aspx (accessed August 19, 2020).

33 Keith G. Bentele and Erin E. O'Brien, "Jim Crow 2.0?" *Perspectives on Politics* 11 (2013): 1088–1116.

34 John Alquist, Kenneth Mayer, and Simon Jackman, "Alien Abduction and Voter Impersonation in the 2012 US General Election," *Election Law Journal* 13 (#4, 2014): 460–475. See also Sharad Goel, Marc Meredith, Michael Morse, and David Rothschild, "One Person, One Vote," *American Political Science Review* 114 (2020): 456-469.

35 See Bentele and O'Brien, "Jim Crow 2.0?"

36 Lonna Rae Atkeson, Lisa Ann Bryant, Thad E. Hall, Kyle Saunders, and Michael Alvarez, "A New Barrier to Participation," *Electoral Studies* 29 (2010): 66–73, and Ariel R. White, Noah L. Nathan, and Julie K. Faller, "What Do I Need to Vote?" *American Political Science Review* 109 (2015): 129–142.

37 Matt Apuzzo, "Students Joining Battle to Upend Laws on Voter ID," *New York Times,* July 6, 2014, p. A1. In 2011, the Texas legislature, for example, voted that licenses to carry concealed handguns, but not student university ID cards, are a valid form of voter ID.

38 The U.S. Government Accountability Office reported ("Elections: Issues Related to State Voter Identification Laws") that voter ID laws in Tennessee and Kansas caused decreases in turnout, especially among blacks and young people: https://journalistsresource.org/studies/politics/elections/voter-id-laws-empirical-evidence-government-accountability-office/ (accessed August 19, 2020).

39 Vanessa Williams, "Congressional Democrats Launch Campaign to Rally Public Support for Voting Rights Protections," *Washington Post,* November 4, 2015, p. A1.

40 Henry E. Brady and John E. McNulty, "Turning Out to Vote," *American Political Science Review* 105 (2011): 115–134.

41 Sam Levine, "Voter Purges," *The Guardian,* December 31, 2019, www.theguardian.com.

42 Special Counsel Robert S. Mueller III, "Report On the Investigation into Russian Interference in the 2016 Presidential Election," March 2019, https://www.justice.gov/storage/report.pdf (accessed August 19, 2020).

43 Tim Elfrink, "It Is Not Letting Me Vote for Who I Want," *Washington Post,* August 28 2019, https://www.washingtonpost.com/nation/2019/08/28/mississippi-election-machine-changes-votes-video/ (accessed August 19, 2020).

44 On the problems with American elections, see Pippa Norris, *Why Elections Fail* (New York: Cambridge University Press, 2015).

45 See Justin Buchler, Matthew Jarvis, and John E. McNulty, "Punch Card Technology and the Racial Gap in Residual Votes," *Perspectives on Politics* 2 (2004): 517–524.

46 See Fernanda Santos, "In Arizona, Voters Demand: Why the Lines?" *New York Times,* March 25, 2016, p. A13.

47 David C. Kimball and Martha Kropf, "The Street-Level Bureaucrats of Elections," *Review of Policy Research* 23 (2006): 1257–1268.

48 See Michael Tomz and Robert P. Van Houweling, "How Does Voting Equipment Affect the Racial Gap in Voided Ballots?" *American Journal of Political Science* 47 (2003): 46–60.

49 Enrijeta Shino, Mara Suttmann-Lea and Daniel A. Smith, "Here's the Problem with Mail-in Ballots," *Washington Post,* May 21, 2020, https://www.washingtonpost.com/politics/2020/05/21/heres-problem-with-mail-in-ballots-they-might-not-be-counted/ (accessed August 19, 2020).

50 Gil Aegerter, "Cyberattack on Florida Election Is First Known Case in US, Experts Say," *NBC News*, March 18, 2013, http://investigations.nbcnews.com/_news/2013/03/18/17314818-cyberattack-on-florida-election-is-first-known-case-in-us-experts-say (accessed August 19, 2020).

51 Abby Goodnough, "Lost Record of Vote in '02 Florida Race Raises '04 Concern," *New York Times*, July 28, 2004, p. 1.

52 Walter Dean Burnham, "The Changing Shape of the American Political Universe," *American Political Science Review* 59 (1965): 7–28.

53 Because of the difficulties in estimating American turnout, many "official" turnout figures *underestimate* it. The percentages here and in Figure 8.2 correct for this underestimation. Their denominator is an effort to estimate the *eligible* population: the voting-age population minus the number of noncitizens living in the United States. The numerator of the turnout fraction is the number of voters who cast a vote for president or for the office with the highest vote in midterm elections. See Walter Dean Burnham, "The Turnout Problem," in A. James Reichley, ed., *Elections American Style* (Washington, DC: Brookings, 1987), pp. 97–133; and Michael McDonald, "United States Elections Project," at www.electproject.org/home/voter-turnout/voter-turnout-data (accessed November 25, 2019).

54 Unless otherwise indicated, turnout figures are those of Michael McDonald (see note 53).

55 Richard A. Brody, "The Puzzle of Participation in America," in Anthony King, ed., *The New American Political System* (Washington, DC: American Enterprise Institute, 1978), pp. 287–324.

56 See John H. Aldrich, "Rational Choice and Turnout," *American Journal of Political Science* 37 (1993): 246–278.

57 See, for example, John H. Aldrich, Jamie L. Carson, Brad T. Gomez, and David W. Rohde, *Change and Continuity in the 2016 & 2018 Elections* (Los Angeles, CA: Sage, 2020), Chapter 4.

58 Rachel Milstein Sondheimer and Donald P. Green, "Using Experiments to Estimate the Effects of Education on Voter Turnout," *American Journal of Political Science* 54 (2010): 174–189; and Robert A. Jackson, "Clarifying the Relationship between Education and Turnout," *American Politics Quarterly* 23 (1995): 279–299.

59 See Jan E. Leighley and Jonathan Nagler, *Who Votes Now?* (Princeton, NJ: Princeton University Press, 2013).

60 See Sidney Verba, Norman H. Nie, and Jae-On Kim, *Participation and Political Equality* (Cambridge: Cambridge University Press, 1978).

61 Cliff Zukin, Scott Keeter, Molly Andolina, Krista Jenkins, and Michael X. Delli Carpini, *A New Engagement?* (Oxford: Oxford University Press, 2006).

62 Karl T. Kurz, Alan Rosenthal, and Cliff Zukin, "Citizenship: A Challenge for All Generations," 2003, www.ncsl.org/Portals/1/documents/public/trust/citizenship.pdf (accessed August 19, 2020).

63 Kim Parker, Nikki Graf and Ruth Igielnik, "Generation Z Looks a Lot Like Millennials on Key Social and Political Issues," January 17, 2019, https://www.pewsocialtrends.org/2019/01/17/generation-z-looks-a-lot-like-millennials-on-key-social-and-political-issues/ (accessed August 19, 2020).

64 Bernard L. Fraga, *The Turnout Gap* (Cambridge: Cambridge University Press, 2018).

65 D'Vera Cohn, "It's Official," Pew Research Center, June 23, 2016, www.pewresearch.org/fact-tank/2016/06/23/its-official-minority-babies-are-the-majority-among-the-nations-infants-but-only-just (accessed August 19, 2020).

66 Scott D. McClurg, "The Electoral Relevance of Political Talk," *American Journal of Political Science* 50 (2006): 737–754.

67 Nancy Burns, Kay Lehman Schlozman, and Sidney Verba, "The Public Consequences of Private Inequality," *American Political Science Review* 91 (1997): 373–389.

68 See Steven J. Rosenstone and John Mark Hansen, *Mobilization, Participation, and Democracy in America* (New York: Longman, 2003), pp. 141–156.

69 Lyn Ragsdale and Jerrold G. Rusk, "Who Are Nonvoters?" *American Journal of Political Science* 37 (1993): 721–746.

70 Robert A. Jackson, "The Mobilization of U.S. State Electorates in the 1988 and 1990 Elections," *Journal of Politics* 59 (1997): 520–537.

71 See Danny Hayes and Jennifer L. Lawless, "As Local News Goes, So Does Citizen Engagement," *Journal of Politics* 77 (2015): 447–462.

72 Cindy D. Kam and Stephen M. Utych, "Close Elections and Cognitive Engagement," *Journal of Politics* 73 (2011): 1251–1266.

73 Heather K. Evans, Michael J. Ensley, and Edward G. Carmines, "The Enduring Effects of Competitive Elections," *Journal of Elections, Public Opinion and Parties* 24 (2014): 455–472.

74 See Donald P. Green and Alan S. Gerber, *Get Out the Vote!* (Washington, DC: Brookings Institution, 2004); and Kevin Arceneaux and David W. Nickerson, "Who Is Mobilized to Vote?" *American Journal of Political Science* 53 (2009): 1–16.

75 Thomas Patterson, press release from the Vanishing Voter Project, John F. Kennedy School of Government, Harvard University, November 11, 2004.

76 See Jan E. Leighley and Jonathan Nagler, "Unions, Voter Turnout, and Class Bias in the U.S. Electorate," *Journal of Politics* 69 (2007): 430–441.

77 Jack Citrin, Eric Schickler, and John Sides, "What If Everyone Voted?" *American Journal of Political Science* 47 (2003): 75–90.

78 See "The 100 Million Project: The Untold Story of American Non-Voters," The Knight Foundation, February 2020, https://knightfoundation.org/wp-content/uploads/2020/02/The-100-Million-Project_KF_Report_2020.pdf (accessed August 19, 2020).

79 Ryan D. Enos, Anthony Fowler, and Lynn Vavreck, "Increasing Inequality," *Journal of Politics* 76 (2014), and David W. Nickerson, "Do Voter Registration Drives Increase Participation?" *Journal of Politics* 77 (2015): 88–101.

80 Adriel Bettelheim, "Youth's Long-Term Role in Politics," *CQ Weekly*, November 10, 2008, p. 2973.

81 APSA Task Force Report, "American Democracy in an Age of Rising Inequality," *Perspectives on Politics* 2 (2004): 658.

82 Jan E. Leighley and Jennifer Oser, "Representation in an Era of Political and Economic Inequality," *Perspectives on Politics* 16 (June 2018): 328–344; see also Zachary Mohr, JoEllen V. Pope, Martha E. Kropf, and Mary Jo Shepherd, "Strategic Spending," *American Journal of Political Science* 63 (April 2019): 427–438.

PART FOUR

Parties, Nominations, and Elections

The party organization, the party's candidates, and their party identifiers are most likely to pull together at election time, because they can all benefit by doing so, even though they don't always march to the same drummer at other times. When candidates run more effective campaigns, they improve not only their own ability to attract money and other resources but also that of their party organization. When candidates are elected, their party's activists are more likely to see action on the issues that drew them to the party. When a party's identifiers feel enthusiastic about its candidates, they may be more inclined to contribute to the party organization and to bring their friends to the polls to support the whole party slate.

All this cooperation does not come easily, however. Almost every aspect of elections can pit the needs of one part of the party against those of another. When primaries are used to select a party's candidates, at times party voters will choose a nominee who is regarded as a disaster by party leaders. Recall from Chapter 4 the plight of Delaware Republican Party leaders when Republican primary voters rejected a longtime U.S. Senator in favor of a candidate who admitted dabbling in witchcraft when she was younger (and who felt the need to reassure voters in her first campaign ad that "I'm not a witch").

Candidates sometimes emphasize issues that conflict with the image their party as a whole wants to present to the public. After they win, some candidates may ignore or downplay issues that matter a lot to their party's activists. Efforts by the party organization to raise money will compete with its candidates' own fund-raising.

In addition to this competition within each party, the parties also compete on the larger electoral stage. Groups such as super PACs, labor unions, religious lobbies, insurance companies, and other corporations involve themselves in campaigns, sometimes very aggressively, to achieve their political goals. Democratic Party leaders, for example, will probably compete as well as cooperate with environmental, women's rights, and civil rights groups, and unions representing trial lawyers and government employees for the attention of a Democratic candidate. This competition and cooperation is guided by a set of rules, ranging from laws to standard practices. These rules include the widespread use of primary elections, laws governing campaign fund-raising, big shifts in the media environment, and rapid advances in the micro-targeting technology used to reach specific types of voters.

The first two chapters in this section focus on parties' involvement in nominating candidates. Chapter 9 explores the nomination process in general, and Chapter 10 considers the fascinating and unusual practices with which the American major parties select their presidential candidates. In Chapter 11, we turn to the role of parties in general elections. Chapter 12 traces the flow of money into campaigns and considers how it can both expand and limit the influence of parties on their candidates.

CHAPTER 9

How Parties Choose Candidates

If you want to hold public office in most nations, you'd need to impress your party's leaders or members of the party in government, because they are the people who choose the party's candidates. In the U.S., you would bypass the party's leaders and run in a primary election (known formally as a direct primary) instead. In a primary, the party's identifiers—the party in the electorate—decide which candidates will run for office under the party's label. Then, in a later general election, all voters can choose between the parties' nominees for each office. Although a number of democracies have been moving toward selecting their leaders in more inclusive ways, most democratic systems don't let voters tell the party organization who its candidates will be.[1]

Choosing candidates through primaries has changed the American parties' relationships with their candidates. It limits party organizations' ability to hold elected officials accountable. It lengthens campaigns and increases their costs. In areas where one party dominates, the real choice of elected officials will be made in the primary. Primaries also demand a great deal from the voting public. In addition to having to vote on two different occasions to elect someone to the same public office, primaries ask citizens to forsake their reliance on party identification—the main device people use to choose candidates—because in a party primary, all candidates share the same party ID. What led to the use of this unusual, two-step election process? How does it work, and how well does it serve the needs of voters, candidates, and parties? And why, if primaries make nominations more open and democratic, have the parties become even more widely disliked?

How the Nomination Process Evolved

For the first 110 years of the American republic, candidates for office were nominated by party caucuses and later by party conventions. In both cases, the leaders and activists of the party organizations chose the party's nominees, not the rest of the voting public.

Nominations by Caucus

In the early years, as the parties built local organizations, they held local party meetings, called caucuses, to choose candidates for county offices. Caucuses of like-minded partisans in Congress nominated presidential and vice-presidential candidates. Similar party caucuses in state legislatures chose candidates for governor and other statewide offices. These caucuses were generally informal, and they did not necessarily include all the major figures of the party.[2]

Nominations by Convention

As pressure for popular democracy spread, critics condemned the caucuses as an aristocratic elite—"King Caucus"—that ignored public opinion. In 1831, a minor party called the Anti-Masons held a national convention to nominate its presidential candidate, hoping to get enough press attention to gain major party status. The Jacksonian Democrats adopted the idea in 1832. From then on, through the rest of the 1800s, conventions were the main means of nominating presidential candidates. These conventions were composed of delegates chosen by state and local party leaders, often at their own lower-level nominating conventions.

These large and chaotic conventions looked more broadly representative than the caucuses but often were not. Party leaders chose the delegates and managed the conventions. Reformers denounced the convention system as yet another form of boss rule. By the end of the 1800s, the Progressive movement led the drive for a new way of nominating candidates.[3]

Nominations by Direct Primaries

The Progressives argued that voters should be able to directly select their party's candidates for each office; party leaders (who at that time included the "bosses" of the urban party machines) should not have that power. This direct, primary (meaning "first") election reflected the Progressives' core belief that the best way to cure a democracy's ills was to prescribe larger doses of democracy. Robert M. La Follette, a Progressive leader, wrote that in a primary, "The nomination of the party will not be the result of 'compromise' or impulse, or evil design [as he felt it was in a party-run caucus/convention system] … but the candidates of the majority, honestly and fairly nominated."[4]

Some southern states had already used primaries in local elections after the Civil War, to legitimize the nominees and settle internal disputes in their one-party Democratic systems. In the first two decades of the 1900s, all but four other states adopted primaries for at least some of their statewide nominations. This was a time when one party or the other dominated the politics of many states. It might be possible to tolerate the poor choices made by conventions when voters have a real choice in the general election, but not when the nominees of the dominant party had no serious competition. So the Progressives, who fought economic monopoly with antitrust legislation, used the direct primary as a weapon against political monopoly.

Although the primary was designed to democratize the nominating process, many of its supporters hoped that it would have the further effect of crippling the political parties. Primaries would take away the party organization's most important power—the nomination of candidates—and give it instead to party voters. In fact, some states, such as Wisconsin, adopted a definition of the party electorate so broad that it included any voters who chose to vote in the party's primary.

Primaries were not the first cause of party weakness in the U.S. If party leaders had been strong enough throughout the country when primaries were proposed, then they would have been able to stop the spread of this reform and keep control of the nominations themselves. But primaries did undermine the party organizations' power even further. Elected officials who owed their nominations to primary voters might not feel as loyal to the party organization as officials who were nominated by party leaders. Because of the existence of primaries, party leaders in the U.S. have less control over who will receive the party nomination than in most other democracies. In some states, the reforms required that even the party organization's own leaders be chosen by primary voters, so the parties risked losing control over their own internal affairs.

On the other hand, as some parties in other democracies are learning, giving larger numbers of partisans a chance to select their nominee can also give the party a lot of information about who those partisans are, what they want, and where they can be found. Voters in a general election don't have to declare their party preference, but voters in many primaries do; this provides party organizations with a list of their supporters. Primaries also provide the party's workers with practical training in campaigning in advance of the general election—an especially valuable benefit for the weaker party in a nation.[5]

The Current Mix of Primaries and Conventions

Although nominating conventions are no longer common, they are still used most visibly in presidential races as well as in a few states. Because states have the legal right to design their own nominating systems, the result is a mixture of primaries and conventions for choosing candidates for state offices.

Every state now uses primaries to nominate at least some statewide officials, and most states use this method exclusively.[6] In four southern states, the party may choose to hold a convention instead of a primary, but only in Virginia has the convention option been used recently, typically when activists with more extreme views hope to win the nomination for their preferred candidate. Other states use conventions to screen candidates for the primary ballot.[7] In Iowa, for instance, if no candidate wins at least 35 percent of the primary vote for the U.S. House, then a district party convention selects the nominee. This variety of choices reminds us again that, in spite of the national parties' growing strength (see Chapter 4), the state and local parties still make a lot of important decisions on their own.

Types of Primaries

Primaries come in many different forms, based on who is allowed to vote in them.[8] In states with so-called closed primaries, only voters who have formally declared their affiliation with a party can participate. This makes it easier for party activists and identifiers to keep their party's choice of nominees in their own hands. Voters in states with "open" primaries have more freedom to choose which party's primary they want to vote in. And in a few states, Democratic and Republican candidates for state and local offices all run on the same primary ballot, so a voter can select some candidates of each party.

Closed Primaries

Nine states hold a **fully closed primary**, in which voters have to register as a Democrat or a Republican prior to the election.[9] When they come to vote, they receive the primary ballot of only their own party. If they want to vote in the other party's primary, they must formally change their party affiliation on the registration rolls before the primary. States with traditionally strong party organizations, such as New York and Pennsylvania, are among those that have been able to keep their primaries fully closed. Seven other states, called partially closed, let independent voters into their primaries as well.

In many other states, whose primaries are often called *partially open*, voters can change their party registration when they come to vote, or they can simply declare their party preference at the polling place. They are then given their declared party's ballot and, in a few of these states, considered to be enrolled in that party. From the voter's point of view, these primaries are not very different from an open primary. The difference is important from the party's perspective, however, because in many partially open primaries, the names of the people who took the party's ballot are then available to party organizations to target in the general election.

Open Primaries

Citizens of most of the remaining states can vote in the primary of their choice without having to state publicly which party they favor.[10] In open primaries, voters receive either a consolidated ballot or ballots for every party, and they select the party of their choice in the privacy of the voting booth. They can vote in only one party's primary in a given election. Many of these states have histories of Progressive strength, such as Wisconsin and Minnesota.

Blanket Primaries

The state of Washington adopted the blanket primary in 1935. It gives voters even greater freedom. The names of candidates from all parties appear on a single ballot in the primary, just as they do in the general election, so that in contrast to an open primary, a voter can choose a Democrat for one office and a Republican for another. Alaska's Democrats adopted the blanket primary for a time as well.

California voters approved an initiative in 1996 to hold a blanket primary. Proponents said it would bring more voters to the polls and encourage the choice of more moderate candidates.[11] Party leaders saw it differently. They claimed the plan prevented the party's loyal supporters from choosing the candidates who best represented their views. That, they said, violated their First Amendment right to freedom of association and kept the party from offering a clear and consistent message to the voters. (See box, "Why Shouldn't I Be Able to Vote in Both Parties' Primaries?" below.) In 2000, the U.S. Supreme Court sided with

Why Shouldn't I Be Able to Vote in Both Parties' Primaries?

The argument that voters, not party insiders, should be able to select a party's candidates is so compelling that many people wonder why they should be limited to voting in only *one* party's primary election. Even in open primaries, a voter must confine herself to choosing among one party's candidates, not both. If primaries give us a dose of democracy, wouldn't two doses be better?

The Supreme Court has agreed with party leaders that the answer is no. Although the U.S. Constitution grants the right to vote, it doesn't guarantee voting rights in primary elections; in fact, primaries weren't created until a century after the Constitution was ratified. Nor does the Constitution mention political parties. They have developed as partly private institutions that the Court sees as having the *right to freedom of association,* or *assembly.* In short, the Court sees parties as voluntary groups of people who, like other voluntary groups, form to express their common interests. Therefore,

parties must be able to support candidates who reflect their party's own views on issues. In several decisions, then, the Court has given party organizations the power to decide who gets to choose their candidates—who gets to vote in their primaries—and to exclude those the party doesn't recognize as its "members" or identifiers.

Parties' free association rights are not unlimited. Efforts by white southern Democrats in the early 1900s to make the Democratic Party into a whites-only club (the "white primary") were thwarted by several Court rulings in the 1930s and 1940s. And party organizations may *choose* to open their primary elections to independents (in partially closed primaries) or even the other party's identifiers. Party leaders sometimes do so to select candidates most likely to win support in the general election, though they then risk the possibility that voters of the other party will vote for the weakest candidate in the field ("raiding").

Sources: Seth Masket, "A Case for Keeping Primary Voting Confined to Party Members," Pacific Standard, March 19, 2018, https://psmag.com/news/a-case-for-keeping-primary-voting-confined-to-party-members; and Justia, "Right of Association," undated, https://law.justia.com/constitution/us/-amendment-01/10-right-of-association.html (both accessed August 20, 2020).

the parties and gave the right to decide who votes in a primary, at least in California, back to the party organizations.[12]

"Top Two" Primaries

In 2008, the state of Washington moved to a type of blanket primary called a top two (or nonpartisan) system. Like a blanket primary, all candidates' names appear on the same ballot. Unlike a blanket primary, the top two vote getters for each office, regardless of party, advance to the general election. The party organization can still endorse a candidate, but if voters prefer (and they sometimes do), they can select two Democrats, or two Republicans, to run against one another in the general election. California voters adopted a similar system two years later. The purpose of the change was to force candidates to appeal to all voters, not just to the extremes of their own party. Observers disagree on whether the top two system has succeeded in producing more moderate candidates and increasing voter participation.[13]

Louisiana uses a version of this system for state and local elections: If one candidate for an office wins more than 50 percent of the votes in the nonpartisan primary, he or she is elected to that office immediately. If no candidate for the office wins an outright majority in the primary, then the two top candidates (again, regardless of party) face one another in a runoff. Not surprisingly, the major national parties oppose the use of nonpartisan or top two systems and prohibit states from adopting them in their presidential primaries.

When states shift from one type of primary to another, it is usually because state party leaders are trying to protect their party's interests in the nominating process under changing political conditions. Some state parties have attempted to attract independent voters by switching to an open primary. In others, party leaders have urged the legislature to adopt new primary rules that would advantage candidates the party leaders favor in a particular election year. Sometimes, change has been prompted by nonparty or antiparty groups, as happened in California. And it's not unusual for state parties to use one set of primary rules for state races and a different set of rules for presidential races (see Chapter 10).

Why Does the Type of Primary Matter?

These varieties of primaries represent different answers to a long-standing debate: Is democracy better served by competition between strong and disciplined parties or by a system in which parties have relatively little power? The closed primary reflects the belief that citizens benefit from having clear choices in elections, which can best be provided by strong, internally unified parties; therefore, it makes sense for a party's candidates to be selected only by that party's loyal followers. In contrast, open and blanket primaries are based on the view that rigid party loyalties can harm a democracy, so candidates should be chosen by all voters, regardless of party.

Most party organizations prefer the fully closed primary in which voters must register by party before the primary. It pays greater respect to the party's right to select its candidates. Further, the closed primary limits the greatest dangers of open and blanket primaries, at least from the perspective of party leaders:

crossing over and raiding. Both terms refer to people who vote in the primary of a party that they do not generally support. They differ in the voter's intent.

Voters **cross over** to take part in a more exciting race or to vote for a more appealing candidate in the other party. Crossing over is common in open primaries, especially in a presidential primary when there is no competition for their own party's nomination. Partisans rarely cross over in off-year gubernatorial primaries because that would keep them from having a voice in other state and local-level party contests.

Raiding is a conscious effort to weaken the other party by voting for its least attractive candidates. For instance, when President Trump was largely unopposed in the 2020 Republican nomination contests, he urged South Carolina Republicans to vote in the Democratic open primary for the candidate they considered the weakest. Few Republicans did so, however. Studies of open primaries have found little evidence of raiding. Voters usually cross over to vote for their real preferences rather than to weaken the party in whose primary they are participating.[14] But even the non-strategic crossover voters often support a different candidate than the party's partisans do.

For that reason, candidates take each state's type of primary into account in building their campaign strategies. Candidates who are outside of their party's mainstream typically spend more time campaigning in states with open primaries, so that independents can vote for them. As Figure 9.1 shows, Sen. Bernie Sanders expected more support from independents in 2020 than from strong Democrats, so he worked especially hard in open primary states such as Michigan, where independent voters were permitted in Democratic primaries. Sanders did much better there compared with his chief rival, Joe Biden, than in closed primary states such as Florida, though the two states voted just a week apart. Candidates such as Sanders may even encourage crossovers in these open primaries by discussing issues that appeal to independents or the other party's voters.[15]

How Candidates Qualify

States also vary in the ease with which candidates can get their names on the primary ballot and in the support required to win the nomination.

How Do Candidates Get on the Ballot?

In most states, candidates get on the primary ballot by filing a petition. State election laws specify how many signatures the petition has to contain—either a specific number or a percentage of the vote for the office in the last election.[16] States vary a lot in the difficulty of this step. Some have complicated rules requiring a lot of signatures, designed to favor party insiders. In other states, a candidate needs only to appear before the clerk of elections and pay a small fee. A few states even put presidential candidates on the ballot if they are "generally recognized" to be running.

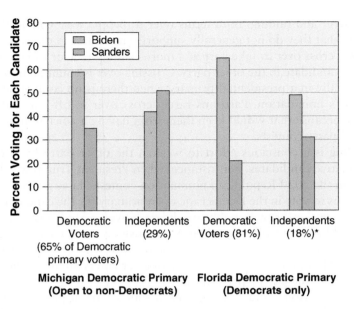

FIGURE 9.1 Voting in Open Primaries Differs from Closed Primaries: Biden vs. Sanders, 2020

Note: Bars show the percentage of Democratic and independent voters in Michigan's Democratic primary, in which independents can vote, and Florida's closed Democratic primary who cast a ballot for Joe Biden and Bernie Sanders.

*But 18 percent of the registered Democratic voters in the primary told exit pollsters that they now consider themselves independents.

Source: Exit polls at https://www.cnn.com/election/2020/entrance-and-exit-polls/michigan/democratic and https://www.cnn.com/election/2020/entrance-and-exit-polls/florida/democratic (both accessed August 20, 2020).

These simple rules have consequences for parties. The easier it is for candidates to get on the ballot, the more likely it becomes that dissident, or even crackpot, candidates will enter a race and engage the party's preferred candidates in costly primary battles. In states with easy ballot access, citizens can be treated to grudge campaigns, in which people file to oppose the sheriff who arrested them, for instance, or who simply enjoy the thought of wreaking havoc in a primary.

Runoffs: When Too Many Candidates Get on the Ballot

What if the leading candidate in a primary gets less than a majority of the votes? In most states' primaries, a plurality is enough. Almost all southern and border states, however, hold a runoff between the top two candidates if one candidate does not win at least 40 or 50 percent of the vote. During the long period of one-party Democratic rule of the South, Democratic factionalism often produced three, four, or five serious candidates for a single office in a primary. The runoff was used to ensure a majority winner to present a unified face to the electorate and to ward off any challenges in the general election from blacks and other Republicans.

The southern runoff primary has long been controversial. Citing instances in which black candidates who received a plurality in the first primary lost to whites in the runoff, studies show that runoffs disadvantage minority groups.[17]

What Parties Don't Like about Primaries

The Progressives designed the direct primary to break the party organization's monopoly control of nominations. In important ways, it did. In the process, it challenged parties' effectiveness in elections more generally.

Difficulties in Recruiting Candidates

Candidate recruitment has never been an easy job, especially for the minority party. The direct primary makes the challenge even harder. If an ambitious candidate can challenge the party favorite in the dominant party's primary, he or she is less likely to consider running for office under the weaker party's label. So, some argue, the weaker party will find it even harder to recruit good candidates for races it is not likely to win. Little by little, the majority party becomes the only viable road to success, and the other party atrophies.[18]

This argument should not be taken too far. One-party politics declined after primaries became more common. And even in areas dominated by one party, the internal competition promoted by primaries can keep officeholders responsive to their constituents.[19] Nevertheless, the fact that party organizations cannot guarantee the outcome of their own primaries means that they have less to offer the candidates they are trying to recruit.

The Risk of Unappealing or Extremist Nominees

Normally, only about half as many voters turn out for a primary as for a general election. That can pose a problem: if primary voters aren't typical of their party's identifiers more generally, then they may choose candidates who are less appealing—for example, more ideologically extreme—to general election voters.[20] Party leaders try to avoid this risk; research shows that they often support the more moderate candidate in a primary, at least in part to protect the party's chance of victory.[21] But they don't always succeed in recruiting the candidates they'd like, or in convincing primary voters to follow their lead.

Another reason why primary voters might choose a weak candidate is that in a race in which all the candidates are of the same party, voters cannot use their party identification to select candidates, and many voters will not have any other relevant information available. They may choose a candidate because his or her name is familiar or may simply vote for the first name listed on the ballot. Or the candidate may be unopposed for the nomination, as in the case of most of the 2020 candidates aligned with the "Q Anon" movement, which saw President

Trump as fighting a "deep state" that runs a satanic child sex-trafficking ring.[22] If a party convention chose the nominees, it could be argued, convention delegates would know the prospective candidates better, so they would not be prone to these misjudgments.

Divisive Primaries

When parties hold primaries, their internal conflict becomes public. In some cases, activists who supported the losing candidate may sit out the general election rather than work for their party's nominee. That affected the support for Democrats Hillary Clinton in 2016 and Joe Biden in 2020 when they emerged from hard-fought primary races.[23] The charges raised by a candidate's primary opponent are often reused by the opposition in the general election, a source of free campaign help to the other party. In 2016, some of Clinton's most hard-hitting campaign ads against Donald Trump featured attacks on Trump by his Republican primary opponents. If a divisive primary is expensive, it may eat up much of the money the primary winner needs to run an effective campaign in the general election.[24]

A divisive primary could be especially damaging if the losing candidate refuses to take "no" for an answer and runs in the general election anyway, as an independent or minor party candidate. The sore loser could draw enough support to destroy the chances of his or her former primary rival. In the great majority of states, however, "sore loser" laws and simultaneous filing deadlines prevent primary losers from using this kind of end run to get on the general election ballot.

Despite these concerns, divisive primaries don't always weaken a party. Running in a competitive primary might make the winner an even stronger candidate in the general election. It gives the winner a chance to test his or her campaign organization in anticipation of the general election race. And at times, when an incumbent candidate has been slipping as a result of scandal or change in the district, the national party has encouraged viable challengers. Although that might provoke a divisive primary, it could also produce a party nominee who is better able to hold the seat for the party in the fall.

The large numbers of safe House races can make divisive primaries more common. When the redistricting that followed the 2010 U.S. Census increased the numbers of safe congressional seats, several ambitious candidates saw primary elections as their best and least expensive way to win a House seat. That attracted the attention, and the lavish spending, of dozens of interest groups aiming to change the ideological orientation of Congress. The Democrats are famous for their internal disputes, but we can see just as many divisive primaries in the Republican Party: for instance, when far-right candidates challenge incumbents they call Republicans In Name Only (RINOs).[25] Other groups, including the Club for Growth, have financed primary campaigns as a way to warn other Republicans that they will face a primary opponent if they don't take the strictest possible anti-tax position.[26]

Problems in Holding Candidates Accountable

When candidates are chosen in primaries rather than by party leaders, the party loses a powerful means of holding its candidates and officeholders accountable for their actions. In England, for example, if an elected official breaks with the party on an important issue, party leaders can usually keep him or her from being renominated. If the party cannot prevent the renomination of a maverick officeholder, then it has no way of enforcing loyalty. That, of course, is just what the Progressives had hoped. Thus, primaries have these drawbacks:

- Primaries permit the nomination of candidates hostile to the party organization and leadership, opposed to the party's platform, or out of step with the public image that party leaders want to project.
- Primaries greatly increase nomination spending. The cost of a contested primary is almost always higher than that of a convention.
- Primaries extend political campaigns, already longer in the U.S. than in other democracies, to a degree that can try many voters' patience.

The Party Organization Fights Back

Parties are clearly aware of the threats posed by primary elections, but they are just as aware that a direct attempt to abolish primaries would fail. So party organizations have developed a range of strategies for trying to limit the damage primaries can cause.[27] The success of these strategies varies. As we will see in Chapter 10, the presidential nomination process has often been dominated by party leaders, and some local parties have been able to influence primaries effectively. Other party organizations have neither the strength nor the will to try.

Persuading Candidates to Run (or Not to Run)

The most effective way for a party organization to control a primary is to make sure that the party's favored candidate has no opponent. Some party organizations try to mediate among prospective candidates or coax an attractive but unwilling candidate to run. If they have a strong organization, they may be able to convince less desirable candidates to stay out of the race. Even if they have little to offer or withhold, many party leaders have the opportunity to influence prospective candidates' decisions; researchers have found that almost 70 percent of nonincumbent state legislative candidates discussed their plans to run with local party leaders before announcing their candidacy.[28]

Endorsing Candidates

Some of the stronger state parties, such as those in Massachusetts and Minnesota, endorse preferred candidates before the primary, to try to affect voters' choices. Recall that in several states, at least one of the parties holds a convention to formally endorse candidates for state office. Usually, a candidate who gets a certain percentage of the convention's vote automatically gets his or her name on the primary ballot. Endorsements sometimes come with campaign money and organizational help. In some other states, party leaders may meet informally to endorse some candidates.

Do these endorsements influence voters? The record is mixed. Formal endorsements can often discourage other candidates or well-funded interest groups from challenging the party's choice in the primary. Besides, the process of winning a formal endorsement usually involves the candidate in so many face-to-face meetings with party activists that the resulting visibility, and the resources that the endorsing party can provide, give the endorsed candidate some vote-getting benefits.[29] Studies find that when party leaders unify to support one candidate in a primary, that candidate usually wins.[30]

But some states' laws prevent parties from endorsing candidates prior to the primary. In these cases, informal party endorsements are less effective. Only the most politically attentive voters are likely to know that the party is supporting a particular candidate, and they are the ones least in need of the guidance provided by the party's endorsement.[31] And party endorsements make a difference only for some types of candidates and to some types of voters.[32]

Providing Tangible Support

If the party can't prevent a challenge to its preferred candidates, then it must find ways to make those candidates more attractive to voters. It may offer party money and expertise to its favored candidates, urge party activists to circulate their nominating petitions, and encourage campaign donors and talented campaign workers to support them.[33] The party may advertise its endorsements or print reminder cards that voters can take into the polling booth.

State and local parties vary in their efforts to influence primaries, but recruiting candidates is probably the most frequent activity. Trying to clear the field for a favored candidate is less common. In most parts of the country, parties are only one of the groups encouraging men and women to run for office. Local business, professional, and labor groups; civic associations; ethnic, racial, and religious organizations; and other political groups and officeholders may also be working to recruit candidates. The party organizations best able to control candidate recruitment are generally those that endorse and support candidates in the primary itself.

Candidates and Voters in the Primaries

Two facts help make the primaries more manageable for the parties: Often only one candidate runs for each office in a primary, and most Americans do not vote in them. The party may be responsible for one or both of these situations. There may be no competition in a primary, for example, because of the party's skill in persuading and dissuading potential candidates. The result is that nominations can be more easily controlled by aggressive party organizations.

Many Candidates Run without Competition

Many candidates have no opponent in their primary race. Probably the most important determinant of the competitiveness of a primary is the party's chance of winning the general election. There is not usually much competition for the nomination of the party likely to lose. Primaries also tend to be less competitive when an incumbent is running (unless the incumbent is already thought to be vulnerable), when parties have made preprimary endorsements, and when the state's rules make it harder to get on the ballot.[34]

The power of incumbency to discourage competition is one of the many ironies of the primary. In an election in which voters cannot rely on the party label to guide their choices, name recognition and media coverage are important influences. Incumbents are more likely to have these resources than challengers are. To dislodge an incumbent, a challenger will usually need large amounts of campaign money, but few challengers can raise large campaign budgets. By weakening party control of nominations through the direct primary, then, Progressive reformers may have unintentionally made it harder to defeat incumbents.

... And Voters Are in Short Supply

If competition is scarce in primaries, so are voters. Turnout tends to be especially low in the weaker party's primary, in primaries held separately from the state's presidential primary, and in elections in which independents and the other party's identifiers are not allowed to vote.[35] In addition to the lack of competition in many primary contests, the fact that no one is elected in a primary probably depresses turnout. A race for the nomination lacks the drama inherent in a general election that is followed by victorious candidates taking office.

Southern primaries in earlier years were the one great exception to the rule that few people vote in primaries. Because winning the Democratic nomination in a one-party area is tantamount to winning the office itself, competition and turnout in Democratic primaries were relatively high. When the Republican Party became more competitive in the South, however, the Democratic primaries lost their special standing. The result is that participation has declined in southern primaries. Republican primaries are attracting many more voters now because their candidates' prospects in the general election have greatly improved, but the GOP increase has not been big enough to offset the drop in Democratic turnout.[36]

The primary electorate is distinctive in several ways. Many primary voters are strong party identifiers and activists, which makes them more responsive to party endorsements of certain candidates. As would be expected, people who vote in primaries have higher levels of education and political interest than non-voters do. Recent evidence suggests that primary voters are more ideologically extreme, intense, and more consistent in their views than are people who vote only in the general election, and they tend to be more hostile toward the opposition party.[37] But because primaries have such small turnouts, they can be more easily dominated by well-financed organized interests, such as anti-tax or pro-gun groups, than can general elections.

Primary voters often make unexpected choices. Because primary campaigns don't get much media coverage, the candidates are often not well known. Thus, the voter's choice in a primary is not as well-structured or predictable as that in a general election. Many voting decisions are made right in the polling booth. It is small wonder that parties are rarely confident about primary results, and pollsters find it hard to predict them accurately.

The Impact of the Direct Primary

On balance, how has the use of primary elections affected us? Has the primary democratized nominations by taking them out of the hands of party leaders and giving them to voters? Has it weakened the party organizations overall?

Has It Made Elections More Democratic?

Many more people vote in primaries than take part in conventions or caucuses. In that sense, the process has been made more democratic. But the democratic promise of primaries is reduced by the number of unopposed candidates and the low levels of voter turnout. If voters are to have meaningful alternatives, then there must be more than one candidate for an office. If the results are to be meaningful, then people must go to the polls.

It is not surprising that turnout in primaries is low. Adopting the direct primary doubled the number of elections in the U.S. Primaries may have given citizens more opportunities to take part in politics than they would have preferred. Because party ID can't be used as a shortcut to make voting decisions in a primary, participants have to do more work to cast an informed ballot. Would-be candidates are put off by the cost of an additional race, the difficulty of getting on the primary ballot, and the need to differentiate themselves from other candidates of their party. If greater competition for office and extensive public participation in the nominating process were goals of the primary's architects, then they would be seriously disappointed.

In addition, as we have seen, party organization leaders can often influence the results of primaries. If only 25 percent of eligible voters go to the polls, then 13 percent will be enough to nominate a candidate. Parties count on the fact that a large part of that group will be party loyalists who care about the party leaders' recommendations. Thus, strong party organizations—those able to muster the needed voters, money, activists, and organization—can still make a difference in the outcome. But working to influence primary elections is very costly and time consuming, even for strong parties. The large number of elected offices in the U.S., from senator to surveyor, forces party organizations to be selective in trying to affect primaries. Parties sometimes stand aside because picking a favorite in the primary might produce resentment (see Chapter 4). Of course, party leaders' greatest fear is that if they support one candidate in a primary and another candidate wins, they could lose all influence over the winning officeholder.

In some ways, then, the primary has been a democratizing force. In competitive districts, especially when no incumbent is running, voters have the opportunity for choice envisioned by the reformers. In all districts, the primaries place real limits on the power of party leaders. Parties, even strong ones, can no longer award a nomination to anyone they choose. Compared with systems where party leaders select the candidates, primaries can help the weaker party choose a candidate with greater voter appeal.[38] And the primary gives dissenters a chance to take their case to the party's voters, so it offers them a potential veto over the party leaders' preferences.

How Badly Has It Harmed the Parties?

On the other hand, is it possible to say that the direct primary has strengthened democracy in the U.S. if it weakens the political parties? From the risk of divisive primaries to the added campaign funding and voter mobilization they require, primaries strain party resources and create headaches for party leaders. Party organizations can affect the results of their primaries through their efforts to recruit and help fund candidates, make preprimary endorsements, and hold conventions to nominate some candidates. But the bottom line is this: When a party organization cannot choose who will carry the party label into the general election, the party has been deprived of one of its key resources.

The direct primary has redistributed power within the parties. The Progressives' goal was to shift the power to nominate candidates from the party organization to the party in the electorate, but a funny thing happened along the way. Because candidates (especially incumbents) can win the party's nomination even when they defy the party organization, the idea of party "discipline" loses credibility. Just as the direct primary undercuts the ability of the party organization to recruit candidates who share its goals and accept its discipline, it prevents the organization from disciplining partisans who already are in office. The primary, then, empowers the party's candidates and the party in government at the expense of the party organization. This sets the U.S. apart from many other democracies, in which the party organization has real power over the party in government. In all these ways, the direct primary has gone beyond changing the nominating process. It has helped to reshape the American parties.

Is the Primary Worth the Cost?

How to nominate party candidates has been a controversial issue since political parties were first formed in the U.S. It raises the fundamental question of what a political party is. Are parties only alliances of officeholders—the party in government? That seemed to be the prevailing definition in the early years when public officials nominated candidates in legislative party caucuses. Should the definition be expanded to include the party's activists and organizational leaders? The change from a caucus to a convention system of nominations, in which the party organization played its greatest role, reflected this change in the definition of party.

The use of primaries defines parties as including those citizens who identify with the party—the party in the electorate—a definition that few other democracies accept. In fact, many states have taken this definition even further; states with open primaries and "top two" elections give any registered voters a say in the party's nominations. And in practice, open primary states allow some of the party's opponents to cross over and influence the nomination, even though the Supreme Court insists that the parties' freedom of association is vital.

The methods we use to nominate candidates have a far-reaching impact. The Jacksonians promoted the convention system to gain control of the party from congressional party leaders. Progressives used their preference for the direct primary as a weapon to wrest control of the party and, ultimately, the government from the party organization. Because of the importance of nominations in the political process, those who control the nominations have great influence on the political agenda and, in turn, over who gets what in the political system. The stakes in this debate, as a result, are extremely high.

Notes

1 See Jean-Benoit Pilet and William Cross, eds., *The Selection of Political Party Leaders in Contemporary Parliamentary Democracies* (New York: Routledge, 2014).
2 Stephen J. Wayne, *The Road to the White House 2008* (Belmont, CA: Wadsworth, 2008), pp. 6–8.
3 See Chapters 7 and 21 in Marjorie Randon Hershey, ed., *Guide to U.S. Political Parties* (Los Angeles, CA: Sage, 2014).
4 Robert M. La Follette, *La Follette's Autobiography* (Madison, WI: R. M. La Follette, 1913), pp. 197–198.
5 Sasha Issenberg, "America Exports Democracy, But Not the Way You Think," *New York Times,* March 16, 2014, p. SR4.
6 Some states allow third parties to nominate their candidates through conventions.
7 See Mark D. Brewer and L. Sandy Maisel, *Parties and Elections in America*, 8th ed. (Lanham, MD: Rowman & Littlefield, 2018), Chapter 6.
8 The National Conference of State Legislatures lists the states' various primary election systems at http://www.ncsl.org/research/elections-and-campaigns/primary-types.aspx (as of June 26, 2018; accessed August 20, 2020).
9 Note that experts disagree on what to call different types of primaries, and states sometimes move from one type to another or allow different parties in the same state to use different types of primaries.
10 A 1986 Supreme Court decision (*Tashjian v. Republican Party of Connecticut*) upheld the Connecticut party's efforts to establish an open primary. However, many state parties would prefer a closed primary to an open one.
11 Researchers differ as to whether closed primaries are more likely to produce ideologically extreme candidates. Compare Karen M. Kaufmann, James G. Gimpel, and Adam H. Hoffman, "A Promise Fulfilled?" *Journal of Politics* 65 (2003): 457–476, with David W. Brady, Hahrie Han, and Jeremy C. Pope, "Primary Elections and Candidate Ideology," *Legislative Studies Quarterly* 32 (2007): 79–106.
12 *California Democratic Party v. Jones* (2000). On blanket primaries, see Bruce E. Cain and Elisabeth R. Gerber, eds., *Voting at the Political Fault Line* (Berkeley, CA: University of California Press, 2002).

13 Eric McGhee and Boris Shor, "Has the Top Two Primary Elected More Moderates?" *Perspectives on Politics* 15 (November 2017): 1053–1066. See also R. Michael Alvarez and J. Andrew Sinclair, *Nonpartisan Primary Election Reform* (Cambridge: Cambridge University Press, 2015).

14 Gary D. Wekkin, "Why Crossover Voters Are Not 'Mischievous' Voters," *American Politics Quarterly* 19 (1991): 229–247.

15 Lynn Vavreck, "The Reasoning Voter Meets the Strategic Candidate," *American Politics Research* 29 (2001): 507–529.

16 See the monthly newsletter *Ballot Access News*, www.ballot-access.org.

17 See, for instance, Thomas A. Reitz and Rebecca B. Morton, "Majority Requirements and Minority Representation," *NYU Annual Survey of American Law* 63 (2008): 691–725.

18 V. O. Key, Jr., *American State Politics: An Introduction* (New York: Knopf, 1956), p. 195.

19 John G. Geer and Mark E. Shere, "Party Competition and the Prisoner's Dilemma," *Journal of Politics* 54 (1992): 741–761.

20 Andrew B. Hall, "What Happens When Extremists Win Primaries?" *American Political Science Review* 109 (2015): 18–42. See also Brady, Han, and Pope, "Primary Elections and Candidate Ideology."

21 Hans J. G. Hassell, "Principled Moderation," *Legislative Studies Quarterly* 43 (#2 2018): 343–369.

22 See, for example, Mike Baker, "G.O.P. Voters Back Q Anon Conspiracy Promoter for U.S. Senate," *New York Times*, May 20, 2020, https://www.nytimes.com/2020/05/20/us/oregon-senate-perkins-qanon.html (accessed August 20, 2020).

23 See William G. Mayer, "The Nominations," in Michael Nelson, ed., *The Elections of 2016* (Thousand Oaks, CA: CQ Press, 2018), Chapter 2.

24 See Alexander Fouirnaies and Andrew B. Hall, "How Divisive Primaries Hurt Parties," *Journal of Politics* 82 (January 2020): 43–56.

25 Paige L. Schneider, "Factionalism in the Southern Republican Party," *American Review of Politics* 19 (1998): 129–148.

26 Matt Bai, "Fight Club," *New York Times Magazine*, August 10, 2003, pp. 24–27.

27 See Hans J. G. Hassell, *The Party's Primary* (Cambridge: University of Cambridge Press, 2018).

28 Gary F. Moncrief, Peverill Squire, and Malcolm E. Jewell, *Who Runs for the Legislature?* (Upper Saddle River, NJ: Prentice Hall, 2001), p. 39.

29 Sarah McCally Morehouse, *The Governor as Party Leader* (Ann Arbor, MI: University of Michigan Press, 1998), pp. 22–23.

30 Hans J. G. Hassell, "Party Control of Party Primaries," *Journal of Politics* 78 (2016): 75–87.

31 L. Sandy Maisel, Linda L. Fowler, Ruth S. Jones, and Walter J. Stone, "Nomination Politics," in L. Sandy Maisel, ed., *The Parties Respond* (Boulder, CO: Westview, 1994), pp. 155–156.

32 Thad Kousser, Scott Lucas, Seth Masket, and Eric McGhee, "Kingmakers or Cheerleaders?" *Political Research Quarterly* 68 (2015): 443–456.

33 See Hassell, "Party Control."

34 See Jay Goodliffe and David B. Magleby, "Campaign Finance in U.S. House Primary and General Elections," in Peter F. Galderisi, Marni Ezra, and Michael Lyons, eds., *Congressional Primaries and the Politics of Representation* (Lanham, MD: Rowman & Littlefield, 2001), pp. 62–76.

35 See Molly Rockett and Austin Plier, "2016 Presidential Primary Voter Turnout Analysis to Date," *Fairvote*, May 6, 2016, https://www.fairvote.org/2016_presidential_primary_voter_turnout_analysis_to_date (accessed August 20, 2020).

36 For instance, see Chris Kromm, "Democratic Turnout Plummets in Southern Primaries," *Facing South*, March 4, 2016, https://www.facingsouth.org/2016/03/2016-elections-gop-turnout-soars-democratic-turnou (accessed December 1, 2019).

37 Michael P. McDonald and Thessalia Merivaki, "Voter Turnout in Presidential Nominating Contests," *The Forum* 13, 4 (February 2016): 597–622; Marjorie Randon Hershey and Nathaniel E. Birkhead, "Assessing the Ideological Extremism of American Party Activists," *Party Politics* 25 (July 2019): 495–506.

38 James Adams and Samuel Merrill III, "Candidate and Party Strategies in Two-Stage Elections Beginning with a Primary," *American Journal of Political Science* 52 (2008): 344–359.

CHAPTER 10

Choosing the
Presidential Nominees

Here's the first thing you need to know about presidential nominations: No sane person would intentionally devise a nomination system like that of the American parties. As you'll soon find out, it has evolved into a very complicated process, hard to understand, easy to criticize, and occasionally inclined to produce odd results. The process itself has not changed fundamentally since the early 1970s. But recent changes in the American political environment have made an already convoluted and decentralized nominating system even harder to explain and predict. Because of the big increase in media coverage (including partisan and social media), the growth in partisan hostility, and the steep increase in free-spending super PACs, candidates who might not have been considered seriously in earlier presidential races have now been able to gain media exposure and attract other resources. In this more fluid political environment, what does it take to gain a party's presidential nomination?

The "Invisible Primary"

Most serious presidential candidates begin several years before the election to take polls, raise money, identify active supporters in states with early contests, and compete for the services of respected consultants (see box "How a Presidential Candidate Is Chosen" on page 216). The competition heats up during the months before the first primaries and caucuses. Journalists are competing at this time as well; they each want to be the first to predict who will win the nomination. The indicators they use are candidates' standing in polls, their fund-raising success, and the endorsements made by prominent political figures. This process of early fund-raising and jockeying for media attention and support has become so important to the eventual result that it has come to be called the **invisible primary** or the "money primary."[1]

Party leaders and activists and interest groups closely linked with the party are watching carefully as well. They want to determine which candidates would best serve their interests. Although party leaders have no formal power over the nominating process, they can communicate their choices to party activists by publicly endorsing particular candidates. In most presidential races until recent

How a Presidential Candidate Is Chosen

Step 1: Assessing Their Chances. Many people who think they might stand a chance—governors, senators, House members, people well-known in another field—consider running for president. They take private polls to see how prospective voters view them. To assess their likelihood of getting the resources they'd need, they contact fund-raisers and potential donors and try to get well-respected consultants to commit to their candidacy. (Donald Trump was a rare exception in 2016, because he planned to use his own fortune to pay for most of his nomination campaign in that year.) They visit states with early primaries and caucuses to gain support from local officials.

Timing: Typically, several years before the presidential election.

Step 2: Entering the Race. Those who feel they have a good chance—and some who don't—set up exploratory committees to raise money for advertising and fund their increasingly frequent trips to Iowa, New Hampshire, and other states with early delegate selection events. Then they formally declare their candidacy and work to get on every state ballot.

Timing: Typically, at least a year before the presidential election.

Step 3: Primaries and Caucuses. Voters cast a ballot in their states for the candidate they want their party to nominate for president. Most states hold primary elections for this purpose; the rest use participatory caucuses and state conventions. Delegates are chosen to represent each state and to vote in the party's national convention for the candidate(s) selected by their state's voters.

Timing: Between February and June of each presidential election year.

Step 4: National Nominating Conventions. The delegates vote in their party's convention for the presidential candidate(s) chosen by the voters in their state's primary or caucuses (see Step 3). Then they vote for the winning candidate's choice of a vice presidential nominee and to adopt a party platform.

Timing: By tradition, the party that does not currently hold the presidency schedules its convention first, in July or August; the other party's convention is held soon after.

Step 5: General Election. The two major parties' candidates run against one another.

Timing: From the conventions until the first Tuesday after the first Monday in November.

years, voters in the primaries and caucuses have nominated the consensus choice of the party's leaders and activists.[2] Especially in this early phase of the process, many partisans don't know much about the prospective candidates and welcome these recommendations. But as Donald Trump's successful nomination race in 2016 showed, party leaders aren't always able to thwart the appeal of an outsider with exceptional resources—in particular, in Trump's case, the ability to generate near-constant media coverage.

Candidates who fall behind in funding and endorsements, and thus in media coverage and polls, are likely to be winnowed out of the race even before most Americans have the chance to evaluate them. In contrast, those who raise more money than expected can greatly improve their chances. The candidates who survive this first testing period must then face a gauntlet of state party primaries and caucuses. Their aim is to win delegates who will vote for them at the party's national convention. This process, which continues to evolve, challenges the strategic capabilities of every presidential candidate.

The Adoption of Presidential Primaries

In the early years of the U.S., prospective presidential candidates needed to impress their colleagues in Congress, because presidential nominees were chosen by the congressional party caucuses. When the parties started nominating their presidential candidates in national conventions in the 1830s, as Chapter 1 showed, the real power in the process moved to the local and state party leaders. They chose their state's delegates to the national convention and told those delegates which presidential candidate to support. The selection was usually done in a series of party-controlled meetings, called caucuses, held first at the local level and then in statewide conventions.

At the urging of Progressives, who aimed to weaken party leaders' power, Florida passed the first presidential primary law in 1901 to let voters pick the party's candidate. Many other states followed. The parties later struck back; by 1936, only 14 states were still holding primaries to choose their delegates to the national conventions. That number had hardly changed by 1968.[3] Even in many states that held primaries, voters could take part in only a non-binding "beauty contest" to express their preferences about presidential candidates; the delegates who went to the national convention and actually chose the candidates were selected elsewhere. A fascinating story began to unfold in 1968, however, in which the national Democratic Party took control of the delegate selection process away from the state parties and gave new life to the use of presidential primaries.

Turbulence in the Democratic Party

Rioters fought with police in the streets outside the 1968 Democratic convention. The party was torn by disputes over civil rights and American involvement in the Vietnam War. When the convention nominated the party leaders' choice, Vice President Hubert Humphrey, as the Democratic presidential candidate, antiwar Democrats protested that the nomination did not fairly reflect the views of most grassroots party activists. Humphrey hadn't run in even one state primary, they complained. To try to make peace with these activists, the national party leaders agreed that the next convention's delegates would be selected in a more open and democratic manner.

The party created a reform commission chaired by liberal Senator George McGovern (and later by U.S. Representative Donald Fraser and known as the **McGovern–Fraser Commission**). It recommended, and the Democratic National Committee (DNC) and the next Democratic convention approved, major changes to increase the influence of insurgent Democrats in the 1972 presidential nominating process. One of the striking elements of this story is the remarkable ease with which state Democratic Party leaders accepted rule changes that greatly reduced their power over the awarding of the party's greatest prize, the presidential nomination.[4]

In trying to comply with the complicated new McGovern–Fraser rules, many states stopped using caucus-convention systems and reinstituted primaries. The remaining caucuses were guided by strict party requirements that delegates be selected in open and well-publicized meetings. Techniques formerly used by state party organizations to control the caucuses were outlawed. In the process, not only were the delegate selection procedures democratized but also the principle was established that the national party, not the states or the state parties, has ultimate control over the rules for nominating presidential candidates.

Once the reform genie was let out of the bottle, it was hard to contain. The Democrats tinkered with their nomination rules prior to almost every election for the next 20 years. First, they used national party leverage to make the process more open and more representative of women, blacks, and young people. Then, the Democrats required the use of proportional representation, so that voter support for candidates was more faithfully represented in states' delegations. Starting in 1980, to bring party leaders (and their personal knowledge of candidates) back into the process, many Democratic elected and party officials were guaranteed a vote at the convention as uncommitted "superdelegates" (now called "automatic delegates," to be discussed later in this chapter).

The results dramatically transformed the process by which the Democrats select their presidential nominees. Many state legislatures responded to the new Democratic rules by changing state election laws to require primary elections in both parties. Thus, the Republicans became the unwilling beneficiaries of the Democratic reforms. Until recently, the Republicans preserved their tradition of giving state parties wide latitude in developing their own rules for selecting delegates. Since 2012, however, the Republican National Committee (RNC) has become more active in constraining the choices of the state party organizations.

Presidential Primaries and Caucuses Today

Each state decides whether to choose its delegates to the parties' national conventions in a primary election or a series of caucuses. Although primaries are more common, states can change their method of selection from one presidential

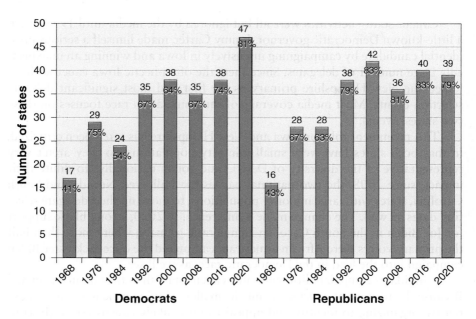

FIGURE 10.1 Change in the Number of Presidential Primaries, 1968–2020

Note: The number above each bar is the number of states that scheduled primaries to select delegates in that year; inside the bar is the percentage of convention delegates elected in those primaries. Percentages are based on total numbers of delegates, including Democratic automatic delegates and Republican unbound delegates. All 50 states plus Washington, DC, are included, but not the territories (American Samoa, Guam, Puerto Rico, Virgin Islands) or Democrats Abroad.

Sources: For 1968–1992, Michael G. Hagen and William G. Mayer, "The Modern Politics of Presidential Selection," in William G. Mayer, ed., *In Pursuit of the White House 2000* (New York: Chatham House, 2000), pp. 11 and 43–44. Figures for 2000 and 2004 were kindly provided by Mayer. Figures for 2008–2020 were calculated by the author from data provided by two parties' Calls for their national conventions.

election to the next (see Figure 10.1). When an incumbent president seems assured to win renomination, for instance, many states cancel that party's primary to save money or to ensure that opposition will not arise later in the process. And in the extraordinary circumstances of 2020, large numbers of state nominating events occurring after mid-March were postponed because of the corona virus pandemic.

A state holding a primary selects a date on which its eligible voters can go to a polling place (or cast a mail or absentee ballot) and choose who they'd like to be their party's presidential nominee. The popular vote for each candidate determines how many of the state's pledged delegates will go to the party's national convention supporting that candidate.

Other states use a longer delegate selection process that begins with precinct caucuses. In these meetings, party identifiers are invited to gather, often for an hour or more, to debate which candidate for president will best represent their party and the issues they believe in. Then they choose delegates to communicate their presidential preference to meetings at higher levels, typically at the county, congressional district, and then the state level. The state's final delegate slate for the national convention can be determined at the higher-level conventions.

Caucus states' activities were all but ignored by the media until 1976, when a little-known Democratic governor, Jimmy Carter, made himself a serious presidential candidate by campaigning intensively in Iowa and winning an unexpectedly large number of delegates. Since then, the often-hectic Iowa caucuses have joined the New Hampshire primary as the first and most significant delegate selection events. Most media coverage of the nomination race focuses on these two states' events.[5]

This prominent role for Iowa and New Hampshire has often been criticized, in that both states have very small minority populations, so they aren't very representative of the diversity of Democratic voters nationally. To dilute their impact, since 2008, the two national parties have allowed Nevada and South Carolina, states with large minority populations, to move up their delegate selection dates as well. The change made a difference. In 2020, strong black support for Joe Biden in the South Carolina Democratic primary, where more than half the primary voters were African-American, catapulted the once-lackluster Biden campaign into the lead in the Democratic race, as we'll see.

Candidates campaign differently in a caucus state than they do in a primary. Because the turnout at caucuses is much smaller, winning caucuses requires extensive organizing to identify and appeal to these likely caucus goers. (In contrast, media ads are better suited to reach the bigger turnout in a primary.) In 2020, several of the remaining caucus states switched to primaries instead, partly because caucus results can be challenging to compile, as Iowa Democratic leaders in 2020 would confirm, and harder for the media to report.

The Race for Delegates: Timing and Momentum

Joe Biden almost missed his chance in 2020. Candidates who survive the "invisible primary" know that they can create momentum by winning states whose contests are held early in the nominating process. These early wins attract more media coverage for the candidate and, in turn, more name recognition among voters. The candidate looks more and more unstoppable, so it is easier to raise money, which makes later victories more likely. This happens especially in contests when winner-take-all rules are used. Because the other candidates aren't winning any delegates, they fall further and further behind.

Biden performed miserably in Iowa and New Hampshire in the 2020 Democratic nomination race, coming in fourth and fifth, respectively. But the quick succession of other early primaries and caucuses gave him a second chance. After a credible finish in the Nevada caucuses, Biden swept the South Carolina primary. Widespread Democratic concern about the electability of Biden's strongest opponent, Vermont Sen. Bernie Sanders, led to a dominating Biden win in the many Super Tuesday primaries and caucuses on March 3. On that early date, Biden became the presumptive Democratic nominee (see box "Momentum in Presidential Nominations" on page 221). The general election was still eight months away.

Momentum in Presidential Nominations

Each state's party organization decides how and when its voters will select their delegates to the national nominating conventions, within limits set by the national party. In 1976, only half of the states' primaries and caucuses had been held by early May. But in recent years, many states moved their primary or caucuses close to the start of the election year, when they would get more media coverage, bring in more money from campaign ads, and give the state's voters more of a chance to influence who would be their parties' nominees. The high point of this "front-loading" came in 2008, when the midpoint of the nominating season took place in early February. That dragged out the nominating process and wore out the contenders. Since 2012, the national parties have shortened the nominating season somewhat by ruling that no nomination contest could be held before early February.

Even so, the first few nominating events still received much more attention in 2020 than did later state events. The first two states to vote—Iowa and New Hampshire—are not very typical of the American population as a whole. Both states are almost entirely white, with few urban centers. In Iowa, most Republican caucus voters are evangelical Christians. These two early states are even more atypical of Democratic voters; if the nomination calendar were scheduled according to the similarity between their Democratic voters and the party's national voter base, the first nominating events would be held in Illinois, New Jersey, New York, and Florida.

Yet, despite their atypical characteristics, Iowa and New Hampshire voters narrowed the list of candidates for other voters to consider. Three Democratic candidates left the race right after the 2020 New Hampshire primary. Voters in the early primaries, then, had a much wider range of candidate choices than did voters whose primaries were held in May or June. And for primary voters whose aim is to choose the strongest possible candidate for their party, the results of early-state events can give them their answer by creating momentum for the winner. Former vice president Joe Biden's showing in Nevada and his much bigger victory in South Carolina signaled to Democratic primary voters that Biden had the breadth of party support needed to warrant their votes. The result was described as "one of the most remarkable presidential campaign turnarounds in U.S. history."[6]

This curious nominating schedule, which owes its existence to tradition rather than careful planning, is often described as being biased and unrepresentative. Some reformers prefer replacing it with a national primary, with all states voting for their party's presidential nominee on the same day. A national primary wouldn't eliminate the role of momentum; instead, the momentum would come from the "invisible primary," advantaging the candidates who led in the polls just prior to the primary. The present sequential system, despite its flaws, does permit some lesser-known candidates to build support in Iowa and New Hampshire, which are small enough for one-on-one, "retail" voter contact.

Sources: Larry M. Bartels, *Presidential Primaries and the Dynamics of Public Choice* (Princeton, NJ: Princeton University Press, 1988) and David P. Redlawsk, Caroline J. Tolbert, and Todd Donovan, *Why Iowa?* (Chicago, IL: University of Chicago Press, 2011), Chapter 8; but see Joshua D. Clinton, Andrew M. Engelhardt, and Marc J. Trussler, "Knockout Blows or the Status Quo?" *Journal of Politics* 81 (July 2019): 997–1013.

One reason why so many states hold their nominating events early in the election year is that state legislatures see the benefits their state can derive from an early primary or caucus. The media interest generated by an early contest brings large numbers of journalists and campaigners (who spend money on food, lodging, and other needs) into the state. The media put the state's concerns in the national spotlight. Iowa's first-in-the-nation status, for example, means that ethanol use, favored by Iowa's corn farmers, gets more notice from presidential candidates than it would receive otherwise. Thus, the nomination process became **front-loaded**, as states moved their primaries and caucuses closer to the beginning of the nominating season.

Candidates' Strategic Choices

As candidates approach these primaries and caucuses, they must make vital decisions. How much effort and money should they put into each state? Which of their issue stands and personal qualities will be most persuasive to which voters? Different types of candidates face different challenges. An early front-runner, for example, normally has to demonstrate overwhelming support in the first few delegate selection events, or his or her supporters' and contributors' confidence may be so badly shaken that the candidate's chances fade. Many other formal and informal "rules" structure the nominating process and affect campaigns' strategies.

The Democrats' rules differ from the Republicans'. Recall that the Democrats' nomination reforms require the use of proportional representation (PR), so that candidates with significant support will not be shut out in any state. Since 1988, any candidates who win at least 15 percent of the vote in a state's primary or caucus get approximately the same share of the delegates as they received of the popular vote. Until 2012, the Republicans had no national rules as to how to count these votes, but most states' Republican parties used some form of a winner-take-all system: The candidate who gets the most votes in a state primary or caucus wins all or most of the state's delegates.

A winner-take-all rule produces very different results from a PR rule (see Chapter 2).[7] Because whoever gets the most votes in a winner-take-all election receives *all* the delegates from that state, he or she can quickly build an unbeatable lead. Second- and third-place candidates do better in states with PR rules, because they can keep winning at least some delegates in states where they get at least 15 percent of the vote. That lets them stay in the race longer. But even under PR rules, once the leading candidate has pulled ahead, the rules can become a stumbling block for the other candidates, because they won't be able to catch up with the leader by winning a plurality in a big state. As one reporter noted, "the Republican who kills the buffalo gets all the meat; the Democrat has to crouch around the campfire and share it with his brethren and sistren."[8]

What Is the Party's Role?

The party organizations' interests in the nominating process are not necessarily the same as those of the presidential candidates. State and local parties want a nominee who will bring voters to the polls to support the party's candidates for state and local offices. A weak presidential candidate may hurt their chances. Party leaders also worry that a hotly contested nomination race could lead to conflict within local and state parties, which might weaken them in the general election.

Historically, some state parties protected their interests by selecting delegates uncommitted to any candidate and then casting the state's delegate votes as a bloc for a particular nominee. The ability to swing a bloc of delegates to a candidate could increase the state party's influence at the convention. But the current nominating system makes it difficult for state parties to send an uncommitted delegation. In many primary states, the candidates set up their own delegate slates, so the delegates' first loyalty is to the candidate. In caucus states, delegates committed to a candidate usually have greater appeal to caucus-goers than do uncommitted delegates.

Besides, interest groups such as labor unions, environmentalists, business groups, and evangelical Christian organizations urge their activists to take part in caucuses and primaries to push for a nominee committed to their goals rather than an uncommitted slate. Democratic presidential candidates Tom Steyer, Elizabeth Warren, and Andrew Yang, for example, stressed some issues such as climate change during the 2020 nomination season, not because it was a priority for many primary voters but because it mattered a great deal to environmentalists concerned with the Democratic presidential nomination.

The DNC also added a new hurdle in 2020 for presidential candidates who hoped to take part in the party's monthly pre-election debates. Not only did candidates need to exceed a small percentage of support in polls; they also had to attract thousands of small donors. But even with this effort at winnowing, Democratic opposition to President Trump was so intense that more than 20 Democrats competed during the invisible primary, and 11 were still in the race by the time of the Iowa caucuses. Party leaders, then, have a harder time protecting the party's interests in a nominating process that is dominated by the candidates and their group and individual supporters.[9]

The Democrats tried to enhance the party's role in 1980 and to a greater extent in 1984 by adding delegate seats at the national convention for elected and party officials. These **superdelegates,** now officially termed "automatic delegates"—all Democratic governors and members of Congress, current and former presidents and vice presidents, and all members of the Democratic National Committee—were meant to be a large, uncommitted bloc now totaling about 16 percent of all delegates, with the party's interests in mind (see Table 10.1).

The closeness of the delegate count during the 2008 and 2016 Democratic contests raised concerns that the superdelegates' votes might actually decide the race. This elicited charges of "boss rule," especially by proponents of candidates who did not have majority support among superdelegates. But their suspicions were largely unfounded. All the superdelegates are either elected officials, who have a natural interest in maintaining constituent support, or party leaders, who want to choose the nominee who appeals to the most voters. For example, in 2016, although Bernie Sanders supporters feared that superdelegates were

TABLE 10.1 Who Were the "Superdelegates" in 2020?

Affiliation	Number	% of all Superdelegates
All Democratic National Committee (DNC) members*	436	56.5
Party enthusiasts chosen by each state's party organization 51% male, 58% white, 23% black, 12% Hispanic American, 7% Asian American or other		
All Democratic members of the U.S. House of Representatives	234	30.4
55% male, 50% white, 23% black, 20% Hispanic American, 7% Asian American or other		
All Democratic U.S. senators	47	6.1
66% male, 81% white, 6% black, 4% Hispanic American, 6% Asian American or other		
All Democratic governors	28	3.6
71% male, 79% white, 4% black, 7% Hispanic American, 11% Asian American or other		
Distinguished party leaders	26	3.4
Democratic current and former presidents and vice presidents, former DNC chairs, former House and Senate Democratic leaders		
88% male, 88% white, 8% black, 4% Hispanic Americans		
Total Democratic superdelegates	771	100

*Excluding the DNC members who are current governors and U.S. Senate and House members, who are counted in those categories. Note that the DNC includes members from all states and Washington, DC, Puerto Rico, American Samoa, Guam, the Northern Marianas, the U.S. Virgin Islands, and Democrats Abroad.

Source: Calculated by the author from data provided by the DNC.

unfairly tipping the convention vote toward Hillary Clinton, the superdelegates were actually on the same side as the party's voters; Clinton had also won many more popular votes than Sanders in state primaries and caucuses.

So in practice, superdelegates have not played an independent role in the nominating process as a voice for the party's interests.[10] Even so, amid continuing charges of "boss rule," the DNC limited the superdelegates' role in 2020. Superdelegates would be allowed to cast votes at the convention only if the delegates could not agree on a nominee on its first ballot.[11] Biden's first-ballot victory left the superdelegates without real impact.

The Republicans took a different path. After Barack Obama beat John McCain in the 2008 presidential election, Republican Party leaders suspected that the front-loading of the nomination race had led to McCain's winning the party's nomination too quickly. So they changed the rules for the 2012 nomination to slow the race down. Breaking with its usual states' rights policy, the Republican National Committee (RNC) mandated that any Republican nomination events held before April 1 must use some form of PR in allocating delegates to presidential candidates. That would help candidates other than the front-runner stay in the race longer. The new rule would also give states a reason not to front-load their caucuses and primaries. That, Republican leaders hoped, would give party voters more time to get to know the candidates, so they could pick the strongest nominee.

The change did stretch out the Republican nomination race. But the eventual nominee, Mitt Romney, lost the 2012 general election to Obama. The RNC concluded that the reformed nominating season had taken *too* long; it delayed the party in uniting behind Romney. So the RNC recommended a shorter, more streamlined system for 2016. Only states with nominating events between March 1 and March 14 would have to use PR rules. The national convention was moved up to mid-July, to give the party's candidate more time to campaign for the general election.[12] And the Republican nominee, Donald Trump, won the presidential race this time. Their 2016 win, as wins usually do, convinced the Republicans to keep almost the same system in 2020.

Party leaders often develop strategies in reaction to their most recent campaign experiences. But in the case of presidential campaigns, the long, four-year interval between campaigns allows for so many changes in the political environment that what's learned from the last election doesn't necessarily work in the next. In the immortal words of Yogi Berra, "It's tough to make predictions, especially about the future."

One big message emerges from this welter of reforms and re-reforms: The modern process of selecting the parties' presidential candidates has not been friendly to the party organization. Donald Trump's success in winning the Republican presidential nomination in 2016 is an excellent example. When Trump announced his candidacy, most Republican Party leaders didn't take him seriously. Even after a large proportion of states had held their primaries and caucuses that year, Trump's endorsements by prominent Republicans could be counted on one hand with a few fingers to spare. The Republican Speaker of the U.S. House held back on supporting Trump even after all his opponents had withdrawn from the race.

If Republican Party leaders didn't want Trump as their candidate, then why did he win the party's nomination? Perhaps the fact that there were 17 contenders for the nomination kept the field divided rather than letting one Republican face Trump head-on. Perhaps Republicans failed to take Trump seriously until it was too late to stop him. A more likely reason is that the RNC and the Republican Party in government do not control the party's presidential nomination process. Voters in Republican primaries and caucuses do, and in 2016, a plurality chose Trump.

Many observers are not happy with this limit on the parties' role in presidential elections. Some argue that political professionals such as party leaders and elected officials are better positioned to determine whether candidates have the skills needed to govern capably. These pros have more experience in coalition-building, so they can make sure that a nominee will represent all the major elements of the party. Party identifiers, they suggest, can't be expected to manage all these requirements at the same time.[13] But it's hard to imagine any successful challenge to the current reliance on primaries in the U.S. nominating system.

Voters' Choices in Presidential Nominations

The move to primaries and participatory caucuses has increased citizen involvement in nominating a president. What determines the level of voter turnout and guides voters' choices in these contests?

Who Votes?

Turnout varies a great deal from state to state and across different years in any one state. Media attention to the early contests tends to produce higher turnouts in those states. Turnout is greater in states with a better-educated citizenry and a tradition of two-party competition—the same states where there is higher turnout in the general election. The nature of the contest matters, too. Voters are more attracted to races that are closely fought and in which the candidates spend more money and the excitement is high, all of which increase interest in the election. The same is true of non-presidential primaries (see Chapter 9).[14]

Are Primary and Caucus Voters Typical?

However, primaries have lower turnout than general elections do, and caucuses have lower turnout still. Are the people who turn out to vote in these events, and who therefore choose the nominees for the rest of the public, typical of other citizens? Critics of the reforms have charged that they are not and, thus, that candidates are now being selected by an unrepresentative group of citizens.

We can explore this question in several ways. When we compare presidential primary voters with nonvoters, we find that those who vote in primaries are, in fact, better educated, wealthier, and older, but then, so are general election voters. A more appropriate comparison is with party identifiers because primaries are the means by which the party electorate chooses its nominees. Using this comparison, just as is the case with primary voters more generally, voters in presidential primaries tend to be slightly older, better educated, more affluent, better integrated into their communities, somewhat more partisan and interested in politics, and less likely to be black or Hispanic. The differences are not substantial, however.[15]

Do Voters Make Informed Choices?

Another criticism of primaries is that voters don't make very well-informed decisions. Compared with voters in the general election, primary voters tend to pay less attention to the campaign and know less about the candidates. Especially in the early contests, voters are influenced by candidate momentum, as support builds for at least some candidates who have won unexpectedly or by a large margin.

Candidates' personal characteristics influence voters in the primaries,[16] but issues often have only a minor impact. The result, so the argument goes, is a series of contests decided mainly on the basis of short-run, superficial considerations.[17]

Many analysts think that this is too strong an indictment. They feel that voters respond with some rationality to the challenge of having to choose among several candidates without the powerful guidance provided by party labels.[18] Although it may seem pointless to support a candidate simply because he or she has momentum, primary voters often find only minor issue differences among their party's candidates and just want to pick the candidate with the best chance of winning the presidency for their party. Momentum seems to matter especially when voters are being asked to sort through a pack of candidates about whom they know little[19] and when there is no well-known front-runner.[20] Even then, the candidates who move to the head of the pack are usually subjected to more thorough evaluation, which gives voters more reasons to support or oppose them. In short, even though primary voters often know less about the candidates than do general election voters, the quality of their decisions may not differ very much from those in general elections.[21]

Do Primaries Produce Good Candidates?

The current primary-dominated system has produced some talented candidates and some less distinguished nominees, just as the earlier nominating system did. The pre-reform nominating system tended to favor mainstream politicians who were acceptable to the party's leaders, including some candidates who had earned their nomination through party loyalty rather than through their personal appeal or their skills at governing. Primaries are more likely to give an advantage to candidates whose names are well known to the public and those who have the support of issue activists and people with intensely held views.[22]

Compared with the earlier nominating process, the current system gives presidential candidates more opportunities to demonstrate their public support, raise more campaign money, and test their stamina and ability to cope with pressure. On the other hand, candidates' performance in the primaries may not be a good indicator of their likely competence in the White House.

The National Conventions

Once the states have chosen their delegates in primaries and caucuses, the delegates go to their party's national convention and vote for a presidential nominee. But the conventions function much differently now than they did at their origins in the 1830s.

How the Conventions Began

The national party convention is an old and respected institution, but it began, at least in part, as a power grab. In 1832, Andrew Jackson's nomination as the

Democratic–Republican candidate for president was a foregone conclusion, but state political leaders wanted to keep Henry Clay, the favorite of the congressional caucus, from being nominated as vice president; they preferred Martin Van Buren. So these leaders pushed for a national convention to make the nominations. In doing so, they wrested control of the presidential selection process from congressional leaders. By the time the Republican Party emerged in 1854, the convention had become the accepted means by which major parties chose their presidential candidates. Since 1856, both major parties have held national conventions every four years.

Before the nomination reforms of the 1970s, the delegates who would select the party's nominee in the national convention were chosen by state and local party leaders, not by voters. When the first round of balloting did not produce a majority for one candidate, intense bargaining would follow among state party leaders and the remaining candidates. The leading candidates would work to hold their supporters while negotiating for the votes of state delegations that had come committed to other candidates. In recent years, however, one candidate has won a majority of delegate votes well before the convention starts, so the last time a convention went beyond a single round of balloting was in 1952.

Convention delegates (except for superdelegates) are bound by state or party rules to vote for the candidate their state's voters told them to support on the first convention ballot. If no candidate gets a majority, then on the second ballot almost 60 percent of the delegates would be freed to vote for any candidate they choose. This rule affects the outcome as well. In 2016, some delegates sent by their states to vote for Trump actually preferred another candidate. If the convention had needed a second ballot, then Trump would have probably lost the nomination. But a series of Trump victories in late primaries convinced his remaining competitors to drop out of the race, and the first-ballot tradition was preserved.

What Conventions Do

Conventions have several important tasks in addition to showcasing the party's presidential candidate. Each party's convention starts by taking advantage of this national media exposure to spotlight the party's most popular figures and to introduce its most exciting new candidates and office-holders. Then they roll out the convention's star in what they hope will be a rousing and persuasive blastoff for the general election campaign.

Formalizing the Presidential Nomination   Conventions must bring supporters of defeated primary candidates back into the party fold. So the winning nominee will stress unifying themes and party traditions as well as the major goals he or she will stress in the general election. Films will be shown depicting his or her appealing childhood and family life and linking the candidate with the party's most beloved figures, both historical and current.

Approving the Vice Presidential Nominee   The day after the presidential nomination is ratified, delegates vote again to select the vice presidential candidate. This, too, is ceremonial; presidential nominees choose their own running mates and conventions ratify their choice.[23] In years past, the vice presidential nominee was selected by the (usually exhausted) presidential candidate at the time of the convention. Now, presidential nominees announce their "veep" choice before the convention begins, often to increase their support among some groups of voters. Joe Biden's selection of Senator Kamala Harris in 2020 reflected the importance of black women in the Democratic coalition, just as Donald Trump's choice of Mike Pence in 2016 demonstrated the vital role of evangelical Christians among Republican voters.

Approving the Platform   In addition to nominating candidates, the convention's main job is to approve the party's **platform**—its statement of party positions on a wide range of issues. The platform committee often asks for public comments, online as well as in hearings, long before the convention opens. The finished platform is then presented to the convention for its approval.

Because they are approved in nominating conventions whose main purpose is to promote a presidential candidate, platforms usually reflect the candidate's views or the bargains the candidate has made to win support or preserve party harmony.[24] So a platform usually lists the policy preferences of various groups in the party's (and the candidate's) supporting coalition. Platforms are also campaign documents, intended to help the party's candidates win their races.

Yet platforms are much more than just a laundry list of promises. They often define the major differences between the parties, as the leading scholar of party platforms shows.[25] As a result, they can provoke spirited debates at the convention because many delegates care deeply about this statement of the party's beliefs on such issues as abortion, taxes, climate change, and American involvement in the world (see Chapter 15).

Launching the General Election Campaign   The final business of the convention is to present the party's presidential candidate to the American public. Candidates hope that their glowing portrayal in the convention will boost their public support, known as a "convention bounce."

Many other events took place at the conventions as well, when they were held in person. Lobbyists hosted lavish dinners and receptions to curry favor with elected officials. Even though conventions are partly funded by tax dollars, most of their costs have been paid by big donors with an interest in federal policies—corporations (especially for the Republicans), unions (for the Democrats), and wealthy individuals.

Who Are the Delegates?

Convention delegates help to shape the public's image of the two parties. What kinds of people represent their parties at these events?

Apportioning Delegates among the States

The national parties determine how many delegates each state can send to the convention. The two parties make these choices differently. The Republicans allocate delegates more equally among the states; the Democrats weigh more heavily the size of the state's population and its record of support for Democratic candidates.

These formulas affect the voting strength of various groups within the party coalitions, as they do in the two national committees (see Chapter 4). The GOP's decision to represent the small states more equally with the large states has advantaged its conservative wing. In contrast, by giving relatively more weight to the larger states with stronger Democratic voting traditions, the Democrats have favored the more liberal interests in their party, and in particular, urban areas with large minority populations.

How Representative Are the Delegates?

The delegates to the Democratic and Republican conventions have never been a cross-section of Americans or even of their party's voters. White males, the well-educated, and the affluent are traditionally overrepresented in conventions. Reflecting their different coalitional bases, since the 1930s, Democratic delegations have had more labor union members and black Americans, and Republican conventions have drawn more Protestants and small business owners.

Demographics   The Democrats used affirmative action plans starting in 1972 to increase the presence of women, blacks, and, for a brief time, young people. We can see the results in surveys of convention delegates. At recent Democratic conventions held in person in host cities, more than a third of the delegates were people of color (compared with only about 5 percent of Republican delegates), and since 1980, the DNC has required that half of the delegates be women. The percentage of female delegates at Republican conventions increased during this period as well, without party mandates. The DNC urged state parties to recruit more low- and moderate-income delegates, but their lesser political involvement and the high price of attending a convention stood in the way. As a result, in-person conventions remained meetings of the wealthy and well educated. In recent conventions, a quarter to a third of both parties' delegates said they were millionaires, and most had post-graduate education.[26]

Political Experience   We might assume that delegates would be recidivists, chosen for this honor again and again. That has not been the case. After the reforms, the percentage of convention first timers jumped to about 80 percent. Even after the Democrats began granting convention seats to politically experienced superdelegates, most of the delegates were newcomers. However, the great majority are long-time party activists. Many have been active in their party for at least 20 years, and most currently hold party office.

Issues   Convention delegates tend to be more extreme in their views and more aware of issues than most other voters are. They are also, as you might expect, very polarized by party. Democratic delegates tend to be more liberal than the average Democratic voter, and many more Republican delegates call themselves "very conservative" than do other GOP voters. For instance, the overwhelming majority of Democratic delegates in recent presidential conventions have favored providing health care coverage for all Americans even if taxes go up, whereas fewer than 10 percent of Republican delegates have agreed. Most Democratic delegates have favored same-sex marriage, unrestricted abortion rights, and stricter gun control laws, while the proportion of Republican delegates holding those views is only about 5 percent. The two parties' delegates have differed most from one another in their views on health-care coverage and tax cuts. Although using primaries and caucuses was intended to make the conventions more representative of the parties' grassroots supporters, delegates' views reflect the perspectives of party activists—not surprisingly, given that they regularly participate in delegate selection events—more than the average party identifier.

Purists or Pragmatists?   The Democratic Party reforms of the 1970s hoped to give greater voice in the nominating process to party purists—those described in Chapter 5 as attracted to politics by issues, more insistent on internal party democracy, and less willing to compromise. That aim was successful; there were more purists in the 1972 convention than there had been in 1968. The proportion of pragmatists—those who hold long-term commitment to the party and who are more willing to compromise on issues to win the general election—went down.[27] As we have seen, the Democrats later modified this trend by adding superdelegates, to bring the skills of party professionals and elected officials back into the nomination process. Research shows that both before and after the reforms, delegates remained strongly committed to the parties and their goals.[28] It may be that for both pragmatists and purists, involvement in this very public party pageant strengthens delegates' commitment to both the party and its ideals.

Who Controls the Delegates?   It would not matter how representative delegates are if they act as pawns of powerful party leaders. For most of the history of party conventions, that is exactly how the state delegations behaved. But state party leaders no longer control their state delegations. When the Democrats eliminated their long-standing unit rule in 1968, through which a majority of a state delegation could throw all the delegation's votes to one candidate, they removed a powerful instrument of leadership control. Perhaps the strongest force preventing state party leaders from controlling the conventions is the fact that the delegates in both parties are now already committed to a candidate by their state's primary or caucuses. That makes them unavailable for "delivery" by party leaders. If anyone controls modern conventions, then, it is the party's prospective nominee for president, not leaders of the state parties.

How Media Cover Conventions

Media coverage of conventions has also changed significantly. Conventions have been reshaped and rescheduled to meet the media's needs.[29] Ironically, as a result, media attention to the conventions has declined sharply.

Beginning with the first televised national party conventions in 1948, TV journalists and politicians found ways to serve one another's interests. In the early days of television before the convenience of videotape, networks were desperate for content to fill broadcast time, so they covered the party conventions live, from beginning to end. The convention became a major story, like the Olympics, in which TV news could demonstrate its skill and provide a public service. Reporters swarmed through the convention halls, covering the strategic moves of major candidates, the actions of powerful party leaders, and the reactions of individual delegates.

For party leaders, television coverage offered a priceless opportunity to reach voters and launch the presidential campaign with maximum impact. So they reshaped the convention into a performance intended as much for the national television audience as for the delegates. Party officials gave key speaking roles to telegenic candidates, speeded up the proceedings, and moved the most dramatic convention presentations into prime-time hours. More and more, the aim of the convention shifted from the conduct of party business to the wooing of voters.

But once the McGovern-Fraser reforms took effect, the parties' presidential candidates were named before the convention started. Conventions lost most of their suspense. To hold viewers, media searched the conventions for new sources of excitement, such as potential conflicts. But party leaders had no interest in making their disputes public; that would interfere with the positive message they were trying to convey. As the conventions became more scripted, and therefore less exciting to the public, the major networks cut their coverage markedly. The major networks (ABC, CBS, and NBC) devoted about 60 hours of television time to broadcasting each convention in 1952, but when the corona virus pandemic forced both conventions into a virtual format in 2020, the broadcast networks provided only about four hours of live coverage per convention.

Reactions to the virtual party conventions in 2020 were generally positive.[30] Both parties presented highly produced celebrations of their candidates and traditions, mixing live and taped segments. Both conventions were faster-paced than their earlier in-person versions had been, and party leaders benefited because the online presentation kept party dissidents from calling attention to themselves. So although partisans may have missed the pageantry and networking of an in-person convention, it seems likely that future nominating conventions will be at least partly virtual.

Effects of the Nomination Reforms

The reforms of the nominating process in recent decades have greatly changed the way we select presidential candidates and the types of candidates we select. Many more voters currently have a chance to influence the choice of their party's nominee, though the proportion of eligible voters who take advantage of that opportunity remains disappointingly small. Compared to earlier times when party leaders, who were largely older white males, had the power to select nominees, the reformed process has opened the door to participation by people of color, women, young people, and other groups previously left out of this vital choice.

Further, the reforms have made issues all the more important in the nominating process. Candidates for president must mobilize groups of activists and voters to win primaries and caucuses, and most of these groups are concerned with particular policies. So presidential candidates can't as easily avoid declaring where they stand on issues important to very active groups, ranging from gun rights proponents to teachers' unions. The pressures exerted by Christian conservatives in the Republican nominating process since the 1970s to preserve the party's stated opposition to same-sex marriage, transgender rights, and abortion are a good illustration, as was the emphasis on minority rights, and the Black Lives Matter movement in particular, in the Democratic convention.

The power of these organized groups in American political life is nothing new, of course. But depending on the political environment at the time, the reforms have enhanced the ability of organized interests to affect and sometimes even dominate political parties.[31]

Should We Reform the Reforms?

The McGovern–Fraser reforms were part of a time-honored pattern in American politics: reformers trying to break up concentrations of power in the party leadership. But the reforms have had many unintended effects as well. Primaries can create internal divisions in party organizations that may not heal in time for the general election. The low turnouts in many primaries and caucuses can increase the influence of well-organized groups on the ideological extremes: the right wing of the Republican Party and the left wing of the Democrats. The results of a few early contests in states not very representative of the nation have a disproportionate effect on the national outcome.[32] In most years, by the time most voters know enough about the candidates to make an informed choice, the nominees have already been chosen. And candidates must invest such an enormous amount of time, energy, and money in the nomination process that the winning candidates are bone-weary—just in time for the general election campaign to begin.

There is no going back to the old system, however. As the reformers charged, it was controlled by state and local party leaders who were often out of touch with the electorate. It kept many party voters and even party activists out of the crucial first step in picking a president. It violated the desire for a more open, democratic politics, and it did not help presidential candidates learn how to prepare for the most powerful leadership job in the world.[33]

What Could Be Done?

Critics of this complicated, lengthy process have often proposed further reform.[34] A Republican task force in 2013 recommended that the long march of primaries and caucuses be compressed into four regional events, in which the states in a given region would all schedule their primaries or caucuses on the same day. The enormous strain on the candidates would be reduced by short-ening the nomination season and holding elections on only four days. That has been tried in part; beginning in the late 1980s, most southern states have held their primaries on the same day in early March, called Super Tuesday. Their aim was to encourage Democrats to nominate moderate candidates who shared southern concerns. But a set of regional primaries doesn't solve many problems. The first region to vote, with its peculiarities and specific concerns, would dis-proportionately influence the nominations. Regional primaries could still lead to internal party divisions; in fact, they might heighten a sense of regional party polarization.

And as we have seen, holding a national primary in which all the states' primaries and caucuses take place on a single day poses big problems as well. It advantages the candidates who start with the most money and name recog-nition, those capable of campaigning in dozens of states at the same time. It limits the roles of the party organizations and the states in selecting presidential candidates.

The benefits of primaries—challenging candidates to organize their cam-paigns and appeal to voters under changing conditions over several months—could be combined with rules that balance their drawbacks. For instance, candidates could qualify to run in primaries and caucuses by winning the sup-port of a specified minimum of state and local officials, as happens now in France.[35] That would allow experienced leaders to vet the governing capabilities of candidates, as an additional piece of information for voters. As is so often the case in politics, there is no "right" answer here—just a series of options, each of which favors some kinds of candidates and interests and disadvantages others.

Notes

1 Marjorie Randon Hershey, "Shedding Light on the Invisible Primary," in Larry J. Sabato, ed., *Get in the Booth! The Presidential Election of 2004* (New York: Long-man, 2004), pp. 27–47.

2 Marty Cohen, David Karol, Hans Noel, and John Zaller, *The Party Decides* (Chicago, IL: University of Chicago Press, 2008), especially Chapter 9.

3 See John S. Jackson III and William J. Crotty, *The Politics of Presidential Selection*, 2nd ed. (New York: Longman, 2001), Chapters 3 and 4.

4 See Larry M. Bartels, *Presidential Primaries and the Dynamics of Public Choice* (Princeton, NJ: Princeton University Press, 1988), pp. 17–21. On the evolution of the presidential primary process, see Caitlin E. Jewett, *The Primary Rules* (Ann Arbor: University of Michigan Press, 2019.

5 William G. Mayer and Andrew E. Busch, *The Front-Loading Problem in Presidential Nominations* (Washington, DC: Brookings Institution Press, 2004), pp. 24–25.

6 Bill Barrow and Nicholas Riccardi, "5 Primary Takeaways: Joe Biden Is Demo-crats' Antidote," March 18, 2020, https://www.nbcwashington.com/news/health/5-primary-takeaways-joe-biden-is-democrats-antidote/2245015/ (accessed August 21, 2020).

7 See John H. Aldrich, *Before the Convention* (Chicago, IL: University of Chicago Press, 1980); and Paul-Henri Gurian and Audrey A. Haynes, "Campaign Strategy in Presidential Primaries," *American Journal of Political Science* 37 (1993): 335–341.

8 John M. Broder, "Show Me the Delegate Rules and I'll Show You the Party," *New York Times,* February 17, 2008, Week in Review, p. 1.

9 Julia Azari and Seth Masket, "The DNC's Debate Rules Won't Make The 2020 Primaries Any Less Chaotic," February 20, 2019, https://fivethirtyeight.com/features/-the-dncs-debate-rules-wont-make-the-2020-primaries-any-less-chaotic/ (accessed August 21, 2020).

10 Kim Fridkin, Patrick Kenney, and Sarah Gershon, "Comparing the Views of Super-delegates and Democratic Voters in the 2008 Democratic Nomination Campaign," *Party Politics* 18 (2012): 749–770. The Republicans send a smaller number of un-pledged delegates, including state party chairs, to their national convention.

11 Jonathan Rauch and Ray La Raja, "Too Much Democracy Is Bad for Democracy," *The Atlantic,* December 2019, https://www.theatlantic.com/magazine/archive/2019/12/too-much-democracy-is-bad-for-democracy/600766/ (accessed August 21, 2020).

12 Team GOP, "The Official Guide to the 2016 Republican Nominating Process," October 8, 2015, at www.gop.com/the-official-guide-to-the-2016-republican-nominating-process/ (accessed August 21, 2020).

13 See Rauch and La Raja, "Too Much Democracy."

14 See Barbara Norrander, "Primary Elections and Caucuses," in Marjorie Randon Hershey, ed., *Guide to U.S. Political Parties* (Los Angeles, CA: Sage, 2014), Chapter 21.

15 Barbara Norrander, *The Imperfect Primary* (New York: Routledge, 2010), p. 63.

16 Mark J. Wattier and Raymond Tatalovich, "Gods, Generals, and the Confederate Flag," *The Citadel Symposium on Southern Politics,* Charleston, 2004.

17 See John G. Geer, *Nominating Presidents* (New York: Greenwood Press, 1989).

18 Samuel L. Popkin, *The Reasoning Voter* (Chicago, IL: University of Chicago Press, 1991), Chapters 6–8.

19 Bartels, *Presidential Primaries and the Dynamics of Public Choice,* Chapter 4.

20 Paul R. Abramson, John H. Aldrich, Phil Paolino, and David W. Rohde, "'Sophisticated' Voting in the 1988 Presidential Primaries," *American Political Science Review* 86 (1992): 55–69.

21 See Walter J. Stone, Ronald B. Rapoport, and Alan I. Abramowitz, "Candidate Support in Presidential Nomination Campaigns," *Journal of Politics* 54 (1992): 1074–1097.

22 Michael G. Hagen and William G. Mayer, "The Modern Politics of Presidential Selection," in William G. Mayer, ed., *In Pursuit of the White House 2000* (New York, NY: Chatham House, 2000), pp. 17–21.

23 See Lee Sigelman and Paul J. Wahlbeck, "The 'Veepstakes'," *American Political Science Review* 91 (1997): 855–864.

24 L. Sandy Maisel, "The Platform-Writing Process," *Political Science Quarterly* 108 (1993–1994): 671–699.

25 Gerald M. Pomper, "Party Responsibility and the Future of American Democracy," in Jeffrey E. Cohen, Richard Fleisher, and Paul Kantor, eds., *American Political Parties: Decline or Resurgence?* (Washington, DC: CQ Press, 2001), pp. 170–172.

26 These data and those cited in the rest of the chapter come from the *New York Times*/CBS News Polls of Democratic and Republican National Convention delegates.

27 See John W. Soule and Wilma E. McGrath, "A Comparative Study of Presidential Nomination Conventions," *American Journal of Political Science* 19 (1975): 501–517.

28 Geoffrey C. Layman, "Party Activists," in Hershey, ed., *Guide to U.S. Political Parties*, Chapter 16, and Kenny J. Whitby, *Strategic Decision-making in Presidential Nominations* (Albany, NY: SUNY Press, 2014). See also Priscilla L. Southwell, "A Backroom without the Smoke?" *Party Politics* 18 (2012): 267–283.
29 Shafer, *Bifurcated Politics*, Chapter 8; and Costas Panagopoulos, ed., *Rewiring Politics* (Baton Rouge, LA: Louisiana State University Press, 2007).
30 See, for example, Peter Marks, "This Convention Isn't Just Efficient," *Washington Post*, August 21, 2020,
31 See Nelson W. Polsby, *Consequences of Party Reform* (Oxford: Oxford University Press, 1983), and Cohen, Karol, Noel, and Zaller, *The Party Decides*.
32 See Emmett H. Buell, Jr., "The Changing Face of the New Hampshire Primary," in William G. Mayer, ed., *In Pursuit of the White House 2000* (New York: Chatham House, 2000), pp. 87–144.
33 Polsby, *Consequences of Party Reform*.
34 See Caroline Tolbert and Peverill Squire, eds., "Reforming the Presidential Nominating Process," *PS: Political Science and Politics* 42 (2009): 27–79.
35 See Rauch and La Raja, "Too Much Democracy."

CHAPTER 11

The General Election

A sign at a Bernie Sanders campaign rally in Washington State read, "Obi-Wan Bernobi—He's our only hope." Hundreds of thousands of young Americans came out to support Sen. Sanders in his campaign for the 2020 Democratic presidential nomination, energized by Sanders's focus on income inequality, his fighting spirit, and his rebellion against "the establishment."[1] The enthusiasm Sanders generated worried many other Democratic elected officials. Though he was the Democratic front-runner in the first two nominating events in Iowa and New Hampshire, several Democratic party leaders warned that Sanders's outspoken defense of democratic socialism and questions about his health would make his nomination a disaster. The party would squander its opportunity to defeat Donald Trump, they insisted, unless Sanders left the race. If his party leadership wanted Sanders to stop running, then why didn't he? Because the party leaders don't run today's campaigns. The candidates and their supporters do. And candidate Sanders vowed to keep on campaigning.

This isn't the way campaigns used to work. Most campaigns were **party centered** until the mid-1900s: party leaders managed candidates' campaigns with the party's interests as their main focus, just as they do today in most other democracies. State and local party organizations provided most of the money and volunteers used by candidates.

But a series of changes were undermining parties' control over campaigns. Reformers pushed for greater use of primary elections. Because it is risky for a party to take sides in a primary (see Chapter 4), candidates had to compete for their party's nomination by creating their own campaign organization, which they usually keep and expand after winning the primary. State and local party organizations were weakened by other reforms, ranging from civil service laws to nonpartisan elections, and their flow of volunteers dried up (see Chapter 3). Some public relations experts specialized in political consulting and provided the services—for a fee, of course—that the parties had provided for free (or at least for no monetary payment) in earlier years.

These changes freed candidates from having to depend on their parties for money, volunteers, and advice. Campaigns became more **candidate centered,** directed by the candidates and their staffs and consultants rather than by the party organizations and focusing on the candidate's needs, not the party's. But as they have throughout their long lives, the parties adjusted to these changes.[2] This chapter will look at the technologies, information sources, and means of persuasion that candidates now have, which contribute to the candidate-centered nature of most campaigns. But party organizations have been able to reclaim an important role in at least some campaigns, which we'll explore as well.

Campaign Strategy

Designing strategy for a general election campaign[3] differs in several ways from that in a primary. Campaigning in a primary election focuses mainly on party voters, especially in states with closed primaries (see Chapter 9). In contrast, the general election audience is much larger, more diverse, and can observe the candidates for a longer time. The general election campaign is also powerfully affected by whether the candidate's party is in the majority or the minority in that district (see box "Getting Out the Base in 2020—and 2024?" on page 239).

In both primary and general election campaigns, however, one of the best ways to win is to already hold the office you seek.[4] Incumbents normally have greater name recognition and more success in attracting (usually favorable) media coverage than do their potential opponents. Their constituent service and paid travel back to the district give them a substantial edge over their challengers, unless they throw it away due to scandal. Their access to power makes it easier for incumbents to raise as much campaign money as they think they need, and their experience helps them use it effectively. Also, incumbents are usually part of the majority party in the district. Because of these advantages, in both primaries and general elections, incumbents often need to do little more than stress their understanding of the district, their trustworthiness, and their commitment to widely shared values—that is, unless their opponent's party runs the table in a national sweep (an increasingly frequent event).

Challengers face a much harsher campaign environment. Especially if they have not won any other political office before, challengers do not start with an experienced organization, proven fund-raising skills, or the other incumbent advantages.[5] In the days when party organizations ran campaigns, this might not have been a problem. At a time of candidate-centered campaigns, it is. One obvious answer might be to purchase an experienced campaign organization by hiring skilled consultants, but most challengers don't have the money. Thus, the predictable cycle begins: The challenger lacks an existing organization and enough money to attract the interest of well-known consultants and buy media time, so he or she cannot reach many voters. Without these vital resources, a challenger will not rise in the polls or raise enough money to become better known.

No matter how resource-poor they are, however, challengers can raise issues. Thus, policy issues such as abortion, health care, and taxes are more important tools for challengers than they are for incumbents.[6] Researchers find that challengers usually do better when they campaign on issues "owned" by their party, such as health care and Social Security for Democrats and national defense and taxes for Republicans.[7] But even the most powerful issues won't do a challenger much good if he or she can't attract the money or media coverage needed to publicize them.

Candidates for open seats (those where no incumbent is running) are more likely to run competitive races. Typically, people who choose to run for highly

Getting Out the Base in 2020—and 2024?

President Trump's campaign strategists knew that he had a very loyal base of support: older white men, conservatives, Christian evangelicals. The strategists also knew that these groups were not a majority of voters. In these polarized times, campaigners must evaluate two approaches to winning office. One is the "base strategy": identify the people who already support your candidate, make sure they're registered, and motivate them to get out and vote (and mobilize their friends as well). The other is a persuasion strategy: locate people who are undecided or only weakly committed, show them why your candidate serves their needs, and get them to the polls.

Lots of evidence convinced the Trump staff that a base strategy was their best choice. Feelings about the president had remained unusually stable over four years; his public approval rating rarely rose above or dipped below the low 40s. Most Republicans adored him; their Trump approval averaged almost 90 percent. And most Democrats abhorred him. These attitudes hardened and weaponized during the impeachment process in 2019–2020. Not many Americans were undecided as to whether they liked Donald J. Trump. If there weren't many voters open to persuasion, then the logical plan was to focus laser-like on Trump's supporters and, in a nation with comparatively low voting turnout, make sure they got to the polls.

But there was an alternative argument. Researchers using data from Catalist, which maintains a mammoth database of voter records and preferences, reported in 2019 that most of the Democratic gains in the 2018 midterms came from among people who had reluctantly supported Trump in 2016. They had either disliked Hillary Clinton more or they valued Trump's hard-charging anti-immigration, pro-life, and other conservative stands, even though they disliked Trump himself. For some of these reluctant Trump voters, two years of the Trump administration changed their minds and led them to vote Democratic in 2018. If even 10 percent of prospective voters could be influenced like this in 2020, then a persuasion strategy must be added.

The Trump campaign had enough money to do both. To a lesser extent, so did the campaign of his Democratic rival, Joe Biden. Below the presidential level, most campaigns don't. They study the data; they assess whether their candidate is more at home with a base or a persuasion strategy, and then they make their choice. That choice—whether to rely primarily on mobilizing their base or persuading the persuadable—may determine their candidate's fate. Then, if they have the resources, they will keep polling for signs that the number of persuadable voters is growing or shrinking and adjust their plans accordingly.

If you are managing a 2024 presidential campaign, which approach would you take? On the Republican side, will appeals to your conservative Christian base weaken your support among the growing numbers of minority voters? If you're a Democrat, can you motivate your base to go to the polls without prompting a counter-mobilization among Republicans? If your strategy works, you'll be hailed as a genius, and your party's candidates in 2028 will compete to hire you. If it doesn't, expect to be a frequent butt of jokes on social media.[8]

visible offices—the presidency, governorships, Senate seats—already have considerable name recognition, which increases because of the attention given to an open seat race. They can attract enough funds to pay for extensive media campaigns. Their major challenge will be to spend their money effectively and to define themselves to the voters before their opponent gets the chance to define them.

How Campaigning Has Changed

Candidates now have campaign tools that would have been the envy of campaigners decades ago. Advances in data analytics, social media, voter targeting, and fund-raising have revolutionized campaigning.

Sources of Information

Polls and Big Databases   In big and competitive races, campaigns want to gather as much information as they can about each prospective voter, from issue attitudes to voting histories. Voting records, social media, and public opinion polls are the chief sources of this information.[9] The national party organizations also combine information gained from "frequent shopper" cards, other consumer databases, and the tracking of individuals' Internet browsing into massive databases on voters' attitudes, as you'll soon see.

Computers   The resulting databases are mined for patterns, such as which types of voters get triggered by which issues, what mobilizes them, and how they feel about the campaign. Before computers were used in campaigns, candidates relied on guesswork and the opinions of highly regarded political advisers to guide their choices. Now, big-budget campaigns can test the predicted effects of hundreds of alternative strategies on their computerized voter models. Campaign strategists can then create evidence-based plans for buying media time and selecting ad content. Fund-raisers can compare the amounts of money raised by different appeals. Opposition ("oppo") researchers can locate statements made by the opposing candidate on any conceivable issue. Social media marketing campaigns can be analyzed for impact and then fine-tuned.

Professional Consultants

Political consultants specialize in particular campaign services.[10] Some consultants buy media time for advertising, focusing on what programs or times of day will benefit each of their candidate clients. Others deal mainly with web-page design or canvassing or direct-mail fund-raising. Professional consultants usually work for several different campaigns at a time, but they almost always work with clients from only one party. Some consultants restrict themselves even further to one ideological grouping within the party. Although they function independently of the party organization, they normally try to keep a cooperative relationship with the party's leaders. National party committees often play a matchmaking role in bringing together consultants and candidates.

Methods of Persuasion: The Air War

Because of the large size of most state and federal election districts, candidates (and national parties as well) make extensive use of mass media, especially television, radio, and the Internet.

Television

Television consumes most of a typical campaign's budget. In the early and inexpensive days of TV, candidates bought large chunks of time to air entire speeches to a wide audience. Now, because of TV's increased cost and voters' shorter attention spans, campaign messages are compressed into 30-second spot ads that can be run frequently.[11] Media specialists carefully target the placement of these ads. If a candidate wants to appeal to middle-aged men, for instance, then the specialist might run ads on *NCIS* and *Monday Night Football*. In midterm congressional races, where older people are a larger proportion of voters than in presidential elections, consultants reach older viewers by placing ads on *Good Morning America, Today*, and *CBS This Morning*. The value of broadcast advertising has been reduced by technology that can screen out campaign ads, from the "mute" button to TV Ad Blocker, but these ads remain a staple of campaigns that can afford them.

Cable TV is a cost-effective alternative to the traditional networks and works especially well in local campaigns, whose constituencies are too small to warrant buying time in major media markets. Most cable stations, such as Fox News and CBN (Christian Broadcasting Network), have more specialized "niche" audiences than do the bigger networks. This makes it easier for campaigns to target their ads to types of viewers likely to support them (called **narrowcasting**).

Campaigns also try to get as much **free media** coverage as possible on TV, radio, and online news and in newspapers. (Campaigners prefer to call it **earned media.**) When newscasts and print reporters cover a candidate, the information may seem more credible and "objective" than if it is conveyed through the campaign's own ads.

To get free media coverage, campaigns need to provide material that meets the media's definition of "news."[12] If "news" is that which is dramatic, controversial, and immediate, then a candidate is not likely to earn media coverage by delivering the same speech one more time, no matter how important the issue. Dave Barry offers this illustration:

> Let's consider two headlines. FIRST HEADLINE: 'Federal Reserve Board Ponders Reversal of Postponement of Deferral of Policy Reconsideration.' SECOND HEADLINE: 'Federal Reserve Board Caught in Motel with Under-age Sheep.' Be honest, now. Which of these two stories would you read?[13]

Candidates who depend on free media need to stage campaign events that use the tamer, political equivalent of the underage sheep: dramatic confrontations, exciting settings, or meetings with well-known or telegenic people.

But free media coverage of campaigns is all too brief. Even close to Election Day, viewers are typically exposed to less than two minutes of election news during a 30-minute local newscast, most of it discussing strategy and polls, compared with four and a half minutes of paid political ads.[14] And the shrinking number of local newspapers, covering less political news, allows more Americans to avoid political news altogether. The political information these news avoiders receive, then, comes entirely from campaign ads and entertainment programming.[15] This decline in local political coverage has been linked to less political knowledge and lower voter turnout.[16]

The Internet

First used by candidates in 1996, websites are now a part of every major campaign and many local races as well. Campaigns can reach their supporters directly on the Internet, thus bypassing the choices made by the broadcast media. Many websites ask visitors to register, which allows the campaign to contact them later. By loading ads online—on YouTube, for instance—campaigners can get their messages distributed nationally without paying for costly TV time.

Media buyers also place campaign ads as pop-ups on other Internet sites, or as "pre-rolls" on YouTube. Both parties buy ads on Google, so that when someone enters a search term indicating her political sympathies (for instance, "Black Lives Matter"), a pop-up ad could appear later featuring the party or candidate closest to those views. People clicking on the ad are directed to a page where they can donate funds. By examining the "take," a consultant can measure which search terms brought the best results. Campaigns now create ads designed specifically for online use, rather than just posting made-for-TV ads on social media or other platforms. And although people under the age of 30 are most likely to be Internet users, older adults who use the Internet are increasingly likely to watch political videos and share election news online.[17]

In short, the broadcast media are an efficient way to reach large numbers of prospective voters. Their greatest strength, however—the breadth of their reach—is also one of their greatest weaknesses. (The other is their high cost.) If you were running for office, you would want to target different messages to different kinds of people so that you could speak to each individual about the issue that most concerns him or her.

Direct Contact by Mail, Text, and Social Media

Direct Mail   By merging postal mail lists of people who are of special interest to a campaign, consultants can direct personalized letters to millions of people who might be inclined to respond to a particular appeal. A candidate who wants to appeal to pro-gun voters, for example, could send computer-generated letters to people on mailing lists of the National Rifle Association, donors to other pro-gun candidates, and subscribers to hunting magazines. Because these messages are designed to be read by like-minded individuals in the privacy of their homes, direct-mail appeals can be highly emotional and inflammatory, appeals that would not work as well in the broadcast media.

E-mail   E-mail has the great advantage that it is cheaper than regular mail; fund-raising using e-mail and websites costs about one penny for each dollar raised, compared with about 40 cents per dollar raised by direct (postal) mail.[18] Online fund-raising remains the primary source of donations in federal campaigns and for many state and local candidates as well. The 2020 Trump reelection campaign took online fund-raising to new heights, raising $8.5 million in just two days after House Speaker Nancy Pelosi announced the effort to impeach Trump.[19] Joe Biden, who didn't secure his party's nomination until months later, had to work hard to catch up.

Text Messaging   Because postal mail misses large numbers of young people whose addresses change from year to year, campaigns increasingly use texting to contact supporters.[20] One of the most recent innovations is the use of "peer to peer" texting apps, in which a campaign volunteer can send hundreds of messages an hour, avoiding federal regulations by clicking "send" one message at a time, and keeping the source of the text anonymous. The Trump campaign used social media in 2020 to collect phone numbers and other contact information from prospective supporters, ironically, to work around Facebook and Google, which they believed were biased against them. Trump staffers offered campaign gear to attenders at rallies in return for cell numbers, claiming that their phones would turn them into "the army of Trump."[21] Biden's campaign gathered phone numbers by announcing that he'd reveal his vice-presidential pick by text.

Facebook   Nevertheless, social media remain central to campaigning. About 220 million U.S. users log in to Facebook each month, and in doing so they provide the platform with a rich stock of information about their personal lives: what they like, where they travel, what groups they associate with. Campaigns can use these data to direct appeals to very specifically targeted types of people, without making their strategy more broadly known. By urging each recipient to forward an appeal to an individual's friends on this or other social networks, a campaign can increase its reach exponentially at low cost, called viral marketing. In 2016, the Trump campaign spent $70 million testing literally hundreds of thousands of different messages to see which ones went viral.[22] Younger people relied more on Tik Tok and YouTube for campaign information; Tik Tok users actually reduced the audience at Trump's first post-shutdown campaign rally in 2020 by reserving massive numbers of seats and then not showing up.

Twitter   Although Facebook has a broader audience, politically minded Twitter users are more apt to follow breaking news on the site than are similarly interested posters on Facebook. Campaigns can segment the Twitter audience according to individuals' expressed interest, just as they can on Facebook. Posts on both of these sites carry much more negative messages about the candidates than do the mainstream media.[23] Both social networking sites have exploded as information sources; Twitter's active users have been growing by about 20 percent a year recently.[24] So candidates rely increasingly on Twitter; Trump, for instance, began his presidency by tweeting an average of 100 times a month, but by late 2019, he was averaging over 700 a month, with more than 400 tweets in one week in December.[25] These tweets in turn generated lavish free media coverage for Trump, whose pronouncements on Twitter were like catnip for journalists. Biden was much less active on Twitter, averaging only six to ten tweets a day.

The Ground War: "Under the Radar"

One of the most effective ways to persuade voters is to talk with them one-on-one. House-to house canvassing and phone calls to selected individuals are known as the **ground war.** Canvassing has been reinvigorated in the 2000s, now that it has been married to high-tech advances in voter targeting. However, canvassers in 2020 had to adapt to social distancing measures that reduce its impact.

Canvassing and Phone Banks

In the days of machine politics, party organizations sent their patronage workers and other activists to the homes of people who might vote for party candidates, to tell them about the party ticket. Democratic local party organizations were especially adept at door-to-door canvassing, often using labor union volunteers. These efforts declined in the late 1900s, because parties found it harder to enlist willing workers. But the recent increase in party polarization has motivated new volunteers. And arming canvassers with extensive information about the individuals they are trying to persuade gives the ground war a powerful new weapon. The Republicans moved first, experimenting with a canvassing program in the 2002 midterm elections. They flooded precincts in some competitive states with volunteers and paid staffers, especially during the last 72 hours of the campaign. This **72-hour project** was expensive, costing $200 million, but observers felt that it increased Republican turnout by about 3 percent over that of the last midterm election. Republicans won most of the close contests, maintained control of the House, and narrowly regained control of the Senate.[26] Thus, they greatly expanded the 72-hour project in 2004 based on the concept of **micro-targeting** or "niche marketing."

Micro-Targeting

If you knock on every door in a big city, you'll reach a lot of Democrats. Republican voters are not as concentrated geographically as Democrats tend to be. So Republican strategists determined in the early 2000s that they would have to use more high-tech means to locate likely Republican voters. Drawing on market research techniques developed by their business allies, the national Republicans turned to micro-targeting: using electoral and consumer data to pinpoint the interests of individuals and then delivering a message tailored to their particular concerns.[27] Republicans collected data on millions of people's voting histories, viewing habits, magazine subscriptions, and buying preferences. They entered these data into a national Republican database called **Voter Vault**. Analysis of the data showed, for instance, that people who tune in to country or religious stations, Fox News, or the Golf Channel, and drive BMWs rather than Chevys, are more inclined to support Republicans. Although these consumer preferences may not be as predictive of political behavior as are strictly political data (such as voter registration lists in states where people register by party), they can help to flesh out a picture of each voter (see box "What the National Parties Probably Know about You" on page 246).

With these massive databases, the campaign and the Republican National Committee (RNC), in coordination with Republican state and local parties, worked to cherry-pick likely Republican voters in the 2004 election. They focused especially on seven million likely Republicans and ten million conservative-leaning independents who had not voted regularly in the past. Then they classified these targets into a series of types and determined which issues were most likely to activate voters in each type. One voter type could be approached with a personal contact or phone call dealing with same-sex marriage; another might receive an appeal about terrorism.

This Republican success in the ground war led the national Democrats to ramp up their own program beginning in 2008. Democrats quickly developed the staff; the experts with particular skill at cutting-edge data analytics tended to be social liberals, and in 2008 and 2012, they were hired in large numbers by the Obama campaign, where they transformed the ground war. In 2012, for instance, Obama's presidential campaign claimed to have recruited 2.3 million volunteers and knocked on seven million doors on one day alone.[28] The program seemed effective; one careful study found that in 2012, the two presidential candidates' canvassing, phoning, and mail appeals to voters increased turnout by 7 percentage points in battleground states.[29]

Then the Republicans regained the lead. Americans for Prosperity, a tax-exempt non-profit conservative group organized by oil billionaires David and Charles Koch, helped Republicans expand their data collection for 2014 and 2016. The RNC funded much of the effort.[30] Although barebones in many other ways, the Donald Trump campaign in 2016 put extensive effort into gathering voter information using Facebook. As one reporter noted about the 2020 Trump campaign,

> These days, campaigns can carve the electorate into creepily thin segments: Gold Star moms near military bases, paintball-playing widowers in the Florida Panhandle, recovering addicts in Michigan's Upper Peninsula. And, for anyone who wants to reach a specific audience with an actionable message, there has never been a platform as potent as Facebook.[31]

What the National Parties Probably Know About You

The two national parties know more about you than many of your friends do. For starters, both parties' national committees have probably bought or received from state election officials all the information you provided if you registered to vote. The information varies by state, but it likely includes your name, address, sex, age, whether you asked for a Republican or Democratic ballot in primary elections, whether or not you voted in previous general elections (though not *how* you voted), and in some states, your party affiliation and race. To this base of information, the national parties add data they buy from vendors, such as your contact information, any campaign contributions you've made, and Census data about your area's demographics and voting trends, as well as whether you hold a hunting or fishing license. Three of the most common bits of information are your education, your income, and your religious affiliation. In 2020, the Trump campaign, for instance, claimed to have 3,000 bits of information about each American. Even if you have not registered to vote, you are still likely to be in the parties' databases, minus the information gathered when people register.

The national parties may then choose to add more personalized information about you. When a party canvasser comes to your door, he or she may ask about your issue and candidate preferences and add them to your record in the party's database. Your online viewing habits can be tracked by the parties, just as they are by a variety of advertisers. By buying data from supermarkets and other merchandisers using "customer loyalty" cards, they can find out about your consumption patterns and your credit history. So the parties are likely to know whether you answer e-mail and, if so, at what time of day; whether you prefer Coors or Miller beer, own a gun, belong to a church, a mosque, or Hillel, and what issue angers you the most.

Why do the parties want to know all this about you? Because campaigns and party organizations can use these data to predict the chance you'll vote in a primary or general election, whether you are a likely supporter, and the types of campaign appeals to which you'll respond most positively. That lets the party determine whether to contact you, how often, and the issues most likely to trigger your support. It can also use micro-targeting to send you a different message from the one sent to your neighbor. As a journalist noted,

> An ad that calls for defunding Planned Parenthood might get a mixed response from a large national audience, but serve it directly via Facebook to 800 Roman Catholic women in Dubuque, Iowa, and its reception will be much more positive.... micro-targeting allows candidates to sidle up to millions of voters and whisper personalized messages in their ear.[32]

Some of the data in your file is likely to be false; when parties buy data from many different sources, some will include mistakes. But by assembling hundreds of bits of information about you, the national parties (as well as a variety of corporations) can develop a fairly accurate picture of your interests and behavior.

Data Trust, a private corporation founded by conservatives in 2011, became the platform used by the Trump campaign, the RNC, and other Republican and conservative groups to expand Republicans' voter database.

The Democrats' advantage had faded after 2012. Therefore, Democratic groups and individuals began again in 2019 to rebuild their voter database. Groups such as the Democratic Data Exchange, the nonprofit group Alloy, and data-sharing arrangements among state parties worked to ramp up in time for the 2020 election.

Campaigning During a Pandemic

The corona virus pandemic affected campaigning in 2020, just as it did every other aspect of life. Once a campaign has a huge database of its likely voters, the best way to persuade those voters is through personal contact. But the need for social distancing to limit the spread of the virus made person-to-person canvassing risky at best, and usually, impossible. Campaigners could still use their databases to micro-target through phone calls, direct mail pieces, email, and text, but their inability to canvass door-to-door left many campaigners—local candidates, for instance, who often depend heavily on face-to-face contact with voters—at a loss as to how to win votes.

Media use surged during the pandemic. Candidates with enough resources to buy media ads, then, put increased emphasis on the internet, TV, and radio. The problem was what to say. Incumbents could broadcast messages of reassurance and offer information about local resources during the pandemic. Suppose, however, that you were a challenger at this time. You knew that incumbents' reelection rate is at least 90 percent, so unless you convinced voters that their incumbent was doing a bad job and should be replaced, you stood little chance. Negative ads are typically more memorable than positive ones, but how would attack ads look in a time of crisis? As always, the nature of the political and social environment at the time posed different challenges for some types of candidates from those posed for others.[33]

Canvassing is not a magic bullet under any circumstances. Joe Biden won big victories in Super Tuesday primaries in 2020 even in states where he had no field organization. Canvassing may not hit its intended targets.[34] Campaigns have to select their canvassers carefully; those whose characteristics do not match those of the area they're canvassing can do more harm than good. But when combined with micro-targeting, the ground war can be effective in changing attitudes under some conditions[35]; it's another example of "old politics" becoming cutting-edge again.

In addition to door-to-door canvassing, many campaigns bring supporters to a central location (a **phone bank**) with telephones—often a business, union, or party or campaign headquarters, or even an empty building where volunteers can use their smartphones—to dial lists of numbers identified by the campaign's micro-targeting. Phone banking is cheaper than door-to-door contact, though usually not as persuasive. Even cheaper are virtual phone banks, where supporters anywhere in the nation go online to get a list of phone numbers and a script to read, and **robocalls,** in which volunteers or computers can direct automated phone calls to large numbers of people on a campaign's target list. Robocalls are often used to send a negative message or to do **push polling**—attack messages disguised as public opinion polls. In high-profile races, households may receive several of these calls a night as the election approaches. These techniques have limits, too: Caller ID lets people screen their calls, and the growing number of cell-phone-only individuals makes calling more costly.

Negative Campaigning

Negative campaigning is nothing new; political figures have been viciously attacked personally as well as ideologically since the U.S. began. But negative advertising seems to be on the increase recently. News media cover negative ads more than positive ads, because conflict and controversy better fit the media definition of "news." Media coverage of these negative ads then carries their message to even more people.[36] Party independent spending, super PACs (see Chapter 12), and other outside groups have been responsible for most of the negative ads. This benefits candidates, who don't have to take the blame for "going negative" because the damaging information is being aired by others.[37]

Much recent evidence suggests that negative campaigning can be effective under some conditions. Negative ads are often particularly memorable and emotionally engaging; that can increase voter information and turnout. Attack ads probably do their worst damage to candidates who are less well known to the public—challengers, for instance—because their public images are not yet fixed. The timing of the ads matters as well. Before an individual chooses a candidate, negative ads can be informative and useful. After the individual has made his or her choice, attack ads are more likely to depress turnout, especially among people who are not strong partisans.[38] But negative ads by parties or outside groups are more risky for a campaign when they emphasize an issue the candidate doesn't want to stress or when their tone is harsh enough to offend viewers.

Putting These Tools to Work

These campaign tools have been used in a variety of ways in recent elections. In addition to the innovations in online and ground-war techniques, the environment of American campaigns has changed fundamentally.

Democrats Recover in 2012 from a "Shellacking"

Democratic candidates had experienced major losses in the midterm congressional elections of 2010. President Obama's approval rating had slipped below 50 percent; Republicans, led by the anti-tax Tea Party, reviled Obama's signature health insurance program (the Affordable Care Act, which Republicans called "Obamacare"), and the economic recovery from the Great Recession of 2007 was proceeding only slowly. So even though Democrats outspent and won more House votes than Republicans did, Republicans gained a House majority by winning 66 seats against only three losses—the biggest gain by either party since 1948. The GOP gained six Senate seats (but not majority control) and six governorships, plus more than 700 state legislative seats. It was, as Obama called it, a "shellacking."

Yet the parties' voter support was still balanced enough that the Democrats were able to regain strength in 2012. Although real incomes were only slightly higher than four years earlier and the unemployment rate remained high, the income growth rate increased in September, just in time to allay some of the economic pessimism and boost Obama's prospects of reelection.[39] And much of the public pinned the lion's share of the blame for the recession on George W. Bush, Obama's predecessor.

But the Obama campaign knew that economic confidence was still low in 2012 and the president's approval ratings remained marginal. So they began their air war very early, in May, with heavy ad spending to define Republican nominee Mitt Romney to a national audience before Romney had the chance to define himself. Obama ads portrayed the Republican as a super-rich, heartless corporate raider with little understanding of ordinary people's lives. Romney inadvertently confirmed the image by commenting at what he thought was a private fund-raiser that 47 percent of Americans think government has a responsibility to provide them with health care, food, and housing, so they don't take personal responsibility for their own lives. The comments went viral.

The Obama campaign emphasized its ground game as well, with an elaborate network of field offices. Obama's organization relied on a massive, integrated database to mobilize occasional voters inclined to favor Obama and to raise unprecedented sums from small donors. Romney got more help than Obama from very well-funded outside groups, but the Republicans' post-election self-study concluded that this funding, spent mainly on TV advertising (the air war), had not brought enough of a return in votes.[40]

Obama won reelection, but most demographic groups gave him less support in 2012 than in 2008. Latino Americans were an important exception. Romney took a hard line on immigration, suggesting that undocumented immigrants "self-deport." One Republican activist complained that increasing the Republican vote among Latinos is impossible when "some Republicans talk as if they're for the deportation of your mother or your aunt."[41] Romney found himself in a difficult spot on this and other issues. Because his main primary competitors were extremely conservative, he was pushed to take far-right positions to win Republican primaries and caucuses. But that left him unable to appeal effectively in the general election campaign to Latinos and others who rejected these positions.

Republicans Strike Back in 2014

The Democrats faced a more hostile terrain in 2014. President Obama's approval ratings were dropping. Polls showed that Republican voters were much more engaged in the campaign than were Democrats. The midterm electorate would be more receptive to Republicans. The Senate incumbents who were up for reelection had last been elected in the Democratic wave of 2008, leaving many of them "exposed." Democrats had to defend 21 Senate seats in 2014, seven of them in states won by Romney in 2012; Republicans had to defend only 15. On top of all these disadvantages, the states electing senators in 2014 tended to be smaller and more conservative than the states comprising the other two Senate election cycles.

Republicans used their improved data analytics to tie each Democratic candidate to President Obama and to public discontent with "Obamacare." Spending by both party and non-party groups reached new heights (see Chapter 12). "Dark money" groups (nonprofit, tax exempt "social welfare" organizations allowed by federal law to keep the names of their donors secret), and super PACs, both of which can accept unlimited donations from individuals, corporations, and unions, blanketed the airwaves.

Then a series of frightening news stories appeared just before the election: terrorism by the Islamic State, a major outbreak of the Ebola virus in Africa, a rush of undocumented children crossing into the U.S. from Mexico. Everything pointed to a Democratic defeat, but the outcome was even worse than Democrats feared. Republicans gained a net 13 seats in the House, for a total of 247, their biggest House majority since the 1920s. With a switch of nine Senate seats from Democratic to Republican, the Republicans now held majorities in both houses of Congress, though the Senate majority was slim.

2016: The Unprecedented Campaign

Then came the strangest nomination race in years. The Republican field was exceptionally large; 17 candidates sought to replace the retiring President Obama. The most unusual of these was real-estate mogul Donald Trump, a billionaire businessman and reality TV star (*The Apprentice*) with a talent for attracting media attention with his bombastic comments.

Trump seemed to be breaking all the traditional rules of presidential campaigning. He spent very little on polls and ads until late in the campaign, relying heavily instead on the enormous amount of free media coverage he received. He leveled no-holds-barred attacks on other candidates, as well as Latinos, Muslims, women, and major media outlets. His rhetoric seemed to tap into the anger of many in the Republican base. He campaigned as a big-government Republican, promising not to cut Medicare or Social Security, which deviated from conservative orthodoxy. Because of his unconventional style and his departures from the stands taken by mainstream Republicans, analysts expected Trump's candidacy to flame out quickly. It didn't.

Trump attracted about 45 percent of the vote in Republican primaries and caucuses, but that was enough, in a multi-candidate race that relied mainly on winner-take-all rules, to lock up his party's nomination. His challenges continued, however.

Trump's public image was much more unfavorable than that of any previous presidential candidate. It didn't help that he was frequently caught in outright lies about his businesses, his international experience, and his opponent, to the point where even conservative journalists began referring to him as a "master fabulist" and a "short-fingered vulgarian."[42] His campaign was understaffed and inexperienced, though that helped support his image as an outsider.

The Democratic campaign was unprecedented as well. Former Secretary of State Hillary Clinton became the first woman to win a major party's presidential nomination, after a close race against Sen. Bernie Sanders. Under normal circumstances, this would have been a tough year for Democrats; when one party has held the White House for two terms, the other party is favored to win. And Clinton had the second-worst approval ratings of all recent presidential nominees, coming in just above Trump. In the end, the intense media focus on alleged corruption charges against Clinton, spotlighted by an eleventh-hour FBI investigation, let most Republicans overcome their qualms about their candidate; the percentage of self-identified Republicans supporting Trump was slightly higher than the percentage of Democrats voting for Clinton.

The unprecedented campaign had an almost unprecedented result. Clinton won the popular vote by three percentage points, but Trump won the Electoral College vote on the backs of narrow victories in Michigan, Wisconsin, and Pennsylvania. This was only the fourth presidential race, though the second in 16 years, in which the popular vote winner failed to reach the White House. The pivotal role of those three states led to theories that white, working-class men (typically defined as men without a college degree) put Trump over the top in 2016. Indeed, this group did vote Republican in larger proportions that year than in other recent elections, though studies showed that their support had less to do with their financial struggles than with immigration and racial resentment: the belief that whites were being discriminated against.[43] Whites without college degrees who were more worried about their economic status tended to support Clinton, as did women and those with college degrees.[44]

Yet in contrast to many analysts' claim that Trump had reshaped the Republican coalition, his support resembled the coalitions that had supported previous Republican candidates: voters with higher incomes, rural and exurban whites, and conservative Christians. African-Americans, who characteristically supported Clinton overwhelmingly, turned out to vote less than they had for Obama; black turnout was down almost 8 percentage points from 2012. One analyst suggested,

> In 2016, conservatives who felt disenfranchised were desperate to get back into power. Many would overlook or put up with what they believed were the many leadership shortcomings of Donald Trump if he could help them prevent the continuation of what they saw as the radical misrule of the Obama years.[45]

In short, despite the peculiarities of the 2016 presidential race, party identification continued to shape people's candidate perceptions.

The High-Turnout Midterm of 2018

Just as the 2016 presidential race was all about Donald Trump, so were the 2018 congressional elections. Trump's name wasn't on the ballot, but he overshadowed those who were. Although Republicans had majority control of both the House and Senate, Republican infighting had limited the party's accomplishments in Congress. Trump's main legislative victory, a tax cut directed largely at upper-income people and corporations, proved less than effective as a campaign issue. Yet Republican congressional candidates felt they had little choice but to tie themselves tightly to the lightning-rod president and his white, rural base, focusing on issues of illegal immigration and crime. Democrats, many of whom "found a Trump presidency to be an abomination," instead emphasized jobs and Trump's threats to the Affordable Care Act.[46]

The result was a Democratic wave. The party netted 41 House seats and control of the chamber, the biggest Democratic House gain since Watergate in 1974. Republicans were protected in the Senate by the fact that three quarters of the contested seats were held by Democrats, who kept all but two. The Democratic tide swept state legislative contests as well. Democrats had lost more than 900 state legislative seats during the Obama administration, so the GOP entered 2018 with unified party control of the governorship and both houses of the legislature in 24 states. After the midterm, Republicans retained 22 of those states, but those with unified Democratic control jumped from just 6 to 14.

Both parties' coalitions shifted slightly in 2018, as they usually do in midterm elections. Republican losses stemmed in part from the drop in turnout of whites without college degrees. In two of Trump's key 2016 states, Michigan and Wisconsin, voters replaced Republican governors with Democrats. Women, suburbanites, and college-educated people voted more Democratic than usual, and the numbers of women running for office rose dramatically. Turnout increased across the board, making this the highest turnout midterm in a century. Young people's turnout went way up as well, though not enough to match the turnout of the elderly. But Democrats hoped that the higher youth turnout would carry over into the 2020 elections.

The 2020 Election: The Nightmare on Main Street

Early in 2020, the corona virus pandemic hit the U.S. Tens of thousands got sick; ultimately, hundreds of thousands would die. Climate change was speeding up. And then things got more stressful. The killings of several unarmed black Americans by police—tragically recurrent in U.S. cities—led to massive urban protests from coast to coast. Even before these powerful events, emotions were running high in the presidential election, focusing largely on President Trump. After first trying to downplay the seriousness of the pandemic, Trump outraged many Americans with his inconsistent response to it. Others were outraged by the racial protests or by the police efforts to quell them.[47] In this combustible atmosphere, the Trump Republicans faced off against the Biden Democrats.

The two campaigns' strategies depended heavily on their interpretations of the 2018 midterm results. Many Democratic strategists believed that their party's successes in 2018 were powered by increased turnout, because voters' partisanship and attitudes toward Trump were largely fixed. Other researchers provided different evidence: that the Democratic gains owed more to former Trump voters who had re-thought their choices by 2018, and therefore, enough swing voters remained to offer an attractive target.[48]

But there was no dispute about where the campaign had to be fought. For years, presidential elections had focused on a relatively small number of swing states. In 2020, it was the Democrats' job to expand that number: to put more Republican-leaning states into play. As the pandemic worsened, formerly Republican states such as Arizona, North Carolina, and Iowa leaned toward Biden. Even previously nonpartisan matters such as voting by mail were pulled into the partisan vortex, as Trump claimed repeatedly that the big expansion of voting by mail would be used by the Democrats to commit voter fraud, and therefore that the election results would be phony. At the time of the parties' conventions, a full 86 percent of registered voters said they saw issue differences between the two presidential candidates—the highest percentage in two decades.[49]

These intense differences prompted a higher voter turnout than in almost a century (though still only two-thirds of eligible voters). The biggest change from the 2016 election affected the presidential race. The Biden campaign pulled a few states – Michigan, Wisconsin, Pennsylvania, Arizona, and Georgia – from the Trump column in 2016 to create a Biden victory in 2020.

Below the presidential level, however, Democratic candidates underperformed. Republicans gained seats in the U.S. House and retained a slim Senate majority (pending two runoffs scheduled for January 2021). Democrats had hoped to pick up majority control of several state legislatures in time to redistrict legislative seats after the 2020 Census. However, Republicans kept their lock on most state legislative majorities, thus extending into the new decade a Republican advantage in drawing legislative district lines.

The two parties' campaigns reflected very different views about the state of the nation. The Democrats stressed the need for greater access to health care (including better control of the corona virus pandemic) and racial equality, whereas the Republican coalition put highest priority on economic growth and law and order. Interestingly, counties that had lost jobs during the Trump presidency became slightly more pro-Trump in 2020, suggesting that Trump's appeal was less economic than cultural.

In all, the blue areas got bluer and the red areas got redder. Polarization reigned. The urban-rural partisan divide deepened, except that Democrats gained strength in well-to-do suburbs. And President Trump, as he had foreshadowed, refused to accept the election outcome.

As always, however, the results were interpreted in different ways. After the elections, activists fought to get their preferred interpretation of the outcome accepted, because that process would affect the party's choices in 2022 and 2024[50] (see box "Why Did Joe Biden Win in 2020?" on page 254).

Why Did Joe Biden Win in 2020?

Trump-supporting Republicans argued that voters loved Donald Trump because he stood up to the "liberal media" and elites, but the election was stolen from him. Thus, the party should remain loyal to him.

(The relatively few) Republicans opposing Trump contended that Trump's proportion of the votes had declined since 2016; he was a political liability, and the party needed to move away from populism and back to its roots.

Moderate Democrats felt that their party would have won many more races if some party liberals hadn't scared voters with mentions of democratic socialism and defunding the police. Most Americans reject these ideas as too radical, they said.

Liberal Democrats claimed that Biden Democrats were too timid; the liberals' constituents demanded radical change, including a Green New Deal and defunding the police, and the party lost support by not championing these changes.

It is common for different groups to interpret (or "spin") the meaning of an election differently, in ways that support their own preferred views. Journalists, the targets of the spin, often become cynical about it. Jon Margolis, former national political reporter for the *Chicago Tribune*, claims that he switched to the sports beat because he said he'd never seen a sports story that read, "The Chicago Cubs defeated the St. Louis Cardinals today by a score of 2–2. The Cardinals denied it." Margolis's frustration with politics would have been heightened in 2020, when President Trump denied losing re-election after having lost both the popular and electoral vote.

Sources: Margolis quoted in Ronald D. Elving, "Campaign Data Can Be Calculated Nonsense," *CQ Weekly*, August 19, 1995, p. 2602; Josh Barro, "The Crisis in the Republican Party Is Even Worse Than It Looks," *Business Insider*, May 3, 2016, at https://finance.yahoo.com/news/crisis-republican-party-even-worse-192445687.html (accessed November 11, 2020), with thanks to David Karol.

Do Campaigns Make a Difference?

Many people naturally assume that campaign events are responsible for the election's outcome, probably because campaigns attract so much media attention and massive spending. Yet careful statistical analysis shows that election results can often be predicted fairly well from conditions that existed before the campaign began, such as the incumbent's previous poll ratings, economic conditions, and the distribution of party loyalties in the district. That doesn't leave much room for campaigns to determine the outcome. Instead, it suggests that campaigns simply remind voters of these longer lasting conditions and, in this way, help move them toward a largely predetermined outcome. Does this mean that the candidates' strategies are not important?

The Argument That Campaigns Matter

Candidates certainly believe that campaigns affect election results. That's why they try so hard to raise money, attend events, and avoid gaffes that might turn off some voters. Some evidence does indicate that certain types of campaigning matter. For instance, research shows that canvassing has a small but potentially meaningful effect on both turnout and voters' choices.[51] Researchers find that voters are activated more effectively by door-to-door canvassing than by phone contact, and both kinds of contact are more effective than mailings.[52] The quality of the contact can matter at least as much as the medium.[53] Canvassing probably makes a bigger difference in local elections than in presidential races because there are fewer alternative sources of information in local contests. Where a party canvasses actively, its vote share can increase by a few percentage points, which could be the critical margin in a close race.[54]

As would be expected, television news and advertising can also influence voters' decisions.[55] But the impact of TV ads is usually short lived.[56] Campaign debates and other events make a difference in the election result under some circumstances.[57] All these sources of campaign information, taken together, can improve citizens' knowledge, influence their choices, and affect their turnout.[58]

Some voters are more affected by campaigning than others. For instance, those with limited political interest may pick up only a little information about campaigns, but the few bits of information that break through—often, perceptions of a candidate's likeability—can have a big impact on their attitudes.[59] People whose party ID is weak and who are uneasy about their party's candidate can be especially affected by the campaign communications they receive.[60] The emphasis placed by media[61] and campaigns[62] on different aspects of the race or the candidate can influence what the voters regard as important. And campaigns can affect House races more than Senate and presidential contests.[63]

The Argument That They Don't

On the other hand, there are several reasons why campaigning may have only a limited effect. Television news, ads, and ground war activities offer viewers a wide range of conflicting messages about candidates—positive, negative, and neutral information and opinions. The inconsistency of these messages makes it harder for a campaign to have a single, consistent impact on viewers' minds.[64] In races for high-level offices and open seats, in most cases, both candidates have access to sophisticated campaign techniques. Even in an unusual race such as the 2016 presidential election, the overwhelming majority of voters supported the same party as they had in 2012; most Trump voters in 2016 backed him not because of his unconventional campaigning but because he was the Republican candidate.

Besides, we know that voters pay only selective attention to media and other campaign communications. People interested in politics tend to surround themselves with friends, information, and even personal experiences that support their beliefs and loyalties,[65] and they often ignore information that conflicts with their opinions. The media environment has become highly diversified in recent years, with blogs, newsletters, talk radio, and cable channels presenting a broad array of perspectives. As a result, it is not hard for people to find media outlets that reinforce their views—think of Fox News for conservatives and MSNBC for liberals—and to spread these messages to similarly minded others.[66] Most campaign messages, then, probably reinforce and activate voters' existing political leanings, as they always have.[67] That can explain why so much campaign effort is directed at getting people out to vote—to act on whatever opinions they already hold—rather than at trying to change their voting decision.

Some Tentative Answers

Rather than asking whether campaigns matter, we should ask about the *conditions* under which campaigns are more likely to matter. Campaigns matter more when voters know less about the candidates, when a race is close, and when one candidate is much more resource-rich than the other.[68] That is especially true of local races, where the quality of campaigns varies more.[69] In the information-rich environment of current politics and among the large numbers of weak partisans and independent "leaners," the potential for campaigns to shape voters' perceptions may be at least as great as it has ever been. But some forces will continue to limit campaigns' impact: voters' tendency to pay attention to the messages with which they already agree and their ability to tune out most political messages altogether.

Candidate-Centered or Party-Centered Campaigns?

The campaign techniques explored in this chapter have affected not just voters but also the balance of power in campaigns between parties and candidates. Broadcast media, which need large audiences, tend to focus on individual personalities rather than on institutions such as parties. Tools such as Internet and TV advertising are available to any candidate who can pay for them; they let candidates communicate with voters without the party's help. The technologies that have developed since the mid-1900s, in short, have helped candidates run their campaigns independently of the party organizations. If the American parties had been as strong organizationally as those in many other nations when these technologies developed, then they might have been able to monopolize the use of TV and other media for campaign purposes. But as we have seen, the American parties have always struggled to maintain their power in a political culture hostile to their functioning.

American politics has long been guided by rules that disadvantage political parties.[70] Instead of parliamentary-cabinet government or proportional representation, which would encourage voters to see contests between parties for control of government rather than contests between candidates, the U.S. government has a separation of powers system, which hinders the ability of parties to act collectively. American campaign finance rules make it difficult for parties to coordinate the campaigns of several candidates. And the direct primary, as Chapter 9 shows, allows candidates to run without the party organization's approval.

Consequently, it is the candidates and their advisers, not the parties, who make the strategic decisions in most campaigns. Candidates have their own headquarters and staffers rather than using the party's facilities. Candidates maintain their own relationships with voters rather than rely on the party organization as an intermediary. Party organizations, rather than running campaigns, often work instead to strengthen the appeal of individual candidates. And they must compete with consultants, interest groups, and others for the chance to do so.

Party Influence in Competitive Campaigns

The parties, however, are fighting back. Their greatly expanded fund-raising during the past four decades has let party organizations help individual campaigns with money and other services.[71] As noted in Chapter 4, soft money enabled party organizations to pour millions of dollars into campaign ads in a few battleground states until 2003. Since then, massive party fund-raising and voter contact drives have expanded the party presence in more races, even as the presence of other groups has also expanded (see Chapter 12).

The national parties have become more visible especially in the most competitive Senate and House elections. In some cases, party organizations using independent spending have outspent the candidates themselves. But because independent spending does not allow the parties to explicitly coordinate their efforts with their candidates, much less to run their campaigns, party-funded ads have sometimes stressed different themes from those the campaign preferred to emphasize and, frequently, more negative messages than the campaign's own advertising.[72] Because voters rarely pay attention to the source of any particular message, candidates have gotten blamed for negativity and claims that they have not made. And in most races, the party's role is less noticeable.

The Continuing Struggle between Candidates and Party Organizations

If you value economic efficiency, an expanded party role in campaigns makes sense. Party organizations can distribute appeals for a number of candidates at the same time and register voters to help the entire ticket. Parties can buy media advertising and consultants' services for use by many candidates at cost-effective prices. Party organizations can coordinate Election Day activities for all the party's candidates, provide poll watchers to guard against voting irregularities, send cars to bring people to the polls, and check voter lists to mobilize nonvoters late in the day.

But this efficiency comes at the cost of limiting the candidates' independence. Party organizations and candidates do not always have the same goals. The party, aiming to maximize the number of races it wins, puts its scarce resources into the most competitive campaigns and spends as little as possible on the races it considers hopeless. Each candidate, in contrast, is committed above all to his or her own victory and to gaining the resources needed to achieve it, no matter how unlikely that victory may be. The party, in its drive to win every competitive race, is likely to do whatever it takes, whether through negative or positive campaigning. The candidate, in contrast, has to face the voters; a constant barrage of attack ads may give the candidate a bad image.

The result is a continuing struggle between the party organizations and the candidates—the party in government—for control of campaigns. In most elections, the candidates have won the fight. Although parties have more to offer candidates now than they did just a few years ago, party organizations still contribute only a fairly small percentage of candidates' overall spending in most races. In contrast, European parties often provide more than half the funding for most candidates.

Why should you care? Because candidate-centered campaigning has an important impact on governing. When they control their own campaigns, winning candidates can develop personal relationships with their constituents, unconstrained by party ties. Candidates are free to form close alliances with interest groups, which enhance the ability of these groups to influence public policy. In short, candidate-centered campaigning strengthens the power of the party in government relative to that of the party organization. That leads to an important question: If strong party organizations can help to hold elected officials accountable for their actions, then how much accountability do voters get from a candidate-centered politics?

Notes

1 See, for example, Sean Sullivan and Robert Costa, "Trump and Sanders Lead Competing Populist Movements, Reshaping American Politics," *Washington Post*, March 2, 2020, p. A1.
2 On the American parties' adaptation to reforms, see Seth Masket, *The Inevitable Party* (New York: Oxford University Press, 2016).
3 See Paul S. Herrnson, Costas Panagopoulos, and Kendall L. Bailey, *Congressional Elections*, 8th ed. (Los Angeles, CA: Sage/CQ Press, 2016); and Marjorie Randon Hershey, *Running for Office* (Chatham, NJ: Chatham House, 1984).
4 See Gary C. Jacobson and Jamie L. Carson, *The Politics of Congressional Elections*, 10th ed. (Lanham, MD: Rowman & Littlefield, 2020).
5 Edward I. Sidlow, *Challenging the Incumbent* (Washington, DC: CQ Press, 2003).
6 See Herrnson et al., *Congressional Elections,* pp. 256–269.
7 John R. Petrocik, William L. Benoit, and Glenn J. Hansen, "Issue Ownership and Presidential Campaigning, 1952–2000," *Political Science Quarterly* 118 (2003): 599–926.

8 On general election strategies, see John H. Aldrich, Jamie L. Carson, Brad T. Gomez, and David W. Rohde, *Continuity and Change in the 2016 & 2018 Elections* (Los Angeles, CA: Sage, 2020), Chapter 2.

9 James A. Thurber and Candice J. Nelson, eds., *Campaign Warriors* (Washington, DC: Brookings, 2000).

10 See David A. Dulio, *For Better or Worse* (Albany, NY: SUNY Press, 2004).

11 See Darrell M. West, *Air Wars*, 7th ed. (Los Angeles, CA: CQ Press, 2017).

12 See Doris A. Graber and Johanna Dunaway, *Mass Media and American Politics*, 10th ed. (Los Angeles, CA: CQ Press, 2018), Chapter 4.

13 Dave Barry, "Scandal Sheep," *Boston Globe Magazine,* March 15, 1998, pp. 12–23.

14 Jeff Valenzuela, "Midwest Local TV Newscasts Devote 2.5 Times as Much Air Time to Political Ads as Election Coverage," press release, Joyce Foundation, November 21, 2006.

15 Markus Prior, "News vs. Entertainment," *American Journal of Political Science* 49 (2005): 577–792.

16 Danny Hayes and Jennifer L. Lawless, "The Decline of Local News and Its Effects," *Journal of Politics* 80 (January 2018): 332–336.

17 Amy Mitchell, Jeffrey Gottfried, and Katerina Eva Matsa, "Millennials and Political News," *Pew Research Center,* June 1, 2015, https://www.journalism.org/2015/06/01/-millennials-political-news/ (accessed August 22, 2020).

18 Richard J. Semiatin, *Campaigns in the 21st Century* (Boston, MA: McGraw Hill, 2005), p. 178.

19 Maggie Severns and Alex Isenstadt, "Trump and RNC Raised Massive $125 Million in Third Quarter," *Politico,* October 1, 2019, https://www.politico.com/news/2019/10/01/donald-trump-campaign-millionsfundraising-016251 (accessed August 22, 2020).

20 Allison Dale and Aaron Strauss, "Don't Forget to Vote," *American Journal of Political Science* 53 (2009): 787–704.

21 Alex Thompson, "This is How Donald Trump Stays President for Four More Years," *Politico,* October 24, 2018, https://www.politico.com/story/2018/10/24/trump-2020-reelection-text-messaging-933907 (accessed August 22, 2020).

22 Matea Gold and Elizabeth Dwoskin, "In Elections, Facebook's Reach Has Kept Growing," *Washington Post,* October 9, 2017, p. A1.

23 See Marjorie Randon Hershey, "The Media: Different Audiences Saw Different Campaigns," in Michael E. Nelson, ed., *The Elections of 2012* (Washington, DC: CQ Press/Sage, 2013), pp. 97–718.

24 Zephoria Digital Marketing, "Top 10 Twitter Statistics," February 2020, https://zephoria.com/twitter-statistics-top-ten/ (accessed August 22, 2020).

25 See Marjorie Randon Hershey, "The President and the Media," in Michael Nelson, ed., *Presidents and the Political System*, 12th ed. (Los Angeles, CA: Sage, 2020), pp. 307–333.

26 Paul R. Abramson, John H. Aldrich, and David W. Rohde, *Change and Continuity in the 2000 and 2002 Elections* (Washington, DC: CQ Press, 2003), pp. 261–162.

27 Ruth Igielnik, Scott Keeter, Courtney Kennedy, and Bradley Spahn, "Commercial Voter Files and the Study of U.S. Politics," February 15, 2018, https://www.pewresearch.org/methods/2018/02/15/commercial-voter-files-and-the-study-of-u-s-politics/ (accessed August 22, 2020).

28 Ryan D. Enos and Eitan Hersh, "Party Activists as Campaign Advertisers," *American Political Science Review* 109 (2015): 252.

29 Ryan D. Enos and Anthony Fowler, "Aggregate Effects of Large-Scale Campaigns on Voter Turnout," *Political Science Research and Methods* 6 (October 2018): 733–751.

30 Herrnson, *Congressional Elections*, p. 119.

31 Andrew Marantz, "The Man Behind Trump's Facebook Juggernaut," *New Yorker*, March 2, 2020, https://www.newyorker.com/magazine/2020/03/09/the-man-behind-trumps-facebook-juggernaut (August 22, 2020).

32 Quote from McKay Coppins, "The Billion-Dollar Disinformation Campaign to Reelect the President," *The Atlantic*, February 10, 2020, https://www.theatlantic.com/magazine/archive/2020/03/the-2020-disinformation-war/605530/ (accessed August 22, 2020).

33 See, for example, Alex Rogers, "Campaign Advertising Adapts to New Coronavirus Reality," *CNN*, March 31, 2020, https://www.cnn.com/2020/03/31/politics/-campaigns-advertising-adapts-coronavirus/index.html (accessed August 22, 2020).

34 Paul A. Beck and Erik Heidemann, "The Ground Game from the Voter's Perspective," in John C. Green, Daniel J. Coffey, and David B. Cohen, eds., *The State of the Parties*, 7th ed. (Lanham, MD: Rowman & Littlefield), 2014, pp. 251–169.

35 David Broockman and Joshua Kalla, "Durably Reducing Transphobia," *Science* 352 (April 8, 2016): 220–224.

36 John G. Geer, "The News Media and the Rise of Negativity in Presidential Campaigns," *PS: Political Science & Politics* 45 (2012): 422–227.

37 See Conor M. Dowling and Amber Wichowsky, "Attacks without Consequences?" *American Journal of Political Science* 59 (2015): 19–96.

38 Yanna Krupnikov, "When Does Negativity Demobilize?" *American Journal of Political Science* 55 (2011): 797–713.

39 Larry Bartels, "The Economy and the Campaign," *The Monkey Cage*, January 14, 2013, http://themonkeycage.org/blog/2013/01/14/the-economy-and-the-campaign/#more-26660 (accessed August 22, 2020).

40 "The Full RNC "Growth and Opportunity Project Report," https://www.washingtonpost.com/news/post-politics/wp/2013/03/18/the-full-rnc-growth-and-opportunity-project-report/ (accessed August 22, 2020), p. 49.

41 Quoted in Peter Wallstein, "Republicans Face Murky Political Future in Increasingly Diverse U.S.," *Washington Post*, November 7, 2012, p. 1.

42 Jennifer Rubin, "Donald Trump, Master Fabulist," *Washington Post*, May 2, 2016, https://www.washingtonpost.com/blogs/right-turn/wp/2016/05/02/donald-trump-master-fabulist/ (accessed August 22, 2020).

43 Ann M. Oberhauser, Daniel Drier, and Abdi M. Kusow, "Political Moderation and Polarization in the Heartland," *Sociological Quarterly* 60 (April 2019): 224–244, and Christopher DeSante and Candis Watts, *Racial Stasis* (Chicago, IL: University of Chicago Press, 2020).

44 Perry Bacon, Jr., "Is Trump's Use of Identity Politics Strategic?" July 25, 2019, https://fivethirtyeight.com/features/is-trumps-use-of-white-identity-politics-strategic/ (accessed August 22, 2020).

45 James E. Campbell, "Explaining Electoral Change in the 2018 U.S. Midterm Elections," *The Forum* 16 (#4 2018).

46 Alexander Burns and Jonathan Martin, "Chaos vs. Focus," *New York Times*, November 8, 2018, p. A1. The quote is from Campbell, "Explaining Electoral Change" (see note 47).

47 Dan Balz and Scott Clement, "Biden Strongly ahead of Trump," *Washington Post*, July 19, 2020, p. A1.

48 The latter analysis was by Catalist; see Ronald Brownstein, "Rumblings from Trump's Base Could Shape Democrats' Choice for 2020," *CNN*, June 4, 2019,

https://www.cnn.com/2019/06/04/politics/trump-voters-switch-to-democrats-in-2018-2020/index.html (accessed August 22, 2020).

49 Pew Research Center, "Election 2000," August 13, 2020, https://pewresearch.org/politics/2020/08/13-election-2020-voters-are-highly-engaged-but-nearly-half-expect-to-have-difficulties-voting/ (accessed August 22, 2020).

50 See Marjorie Randon Hershey, ""The Constructed Explanation," *Journal of Politics* 54 (November, 1992): 943–976.

51 See Thomas M. Holbrook and Scott D. McClurg, "The Mobilization of Core Supporters," *American Journal of Political Science* 49 (2005): 689–903, and Seth E. Masket, "Did Obama's Ground Game Matter?" *Public Opinion Quarterly* 73 (2009): 1023–3039.

52 For an overview, see Donald P. Green and Michael Schwam-Baird, "Mobilization, Participation, and American Democracy," *Party Politics* 22 (#2 2016): 158–164.

53 David W. Nickerson, "Quality Is Job One," *American Journal of Political Science* 51 (2007): 269–982.

54 Yard signs have less effect but still can make a difference in very close races; see Donald P. Green, Jonathan S. Krasno, Alexander Coppock, Benjamin D. Farrer, Brandon Lenoir, and Joshua N. Zingher, "The Effects of Lawn Signs on Vote Outcomes," *Electoral Studies* 41 (2016): 143–350.

55 Daron R. Shaw, "The Effect of TV Ads and Candidate Appearances on Statewide Presidential Votes, 1988–86," *American Political Science Review* 93 (1999): 345–351.

56 Alan S. Gerber, James G. Gimpel, Donald P. Green, and Daron R. Shaw, "How Large and Long-lasting Are the Persuasive Effects of Televised Campaign Ads?" *American Political Science Review* 105 (2011): 135–550.

57 Aaron C. Weinshenk and Costas Panagopoulos, "The Dynamics of Voter Preferences in the 2016 Presidential Election," *The Forum* (#1 2018).

58 See Paul Freedman, Michael Franz, and Kenneth Goldstein, "Campaign Advertising and Democratic Citizenship," *American Journal of Political Science* 48 (2004): 723–341.

59 Matthew A. Baum, "Talking the Vote," *American Journal of Political Science* 49 (2005): 213–334.

60 Shanto Iyengar and John R. Petrocik, "'Basic Rule' Voting," in James A. Thurber, Candice J. Nelson, and David A. Dulio, eds., *Crowded Airwaves* (Washington, DC: Brookings, 2000), p. 142.

61 See Joanne M. Miller and Jon A. Krosnick, "News Media Impact on the Ingredients of Presidential Evaluations," *American Journal of Political Science* 44 (2000): 295–509.

62 David A. M. Peterson, "Campaign Learning and Vote Determinants," *American Journal of Political Science* 53 (2009): 445–560.

63 Patrick D. Tucker and Steven S. Smith, "Changes in Candidate Evaluations over the Campaign Season," *Political Behavior* (2020):

64 Russell J. Dalton, Paul A. Beck, and Robert Huckfeldt, "Partisan Cues and the Media," *American Political Science Review* 92 (1998): 111–126.

65 See Paul Allen Beck, "Voters' Intermediation Environments in the 1988 Presidential Contest," *Public Opinion Quarterly* 55 (1991): 371–394.

66 James N. Druckman, Matthew S. Levendusky, and Audrey McLain, "No Need to Watch," *American Journal of Political Science* 62 (January 2018): 99–112.

67 On the lack of campaign effects, see Joshua L. Kalla and David E. Broockman, "The Minimal Persuasive Effects of Campaign Contact in General Elections," *American Political Science Review* 112 (February 2018): 148–166.

68 John Sides, Daron Shaw, Matt Grossman, and Keena Lipsitz, *Campaigns and Elections*, 3rd ed. (New York: W.W. Norton, 2018), p. 397.

69 William J. Feltus, Kenneth M. Goldstein, and Matthew Dallek, *Campaigns* (Los Angeles, CA: CQ/Sage, 2019), p. 26.

70 John H. Aldrich, *Why Parties? A Second Look* (Chicago, IL: University of Chicago Press, 2011), pp. 266–669.

71 See Holbrook and McClurg, "The Mobilization of Core Supporters."

72 See Paul S. Herrnson and Diana Dwyre, "Party Issue Advocacy in Congressional Election Campaigns," in John C. Green and Daniel M. Shea, eds., *The State of the Parties,* 3rd ed. (Lanham, MD: Rowman & Littlefield, 1999), pp. 86–604.

CHAPTER 12

Financing the Campaigns

Campaign finance is steeped in myths. The candidate with the most campaign money *doesn't* always win the election. Individuals, corporations, and labor unions *can't* give unlimited sums *directly* to candidates' campaigns. The cigar-chomping party bosses who chose candidates and handed them cash in the days of the political machine are about as common today as typewriters and the Nintendo Entertainment System.

The real story is at least as dramatic as the myths, however. Money does remain the key to mobilizing the resources needed for a viable campaign. The cost of these resources—huge databases, TV advertising, paid professional consultants, polls—has risen greatly in recent decades. Court decisions have permitted big givers to pump millions of dollars into elections (though not directly into candidates' campaign budgets). These big givers are not college students, nurses, or truck drivers, and their daily lives do not reflect the experiences of the average American.[1] But their spending and that of political parties, organized interests, and many other individuals affect elections. People who run for office, especially at the federal and state levels, are not likely to be taken seriously unless they start with a big campaign budget or a proven talent for fund-raising.

For most of American history, money used in campaigns was collected and spent in secret. Candidates were not required to disclose how they raised funds, and citizens had no way to be sure who was paying for a candidate's campaign or what the givers might be getting in return. Regulations adopted in the 1970s gave us a flood of information about campaign contributions and spending. But as the result of recent court decisions, much of the money spent on campaigns since 2010 is now almost as hard to trace as in the days before the reforms.

Let us clarify this complicated story by first reviewing its main themes. Then the chapter will continue by explaining how campaign finance reached this dismal state.

How Much Money Is Spent on Campaigns?

Campaigns for all levels of office in the U.S. cost over $14 billion collectively in 2020 and $5.7 billion in the midterm elections of 2018[2]—an enormous increase over the amounts spent just two decades ago. Inflation has reduced the purchasing power of the dollar during this period, so the real, inflation-adjusted increase is not nearly as dramatic. But the growth in spending since 1996 is impressive by any standard.

Campaign spending has shot upward for many reasons. Fund raisers have become much more skilled at energizing both small and big donors. A polarized political system has heightened the stakes in elections. The Supreme Court's gutting of campaign finance laws has permitted non-party groups to spend record sums in campaigns. So although federal regulations slowed the arms race in campaign funding from the 1970s to the 1990s, we are back to the days when secretive giving by big contributors threatens the integrity of the electoral process and the effectiveness of the political parties.

Presidential Campaigns

It is now commonplace that each new presidential race is termed "the biggest spending campaign in American history." That was true of 2020 (see Figure 12.1), even though there was no contest for the Republican nomination. In 2016, Donald Trump won despite having been greatly outspent. Democratic nominee Hillary Clinton and her associated super PACs (see later in this chapter) spent about $1.2 billion, compared with "only" $720 million for Team Trump, though spending by the national party organizations and outside interests, in addition to Trump's remarkable ability to draw free media coverage by making controversial statements, helped to level the playing field.

Trump made sure that would not happen again in 2020; he filed for re-election the day after he was inaugurated in 2017, and millions of dollars poured into his campaign coffers right away. More than a year before the 2020 election, his campaign committees had already spent $531 million, and his spending reached $1 billion by the time of the Republican convention. Trump greatly

FIGURE 12.1 Total Spending by Candidates, Parties, and Groups in Presidential Elections, 1960–2020

Note: Estimates are for two-year cycles ending in the presidential election years. Inflation-adjusted figures are computed by deflating the actual expenditures by changes in the price level as measured by the Consumer Price Index yearly averages (with 1960 as the base year).

Sources: FEC data reported by the Committee for Responsive Politics. Data for 2020 are reported as of November 28.

out-raised his Democratic opponent, Joe Biden, during the nomination season, but Biden's fund-raising improved substantially after that. Biden's total spending finally surpassed $1 billion two weeks before election day. This blizzard of campaign money shows no signs of slowing down.

Congressional Campaigns

Nor have midterm elections been left behind (see Figures 12.2 and 12.3). Total spending in the 2018 midterms exceeded $5.7 billion—closer to the level typically seen in a presidential race than in the previous midterm (2014), when spending hit $3.8 billion. Records were shattered in all directions. Challenger spending more than doubled compared with the previous midterm election in 2014, in part because many more incumbents faced challenges. Party-related

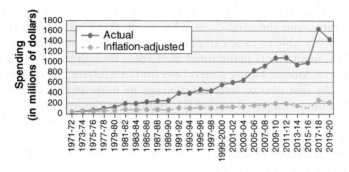

FIGURE 12.2 Total Candidate Spending in House Campaigns, 1971–1972 to 2019–2020

Note: Inflation-adjusted figures are computed by deflating the actual expenditures by changes in the price level as measured by the Consumer Price Index yearly averages (with 1972 as the base year).

Source: FEC data from the Committee for Responsive Politics. Data for 2020 are as of November 30, 2020.

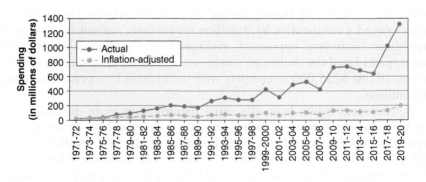

FIGURE 12.3 Total Candidate Spending in Senate Campaigns, 1971–1972 to 2019–2020

Note: Inflation-adjusted figures are computed as in Figure 12.2.

Source: FEC data from the Committee for Responsive Politics. Data for 2020 are as of November 30, 2020.

groups pushed their fund-raising well over $100 million apiece, including the Democratic and Republican Governors' Associations, the National Democratic Redistricting Project, and a major Republican super PAC, the Congressional Leadership Fund. Much of the funding for these party-related groups came in million-dollar increments from extremely wealthy individuals, such as the oil-rich Koch brothers network, which claimed to spend about $400 million in the 2018 congressional elections.[3]

One of the most striking findings in congressional races is that incumbents greatly outraise and outspend their challengers in every election year. Incumbents in safe House seats often spend more than their challengers by a factor of 10, and the incumbent advantage in a safe Senate race is only slightly less. To beat an incumbent, a challenger must expect to come close to the incumbent's spending, which happens only rarely. The campaign budgets of candidates in open seat races—those where no incumbent is running—are normally closer to incumbents' fund-raising levels than challengers, because open seat races attract more attention, and the candidates who run in them are usually more experienced and better able to raise campaign money than most challengers.

In 2018, incumbents maintained their edge, though there were clear differences by party. Among House general election candidates, incumbents outraised challengers by just two to one: the average incumbent House member raised about $2 million compared with $1.1 million for the average challenger (and $1.7 million on average for open-seat races).[4] In Senate contests, the average Senator collected $16.7 million and the average challenger $6.3 million. Open seat Senate candidates raised an average of $10.5 million—in all, tidy sums for an office that pays about $174,000 a year.

Republican candidates normally hold a fund-raising edge over Democrats in congressional campaigns. The size of that advantage in a given election depends on which party has the most incumbents and, therefore, controls each house of Congress. Control of a legislative body is worth a great deal to a party, quite literally. So when Democrats saw a chance to capture control of the House in 2018, Democratic money flowed especially to Democratic House challengers. Among all House general election candidates, Democratic challengers raised a competitive $1.9 million on average, not much less than their Republican incumbent opponents' average of $2.3 million. Their Republican counterparts faced the challenger's more usual, dismal disadvantage, raising an average of just $225,000 to compete with the average Democratic incumbent's $1.6 million.

Senate races broke from the usual pattern even more dramatically. The average Democratic Senate challenger actually outraised his or her incumbent Republican opponent in 2018, though not by much ($14.7 million compared with $14.3 million). And incumbent Democrats outraised Republican challengers, on average, by almost two to one ($17.9 million to $8.6 million).[5] Nonparty groups' funding tilted toward Democratic candidates as well—also a break from the usual Republican advantage. Republicans, in short, focused their contributions on shoring up the chances of endangered Republican House incumbents, at the cost of funding Republican challengers. But the party probably held down its losses with its own considerable fund-raising; the three national Republican Party committees took in more money than the Democratic committees.

State and Local Campaigns

Even though local governments make a major difference in people's daily lives, many local races are still relatively low-spending affairs. But the totals are increasing, with occasional eye-popping results. In 2009, for instance, Michael Bloomberg spent $100 million of his own funds to win a third term as New York City mayor. Campaigns for governor now can cost as much as U.S. Senate races. Most impressive has been the increase in spending by non-party groups, including a large number who do not disclose where their money comes from. Even state Supreme Court elections have become big-spending contests. The all-time record was set in 2015 by Pennsylvania's state Supreme Court elections in which spending totaled just under $16 million. In these judicial races, most of the money comes from business interests and trial lawyers who have a big stake in the judges' rulings.[6]

These figures must be kept in perspective. As substantial as it is, the total cost of all U.S. campaigns is just a fifth of the money Americans spend on lottery tickets each year (see box "Campaign Spending: Too Much or Too Little?" on this page). To the extent that campaigns give us a chance to learn about the strengths and weaknesses of the people who would govern us, the amounts spent on campaign advertising could be considered a real bargain.[7] There are important questions to be asked, however, about the motivations of contributors and the fund-raising disparities among candidates. And although

---

Campaign Spending: Too Much or Too Little?

What will $14 billion buy In the U.S.?

- The amount Americans are estimated to have spent on snacks, TVs, party items, and other supplies for the 2020 Super Bowl.
- Almost half of what the U.S. spent on pet food in 2019.
- About one-fifth of what Americans paid for lottery tickets in 2017.
- Construction of two Nimitz-class aircraft carriers (not counting operating costs).
- All the political campaigns run at all levels of government by and for all candidates in 2020.

Sources: National Retail Federation, "2020 Super Bowl: Consumers to Spend $17.2 Billion," https://nrf.com/insights/holiday-and-seasonal-trends/super-bowl; American Pet Products Association, "Pet Industry Market Size & Ownership Statistics," https://www.americanpetproducts.org/press_industrytrends.asp; Megan Leonhart, "Americans Spend over $1,000 a Year on Lotto Tickets," December 12, 2019, https://www.cnbc.com/2019/12/12/americans-spend-over-1000-dollars-a-year-on-lotto-tickets.html, and http://wiki.answers.com/Q/How_much_does_ an_aircraft_carrier_cost (all accessed August 24, 2020).

tens of millions of people buy lottery tickets, the money that funds campaigns—and whatever influence derives from it—comes from a much smaller number of individuals.

What Is the Impact of Campaign Spending?

Money doesn't necessarily buy victory, but it rarely hurts. In the general election for president, both sides usually have enough money to reach voters with their messages, so the candidate with the largest war chest does not gain a big advantage. Money matters more in the early months of the presidential nomination race, especially in buying the early visibility that is so vital to an underdog. But even then, it is not sufficient in itself; Bloomberg and Tom Steyer each spent phenomenal sums in 2020 ($201 million for Steyer even before the first nomination events were held, about $1.1 billion for Bloomberg) but neither came close to winning the Democratic nomination.

In congressional elections, most researchers find that money does make a difference—for challengers. The more challengers spend when they run against incumbents, the better their chances of victory. The same is not true for incumbents. Gary Jacobson found that the more incumbents spend, the worse they do in the race.[8] In 2018, for instance, incumbent Republican Karen Handel spent a full $8.6 million to keep her Georgia U.S. House seat but lost to Democrat Lucy McBath, who spent only $2.5 million. It is not that incumbent spending turns voters off, but rather that incumbents spend a lot when they face serious competition. A big budget for an incumbent, then, typically means that he or she has (or worries about getting) an unusually strong challenger.

Other researchers disagree and report that when incumbents spend more, they do get a return in terms of votes. The dispute turns on thorny questions about the proper way to estimate the impact of spending,[9] but there is general agreement on three points. First, House incumbents do not usually face a serious challenge for reelection. Second, challengers need a lot of money to have a chance of beating an incumbent. Third, incumbents may not be able to survive a strong challenger by pouring more money into their campaigns.

For political scientists, measuring the effects of campaign spending is a complicated task. For candidates, the answer is simple: More is better—especially at the state level, where the party that spends more is more likely to win a legislative majority.[10]

A Never-Ending Story: How "Interested Money" Flows into Campaigns

It is no surprise that people and groups try to put money into campaigns. Government actions inevitably help some groups and harm others; even the most popular policy proposals (cutting taxes, for example) would cause damage to some people (by reducing the funds available to government to spend on defense

Type of funding	Who gives it?	Who gets it?	$ is spent on

Donations to Candidate's Campaign (amounts limited by law)	Individuals
	Parties
	Traditional PACs
	Candidate's personal
	  funds
		The candidate's campaign	TV and Internet ads
			Staff salaries
			Field work and all
			  other campaign
			  activities

Outside Spending (unlimited amounts)	Parties Traditional and super PACs Nonprofits (527, 501c) Corporations, unions Other organized interests Wealthy individuals	Media outlets consultants	Independent spending ads Issue ads Registering voters Promoting policies

FIGURE 12.4 How Money Flows into Federal Campaigns

Source: Created by the author. Thanks to Jennifer Victor for the presentation.

or to subsidize businesses or poor families). So it makes sense that people and groups will use whatever legal methods are available to ensure that they will be among the winners, not the losers, in government policy making. Money is primary among those methods.

Money now comes into campaigns in two different ways. First, individuals and groups can **give money to a candidate's campaign**. The campaign then decides how to spend the money it receives. Second, groups and individuals (other than candidates) can spend their own money on campaign communications and activities, usually independent of the campaign ("outside spending"; see Figure 12.4). In this case, it is the spenders, not the campaign, who choose how to use the money. Since the early 1970s, money donated directly to a candidate's campaign has been limited by law. But outside spending—called **independent spending** or **express advocacy** and issue ads—is largely unregulated. As a result, outside spending has mushroomed.

The "Wild West" Days of Campaign Finance

Before the campaign finance reforms of the 1970s, American campaign finance laws were weak, inconsistent, and usually ignored. Congressional and presidential candidates could take unlimited sums of money from individuals. Reformers tried periodically to regulate campaign fund-raising and spending. A new episode of reform was under way in the early 1970s when the Watergate scandals broke. Corporations and wealthy individuals were found to have given large sums of money to President Nixon's reelection campaign in 1972 in return for preferential treatment ranging from tax breaks for businesses to ambassadorships for individual big givers. The revulsion caused by these fund-raising scandals led Congress to pass the most extensive federal law on the subject in U.S. history: the Federal Election Campaign Act (FECA) amendments of 1974. The Supreme Court invalidated some of these reforms in 1976. But the resulting legislation put limits on federal campaign contributions and set up a system of public funding for presidential campaigns, as a means of tying a candidate's fund-raising more closely to his or her public support.

The FECA Reforms of the 1970s

FECA mandated significant changes in campaign finance. Here are the most notable:

Limits on Direct Contributions to Campaigns

From Individuals   Among the most vivid Watergate stories were those of big contributions from wealthy, so-called "fat cat" donors who received advantages in public policy in return for their money. In response, FECA limited the amounts of money an individual could give directly to a candidate. Beginning in 1976, individuals were allowed to contribute no more than $1,000 to each candidate per election (counting primary and general as separate elections), and no more than $25,000 to all candidates combined, on the assumption that $1,000 was too small an amount, as a portion of a candidate's total campaign budget, to buy big favors. These limits apply only to federal campaigns—those for president and Congress. These limited funds contributed by individuals (and by parties and PACs) under FECA's rules were called **hard (or federal) money.**

Once the individual contribution limit was in place, candidates found that they needed to entice many more individuals to contribute. They succeeded so well, by using regular mail and the newly developed email to raise small contributions, that even today, most of the money contributed *directly* to candidates comes from individual donors, not parties or PACs. In the 2020 elections, individuals accounted for more than half of the contributions to House candidates and about 75 percent of the money given to Senate candidates.

This expanded group of small donors is not typical of the public as a whole, however; the givers tend to be older, wealthier, male, more Republican, and more ideologically extreme than the average American voter[11] and there is evidence that candidates listen to them more than they do to the average voter.[12] Perhaps the biggest recent change in this profile is that women are contributing more now, and overwhelmingly to Democratic candidates.[13] Both parties have created platforms—ActBlue for the Democrats, WinRed for the Republicans—to make it easier for small donors to give online to multiple candidates of the same party.

From Traditional Political Action Committees (PACs)   Corporations and labor unions had long been prohibited from giving money directly from their own treasuries to political candidates. So beginning in the 1940s, labor unions had sought to make legal campaign contributions by forming political action committees, abbreviated as PACs: political groups whose sole purpose is to raise and spend money to influence elections. Because the PAC's money would be kept in a fund separate from the union's own regular revenues, union leaders figured that their PACs could contribute to federal campaigns without violating the ban on direct union contributions. At the urging of many unions, FECA confirmed the legality of PACs and the right of sponsoring organizations to pay their overhead expenses.

FECA allowed PACs to donate up to $5,000 per candidate per election, with no overall limit on the number of candidates they supported. Because candidates could get five times more money from a PAC than from an individual, PACs became an attractive source of contributions to candidates. The attraction was mutual; seeing the opportunity to contribute legally to candidates' campaigns, corporations and other groups formed thousands of PACs in the 1970s and 1980s. Corporate and trade association PACs (most of which are also business-related) soon came to dominate the PAC universe. In 2020, corporate and trade PACs provided more than 68 percent of all PAC contributions to federal candidates. The heavy hitters are in the fields of finance, real estate, health care, communications, and energy. Although labor unions are now a fairly small proportion of all PACs, and gave only 13 percent of all PAC contributions to candidates in 2020, unions still contribute millions to federal campaigns. Because unions give almost all their PAC money to Democrats, they help compensate for the usual Republican edge in business contributions (see Table 12.1). In addition, as Chapter 4

TABLE 12.1 The Biggest PAC Spenders (in Contributions to Federal Candidates), 2019–2020

Rank	PAC	Contributions to Federal Candidates		
		Total (in millions of $)	To Democrats (%)	To Republicans (%)
1	National Association of Realtors*	$3.5	53	47
2	National Beer Wholesalers*	2.8	53	47
3	Credit Union National Association*	2.6	54	46
4	Operating Engineers Union	2.5	82	18
5	AT&T Inc.*	2.5	53	47
6	American Crystal Sugar*	2.5	56	44
7	Majority Committee PAC*	2.5	-	99
8	Comcast Corporation*	2.4	46	54
9	American Bankers Association*	2.4	31	69
10	National Air Traffic Controllers Association	2.3	67	33

Note: *denotes corporate or other business-related PAC.

Source: Calculated from Federal Election Commission data from the Center for Responsive Politics as of October 23, 2020, www.opensecrets.org/political-action-committees-pacs/2020 (accessed November 28, 2020).

showed, members of the party in government have formed "leadership PACs" from which they are expected to donate to their party's congressional campaign committee as well as to raise money for the party and its endangered candidates.

As they did when FECA was passed, traditional PACs continue to put most of their money into congressional races. In 2020, they gave a total of about $486 million to federal candidates.[14] Because the average House candidate is less well funded than his or her Senate counterpart, PAC donations account for a higher proportion (more than a fifth) of House campaign budgets. Some PACs and corporate interests also donate funds to charities favored by powerful Congress members. Both parties' Hill committees connect their candidates with PACs likely to be sympathetic to their causes. PACs' aim is to gain access to elected officials: the assurance that the legislator's door will be open when the group hopes to plead its case on legislation. Thus, the great majority of PAC contributions go to incumbents. There is little advantage, after all, in getting access to a likely loser.

What PACs get in return is harder to measure. Political scientists don't find much evidence that PAC contributions affect Congress members' roll call votes,[15] although legislators who receive PAC money seem more active in congressional committees on behalf of issues that concern their PAC donors.[16] Because PACs usually give to legislators who have already voted to support that PAC's interests, it isn't clear whether the PAC's money *caused* the legislator to vote that way. Their influence is greatest when they represent powerful interests in the legislator's district, when they don't conflict with his or her party's position, and when the benefit they seek is of little direct concern to anyone else (such as a small change in the tax laws giving a big break to a particular corporation).

From Party Organizations   FECA treated the political party organizations as just another non-candidate group wanting to invest in campaigns, and it restricted the money parties could give to their candidates. So the American parties' role in funding campaigns is much more limited than in most other democracies, where the party organizations, not the candidates, do most of the campaign spending.

Party organizations at the state, local, and national level can give up to $5,000 to each candidate in a House race and larger amounts to Senate candidates. The parties can also spend money *in coordination with* a candidate's campaign to purchase services such as media advertising or polling for the campaign, called **coordinated spending**. This is useful to the party because party committees have more control over how the money is spent than when they give the money directly to candidates. As of 2020, each party was permitted to spend $50,900 per House race, except in states with only one House district, where the limit was $101,900. The state party can spend the same amount or authorize the national party committee to do so. In Senate campaigns, the limit varies with the size of the state's voting-age population: from $101,900 in Delaware to $3.1 million in California.[17] But in most races, this party money still amounts to only a small fraction of the candidate's total spending.

Public Disclosure

The reformers also wanted to make campaign funding more transparent. They felt that voters could make a more informed choice if they knew who had contributed to each candidate. So FECA required that congressional and presidential candidates publicly disclose their spending and the names, addresses, and occupations of all contributors of $200 or more. The Federal Election Commission (FEC) was established to receive candidates' finance reports and make the data publicly available. In recent years, the FEC has been so partisan and dysfunctional that its commissioners deadlocked on whether to serve bagels or doughnuts at its 40th anniversary celebration,[18] but its public files, available online (https://www.fec.gov/), provide a wealth of campaign finance information.

Public Funding of Presidential Campaigns

In a final effort to remove "interested money" from elections, FECA and its amendments in the 1970s provided public funds for presidential candidates. The money comes from voluntary contributions from taxpayers, who could designate a dollar (now $3) of their tax payments to match small contributions to candidates for their party's presidential nomination and to foot most of the bill for the presidential nominees in the general election. To get the money, a candidate for a party's presidential nomination must first demonstrate broad public support by raising $5,000 in contributions of $250 or less in each of 20 states. After that, public funds match every individual contribution up to $250, as a means of encouraging small donations.[19]

The public funding treats minor party candidates differently. They receive only a fraction of that total, and then only after the election if they have received at least 5 percent of the vote. Because candidates need to pay cash for many campaign expenses, this provision of FECA adds to the difficulties faced by minor parties. Only one minor party candidate, Reform Party leader Ross Perot in 1996, has ever qualified for public funding, though some states have experimented with public funding of state or local campaigns.[20]

Spending Limits   The catch is that accepting public funds requires a candidate to abide by low spending limits in each state's primary or caucus and for the nomination and general election races as a whole. These limits have not kept up with the rising cost of presidential campaigns. And because the amount of the public funding is much lower than the figure current candidates have been able to raise for themselves, no recent presidential nominee has accepted those funds. Nevertheless, the availability of public money has helped some lesser-known candidates stay in the nomination race longer, which gives voters more choices.

Congress tried to include provisions in FECA limiting spending in House and Senate campaigns as well. However, the Supreme Court ruled in 1976 that restricting a candidate's spending infringed on the candidate's right to free speech. Those restrictions could be justified only if a candidate accepts public funding. Congress could apply spending limits to its own campaigns, then, only as part of a plan for subsidizing them with public money. That would mean subsidizing their challengers' campaigns as well. For congressional incumbents, who typically outspend their challengers, this was not an appealing idea.

The Loopholes That Ate the Reforms

Not long after Congress passed the FECA reforms, several groups asked the Supreme Court to overturn the law on a variety of grounds: for instance, that tax funds shouldn't subsidize campaigns, and that minor parties were treated unfairly in the reforms. In the landmark case of **Buckley v. Valeo** (1976), the Court's majority expressed a different concern. Although it agreed that Congress could limit the size of individuals' direct contributions to candidates, no such limits could be placed on a candidate's overall campaign spending or on other individuals' or groups' **independent spending**: *ads that are run independently of a candidate's campaign.*[21] In funding their campaigns, the Court ruled, candidates are exercising their free speech right, just as are independent spenders, and that right cannot be limited.

Unlimited Self-Funding by Wealthy Candidates

The Supreme Court said in *Buckley* that Congress can't limit how much federal candidates are allowed to spend of their own personal wealth on their campaigns. Why, when other donors are limited in the amount they can contribute? Because the Supreme Court has ruled that campaign finance limits exist mainly to prevent corruption, and people can't corrupt themselves. The biggest self-funders often lose, however. And because raising funds is closely related to gaining voter support, self-funders can limit their own appeal.

Independent Spending

If you run an ad supporting a candidate or criticizing the candidate's opponent, and if you work with the candidate's campaign in doing so, then the law treats the ad as a campaign contribution, which is limited by FECA. But the Supreme Court wrote in *Buckley* that if you don't consult with the campaign about the ad—if it is run *independently* of the campaign—then your right to free speech allows you to spend unlimited sums on your advertising. The Court majority's reasoning was that free speech is fundamental in a democracy—more important than is limiting political corruption—and because "free" speech costs money to disseminate through TV and other media, Congress can't limit the amount that groups and individuals spend on ads, as long as they are not run in collaboration with a campaign. The Court said in 1996 that political parties could also spend independently on campaign ads and, in 2003, applied this to publicly financed presidential campaigns as well.[22]

Because independent spending is unlimited, parties can use it to greatly expand their role in targeted campaigns. As a result, the national parties have put most of their campaign money into independent spending. In especially competitive House races, it isn't unusual for independent spending by parties and interest groups to dwarf the advertising funded by the candidates themselves.

Non-party groups have greatly expanded their independent spending too. In 2018, successful House challengers (all of whom were Democrats) raised an average of over $4.6 million for their own campaigns and also benefited from an average of more than $5.2 million in independent expenditures, of which more than half came from groups other than party organizations.[23] The Campaign Finance Institute found that in 16 states in 2005–2006, over $180 million was spent independently. By 2017–2018, that sum had tripled.[24]

Independent spending poses many challenges for a democracy. Most independent spending funds negative ads. If a *candidate* launches an outrageous attack, citizens can protest by voting for his or her opponent. If a party, interest group, or individual runs an outrageous ad as an independent spender, who can be held responsible? The independent spender can't be punished at the polls; he or she isn't running for anything. Thus, independent spenders are free to say whatever they wish, and neither they nor the candidate they favor can be held accountable. Nor is the spending really "independent." Campaigns often put ad footage on YouTube, which can then be picked up by "independent" super PACs in their own ad campaigns,[25] or find other means to communicate their strategies to outside spenders.

Soft Money

To strengthen state and local party organizations, Congress amended FECA in 1979 to let them raise and spend unlimited amounts of money on party building and voter mobilization activities. This unlimited fund-raising came to be called soft money, and it was interpreted as extending to national party committees as well. As a result, citizens could give unlimited amounts of money to party organizations for "party building," though these same citizens' and PACs' contributions to federal candidates were strictly limited. Parties could not give this soft money directly to federal candidates, but they could pay for any nonfederal portion of a campaign effort, and the money had a tendency to migrate wherever it was needed.

In effect, then, soft money became a way for individuals and groups to launder large campaign contributions through a party organization. The parties pushed hard to get the money. In a letter made famous by a Supreme Court case, for example, then-Republican National Chair Jim Nicholson sent a draft of the party's health-care proposals to the drug company Bristol-Myers Squibb and asked for any suggested changes—and a $250,000 soft-money contribution to the RNC.[26] Fat cats had reentered the building. It was not the law's stated intention for soft money to become an end run around the FECA contribution limits, but the difficulty of monitoring the uses of these funds made it so. In most states, soft money could be raised not only from individuals and PACs but also from corporate treasuries and labor union dues—funds that could not be donated directly to federal candidates under FECA.[27]

Tremendous sums flowed through the soft-money conduit from the early 1990s until 2002, when it was banned at the federal level (see BCRA). Soft money had become so attractive a source of funding, especially for the Democrats, who did not have as many hard-money donors, that in 2002 it comprised more than half the Democratic Party's receipts and more than one-third the Republicans'.[28] When the 1970s reforms were passed, party organizations didn't have enough money to be big players in congressional or presidential races. But the national parties have since become much more effective fund-raisers. Even after Congress prevented party committees from collecting unlimited soft money, the two parties have been able to raise more than $1 billion in each election. Their role in campaigns has grown correspondingly, especially in hard-fought races.

Issue Advocacy Ads

Issue advocacy ads (issue ads, for short) were originally defined as any political advertising that did not include the terms "elect," "vote for," "support," "oppose," or similar terms. As long as a political ad did not say these "magic words," courts held that the ad was not a campaign ad, because it did not *expressly advocate* electing a candidate. Courts again cited the vital importance of free speech in ruling that these issue ads could be aired by individuals or groups using unlimited funding, even while a campaign was in progress.

In 1996, the Democratic National Committee (DNC) argued that issue ads were actually a form of party-building and voter mobilization, so they should be able to use soft money to pay for issue ads supporting President Bill Clinton's reelection.[29] The issue ads sounded very much like campaign ads. For example, a later issue ad by Hillary Clinton's opponent in the 2000 New York Senate race featured several photogenic babies wearing New York Yankees caps, while a voice intoned, "Every one of these babies has lived in New York longer than Hillary Rodham Clinton." The ad's intent was clear. But because it did not explicitly say "vote against" Clinton or "vote for" her opponent, it was considered to be issue advocacy and thus could be funded with unlimited soft money.

From the candidate's perspective, issue ads were a mixed blessing. As with independent spenders, the issue ads run by outside groups sometimes conveyed different messages than the campaign would prefer. But they were a boon for the parties, who now had a legal way to use big donations from corporations, unions, and individuals in federal elections, and to get around FECA's spending limits for party organizations.

What Did the 1970s Reforms Accomplish?

By 2002, then, groups and parties had found impressive loopholes in FECA, including independent spending and issue ads, paid for largely by unregulated soft money. But the limits on direct contributions to federal candidates remained.

Intended and Unintended Effects   At first, the FECA reforms achieved most of their goals. They slowed the growth of campaign spending by presidential candidates for about three decades. Prior to the reforms, presidential campaign expenditures had tripled between 1960 and 1972. But real spending increased more slowly from 1972 to 2000 and actually declined in three of these eight elections. The contribution limits made small donors more valuable to candidates, which broadened the base of campaign funding. The reforms also opened much of the campaign finance process to public scrutiny.

Like all reforms, however, FECA had some worrisome, unintended effects. Most important was the growing imbalance between donations to candidates, which are limited, and the unlimited outside spending that soft money, issue ads, and independent expenditures made possible. The cap of $1,000 on hard-money contributions held until 2002, although inflation had greatly eroded its value during that time. These relatively low ceilings on individual contributions made soft money and independent spending all the more attractive to parties and interest groups. Both these forms of spending raise real questions of accountability and bring back the types of money—big money from individuals and corporate and union treasuries—that FECA's sponsors had hoped to clean out of federal campaigns.

In the long run, then, the reformers' efforts failed to meet one of their major goals: reducing the influence of interested money. Currently, probably no more than 12 percent of Americans give money to any political candidate or group,[30] and few give $200 or more. The other givers are groups—corporations, labor unions, and other organized interests—that want something specific from lawmakers. Whether they get what they want is not always clear, but we can assume they wouldn't be spending so much if they thought they were getting nothing in return.

Effects on the Parties   For the first two decades of FECA, the prevailing view was that the reforms had harmed the party organizations. By limiting their direct contributions to presidential and congressional candidates, FECA treated the parties as no more privileged in the campaign process than were PACs or other groups. In addition, public funding of presidential campaigns went to the candidates themselves, not to the parties, as it does in most other democracies. That created more distance between the party organization and the presidential campaign.

After 1996, however, the loopholes in the reforms, including independent spending, soft money, and issue advocacy, gave the national parties the means to raise and spend much more money than ever before. Large amounts of party money went into TV and radio advertising and beefed-up voter mobilization programs. State and local parties, energized by money received from the national parties, became more involved in campaigns. Some put major effort into the labor-intensive grassroots work that was the staple of party organizations in an earlier era (see Chapter 11). Soft money allowed the parties to increase their presence in the most competitive races, and the party organizations invested some of their new riches in state and local party building.[31] However, very few of the party-funded issue ads even mentioned the party labels, so they probably did not help to strengthen the parties' ties with voters.[32]

Another Try: The Bipartisan Campaign Reform Act (BCRA)

These unintended effects—soft money in particular—created pressures for new reforms. In 2002, after another set of fund-raising scandals, Congress passed the Bipartisan Campaign Reform Act (known as BCRA, pronounced BICK-ra, or McCain-Feingold, after its sponsors).[33] BCRA banned soft-money contributions to national parties. State and local parties can still accept money from individuals, corporations, and labor unions in amounts up to $10,000 per donor per year, as well as unlimited donations for use in state elections (see Table 12.2).

BCRA also tried to shrink the issue ad loophole. If an issue ad mentioned a federal candidate but didn't engage in express advocacy (by using the

TABLE 12.2 Limits on Campaign Contributions under Federal Law, 2020

	Limit on Contributions		
	Individual	Political Action Committee	State or National Party Committee
To each candidate or candidate committee per election	$ 2,800	$ 5,000*	$5,000**
To national party committees per year	$ 35,500	$15,000	No limit
(Note: Joint fund-raising committees, which distribute money to a party's organization and candidates, can accept up to about $700,000 from an individual [$1.4 million from a married couple] during a two-year election cycle.)			
To a state or local party committee per year	$ 10,000	$ 5,000	No limit
Total per two-year election cycle to all party committees***	~$700,000	No limit	No limit

Source: Federal Election Commission, "FEC announces 2019–2020 campaign cycle contribution limits," February 7, 2019, https://www.fec.gov/updates/fec-announces-20192020-campaign-cycle-contribution-limits/ (accessed August 23, 2020).

Notes: These are the limits on so-called hard-money contributions for the 2020 elections. Individual limits are indexed for inflation; PAC limits (and individual limits to PACs and state parties) are not.
*If the PAC qualifies as a "multicandidate committee" under federal law by making contributions to five or more federal candidates, the limit is $5,000. Otherwise, the committee is treated as an individual with a limit of $2,800.
**The limit is $5,000 for contributions to presidential and House candidates. The national and senatorial campaign committees can give a combined total of $49,600 to Senate candidates.
***This limit can be augmented substantially by individual contributions to the party's national convention, any election recounts and other legal proceedings, and national party headquarters buildings.

"magic words" such as "vote for," "elect," and "defeat"), and if it aired within 60 days of a general election or 30 days of a primary, then it would be termed an electioneering communication and would be regulated. These "electioneering" ads could not be funded by corporations or unions; they had to be paid for entirely by federally regulated money or by soft money contributed only by individuals. The restriction applied only to broadcast media ads directed at targeted audiences, however, so advocacy groups could continue to use soft money for direct mail, phone banks, and voter registration during this time. Many groups did move their soft money into these activities.[34] In addition, BCRA increased the individual contribution limit to $2,000 for federal campaigns, raised the overall limit on individual contributions to candidates, parties, and other political committees combined, and let these limits rise with inflation.

Although most congressional Democrats voted for the bill, Democratic leaders worried that their party's fund-raising would be seriously undercut by BCRA. For decades, Republicans had been more successful than Democrats in raising hard money; many more of the individuals able to contribute $2,000 to a campaign identified as Republicans. Democrats had been able to narrow the fund-raising gap by attracting soft money from labor unions, which BCRA banned. Sure enough, within a year, the RNC had three times as much cash on hand as did the DNC.

More End Runs: 527 and 501(c) Advocacy Groups

After BCRA, then, Democrats looked for a new way to pour soft money into campaigns. They found it in a class of groups called 527s. This odd name refers to provision 527 of the U.S. tax code, allowing certain tax-exempt groups to accept unlimited contributions and spend without limit on election advocacy— and since 2010 they can expressly call for the election or defeat of specific candidates and coordinate their activities with federal candidates or parties. They can also register voters, run get-out-the-vote drives, broadcast issue ads, send direct mail, and distribute voter guides. A small group of wealthy liberals formed several 527 groups in time for the 2004 campaign as a conduit for the soft money that would have gone to the national parties before BCRA.

Republicans had a harder time building their own network of 527s. Publicity about corporate scandals made business leaders uneasy about contributing to these groups. Then Congress required 527s to disclose their contributors and expenses. The FEC further regulated their fund-raising, treating 527s more like PACs. These groups continue to spend in elections but their spending has declined as a proportion of all campaign spending.

As a result, several organizations, including the U.S. Chamber of Commerce, began to funnel their independent spending through another category of groups organized as nonprofits. These tax-exempt "social welfare" groups, collectively called **501c4s**, have the advantage that they can accept unlimited donations from individuals, corporations, and unions but do not have to disclose the names of their donors publicly, as long as partisan political activity is not their "major purpose." Given that issue ads, even those referring to specific candidates, are not defined as "partisan" activities by law, there are few limits on these groups' campaign activities, as long as they do not contribute directly to candidates. Corporations in particular were attracted by this opportunity to avoid the consumer boycotts they might face if their names were publicly linked with controversial political messages. The sources of these "social welfare" groups' spending are highly concentrated. Most 501c4s are funded by very large (often million-dollar) donations from a very few individuals. These groups' campaign spending was dwarfed in 2020 by that of super PACs (which will be discussed later in this chapter). Yet, 501c4 groups were still able to pump an estimated $107 million into the 2018 campaigns and $80 million in 2020,[35] mainly to support Republican candidates and conservative causes. Some of their contributions are funneled through other nonprofits in a complex web of interconnected organizations. These funds, because they don't have to be publicly disclosed, are often referred to as **dark money**.

Each of these channels (see Table 12.3) is useful for certain kinds of fund-raising and spending. Thus, an organization might set up several different groups: a 501c4 to run ads with money that the givers do not want to disclose, a 527 for advocacy ads and ground war activities, and a PAC to give direct but limited contributions to candidates.

The National Parties Survived BCRA

Although BCRA deprived the national parties of unlimited soft money, the parties adapted again. They developed improved programs for attracting small contributors through the Internet. BCRA's higher limit on individual contributions let the parties raise larger donations. In addition, donors can give much bigger sums to joint fund-raising committees: a series of candidate and party committees linked together. The millions they have been able to raise from members of Congress (see Chapter 4) also helped the national parties survive the loss of soft money.

State and local party organizations had more difficulty adjusting to BCRA. After the ban on soft-money transfers from the national party organizations, state and local parties' fund-raising declined. State Democratic Parties suffered especially. As a result, many state parties stopped running broadcast ads for federal candidates. Most state parties found it difficult to increase their own fund-raising while complying with the complicated provisions of the new law.[36]

Bundling

Another unintended effect of BCRA was to encourage greater use of a practice called bundling. Although individual contributions to a campaign are limited, an individual or group can solicit large numbers of these individual donors, combine ("bundle") their contributions, deliver them to a campaign, and take credit for a much more substantial donation. When BCRA doubled the limit on individual donations, bundling became even more profitable. Groups such as the pro-choice EMILY's List and the anti-tax Club for Growth have given bundled donations totaling hundreds of thousands of dollars to a single candidate.

TABLE 12.3 Types of Non-Party Groups Allowed to Put Money into Election Campaigns

	Can the Group...				
Type of Group	**...donate money directly to candidates?**	**... accept donations?**	**...do independent spending?**	**...regulated by**	**...are donors anony- mous?**
Traditional PAC (Political Action Committee)	Yes	Yes—up to $5,000 per donor per election	Yes	FEC	No
Super PAC (Independent Expenditure- Only Committee)	No	Yes— unlimited amounts	Yes	FEC	No
527 Committee (Political Organization)	No	Yes— unlimited amounts	Yes	IRS	No
501c4 (Social Welfare Organization)	No	Yes— unlimited	Yes, as long as campaign contributions are not the group's primary purpose	IRS	Yes

Source: Federal Election Commission, various materials.

The Clinton campaign in 2016 set records for recruiting bundlers; by late September of 2016, they reported that 1,370 individuals had each bundled $100,000 in contributions. Trump's campaign did not release its numbers. Most of the bundlers are lawyers, lobbyists, finance executives, and developers who, like other big donors, have interests in federal policies.[37] It is clearly an end run around the contribution limits, but bundling remains legal.

Citizens United and Super PACS

The national parties survived BCRA, but BCRA did not survive the Supreme Court. The Court dismantled parts of BCRA with rulings culminating in *Citizens United v. FEC* (2010), just as it had earlier opened up huge loopholes in FECA. A narrow majority in *Citizens United* blocked BCRA's effort to shrink the issue ad loophole. Corporations and labor unions can spend as much as they'd like from their own treasuries at any time, the Court's majority ruled, even close to an election, on ads that expressly advocate the election or defeat of a presidential or congressional candidate. Without this right, the majority argued, corporations' and other groups' free speech rights would be limited.

Many expected *Citizens United* to open the floodgates to massive corporate campaign spending. A vehicle for that spending quickly appeared. A federal court of appeals in *SpeechNow.org vs. FEC* (2010) stated that if a PAC confined itself to independent spending, and gave no direct contributions to candidates, then it could accept unlimited contributions from individuals. Due to *Citizens United*, these independent-expenditure-only PACs, which quickly became known as **super PACs**, could accept unlimited donations from corporate treasuries and labor unions. Super PACs can directly advocate the election or defeat of a candidate through advertising; they can also do other types of campaigning such as opposition research and voter registration.

Super PACs didn't gear up in large numbers in time for the 2010 elections. The great majority of money spent in that election came from candidates' campaigns and party organizations, not from outside groups.[38] But by 2012, over 1,200 super PACs had formed. Most of the money spent by super PACs that year came from conservative groups. This helped Republicans make up for the slight Democratic advantage in candidates' fund-raising. Super PACs were a major reason why non-party groups aired more ads in the 2012 nomination campaign than the candidates themselves did.[39]

In 2016, super PACs raised $1.8 billion[40]—a powerful statement from a set of groups that came into existence only six years earlier. About half the money received by super PACs that year came from a small group of wealthy people who gave at least $1 million apiece. In fact, ten mega-donors were responsible for about 20 percent of the collections of super PACs.[41] Corporate interests such as oil and gas companies were also major contributors. Along with 501c4s, then, super PACs in 2016 were responsible for "an unprecedented concentration of political wealth."[42]

Super PACs are not supposed to coordinate with candidates or parties, but most do. In fact, hundreds of super PACs have been set up to support only one candidate each and led by the candidate's former staffers—and in one Indiana House race in 2016, the candidate's own father. These super PACs, then, functioned as shadow campaign committees. Other types of super PACs are closely allied with the party organizations or with ideological or other interest groups.[43] And most of their money comes from donors who don't live in the district or state where the PAC's money is spent.[44]

These PACs continued to pull in mammoth sums after 2016 (see Table 12.4). They raised $1.6 billion in 2018, though they saved almost half of that sum for the upcoming 2020 elections. The heavy hitters on the Republican side were the Congressional Leadership Fund and the Senate Leadership Fund (both party-related spenders), the Club for Growth, and a Trump-related super PAC (America First Action). The Senate Majority PAC and House Majority PAC led Democratic super PACs in 2018. In 2020 American Bridge became a major player for Democrats as well. In all, super PACs were responsible for more than $1.9 in spending during the 2019–2020 election season.

TABLE 12.4 Top Independent Spenders Among Outside Groups in Federal Campaigns, 2019–2020

Rank	Group (Ideological Leaning)	Type	Spending In millions of $
1	Senate Leadership Fund (Conservative)	Super PAC	$251.8
2	Senate Majority PAC (Liberal)	Super PAC	228.5
3	Congressional Leadership Fund (Conservative)	Super PAC	142.6
4	House Majority PAC (Liberal)	Hybrid/Super PAC	138.8
5	Priorities USA Action (Liberal)	Hybrid/Super PAC	135.8
6	America First Action (Conservative)	Super PAC	133.8
7	Future Forward USA (Liberal)	Hybrid/Super PAC	114.8
8	Preserve America PAC (Conservative)	Super PAC	103.0
9	Club for Growth Action (Conservative)	Super PAC	60.6
10	Independence USA PAC (Liberal)	Super PAC	56.0

Note: Hybrid PACs (Carey Committees) function as both traditional PACs and super PACs, keeping the two types of accounts separate.

Source: Federal Election Commission data from the Center for Responsive Politics as of November 27, 2020, www.opensecrets.org/outsidespending/summ.php?cycle=2020&chrt=V&disp=O&type=I (accessed November 28, 2020).

Like other PACs, super PACs must report who gave them money. But if individuals, groups, or corporations give to 501cs, which do not have to disclose their donors, and the 501cs in turn give the money to super PACs, the original sources of the funds can't be traced. Some groups make this very easy by setting up a super PAC and a 501c nonprofit group as "sister organizations," such as Trump's America First Action, a super PAC, and its 501c sister group, America First Policies. For the Democrats, the Senate Majority PAC is closely aligned with a nonprofit called Majority Forward. One reporter suggested, "In this campaign, every candidate needs his own billionaires"[45] (see box "The One Percent of the One Percent" on page 284).

Will Super PACs Replace Parties?

The massive super PAC spending raised concerns that Court decisions had given super PACs and other non-party groups a tremendous advantage over party organizations in influencing elections. If the rise of super PACs were to come at the parties' expense, the impact might be even more worrisome. Some researchers find that parties tend to promote more moderate incumbents than many outside groups or individual donors do. If so, then a reduced role for parties might elect legislators who further polarize and gridlock state legislatures and Congress.[46]

The One Percent of the One Percent

During the 2018 election cycle, less than half of a percent of the U.S. population gave 70 percent of all the money donated to candidates, parties, and other political groups. Just 100 individuals and families (along with companies they own or control) gave more than $1.6 million *each*, mainly to super PACs and other outside groups, which can legally receive unlimited contributions. A donation of $1.6 million is more than 24 times the median income of American households. These mega-donors' wealth has come mainly from financial services and oil and gas production companies as well as pharmaceuticals and technology industries. And these are only the contributions that were disclosed; many more gave similarly large amounts to 501c4 groups, which don't have to reveal the names of their donors. The *Citizens United* and *SpeechNOW* decisions gave these big donors the opportunity to make their dollars felt in elections for the first time in decades.

The best-known big givers include Sheldon Adelson, who owns hotels, casinos, and drug treatment facilities (he donated $124 million in 2018, almost all of it to Republican candidates and groups), and Michael Bloomberg, the owner of Bloomberg media (he contributed $96 million, almost all of it to Democrats). Brothers Charles and the late David Koch, who made their billion-dollar fortunes in the oil industry, are also longtime fixtures on the Big Donor list. The Kochs' ideology is libertarian—they want an end to many or most government functions—but, as practical investors, they spend their dollars to support Republicans and oppose Democrats. The Kochs developed and help fund a network of groups, most of them nonprofits, which gather annually to meet candidates and discuss strategy. Among the groups in the Koch network are Americans for Prosperity, a 501c (an early backer of the Tea Party movement); Freedom Partners, a 501c; Freedom Partners Action Fund, a super PAC; and the American Legislative Exchange Council (ALEC), which opposes action on climate change. Koch-backed groups have kept their distance from Donald Trump, but they continue to play a key role in conservative politics.

In 2020, virtually the same cast of characters was active again, and about three-quarters of the phenomenal sum (about $2.5 billion) raised by super PACs came from donors who gave at least $1 million each. Massive fund-raising by Republican super PACs helped their candidates keep pace with a tsunami of small-dollar Democratic fund-raising.

Sources: Center for Responsive Politics, "Top Individual Contributors: All Federal Contributions," 2018 election cycle, https://www.opensecrets.org/overview/topindivs.php (accessed August 24, 2020), and Jane Mayer, *Dark Money* (New York: Doubleday, 2016).

The argument that super PACs might supplant the parties' influence rests in part on super PACs' superior ability to raise funds from big givers. Since BCRA, party organizations are no longer allowed to fund their independent spending by raising unlimited funds from individuals and groups. Instead, parties have to raise their money in limited portions from individuals and PACs. Wouldn't you rather raise $1 million from one individual, as a super PAC can, than try to persuade 1,000 people to donate $1,000 each?

However, a later Supreme Court decision helped correct this imbalance. In 2014, the Court in *McCutcheon vs. FEC* overturned the aggregate limits on how much a single donor could give to all federal candidates, parties, and PACs combined. Then Congress increased the amount an individual could give to a party committee under some conditions. The result was that a wealthy couple can now give more than $1.4 million to the national party committee of their choice in a two-year election cycle (depending on how many state parties are part of the agreement), using joint fund-raising "victory" committees and donations to the party's national convention.[47] And the *McCutcheon* decision raised speculation that the Court would remove all ceilings on donations to parties.

To this point, super PACs have not mounted a major threat to the parties' role in elections. In 2012, most of the candidates supported by super PACs lost their races. In 2016, more than half the spending in competitive House races came from the parties,[48] and by January 2020, President Trump had enhanced the Republican Party's fund-raising by attracting more than 1.6 million new donors to the national party.[49] PACs pay much higher rates for media ads than candidates do, so their funds don't go as far as those contributed to candidates. Another weakness is that FEC rules don't allow super PACs to pay for campaign staff, candidate travel, or other organizational aspects of the campaign. So in 2016, two Republican candidates (governors Scott Walker of Wisconsin and Rick Perry of Texas) dropped out of the presidential nomination race even though their super PACs still had $15–20 million in funds. The money available to their super PACs, at least during the invisible primary (see Chapter 10), thus couldn't save candidates who fell short in their own fund-raising and organizational expertise.

In short, super PACs are more capable of supplementing party committees' efforts than of replacing them. Because super PACs typically operate with much less overhead spending than do the RNC and DNC, they can be more nimble and flexible in supporting candidates endorsed by party committees. Beginning in 2016 super PACs were moving increasingly into opposition research, canvassing, and voter turnout in addition to funding media ads. This permits super PACs and party organizations to divide campaign tasks between them, utilizing the strengths of each type of organization. For instance, by combining with 501c groups, super PACs can avoid disclosing the sources of their funds, whereas parties cannot. If parties and super PACs are able to maintain collaborative relationships, then any expansion of super PAC fund-raising should help the party organizations by giving them additional tools to contest elections.

State Regulation and Financing

So far, the chapter has focused mainly on campaign finance for presidential and congressional races. Each state makes its own campaign finance rules for state-level offices. These state laws have gotten more attention recently by default: Because Congress has been so gridlocked by partisanship, big funders are increasingly attracted to state elections. Gaining single-party control over a state legislature and governorship allows state parties and their interest group allies to reshape state policy. Single-party control has led some state legislatures to restrict union activity or slash taxes and others to legalize marijuana. Although most states limit individuals', PACs', corporations', labor unions', and/or parties' contributions to campaigns,[50] their laws differ. State party leaders have taken advantage of these differences to move campaign money from states with more lenient laws to competitive races in other states, particularly those where party control of the legislature could flip. These creative transfers are often accomplished with the help of national groups such as the Republican State Leadership Committee and the two parties' governors' associations.[51]

In 2020, outside political groups spent millions on independent spending in a variety of governors' and state legislative races, helping to affect the agendas of those campaigns. This contributed to the nationalization of state and local elections. To limit the effects of these large sums on their elections, several states and some cities (such as Portland, Oregon and New York City) have provided optional public funding for at least some types of candidates, typically covering only part of the campaign's costs.[52] But most of these programs are small and poorly funded, and in contrast, bills have been introduced in many states to loosen even further the restrictions on state campaign finance.

Has Campaign Finance Regulation Made a Difference?

You have now read much more than you wanted to know about campaign finance reform. These reforms have had an impact. Compared with the "Wild West" period of unregulated campaign finance before FECA, citizens (and candidates' opponents) now have a greater opportunity to learn who is giving money to whom in campaigns. Transparency is far from complete, of course, because 501c4 groups can still hide the names of their donors, and groups running independent spending ads can still form using names ("Citizens for America") that don't tell viewers who they really are. And with the rise of 501c4 groups, the proportion of non-party groups disclosing the names of donors who paid for their political ads has dropped dramatically—and the sums spent have grown tremendously.[53]

Contributions directly to candidates are still limited and reported. But reformers have been frustrated by the ability of corporations, unions, other groups, and individuals to put much larger sums into "independent" spending on ads that look very similar to the ads run by candidates. To those who support recent Supreme Court rulings, that is the way it should be; free speech, they feel, is more important than the effort to limit corruption. Yet as a consequence, many of the reformers' aims—to limit interested money and slow the growth of campaign spending—are almost as far out of reach now as they were before FECA became law.[54] And FECA's aim of tying candidates' fund-raising more closely to their public support has been seriously frustrated by court decisions. Super PACs can raise huge sums for candidates with little public support; all the candidate needs is a supportive billionaire or two.

Money in American Politics

Both before and after these reforms, money has played a bigger role in American elections than in those of most other democracies. In the U.S., the sheer size of constituencies leads candidates to buy expensive mass media time. The large number of elected officials combined with frequent primary and general elections has produced a year-round election industry. Fund-raising occupies a great deal of the candidates' time even after they are elected, which distracts public officials from a thoughtful consideration of the public's needs and may give big contributors undue influence on public policy. Even if elected officials hold relatively safe seats, they are expected to raise a lot of money to help their more vulnerable party colleagues win reelection. And because many contributors have intense views on issues, party polarization is increased.

Campaigns don't have to be funded this way. In the United Kingdom, for instance, the active portion of election campaigns runs for only about six to seven weeks, during which all the public-service TV channels have to show the party political broadcasts.[55] Parliamentary candidates can spend no more than the equivalent of $20,000 each—about what hopeless challengers spend in the U.S. On the other hand, Britons can watch daily and often contentious news conferences by the parties' leaders.

The American system of campaign finance has consequences. The fact that candidates dominate the fund-raising in most American campaigns gives them greater independence from their party organizations once they take office. The parties are working hard to increase their role in the raising and spending of campaign money. Their ingenuity was sorely tested by FECA, BCRA, and now by *Citizens United*, but both parties have shown a lot of resilience in adapting to these reforms so far.

After all this experience with reforms that fall short of their mark, is there any point in continuing to try to regulate campaign finance? Many would argue that it's a useless effort, because interested money will always find its way into the pockets of power. On the other hand, although people continue to steal from others, that is not normally used as an argument for repealing laws against theft. The lifting of all campaign finance rules would lead to unrestricted influence of big money on politics, even if the big money came from other nations or drug cartels. So the struggle to contain interested money will continue.

Notes

1 Benjamin I. Page, Larry M. Bartels, and Jason Seawright, "Democracy and the Policy Preferences of Wealthy Americans," *Perspectives on Politics* 11 (2013): 51–73.
2 These figures combine the amounts spent by candidates, parties, and interest groups. Unless otherwise noted, all figures cited in this chapter come from Federal Election Commission reports, at times (and so noted) via the Campaign Finance Institute or the Center for Responsive Politics (CRP), and in this particular case from the Center for Responsive Politics at https://www.opensecrets.org/overview/cost.php. For excellent analyses of campaign finance, see Michael J. Malbin, ed., *The Election after Reform* (Lanham, MD: Rowman & Littlefield, 2006); and Paul S. Herrnson, Costas

Panagopoulos, and Kendall L. Bailey, *Congressional Elections*, 8th ed. (Los Angeles, CA: Sage/CQ Press, 2020).

3 Ylan Mui, "Conservative Koch Brothers' Network to Spend Up to $400 Million for the Midterm Election Cycle," *CNBC*, January 28, 2018, https://www.cnbc.com/2018/01/27/koch-brothers-network-to-spend-400-million-in-midterm-election-cycle.html (accessed August 23, 2020).

4 FEC data calculated by the Center for Responsive Politics, https://www.opensecrets.org/overview/incumbs.php?cycle=2018&type=G&party=S (accessed).

5 Ibid.

6 Brennan Center for Justice, "Outside Spending Enters Pennsylvania Supreme Court Race," October 16, 2015, at https://www.brennancenter.org/our-work/analysis-opinion/outside-spending-enters-pennsylvania-supreme-court-race (accessed August 23, 2020). On local campaign finance, see Brian E. Adams, *Campaign Finance in Local Elections* (Boulder, CO: Lynne Rienner, 2011).

7 See John J. Coleman and Paul F. Manna, "Congressional Campaign Spending and the Quality of Democracy," *Journal of Politics* 62 (2000): 757–789.

8 Gary C. Jacobson, *The Politics of Congressional Elections*, 7th ed. (New York: Pearson-Longman, 2009), p. 45.

9 See these articles in the *American Journal of Political Science*: Donald Philip Green and Jonathan S. Krasno, "Salvation for the Spendthrift Incumbent," 32 (1988): 884–907; Gary C. Jacobson, "The Effects of Campaign Spending in House Elections," 34 (1990): 334–362; and Kenneth Benoit and Michael Marsh, "The Campaign Value of Incumbency," 52 (2008): 874–890.

10 Andrew B. Hall, "Systemic Effects of Campaign Spending," *Political Science Research and Methods,* 4 (2016): 343–359.

11 Seth J. Hill and Gregory A. Huber, "Representativeness and Motivations of the Contemporary Donorate," *Political Behavior* 39 (#1 2017): 3–29.

12 See, for example, Anne E. Baker, "Getting Short-Changed?" *Social Science Quarterly* 97 (2016): 1096–1107; Michael J. Barber, "Representing the Preferences of Donors, Partisans, and Voters in the US Senate," *Public Opinion Quarterly* 80 (2016): 225–249.

13 Sarah Bryner and Doug Weber, "Women March onto the Ballot in 2018," Center for Responsive Politics, March 2018, https://www.opensecrets.org/news/reports/women-candidates (accessed August 23, 2020).

14 Data from the Campaign Finance Institute.

15 Gregory Wawro, "A Panel Probit Analysis of Campaign Contributions and RollCall Votes," *American Journal of Political Science* 45 (2001): 563–579.

16 See Richard L. Hall and Frank W. Wayman, "Buying Time," *American Political Science Review* 84 (1990): 797–820, and Joshua L. Kalla and David E. Broockman, "Campaign Contributions Facilitate Access to Congressional Officials," *American Journal of Political Science* 60 (2016): 545–558.

17 FEC, "Price Index Adjustments for Contribution and Expenditure Limitations and Lobbyist Bundling Disclosure Threshold," February 7, 2019, https://www.federalregister.gov/documents/2019/02/07/2019-01516/price-index-adjustments-for-contribution-and-expenditure-limitations-and-lobbyist-bundling (accessed December 17, 2019).

18 Rebecca Ballhaus and Brody Mullins, "Party Politics: FEC at Loggerheads on How to Celebrate Anniversary," *Wall Street Journal,* April 16, 2015, https://www.wsj.com/articles/party-politics-fec-at-loggerheads-on-how-to-celebrate-anniversary-1429228827 (accessed August 23, 2020).

19 On public funding, see Michael J. Malbin, "Small Donors, Large Donors and the Internet," cfinst.org/president/pdf/PresidentialWorkingPaper_April09.pdf (accessed August 23, 2020).

20 On New York's public campaign finance system, see Michael J. Malbin and Brendan Glavin, "Small Donor Public Finance in New York State," January 2020, http://cfinst.org/pdf/state/ny/Small-Donor-Public-Finance-in-NY_Jan2020.pdf (accessed August 23, 2020).

21 See Thomas E. Mann, "Linking Knowledge and Action," *Perspectives on Politics* 1 (2003): 69–83.

22 The cases are *Colorado Republican Federal Campaign Committee v. Federal Election Commission* (1996), known as "Colorado I," and *McConnell v. Federal Election Commission* (2003).

23 Michael Malbin, "Massive Amounts Were Spent by the Candidates and Independent Spenders in the Races that Decided the 2018 Midterms," press release by the Campaign Finance Institute, November 9, 2018.

24 Data from the Campaign Finance Institute, https://www.followthemoney.org/research/institute-reports/10-years-after-citizens-united-state-races-transformed-by-explosive-growth-in-independent-spending? (accessed August 23, 2020).

25 See, for instance, John Sides, Daron Shaw, Matt Grossman, and Keena Lipsitz, *Campaigns and Elections*, 3rd ed. (New York: W.W. Norton, 2018).

26 From the record in *McConnell v. Federal Election Commission*, quoted in Adam Cohen, "Buying a High-Priced Upgrade on the Political Back-Scratching Circuit," *New York Times*, September 15, 2003, p. A22.

27 See Anthony Corrado, Sarah Barclay, and Heitor Gouvea, "The Parties Take the Lead," in John C. Green and Rick Farmer, eds., *The State of the Parties*, 4th ed. (Lanham, MD: Rowman & Littlefield, 2003), pp. 97–114.

28 For a different view of the partisan impact of soft money, see Raymond J. LaRaja, *Small Change* (Ann Arbor: University of Michigan Press, 2008).

29 John Kenneth White and Daniel M. Shea, *New Party Politics* (Belmont, CA: Wadsworth, 2004), p. 258.

30 Adam Hughes, "5 Facts about U.S. Political Donations," *Pew Research Center*, May 17, 2017, https://www.pewresearch.org/fact-tank/2017/05/17/5-facts-about-u-s-political-donations/ (accessed August 23, 2020).

31 Raymond J. La Raja, "State Parties and Soft Money," in Green and Farmer, *The State of the Parties*, 4th ed., pp. 132–150.

32 Jonathan Krasno and Kenneth Goldstein, "The Facts About Television Advertising and the McCain-Feingold Bill," *PS Political Science & Politics* 35 (2002): 210.

33 Raymond J. LaRaja, "State and Local Political Parties," in Malbin, *The Election after Reform*, Chapter 4.

34 Michael M. Franz, Joel Rivlin, and Kenneth Goldstein, "Much More of the Same," in Malbin, ed., *The Election after Reform*, Chapter 7.

35 Data estimated from information provided by the Center for Responsive Politics, www.opensecrets.org/dark-money/basics (accessed August 23, 2020). Other 501(c) organizations that can raise and spend unlimited sums on political activity, though subject to legal constraints, include 501(c)3 charities, 501(c)5 labor union groups, and 501(c)6 trade associations, such as the Chamber of Commerce.

36 Joseph E. Sandler and Neil P. Reiff, "State and Local Parties Must Tread Carefully Through the Campaign Finance Minefield," *Campaigns & Elections* 25 (2004), pp. 50–51.

37 Center for Responsive Politics, https://www.opensecrets.org/resources/10things/02. php (accessed August 23, 2020).

38 Michael M. Franz, "The *Citizens United* Election?" *The Forum* 8 (2010): 22.

39 Michael M. Franz, "Interest Groups in Electoral Politics: 2012 in Context," *The Forum* 10 (2012): 62–79.

40 Data from the Center for Responsive Politics, https://www.opensecrets.org/ outsidespending/summ.php?cycle=2016&chrt=V&disp=O&type=S

41 Fredreka Schouten and Christopher Schnaars, "Super PAC Donations Surge Past $1 Billion," *USA Today,* September 21, 2016, p. A1.

42 Matea Gold, "The New Gilded Age," *Washington Post*, April 16, 2016, p. A1.

43 Ibid.

44 James G. Gimpel, Frances E. Lee, and Shanna Pearson-Merkowitz, "The Check Is in the Mail," *American Journal of Political Science* 52 (2008): 373–394.

45 Jane Mayer, "Leader of the PACs," *New Yorker,* February 8, 2012, https://www. newyorker.com/news/news-desk/leader-of-the-pacs (accessed August 23, 2020).

46 Raymond J. La Raja and Brian F. Schaffner, *Campaign Finance and Political Polarization* (Ann Arbor: University of Michigan Press, 2015); Michael J. Barber, "Ideological Donors, Contribution Limits, and the Polarization of American Legislatures," *Journal of Politics* 78 (2016): 296–310.

47 See Michelle Ye Hee Lee and Anu Narayanswamy, "Trump's Reelection Effort Has Spent $983 Million So Far," *Washington Post*, July 20, 2020, p. A6.

48 Gary C. Jacobson, "Congress: Nationalized, Polarized, and Partisan," in Michael Nelson, ed., *The Elections of 2016* (Los Angeles, CA: Sage, 2018), p. 180.

49 On Trump's fund-raising in 2020, see the Center for Responsive Politics, https:// www.opensecrets.org/2020-presidential-race (accessed August 23, 2020).

50 See the National Conference of State Legislatures at http://www.ncsl.org/research/- elections-and-campaigns/campaign-finance-an-overview.aspx (accessed August 23, 2020).

51 See Nicholas Confessore, "A National Strategy Funds State Political Monopolies," *New York Times,* January 12, 2014, p. A1.

52 See Michael Miller, "Gaming Arizona," *PS: Political Science and Politics* 61 (2008): 527–532. The Campaign Finance Institute has researched several types of public financing programs; see www.cfinst.org.

53 Data from the Center for Responsive Politics at www.opensecrets.org/outsidespending/ disclosure.php (accessed August 23, 2020).

54 Raymond J. LaRaja, "From Bad to Worse," *The Forum* 6 (2008): Issue 1, Article 2.

55 See "Campaign Finance: United Kingdom," Library of Congress, July 1, 2015, https:// www.loc.gov/law/help/campaign-finance/uk.php (accessed August 23, 2020).

PART FIVE

The Party in Government

As you may recall from Chapter 1, each *party in government* includes *all the elected or appointed public officials* who see themselves as belonging to that party. They are vitally important to the party as a whole because they, not the party organization or the party electorate, have the power to pass or implement the party's proposals on college student loans, immigration, abortion, and gun rights. Without their party in government, the American parties would be very much like interest groups: lots of preferences, little power to make them into law.

The Republican Party in government, like its Democratic counterpart, is a wide-ranging group. In addition to everyone elected to the House, the Senate, and the White House as a Republican, the Republican Party in government includes Republicans who work for federal, state, and local administrative agencies; Republican governors and state legislators; Republicans serving in local elective and appointive offices; and even judges (and Supreme Court justices) who see themselves as Republicans. In the same way, the Democratic Party in government ranges from Democratic senators to Department of Defense workers and county assessors who consider themselves to be Democrats.

These people share the same party label but they do not always share the same priorities. The design of the American political system works against a unified party in government. Because members of Congress are elected separately from the president, they do not need to act as a single Democratic or Republican "team." They represent different constituencies, so they face different pressures from their constituents as to what they, and the rest of their party, should be doing. Remember that congressional candidates are not chosen to run by their party organization; instead, they become the party's candidates by winning voter support in primary elections. The use of direct primaries combined with the separation of powers and federalism make it very difficult for members of the party in government to unite in support of a single, coherent set of policy goals. In fact, in the few cases of Congress members who represent a district that normally favors the other party, congressional party leaders may encourage them to vote *against* their party on an occasional bill to please their constituents and win reelection.

For decades, reformers have dreamed of an alternative. One is the idea of *party government,* also called *responsible parties.* Its proponents argue that American democracy would be improved if the parties were to offer clearer and fuller statements of their proposed policies, nominate candidates pledged to support those policies, and see to it that their winning candidates enact those programs. Voters would then choose not only between candidates but, more importantly, between alternative sets of policies and be assured that the winning set would be put into effect. That would greatly strengthen the parties' role, and voters, the argument goes, would be better able to hold their government accountable.

Although we do see something close to party government in several other democracies, including Britain, it is not likely to develop fully in the U.S. without fundamental institutional change. Because of the separation of powers, Republicans can hold a majority in Congress while a Democrat sits in the White House, or one party can dominate the House while the other controls the Senate. In fact, in the past half-century, divided party control of government has been the norm at the national level and in several states. That makes it difficult for a party to implement all its preferred policies. Instead, legislation is likely to require compromise—a process that many Americans value in theory but dislike in practice. Even at times when one party controls both Congress and the presidency, the legislative party might not always be in perfect agreement with its White House colleague, as recent (and exasperated) presidents have found. The party organization can't guarantee that all the party's candidates, selected in primary elections in differing constituencies across the nation, will run on the party's platform. And the party electorate is still connected only loosely to the party organization.

Yet the Democrats and the Republicans have been acting more like responsible parties in recent years, even without institutional reform. Congress and state legislatures now divide along party lines more than they have in decades. Partisanship has a major influence on the staffing of top executive offices and the appointment of judges. As more citizens are attracted to party work because of particular issues that concern them, the pressure builds for greater party responsibility.

The chapters in Part V address these questions of party influence in government. Chapters 13 and 14 examine the roles of the parties in the organization and operation of the legislature, the executive branch, and the courts. Chapter 15 looks at the degree to which party government can be said to exist in American politics.

CHAPTER 13

Parties in Congress and State Legislatures

It may surprise you to learn that in many ways, Congress works the way the founders of the United States expected. It moves slowly, because it reflects the divisions as well as the needs of the voting population. Those divisions could be seen even in the first Congresses. Now, the heightened party polarization of the U.S. House and Senate can tie the Congress into knots even more effectively. Yet partisanship is not the only reason why Congress is often gridlocked. It's true that Congress members now vote with their party in Congress (and their party's leadership) more regularly than they have in over a century. The gulf between the two parties in Congress is wider than it has been for decades: Republicans in Congress have become more deeply and consistently conservative, and Democrats have become more consistently liberal. As a result, each party has a stronger motive to keep the other party from passing bills. Yet this would not be enough in itself to produce gridlock; in most legislatures, the majority party would be able to pass its legislation over the minority's objections.

But Congress is not most legislatures. It was designed to put roadblocks in the path of majorities, to protect minority rights. One of the biggest roadblocks is the separation of powers. In a political system without a separation of powers—a parliamentary regime, such as that of Great Britain—the party that wins (or can put together a coalition of parties to win) a majority of legislative seats becomes the governing party; its leader becomes the head of government, and it can win every legislative battle in which it stays together. If a majority of legislators vote against the governing party's major policies, then either the governing cabinet must be reshuffled or the legislature must be dissolved and its members sent home to campaign for their jobs again. That provides a strong incentive for each legislative party to remain united. American legislators do not face these pressures. They can reject the proposals of a president, a governor, or even a leader of their own legislative party without toppling the government and having to face a new election.

And they do at times reject the proposals of their party leaders. In recent years, for instance, very conservative Republican House members who formed the House "Freedom Caucus" have refused to go along with their party's House leadership. They are able to do so because, like many other Congress members, they represent districts considered safe for their party; active Republicans in

293

their districts support their highly conservative stands and reward them with reelection when they resist any efforts at compromise or moderation by the House Republican leadership. As a Republican House member complained in the mid-2010s, "We really don't have 218 votes [i.e., a majority] to determine a bathroom break over here on our side."[1]

To add to these challenges, party control of both houses has shifted frequently, so both parties have tasted majority power in recent years and hope to keep or regain it in the next election. Many Congress members are convinced that their party gains voter support by stressing the contrasts between the parties, rather than by compromising to pass legislation. Every bill becomes a way to "send messages" to party voters.[2] Members of both parties see little point in making long-term policy concessions when they could instead take "Hell, no!" stands that please activists back home.

So party power can't shoulder all the blame for gridlock; the design of Congress, the unusually frequent recent shifts in party control of both houses, and the greater polarization of members and activists all deserve a share. In fact, to some analysts, increased party voting doesn't reflect the power of *party* in legislative life at all. Rather, they suggest, legislators rely on their own issue preferences when they vote, and conservative legislators have sorted themselves into the Republican Party and liberals into the Democratic Party.[3] However, there is ample evidence that changes in the parties outside of Congress, organizational reforms, and party leaders themselves have expanded the legislative parties' importance.[4]

How the Parties Are Organized in Congress

What are the parties in Congress? Recall from Chapter 1 that members of the first Congresses divided into two groupings reflecting their differing views on big issues and to serve their legislative needs. Now, these legislative parties coordinate ideas about public policy, set priorities, divide up the workload in developing legislation, try to get the party's bills passed, hold their leaders accountable, protect the party's reputation, and elect party candidates.[5] The congressional parties are independent of the national, state, and local party organizations but have ties to these organizations.

The members of each legislative party come together in meetings (called caucuses by the House Democrats and conferences by the Senate Democrats and both Republican parties) to select their party's leaders (see box "Party Leadership Positions in the House and Senate" on page 295). They also structure the chamber itself by nominating candidates for its presiding officer (the Speaker of the House or president pro tempore of the Senate) and approving procedures for appointing party members to congressional committees.

The majority party dominates the organization of both houses. In the House, the majority party's elected leader, the Speaker, has extensive power over the chamber's operations. The majority party leadership controls the action in committees and on the floor and chooses the chairs of all the committees. Most of each committee's members come from the majority party, by a margin that

Party Leadership Positions in the House and Senate

Each party creates its own leadership structure in each house of Congress; the individual leaders are elected by the entire party membership of the chamber. At the top of the hierarchy is the party leader (called the **majority** or **minority leader**, depending on whether the party controls the chamber). In the House of Representatives, the **Speaker** ranks above the majority leader as the true leader of the majority party. These party leaders have assistants called **whips**,[6] who tell members the party's position on bills, try to convince them to vote the way the party leadership wants, and keep a head count of each bill's supporters and opponents.

Each congressional party also has several specialized leadership positions.

There is a **conference** or (among House Democrats) **caucus chair** to head the meeting of all party members. Other chairs are selected for the **Policy Committee**, which identifies the party's position on proposed legislation and sets issue priorities; the **Campaign Committee**, which provides campaign support to the party's congressional candidates, and any other committees the legislative party may create. Variations do occur; House Democrats, for example, have a single Steering and Policy Committee, and for Senate Republicans, the Republican Conference assigns members to committees as well as serving other functions.

is often larger than the majority's margin in the chamber. Democrats held the House majority from the early 1950s until 1995, from 2007 to 2011, and again beginning in 2019. In the Senate, the majority leader manages floor action, to the degree that floor action can be managed in that more individualistic institution. Republicans held a Senate majority from 1981 to 1987, for most of the period from 1995 to 2007, and again beginning in 2015.

Changes in the Power of House Party Leaders

Party leaders in Congress are chosen by the votes of all members of their legislative party. Their power is, in effect, delegated to them by their party caucus (or conference), and they serve subject to its approval.[7] Party members' willingness to grant power to their congressional party leaders has changed a lot over time.

The Revolt against "Czar" Cannon   Years ago, power in the House of Representatives was highly centralized in the hands of the Speaker. In the first decade of the 1900s, powerful Speaker Joe Cannon chaired the Rules Committee, the "traffic cop" through which he could control the flow of legislation to the floor. He appointed all standing committees and their chairs, putting his chief supporters in key positions, and generally had the resources and sanctions needed to enforce party discipline.[8]

In 1910, however, dissidents within his own party combined with the minority Democrats to revolt against "Czar" Cannon. For many decades after that, Speakers were not able to muster the level of power that Cannon commanded. Instead, they had to operate in a much more decentralized House in which party discipline could be maintained only through skillful bargaining and strong personal loyalties. Successful Speakers during this era were skilled negotiators rather than commanders.[9]

After Cannon, through most of the 1900s, chairs of the standing committees that dealt with proposed legislation were selected using the seniority rule: The longest-serving member of the majority party on a committee automatically became its chair. Because of this rule, members of the majority party could win a chairmanship simply by being reelected to Congress many times, even if they did not support their party leadership's position on issues—in fact, even if they voted with the other party more often than with their own. That gave long-serving party members—many of them conservative southern Democrats—a base of power in Congress independent of the party leaders. Committee chairs could, and often did, use that power in a dictatorial manner.

Growing Party Coordination   During the 1970s, however, the expanded number of liberals in the Democratic caucus, elected in the wake of the Watergate scandals, called for limiting the committee chairs' independence. They believed that weakening the seniority rule and strengthening the party caucus would let House Democrats achieve greater policy coordination and pass more liberal policies. The House Democratic caucus first gave itself the right to vote by secret ballot on whether each committee chair would be retained. Soon after, the caucus did replace a few chairs with less senior Democrats whose views and behavior were more acceptable to liberals in the caucus.[10] The remaining committee chairs, and those who wanted to become chairs, saw that they needed to pay more attention to the views of the caucus. By reducing the chairs' autonomy, this reform expanded the power of their main competitors, the party leaders. And because the Democrats ran the House, it changed the structure of authority in the chamber as a whole.

The power to assign members to committees—a decision vital to members' careers—was moved to the new Steering and Policy Committee dominated by the Speaker. The Speaker was also allowed to choose, with the caucus's approval, the chair and other Democratic members of the Rules Committee, whose independence had formerly been a thorn in the side of the party leadership. Thus, the Speaker gained more power over other party legislators' futures and the fate of the bills they wanted to pass. The whip system, legislators responsible for informing their party colleagues about the party's stands and for finding out how many members are supporting those stands, was enlarged and made more responsive to party leaders.[11] The majority party leadership became not just a traffic cop but a major source of power and policy development.

The Gingrich Revolution

The Republican minority had no input into the Democratic procedural reforms of the 1970s and 1980s. But in 1994, Republicans won a majority of House seats for the first time in 40 years, after a campaign centered on a set of conservative policy pledges called the "Contract with America." The election of new conservative members made the House Republicans even more cohesive. Most of these newcomers had gotten campaign help from Representative Newt Gingrich, then the second-ranking Republican leader in the House, and credited him with engineering their party's unexpected takeover. They elected Gingrich Speaker and gave him unprecedented authority to push the Republican agenda.

To do so, Gingrich set aside the seniority rule entirely. The party leadership could now choose committee chairs on the basis of their commitment to bringing the party's desired bills to the floor. Each committee chair was limited to a six-year term. Why did the committee chairs agree to such a sharp reduction in their power? Republicans had only a slender majority in the House, and they faced a Democrat, Bill Clinton, in the White House. Perhaps GOP members accepted strong party discipline to have a better chance of achieving the goals of the Contract.[12] Or perhaps the change reflected the chairs' personal loyalty to Gingrich, or even fear for their political careers if they resisted. It was a major step in the expansion of party power in the House, and Gingrich became the strongest Speaker since Cannon.[13]

The result, at least initially, was a level of party discipline with which "Czar" Cannon would have felt comfortable. When the ten sections of the Contract with America came to a vote in the House, out of a possible 2,300 Republican voting decisions (ten provisions times 230 Republican House members), there were only 111 "no" votes; 95 percent of Republican votes supported the party leadership's position. More than in almost a century, the majority party disciplined itself to achieve policy goals.

… And Later Shifts in Party Control

Gingrich's heyday didn't last long; he stepped down as Speaker after GOP House losses in 1998. But his reforms survived and even expanded. Republicans eliminated the term limit on the Speaker and undercut seniority rules even more to move loyal leadership allies into powerful subcommittee chairs.[14] Democrats complained that they were being shut out of conference committees and prevented from offering amendments to bills. The Republican leadership was remarkably effective in pushing legislation through the House.

Although the Democrats restored the practice of letting the party caucus choose committee chairs when the party won control of the House in 2007, and almost all the chairs chosen by the caucus were the most senior Democrats on their committees, incoming Speaker Nancy Pelosi imposed more party discipline on committee chairs than had previous Democratic Speakers. Chairs were now expected to support the party leadership's aims and raise a lot of money for party candidates' campaigns. And the Democratic leadership shut the minority Republicans out of the legislative process with as much zeal as the Republicans under Gingrich had shut out the Democrats.

The 2010 midterms brought a lot of new, very conservative Republicans into the House, who allied with the Tea Party-associated Freedom Caucus and chafed under the Gingrich reforms. Demanding a bigger role in creating policy, these new members insisted on a more open legislative process, with more extensive floor debate and more amendments to bills. When Democrat Nancy Pelosi succeeded to the speakership in 2019, she too had to accommodate the differing interests within her party's caucus, balancing the demands of the left-wingers with those of more moderate Democrats elected in districts that had supported Donald Trump. And Republican party leaders in the late 2010s were often constrained by mixed signals from the White House; Senate majority leader Mitch McConnell promised that he wouldn't call up any bill that didn't have the president's approval, but it was often unclear what President Trump would approve.[15]

Overall, the rules changes have made House members more dependent on their party leadership than they were several decades ago. Congressional committees have less opportunity to deliberate about legislation. In some cases, party leaders have been able to produce legislation behind closed doors, with no input at all from the other party, or even from backbenchers in their own party, as happened when the Republican House leadership created its bill to replace "Obamacare" in 2017. If members want to pass legislation and advance in the House, they need to show considerable loyalty to their party and its leaders. To the extent that their efforts help their party gain or keep majority status in the House, members can better achieve their individual goals.[16]

The trend toward increasing leadership power has not prevented challenges to the party leadership in the 2010s, however. Some House members occasionally express their longing to return to the **"regular order,"** in which committees and subcommittees examine bills and negotiate their content, permitting more participation by rank-and-file members in the work of Congress, rather than party leaders crafting bills without wide consultation. However, the close competition between the parties for control of Congress puts a priority on unified party messaging to rev up the party's base. That can be done most effectively by a strong party leadership.

What Caused This Stronger Party Leadership?

One main reason why individual House members have been more willing to accept strong party leadership since the 1970s is that the members of each party have become more ideologically cohesive—more inclined to agree with their party colleagues on issues.[17] As discussed in Chapter 7, white southern voters were leaving the Democratic Party in increasing numbers since the 1970s, and fewer conservative southern Democrats were being elected to Congress. Democratic House members, then, became more uniformly liberal than had been the case in many decades. This process reached full flower in the mid-1990s. Because of the committee reforms, the remaining conservative southern Democrats lost their strongholds of committee power. The sharp gulf that had separated southern Democrats from northern Democrats during the mid-1900s had dried up. Congressional Republicans were becoming more ideologically unified as well and had been energized by the conservative policy leadership coming from President Ronald Reagan in the 1980s.

When a party is ideologically cohesive, the party caucus finds it easier to agree on a unified position on legislation. The members of a cohesive party can better trust that their leaders will share and promote their policy concerns and protect their reelection interests. In addition, the two congressional parties were more at odds with one another on issues during this period than they had been for some time. So the legislators of each party became more willing to grant power to their legislative party leaders, including the power to pressure straggling legislators to fall in line, to pass the party's legislation and to keep the other party from succeeding.[18]

This account of the reasons for stronger party leadership is called **conditional party government, or CPG**. It stresses that as the two parties' supporting coalitions in the electorate become more polarized—the identifiers of a party become more similar to one another in their preferences and more different from those of the other party—the party members representing them in Congress become more polarized as well. Then, a party's legislators will grant their congressional party leaders more power to pursue their shared policy goals.[19] Party leaders, in turn, will work hard to protect their party's "brand" so as to get more party candidates elected, because they will gain power by doing so; majority leaders can get a lot more done than minority leaders can.[20] Party leaders' staffs and resources have expanded hand in hand with their increased power.[21] Using this same logic, we can explain occasional deviations from stronger party leadership, such as the objections to a strong Speakership by the Republican Freedom Caucus in the 2010s. The growing conflict between conservative and very conservative House Republicans—if not in policy beliefs, then in strategic preferences—led some Republicans to balk at concentrating power in the Speakership (see box "Divisions within a 'Unified Party'," on page 300).

Some party leaders have been more willing than others to make use of these new sources of power. In addition to Newt Gingrich, former House Majority Leader Tom DeLay, nicknamed "the hammer," used the congressional reforms to become a highly assertive Republican leader. A decade later, Republican Speaker Paul Ryan was not as comfortable with aggressive partisanship, but Democratic Speaker Nancy Pelosi, as well as her Republican Senate counterpart Mitch McConnell, have been among the strongest recent leaders by working to keep their caucuses united. Legislative party cohesion and party leaders' power, then, depend not only on party polarization but also on the skills and inclinations of individual party leaders.

Parties in the Senate

Clearly, the job of a House party leader is challenging, but the work of Senate party leaders is more like herding cats.[22] By the mid-1970s, Barbara Sinclair

Divisions within a "Unified Party"

Even as each party in Congress becomes more unified, it also contains the seeds of future splits.[23] Truly competitive, or "swing," seats typically differ from the districts a party expects to win. A typical Democratic House member comes from an urban district with a large minority population, and a typical Republican represents a more rural, whiter, and older district. Swing districts are often more suburban and less homogeneous. Therefore, in "wave elections", when one party wins most of the swing seats, the winning party will be welcoming new members whose constituents differ from those of the party's usual base. Those new members will face different types of pressures from those that drive their safer-seat party colleagues. In the 2018 Democratic wave, for instance, most of the newer Democratic representatives were moderates, chosen by districts that had supported Donald Trump in 2016.

Imagine yourself as Speaker of the House majority party – in 2019, the Democrats. You've won the Speaker's seat due to the influx of new, moderate Democrats who, to get reelected, need to please their own constituents, not those of the more liberal Democratic base. A bill has been introduced to expand federal background checks for people who try to buy a gun. Many of your new, moderate Democratic members support an amendment sponsored by Republicans that would require the Immigration and Customs Enforcement (ICE) agency to be notified when an undocumented immigrant tries to

purchase a gun. The Democratic moderates know that if they don't support the amendment, their next Republican challenger will claim that they are "soft" on illegal immigration. But Democrats elected from more typical Democratic districts in urban areas are outraged by the amendment, arguing that ICE has trampled on individual rights through its raids and mass deportations. Some liberal Democratic House members even threaten to encourage primary challenges to Democrats who voted for the amendment.

As leader of the House Democrats, you find yourself in a pickle. What is your response to this high-profile bill and amendment? Do you side with the party's base and insist that the moderates vote with other Democrats against the amendment? Or do you try to explain to the more liberal Democrats that unless these moderates vote the way their swing districts would prefer, and buck the party's leadership, the Democrats could lose their "majority makers" in the next election (which is just a year away)?

Amendments such as this one are called "gotcha" amendments, because they are crafted by the minority party in Congress for the express purpose of encouraging the majority's moderates to break ranks. The difficult job of the party leader is to shape a position that satisfies the party's base while at the same time letting those swing-district moderates satisfy their own constituents.

Party leadership, in short, is an extremely challenging job. In modern

American politics, where both the Democrats and the Republicans have a shot at winning a majority in both houses of Congress in any given election, it is the swing districts that will decide which party runs each house. But the party that wins those swing districts will therefore be gaining members whose constituencies differ from the party's base. That will increase the chance for splits that weaken the majority party.

---

explains,[24] the U.S. Senate had moved from an institution in which committees dominated the legislative work to a much more individualistic body with a more collegial distribution of power. Increasingly, and with avid media attention, members of the Senate established themselves as national spokespersons on various policy questions. Once they had become political "stars," these senators expected to participate more fully in the Senate's work, on their way, many hoped, to greater glory and higher office.

Add to this individualistic atmosphere the unique Senate rule of the filibuster: the right of extended debate, used to talk a bill or a nomination to death if the votes are not available to defeat it in any other way. It takes 60 votes to stop a filibuster in many cases, a number that is very difficult to achieve. As a result, even the *threat* of a filibuster is enough to stop legislation. Members of the minority have been able to wrest control of the legislative agenda away from the majority by making much more frequent use of such threats, especially since 2007. The Democratic Senate majority finally limited filibusters of most presidential nominations in 2013, and the Republican leadership excluded Supreme Court nominees from the filibuster in 2017, but as of 2020, other legislation can still be stopped by filibuster.

The Senate, then, developed a desperate need for a legislative traffic cop. At the same time, changes in southern politics had led to greater party polarization in the Senate, just as they had in the House. More former House members were being elected to the Senate and bringing with them their experience in that polarized institution.[25] Increasingly, then, the party leadership in the Senate tried to direct the traffic. Individual senators came to depend on their party leaders to promote the legislative party's interests. So the individualism that had developed by the 1970s was constrained by greater party polarization.

The Senate's rules make it harder for the majority to govern than is the case in the House; they do not allow as much centralization of power in the party leadership.[26] The Senate majority leader still defers to committee chairs to a greater extent than his House counterpart (the Speaker) does, and party leaders consult with their party colleagues, rather than command them. But even in the Senate, party leaders now play a more important role.[27] Committee chairs were term-limited in 1996 by the Republican majority, and the Majority Leader has been able to name half the membership of the most valued Senate committees without needing to follow seniority. Fewer amendments are allowed on bills, so individual senators play a smaller role than they once did.

Its increased party polarization and frequent shifts in party control since 1980 have led to such intense partisanship that gridlock and obstructionism now characterize the work of the Senate as well as the House. As one senator described it, "What people want is principled bipartisanship, and what they are getting is unprincipled partisanship."[28] As in the House, Senate committees play a reduced role; that gives individual senators less opportunity to develop expertise on important bills, so they become more inclined to look to their party leaders for guidance. Increasingly, legislative activity is designed to showcase campaign messages rather than to fix policy.

Parties in the State Legislatures

As in Congress, the legislative parties organize the legislatures in almost every state.[29] They structure everything from the legislative leadership to its committees. The power of the legislative parties varies, however, depending in part on the legislature's rules and on the personal skills and resources of the party leaders. In a few state legislatures, daily caucuses and strong party leadership make for a party every bit as potent as in the recent U.S. House. In others, especially the traditionally one-party states, party organization is weaker than it was in Congress before the 1970s reforms.

Most state legislative party leaders have a lot of power over the day-to-day workings of the legislature. They do not usually have to defer to powerful committee chairs. The party leaders can typically choose chairs and members of powerful committees on the basis of their support for the party leader personally or for their views on issues rather than on the basis of seniority. Party leaders also exercise their influence through the party caucus. In many states with strong two-party systems, party leaders call meetings to give members information about upcoming bills, learn whether their membership is united or divided on an issue, and encourage legislators to support the party's position. Leaders in a few of these states may even try to get the caucus to hold a "binding" vote calling on all members to support the party's position on an important issue.[30]

In sum, although the parties' legislative organizations look similar across the states—their party leadership positions are fairly uniform—they differ in their behavior. Party leaders' power can vary even between the two houses of the same state legislature, as do the influence and effectiveness of the party caucus.[31]

Methods of Party Influence

How do legislative parties and their leaders exercise their power? What resources can they use to influence their members' behavior?

Carrots and Sticks

Congressional party leaders can affect the behavior of their party colleagues in several ways. They rely more on incentives than on punishments because the most effective punishments are limited in their use and can backfire. The most powerful punishment would be to remove a maverick legislator from his or her seat in the House or Senate. Except in rare cases, however, party leaders do not have that power. Only the legislator's constituents can do that, and they are not likely to serve as agents of the congressional party leadership. Thus, representatives and senators can normally vote against their party's leadership, or against major bills proposed by a president of their party, without fear of losing their jobs. Legislators in Britain face a much different situation; when 21 Conservative Party members of Parliament voted against their party's leadership's position on British withdrawal from the European Union ("Brexit") in 2019, they were promptly expelled from their parliamentary party.

Perhaps the most famous example of the weakness of party penalties in the U.S. Congress is the story of Phil Gramm, elected as a Democratic representative from Texas in 1978. The House Democratic leadership gave Gramm, a conservative, a seat on the prestigious House Budget Committee in return for his promise to cooperate with party leaders. But in 1983, members of the Democratic caucus were infuriated to learn that Gramm had leaked the details of secret Democratic Party meetings on the Reagan budget to Republican House members. The caucus took away Gramm's seat on the Budget Committee.

Gramm did not accept his fate quietly. He resigned from the House and then ran—as a Republican—in the special election held to replace him. His constituents reelected him to the House and later to the Senate as a Republican. In fact, he was soon back on the House Budget Committee, courtesy of the Republican leadership! As long as legislative party leaders cannot keep a party maverick from being renominated and reelected and in districts where voters are not impressed by a legislator's party loyalty, party influence will be limited. Therefore, this step is taken very rarely.[32]

In short, House and Senate party leaders have only a few punishments at their command when trying to unify their parties, and there is always the risk that punishing a legislator will cause him or her to defect (as one Democrat from a Trump-leaning district did in 2019) or lose reelection. Instead, party leaders rely more on incentives to achieve party loyalty. They can offer or withhold desirable committee assignments and help in passing a member's bills. For instance, Speaker Pelosi offered a number of subcommittee chairs to freshman Democratic representatives in 2019 to ensure their support. Leaders can give members useful information about the status of a bill on the legislative schedule. They can make speeches and raise money for a member's reelection.[33] The parties' congressional campaign committees, with their campaign funds and services, have helped promote party cohesion on legislation.[34] Leaders can also use their personal relationships with party colleagues to cajole them through careful listening or more hard-edged persuasion. On a House vote on school vouchers, for example, a reporter described House Republican leaders surrounding a Kentucky Republican who had opposed the leadership on this bill the week before. A senior Democrat, "Representative David R. Obey (D-WI) took to the microphone. 'Is anyone from the office of the attending physician present?' he deadpanned. 'I understand someone's arm is being broken.'" The Republican did decide to vote for the bill.[35]

Agenda Control

According to cartel theory, another vital source of party leaders' power is their ability to control the legislative agenda.[36] When party leaders can control which bills will come up for a vote, they can stop legislation that could divide their party's members, and they can forward bills that help the party keep its majority. In the House in recent decades, both parties, when they held a majority, have adopted rules that concentrate these powers of agenda control in the party leadership. Bills are normally debated under restrictive rules, set by a leadership-controlled House Rules Committee, which often prevent involvement by the minority party's members. At times, legislation has been combined into "omnibus" bills so broad in scope that individual members have to rely on the party leadership to understand their content. Conference committees, which previously included representatives of both parties to iron out differences between the House and Senate versions of a bill, are now held more rarely and often exclude the minority party. Party leaders negotiate the content of legislation at points in the process that they would not have controlled several decades ago.[37]

Party Influence on Legislative Voting

When is party influence most effective? In voting on a bill, a member of Congress could be swayed by any of several forces: not only by party but also his or her beliefs about the issue at hand or pressures from the president, campaign contributors, or constituents. Yet researchers have found that the parties in Congress play an important role in members' voting, whether due to party leaders' persuasion, the majority party's agenda control, or because of the ability of a member's partisanship to structure issues and create loyalties within his or her own mind.

How Unified Is Each Legislative Party?

Several measures can be used to determine how often members vote with their party. The first, the **frequency of party *votes*,** is the proportion of roll calls on which most Democrats vote one way on a bill and most Republicans vote the other way. The second, party unity scores (or **party *support*),** is the degree to which legislators vote with their party's majority on these party votes.

Party Votes Have Become More Frequent A very demanding test of party voting would be the percentage of all legislative roll calls in which at least 90 percent of one party's members vote yes and 90 percent or more of the other party vote no. By such a strict test, party discipline appears regularly in the British House of Commons and the German Bundestag, but not as often in American legislatures. Under Czar Cannon, about a third of all roll calls in the House met this standard of party discipline. From 1921 through 1948, that dropped to only 17 percent,[38] and it declined steadily to below 10 percent in the 1950s and 1960s. During approximately the same period in the British House of Commons, this striking party division occurred on almost every roll call.

Since the late 1990s, however, there has been a notable increase in "90 percent votes" in Congress, and even in the percentage of votes on which the members of one party unanimously oppose the other party.[39] Since 2009, for example, both houses have divided almost perfectly by party on an increasing number of major issues, including the impeachment of President Trump (see Figure 13.1, Case 1), though on occasion, some Republicans have balked at Trump's actions (Figure 13.1, Case 2).

The 90 percent standard is too strict, however, for a look at the American legislative experience over time. Therefore, researchers have focused on a less demanding measure: the **frequency of party votes,** or the percentage of roll calls in which the *majority* of one party opposed a majority of the other. By this measure as well, congressional party voting has greatly increased.

Let's start where senators think we should—with the Senate. During the late 1960s and early 1970s, a majority of Democrats opposed a majority of Republicans in less than 40 percent of all Senate roll call votes. The figure rose to between 50 and 65 percent during the 1990s and 2000s, under both Democratic and Republican control. Then, party voting went into overdrive during the Obama and Trump administrations, hitting 69 percent in 2017 before dropping in 2018–2019. Votes to confirm presidential nominees were especially partisan, as the Republican majority sought to fill judicial posts that it had refused to fill under Obama.

Party voting has been even more frequent in the House. In the late 1800s, party votes were common (although still far less than in the British Parliament). This was a time when the parties were competitive in most congressional districts, party leaders wielded considerable legislative authority, and Congress was a much less professionalized institution. After 1900, following the development of a more professionalized Congress,[40] the frequency of party votes decreased markedly. The start of the New Deal party system in the 1930s heightened party voting for a time, before it fell again to twentieth-century lows (of 27 percent) in 1970 and 1972.

But since the current party polarization began in the mid-1980s, party votes in the House have reached levels not seen since the New Deal. More than three-fourths of House votes were party votes in 2017, tying a recent record. The proportion dropped in the 2018 election year, when parties try to show voters that they can govern, but returned to 68 percent in 2019 (see Figure 13.2). Overall, since the mid-1980s, "the only line of voting cleavage of any significance in this period was partisan,"[41] and the legislative agenda has been set largely by the White House and the House party leadership.

Case 1: Should President Trump be impeached for abuse of power for soliciting foreign interference in the 2020 U.S. election?

House of Representatives

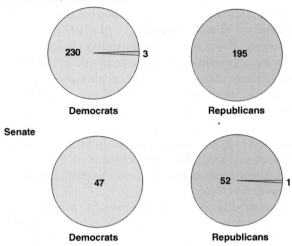

Case 2: Disapprove of president Trump's action lifting sanctions against some Russian companies.

House of Representatives

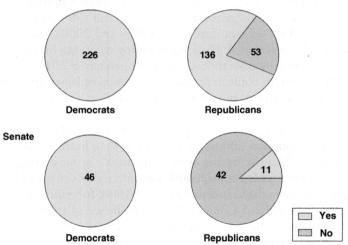

FIGURE 13.1 Congressional Party Unity and Disunity, 2019–2020

Note: The figure shows the numbers of Democrats and Republicans in the Senate and House casting "yes" and "no" votes on the bills named. Senators Bernard Sanders (I-VT) and Angus King (I-ME) are counted as Democrats because they caucus with the Democrats.

Source: New York Times, https://www.nytimes.com/interactive/2019/12/18/us/politics/trump-impeachment-vote.html (accessed August 24, 2020) and *CQ Magazine,* February 10, 2020 (on impeachment), and *CQ Magazine,* February 24, 2020 (on Russian sanctions).

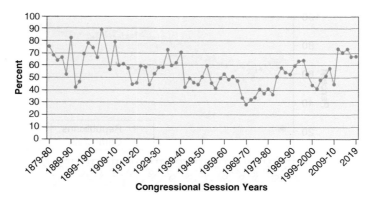

Congressional Session Years

FIGURE 13.2 Party Votes in the House of Representatives, 1879–2019

Note: Entries are the percentage of roll-call votes on which a majority of one party opposed a majority of the other party. Because party votes tend to decrease in the even-numbered years, as an election approaches, the data are averaged across the two sessions of each Congress.

Source: Calculated for 1879–1974 from Jerome B. Chubb and Santa A. Traugott, "Partisan Cleavage and Cohesion in the House of Representatives, 1861–1974," *Journal of Interdisciplinary History 1* (1977): 382–383; more recent data from *CQ Magazine* in December, January, or February issues.

...And So Has Legislators' Party Support   To what extent do legislators support their party on party votes? Beginning in the late 1930s and especially in the late 1960s and early 1970s, conservative southern Democrats often voted with Republicans in Congress to oppose civil rights bills and Democratic labor and education proposals. Their defections were tolerated by the decentralized party leadership of that time. This cross-party alliance was called the **conservative coalition.**

The reshaping of the Democratic Party's supporting coalition in the South seriously undercut the conservative coalition in the 1970s and 1980s. As noted earlier, when the Voting Rights Act brought southern blacks into the electorate, this more diverse southern Democratic constituency began to elect different types of representatives. Some conservative southern House members were defeated by moderate and liberal Democrats who could better appeal to black voters. Other conservative Democrats retired or switched parties. Most of the rest were unseated by the growing number of southern Republican House candidates. Thus, the Democratic Party in Congress lost most of its conservative wing.

The Republicans newly elected from the South beginning in the 1970s were more conservative than most of their continuing Republican colleagues. Since that time, non-southern Republicans have become more conservative as well.[42] As a result, congressional Republicans—whether northern or southern—now tend to represent different types of districts than congressional Democrats do, face different pressures from party activists and organized interests, are recruited from different professions, and hold different views on big issues. As the conditional party government theory suggests, this produced a marked increase in party support, especially after Republicans won control of Congress in 1995

FIGURE 13.3 Average Party Unity Scores, 1961–2019

Note: Entries are the average percentages of members voting in agreement with a majority of their party on party votes—those in which a majority of one party voted against a majority of the other party. Figures for the House and Senate are averaged.

Source: Calculated from *CQ Magazine* Vote Studies, in December, January, or February issues.

(see Figure 13.3). Party organizational reforms, discussed earlier in the chapter, also made it easier for congressional party leaders to unite their party.[43]

The increase in party support has not been uniform. When Democrats regained control of the House in 2007, Speaker Pelosi placed fewer demands for discipline on newly elected, moderate Democrats. The Democratic leadership needed these freshmen to be reelected in their suburban and exurban districts to keep its House majority, and getting reelected would require them to vote a more moderate line than the party leadership would otherwise push.[44] Many of these freshmen joined the "Blue Dog Coalition," a group of about 50 House Democrats from rural and small-town districts, typically in the South and West, who took moderate positions on issues including taxes and business concerns. As polarization spread, however, almost half of the Blue Dogs were defeated in the 2010 midterms, and after another fall and rise, relatively few remained in 2021. To protect the remaining seats, both the Senate and House Democratic leadership encouraged vulnerable Democrats to vote against Democratic bills, criticize President Biden or other Democratic leaders—in short, do whatever it took to get reelected in a difficult political climate.

Similarly, a declining number of Republican moderates in the House (the "Tuesday Group") and a few in the Senate continue to differ from their party on social issues and sometimes on economic issues, because their constituencies differ from those of most of their GOP colleagues. And recall that the most conservative House Republicans have broken with their party leadership on budget issues beginning in 2012, including voting against raising the federal debt limit in 2015, reflecting the hostility toward government spending expressed by Republican activists in their districts. As long as the American parties cannot protect legislators from constituency pressures, and as long as what it means to be a Republican in New York differs from what it means to be a Republican in Mississippi, party cohesion will suffer.

These are the exceptions, however. Party support has been higher in recent years than it has been since the 1950s. In 2019, on party votes, House
Democrats voted with their party's position 95 percent of the time, an all-time
high for the party, demonstrating Speaker Pelosi's remarkable skill at majority-
building. Even the more moderate Blue Dog Democrats fell in line with their
party, though at a slightly lower rate. The comparable figures for the Senate
were 94 percent for Republicans and 84 percent for Democrats.[45] When the
Americans for Democratic Action (ADA), a liberal group, examined how often
legislators voted with the ADA's position on 20 key votes, the average score for
Democratic House members in 2019 was 89 percent and that for Republicans
was 6 percent; 84 House Republicans earned ADA scores of zero. In the Senate,
the comparable scores were 91 and 4 percent.[46]

Greater Polarization of the Congressional Parties

In short, roll-call voting shows that the House and the Senate are more polarized by party now than they have been at any time since the late 1870s (see
Figure 13.4).[47] The center has shrunk; if all members of each chamber are
arrayed along a scale from liberal to conservative, there is almost no overlap
between Republicans and Democrats. In particular, since 2000 each incoming

FIGURE 13.4 Party Polarization in Congress, 1879–2015

Note: Entries are the Common Space DW-NOMINATE scores comparing the polarization of the two parties
in each house for each Congress. These scores rely on the scaling of roll-call votes on a liberal-conservative
dimension. Higher values (closer to 1.0) mean greater ideological difference between the parties.

Source: Keith T. Poole, "New Estimates of Polarization in the 114th Congress," April 15, 2015, https://
voteviewblog.com/2015/04/15/new-estimates-of-polarization-in-the-114th-congress/ (accessed August 24,
2020). See also Clio Andris, David Lee, Marcus J. Hamilton, Mauro Martino, Christian E. Gunning, and John
Armistead Seiden, "The Rise of Partisanship and Super Cooperators in the U.S. House of Representatives,"
Plos One 10 (2015).

class of Republican representatives has been more conservative than those who remain.[48] This has been true of many state legislatures as well, though there is wide variation among the states.[49] And many moderate members have left Congress, in part because they find it harder to get good committee assignments and leadership positions and thus to make a difference on policy.[50] Among Republicans in particular, moderates are more likely to draw primary opposition than deeply conservative members are.[51]

In addition to the marked changes in the parties' supporting coalitions of voters, including the concentration of black Americans in urban areas (Chapter 7) and the creation of majority–minority districts (Chapter 8), other factors have contributed to this polarization. Partisan redistricting can encourage candidates to move to the extreme of their party's distribution, at least in the U.S. House. If a House district has been drawn to favor the incumbent's party, then (as noted in Chapter 2) the most likely source of a successful challenge is an ambitious candidate in the incumbent's party, running against him or her in a primary election. In primaries, Republican incumbents are most likely to be challenged from the right; for Democratic incumbents, from the left. This encourages House members to move toward the extreme of their party rather than toward the center. One study finds that a credible primary challenge moves a typical candidate for Congress fully 10 points along a 100-point conservative-to-liberal scale.[52]

As congressional districts have become more homogeneous in terms of partisanship as well as demographic characteristics, the candidates they elect differ demographically as well. So the two parties show different "faces" in Congress. In 2021, the Republican Party in the House is heavily white, Christian, and male, whereas more than half of the House Democrats are female, African-American, and/or Latino-American. These demographic differences help reinforce citizens' perceptions that the two parties differ dramatically from one another on a wide variety of important qualities.

Note that roll-call voting is only one indicator of Congress members' behavior, and the roll calls that get the greatest attention are generally those where party conflict is the greatest.[53] In addition, these sharp party differences on roll call votes are not necessarily bad. They give voters a clear choice when electing congressional candidates. But they can also produce unsettling policy changes; because the two parties are so closely balanced in strength, a relatively small shift in the political climate can lead to a change in party control of Congress. In 2009–2010, the Democrats had a large enough congressional majority to pass several landmark pieces of liberal legislation, ranging from health-care reform and overhaul of banking regulation to a repeal of the "don't ask, don't tell" rule keeping gay and lesbian personnel from serving openly in the military. After the 2010 elections, when Democrats lost control of the House to the Republicans, the agenda was transformed. Under Republican rule, and especially when 2017 brought unified Republican control, the House focused on repealing the Democratic health care and financial services reforms and on cutting taxes and spending. And when Democrats regained the House in 2019, health care, financial services reforms, and gun control came back onto the House agenda (though these House-passed bills were killed by the Republican-dominated Senate).

What Issues Promote Party Voting?

Students of Congress and state legislatures find that three types of issues tend to prompt more frequent party votes and greater party support: those touching the interests of the legislative party as a group, those involving support of or opposition to an executive program, and those that clearly divide the party's voters.

Issues That Touch the Interests of the Legislative Parties   These produce the greatest party unity. Among the best examples are the basic votes to organize the legislative chamber. In Congress, for instance, it used to be safe to predict 100 percent party unity on the vote to elect the Speaker of the House. When Republican John Boehner lost the votes of two dozen Republican members for reelection as Speaker in 2015, and again when 16 Democrats voted against Nancy Pelosi for Speaker in 2019, it was front-page news.

The parties also tend to be highly unified on issues affecting their numerical strength and on the procedures by which the legislature is run. Votes on procedure show greater polarization than those on the final passage of laws.[54] Party discipline runs high in state legislatures on laws regulating parties and elections and the redrawing of legislative district lines, which touch the basic interests of the party as a political organization.

The Executive's Proposals   Legislators often rally around their party's executive or unite against the executive of the other party. This partisanship has been mounting. In the late 1960s, on average, members of a president's party in Congress voted about 60 percent of the time for issues that he clearly designated a part of his program. In 2019, House Republicans supported President Trump's position a full 91 percent of the time, and Senate Republicans topped their colleagues at 93%.

At the same time, the opposition party's support for a president's program has dropped steadily.[55] Since the 1980s, the opposition has supported the president's proposals only about one-third of the time, on average, and in 2019 House Democrats' support of Trump's proposals dropped to 5 percent, the lowest on record. We can see this party polarization in the two recent cases of presidential impeachment. The House voted to impeach President Clinton in 1998 for lying about his sexual relationship with a White House intern; that and the Senate vote to acquit Clinton were close to being party-line votes. Gary Jacobson wrote, "On what everyone claimed was a conscience vote, 98 percent of Republican consciences dictated a vote to impeach the president, while 98 percent of Democratic consciences dictated the opposite."[56] When the House impeached President Trump in 2019 and the Senate voted to acquit, partisanship had an even more powerful hold on congressional consciences.

When the president's party in Congress marches in lockstep with the president's proposals, then it is important to ask whether Congress plays an independent role in the business of governing. Drops in funding for committee staffs and for research agencies such as the Congressional Research Service and the Government Accountability Office have meant that Congress often lacks information about proposed policies and the resources to oversee the executive branch.[57] The other party's united opposition can be a potential check on the executive, of course, as the Democratic House majority was on President Trump during 2019–2020. But especially when the president's party has a majority in a chamber, the party leadership has often ceded congressional power to the executive branch. The Republican-controlled Senate, for instance, cast aside traditional Republican positions against big federal deficits and high tariffs when their party colleague in the White House, Donald Trump, accepted higher deficits and supported trade wars.

Policies Central to the Party System   Legislative parties are also more unified on issues that fundamentally divide the parties in the electorate—the "label-defining" issues.[58] At the time of the Civil War, the questions of slavery and Reconstruction generated the greatest cohesion within each party and the clearest divisions between the two parties. These issues were displaced by conflicts between farm and industrial interests in the 1890s. Now the parties are most internally cohesive on the role of government in the economy, including taxes and the regulation of business, and on issues such as abortion and LGBTQ rights. In many state legislatures, for instance, an attempt to limit or expand the rights of unions will pit one unified party against another, as will environmental issues and the rights of women, gays, and minority groups. In Congress, a similar set of issues—social welfare, environmental, and tax policy—has produced the most cohesive partisan voting.

What Conditions Produce Strong Legislative Parties?

In sum, what are the conditions most likely to produce strong legislative parties?

Party Polarization and Cohesion   When a party's legislators represent similar constituencies (for instance, when Republicans throughout the state or nation all get significant support from Christian conservatives and very little support from blacks), they are more likely to hold similar views, and party cohesion increases. Combined with greater distance between the two parties in the nature of their constituencies and their views on issues, this encourages legislators to accept strong party leadership to translate these views into policy (recall the theory of conditional party government, discussed on page 299). Legislative party strength has long flourished in California and other states where the two parties have quite different bases of support—where Democratic strength is concentrated among union members and blacks in the big cities and Republican state legislators tend to represent rural and suburban districts that are largely white and conservative.[59] This is especially true of the U.S. House, whose rules, as we have seen, permit greater control by the leadership.[60]

Greater Interparty Competition   There is an interesting relationship between the competitiveness of the two parties and the degree of legislative party voting. At the level of the individual legislator, those from marginal districts, where the two parties have relatively equal shares of the electorate, are generally less likely to vote with their legislative party, and more likely to be responsive to their constituents' preferences, than are those from safer districts.[61] Two characteristics of marginal districts encourage a legislator to be highly sensitive to the constituency. First, both parties in marginal districts often have strong organizations and appealing candidates, so the opposition is a credible threat. Second, in many marginal or swing districts, the groups that support Democrats or Republicans differ from those more typically associated with the party. When party voters in a district hold different views from the national or state party on a big issue, a representative will usually need to bend to constituency wishes to get reelected, even if that means opposing his or her legislative party's position.

As we've seen, party leaders may not insist on the member's party loyalty in such situations; they would rather have a legislator who will at least vote for the party's candidate for Speaker than a totally loyal legislator who is defeated for reelection because his or her constituents do not want what the national party is selling. Where constituency and party point in different directions, most legislators remember that their constituents, not their party leadership, gave them their job.

At the level of the legislature as a whole, however, close party competition can increase party voting. When the two parties in a legislature are relatively evenly balanced numerically, "the majority party must stick together to get legislation passed, and the minority party has some realistic chance of winning if it can remain cohesive."[62] Close party competition gives both parties an incentive to remain unified. In contrast, a comfortable majority can foster internal squabbles. That was true of many legislative parties in the South during the period of one-party Democratic rule. It is true today in state legislatures in which one party has a lopsided majority.

No Competing Centers of Power A legislature's standing committees can be sources of power rivaling the party leaders. This was true of Congress when seniority determined who would become a committee chair. When committee chairs are chosen on the basis of criteria other than party loyalty, then chairs owe less to their party leadership. Seniority is not used as often now in either Congress or state legislatures as a basis for appointing members to powerful positions. Other centers of power in some states—powerful business groups, labor unions, ideological groups, or other big contributors—are often closely allied with one party's leaders. but not always. When the Republican House majority revisited the Affordable Care Act ("Obamacare") in 2017, conservative groups associated with the billionaire Koch brothers offered funding to support Republican House members who voted against their party's leadership's stance.

Other Needed Resources Where the party organization has more to offer a legislator, he or she will be more inclined to follow the party's lead in legislative voting. In Congress and many state legislatures, party leaders can use their power over the legislative agenda to help a member get a desired bill passed. In the states, pork barrel projects in the member's home district can be moved up or down on the agenda by legislative party leaders to help to maintain the loyalty of their party colleagues.

Party organizations outside the legislature can also influence legislative voting if they control important resources. State parties' legislative campaign committees help fund legislative candidates in most states, and legislative party leaders' personal political action committees help in some.[63] Given the shortage of campaign funds at this level, many candidates look beyond the legislative campaign committees to the state parties themselves for campaign money and services. Many states place no ceilings on party contributions to campaigns, so parties can make substantial investments, if they can afford it. Another important resource is the party's influence on nominations. The leaders of many state parties have become more active in recruiting legislative candidates, and some may be able to convince local activists to oppose the renomination of candidates disloyal to the party (although that ability can always be undermined by primary elections).

Lesser Legislative Professionalism Congress has evolved into a highly professional legislative body. Each member controls a sizable personal staff and budget, which can help meet the member's legislative and reelection needs. Serving in Congress is a full-time job with good pay and benefits. Although state legislatures have become more professional as well, very few provide ordinary members with levels of support that even approach those in the Congress. Staff and budgets are usually minimal. Most state legislators are lucky to have as much as a private office and a personal secretary. Many state legislatures meet for only part of the year and pay so little that most members must hold other jobs. With such limited personal resources, legislators in most states welcome party leaders' help in performing their legislative tasks. When a state legislator depends on the party leadership for needed resources, he or she is more likely to listen when a leader calls for party discipline.

Styles of Individual Leaders Legislative party leaders in the states, like those in the U.S. House and Senate, vary in their willingness to use the tools of strong leadership. Their leadership styles interact with the situation of their party—whether it is a powerful majority, a competitive party, or a weakened minority—to determine how effectively they function in uniting their party members and getting their bills passed.

The Power of Legislative Parties

This chapter tells a complex story. On the one hand, parties are at the very center of the legislative process. Some even view them as "legislative leviathans" that dominate Congress to benefit their individual members.[64] Party affiliation explains the legislative behavior of state legislators and Congress members more fully than does any other single factor. Party voting and polarization have increased in recent years in both the houses of Congress.

Yet even now, most American legislative parties are not as unified as those of most other democracies. The fragmenting institutions of American government have left their mark. Separation of powers deprives the party of an institutional need to remain internally cohesive.[65] So even when the same party controls both houses of Congress, majorities aren't necessarily successful in passing laws.[66] Even with stronger party leadership and high levels of party voting, most bills still require bipartisan support to become law.

Under some conditions, such as when a party's legislative constituencies are very similar in their preferences and very different from those of the other party, legislative parties will be more unified and party voting will be common. As increasing party polarization has brought the views of legislative leaders and party voters into closer alignment, members of Congress are less likely to face a difficult choice between party and constituency (see box "Which Would You Choose? Should Your Representative Listen More Closely to the Party or to the Constituents?" below). Party polarization doesn't always lead to legislative grid-lock, in which the congressional parties are unable to move legislation or agree

▰▰▰ WHICH WOULD YOU CHOOSE? ▰▰▰

Should Your Representative Listen More Closely to the Party or to the Constituents?

To the constituents: This sounds like a no-brainer. If we elect members of Congress, they ought to represent the interests of their constituents, right? We have a single-member district system with candidate-centered campaigns; that encourages us to focus on the qualities of individual candidates rather than on the party's platform. We vote for a candidate, and he or she goes to Washington and is then supposed to do whatever we ask. Why should the legislator listen to the party leadership?

To their party: This constituent-centered approach sounds good, but it isn't realistic. How are members of Congress supposed to know what all of their 740,000 constituents want? Isn't it better for the two major parties to offer competing answers on issues, press their legislative party members to pass these policies,

and then let voters decide whether they like the results? That asks less of us as voters and probably corresponds more closely to the (minimal) time we are willing to spend on politics. Besides, by taking a longer view, the parties can look beyond local concerns to a broader national interest.

To both: As we have seen, when the various constituencies that a party's legislators represent become more similar in views and more different from those of the other party, then most legislators don't have to choose between constituents and party. At these times, members can vote with their party colleagues and also speak for the interests and voters who, in their view, sent them to the legislature. So party and constituency are not necessarily in conflict.

on priorities.[67] But when gridlock occurs, the result has been to strengthen the executive branch at the expense of the legislature.

Notes

1 Rep. Charlie Dent, quoted in Ashley Parker, "G.O.P. Is Divided as It Faces a Host of Budget Bills," *New York Times*, March 9, 2015, p. A1.

2 See Frances E. Lee, "Parties as Coordinators: Can Parties Unite What the Constitution Divides?" in Marjorie Randon Hershey, ed., *Guide to U.S. Political Parties* (Los Angeles, CA: Sage, 2014), Chapter 3.

3 Keith Krehbiel, "Where's the Party?" *British Journal of Political Science* 23 (1993): 225–266.

4 Gary W. Cox and Keith T. Poole, "On Measuring Partisanship in Roll-Call Voting," *American Journal of Political Science* 46 (2002): 477–489; and Gerald C. Wright and Brian F. Schaffner, "The Influence of Party," *American Political Science Review* 96 (2002): 367–379.

5 Steven S. Smith, *Party Influence in Congress* (Cambridge, MA: Cambridge University Press, 2007).

6 C. Lawrence Evans, *The Whips* (Ann Arbor, MI: University of Michigan Press, 2018).

7 D. Roderick Kiewiet and Mathew D. McCubbins, *The Logic of Delegation* (Chicago, IL: University of Chicago Press, 1991); Scott R. Meinke, *Leadership Organizations in the House of Representatives* (Ann Arbor, MI: University of Michigan Press, 2016).

8 Even Cannon faced limits, however; see Eric D. Lawrence, Forrest Maltzman, and Paul J. Wahlbeck, "The Politics of Speaker Cannon's Committee Assignments," *American Journal of Political Science* 45 (2001): 551–562. On the history of legislative party leadership, see Bruce I. Oppenheimer, "Ebbs and Flows in the Power of Congressional Party Leaders Since 1910," in Hershey, ed., *Guide to U.S. Political Parties,* pp. 308–323.

9 Steven S. Smith and Gerald Gamm, "The Dynamics of Party Government in Congress," in Lawrence C. Dodd and Bruce I. Oppenheimer, eds., *Congress Reconsidered,* 9th ed. (Washington, DC: CQ Press, 2009), p. 149

10 Gary W. Cox and Mathew W. McCubbins, *Legislative Leviathan*, 2nd ed. (Berkeley, CA: University of California Press, 1993), pp. 279–282.

11 On the Speaker's powers, see Jeffery A. Jenkins and Charles Stewart III, *Fighting for the Speakership* (Princeton, NJ: Princeton University Press, 2012).

12 Barbara Sinclair, *Unorthodox Lawmaking*, 2nd ed. (Washington, DC: CQ Press, 2000), pp. 103–106.

13 Bruce I. Oppenheimer, "Ebbs and Flows," in Hershey, ed., *Guide to U.S. Political Parties* (Los Angeles, CA: Sage, 2014), Chapter 24.

14 Mike Allen, "GOP Leaders Tighten Their Grip on House," *Washington Post*, January 9, 2005, p. A5.

15 Charles Homans, "Opportunity Cost," *New York Times Sunday Magazine*, January 27, 2019, p. 35.

16 Marian Currinder, *Money in the House* (Boulder, CO: Westview, 2009), Chapter 2 and p. 203.

17 David W. Rohde, *Parties and Leaders in the Postreform House* (Chicago, IL: University of Chicago Press, 1991). See also Barbara Sinclair, *Legislators, Leaders, and Lawmaking* (Baltimore, MD: Johns Hopkins University Press, 1995).

18 See, for example, William T. Bianco and Itai Sened, "Uncovering Evidence of Conditional Party Government," *American Political Science Review* 99 (2005): 361–371.

19 See John H. Aldrich, *Why Parties? A Second Look* (Chicago, IL: University of Chicago Press, 2011), Chapter 7.

20 Rohde and Aldrich, "Consequences of Electoral and Institutional Change."

21 Daniel J. Galvin, "The Transformation of Political Institutions," *Studies in American Political Development* 26 (2012): 1–21.

22 Analyst E. J. Dionne goes further, arguing that the Democrats in the U.S. Senate are so ideologically diverse that "the cliché about herding cats does a disservice to how relatively organized felines are." Dionne, "Harry Reid vs. the Smooth Deal," *Washington Post*, March 29, 2015, p. A28.

23 On party factions, see Andrew J. Clarke, "Party Sub-Brands and American Party Factions," *American Journal of Political Science* 64 (2020): 452–470.

24 Barbara Sinclair, "The New World of U.S. Senators," in Dodd and Oppenheimer, eds., *Congress Reconsidered*, pp. 1–22.

25 Sean M. Theriault and David W. Rohde, "The Gingrich Senators and Party Polarization in the U.S. Senate," *Journal of Politics* 73 (2011): 1011–1024.

26 Smith and Gamm, "The Dynamics of Party Government in Congress," pp. 141–164.

27 See Nathan W. Monroe, Jason M. Roberts, and David W. Rohde, eds., *Why Not Parties?* (Chicago, IL: University of Chicago Press, 2008) and Peter Hanson, *Too Weak to Govern* (New York: Cambridge University Press, 2014).

28 Sen. Michael Bennet (D-CO), quoted in Steven Pearlstein, "The Can-Do Senator in a Can't-Do Congress," *Washington Post Magazine,* June 19, 2016, p. 1.

29 The main exception is Nebraska, which is officially nonpartisan.

30 Malcolm E. Jewell and Sarah M. Morehouse, *Political Parties and Elections in American States*, 4th ed. (Washington, DC: CQ Press, 2001), pp. 236–238.

31 Keith E. Hamm and Robert Harmel, "Legislative Party Development and the Speaker System," *Journal of Politics* 55 (1993): 1140–1151.

32 See Robert Harmel, Matthew Giebert, and Kenneth Janda, *American Parties in Context* (New York: Routledge, 2016), Chapter 5.

33 Gregory Koger and Matthew J. Lebo, *Strategic Party Government* (Chicago, IL: University of Chicago Press, 2017).

34 Paul S. Herrnson, Costas Panagopoulos, and Kendall L. Bailey *Congressional Elections*, 8th ed. (Los Angeles, CA: Sage/CQ Press, 2020).

35 Juliet Eilperin, "House GOP Practices Art of One-Vote Victories," *Washington Post*, October 14, 2003, p. A1.

36 See Gary W. Cox and Mathew D. McCubbins, *Setting the Agenda* (Cambridge: Cambridge University Press, 2005) and Jenkins and Stewart, *Fighting for the Speakership*.

37 Barbara Sinclair, "Orchestrators of Unorthodox Lawmaking," *The Forum* 6 (2008), issue 3, article 4.

38 Julius Turner, *Party and Constituency*, rev. ed., Edward V. Schneier, ed. (Baltimore, MD: Johns Hopkins University Press, 1970), pp. 16–17.

39 See Jason M. Roberts and Steven S. Smith, "Procedural Contexts, Party Strategy, and Conditional Party Voting in the U.S. House of Representatives, 1971–2000," *American Journal of Political Science* 47 (2003): 305–317.

40 Nelson W. Polsby, "The Institutionalization of the United States House of Representatives," *American Political Science Review* 62 (1968): 144–168.

41 Aldrich, *Why Parties?* p. 243.

42 Roberts and Smith, "Procedural Contexts."

43 Rohde, *Parties and Leaders in the Postreform House*, Chapter 3. See also M. V. Hood III, Quentin Kidd, and Irwin L. Morris, "Of Byrd[s] and Bumpers," *American Journal of Political Science* 43 (1999): 465–487.

44 On Pelosi's Speakership, see Kathryn Pearson and Eric Schickler, "The Transition to Democratic Leadership in a Polarized House," in Dodd and Oppenheimer, eds., *Congress Reconsidered*, pp. 165–188.

45 "Party Unity Background," *CQ Magazine*, February 24, 2020. See also Karyn Amira, Lauren Johnson, Deon McCray, and Jordan Ragusa, "Adversaries or Allies?" *Perspectives on Politics* 17 (September 2019): 756–771.

46 Americans for Democratic Action, "2019 Congressional Voting Record," https://adaction.org/wp-content/uploads/2020/06/2019.pdf (accessed August 24, 2020).

47 But see David A. Bateman, Joshua D. Clinton, and John S. Lapinski, "A House Divided?" *American Journal of Political Science* 61 (2017): 698–714.

48 This has not been true of Democrats, whose new classes are only slightly more liberal than those who remain. See Edward G. Carmines, "Class Politics, American Style," *Perspectives on Politics* 9 (September 2011): 645–647.

49 Boris Shor, "Party Polarization in America's State Legislatures," in John C. Green, Daniel J. Coffey, and David B. Cohen, eds., *The State of the Parties*, 7th ed. (Lanham, MD: Rowman & Littlefield, 2014), p. 127.

50 Danielle M. Thomsen, *Opting Out of Congress* (Cambridge: Cambridge University Press, 2017).

51 George C. Edwards III, "No Deal: Donald Trump's Leadership of Congress," *The Forum* 15 (#3 2017): 485–486.

52 Barry Burden, "Candidate Positioning in U.S. Congressional Elections," *British Journal of Political Science* 34 (2004): 211–227.

53 See Frank R. Baumgartner, Jeffrey M. Berry, Marie Hojnacki, David C. Kimball, and Beth L. Leech, *Lobbying and Policy Change* (Chicago, IL: University of Chicago Press, 2009), Chapter 5.

54 Stephen A. Jessee and Sean M. Theriault, "The Two Faces of Congressional Roll-Call Voting," *Party Politics* 20 (2014): 836–848.

55 Data from *CQ Magazine* annual vote studies. See also Cary R. Covington, J. Mark Wrighton, and Rhonda Kinney, "A 'Presidency-Augmented' Model of Presidential Success on House Roll Call Votes," *American Journal of Political Science* 39 (November 1995): 1001–1024.

56 Gary C. Jacobson, *The Politics of Congressional Elections*, 7th ed. (New York: Pearson-Longman, 2009), p. 255.

57 See Bill Pascrell, Jr., "Why Is Congress So Dumb?" *Washington Post*, January 11, 2019, Outlook, p. 1.

58 C. Lawrence Evans and Claire E. Grandy, "The Whip Systems of Congress," in Dodd and Oppenheimer, 9th ed., p. 210.

59 Boris Shor and Nolan McCarty, "The Ideological Mapping of American Legislatures," *American Political Science Review* 105 (2011): 530–551.

60 Molly C. Jackman shows the influence of legislative rules on party influence in state legislatures: see "Parties, Median Legislators, and Agenda-Setting," *Journal of Politics* 76 (2014): 259–272.

61 See John D. Griffin, "Electoral Competition and Democratic Responsiveness," *Journal of Politics* 68 (2006): 911–921.

62 Jewell and Morehouse, *Political Parties and Elections*, p. 244.

63 Anthony Gierzynski, *Legislative Party Campaign Committees in the American States* (Lexington, KY: University of Kentucky Press, 1992); and Daniel M. Shea, *Transforming Democracy* (Albany, NY: SUNY Press, 1995).
64 Cox and McCubbins, *Legislative Leviathan.*
65 See Gary Cox, *The Efficient Secret* (New York: Cambridge University Press, 1987).
66 See James M. Curry and Frances E. Lee, "Non-Party Government," *Perspectives on Politics* 17 (March 2019): 47–65.
67 Seth Masket, "Political Polarization Is Not a Driver of Gridlock at the State Level," *Pacific Standard*, May 22, 2019, https://psmag.com/social-justice/political-polarization-is-not-a-driver-of-gridlock-at-the-state-level (accessed August 24, 2020).

CHAPTER 14

The Party in the Executive and the Courts

Ronald Reagan was shot just a few months after his inauguration in 1981, by a disturbed young man trying to impress a Hollywood star. As the nation held its breath, the GOP president was wheeled into surgery. He looked up at his doctor and quipped, "I hope you're a Republican."

The president was kidding, of course; he didn't really expect worse treatment from a physician who didn't share his partisanship. But would you be justified in believing that people's party identification affects the way they perform their duties as mayors? As judges? As testers at the Bureau of Motor Vehicles? As public health officials? Most Americans think of courts as being nonpartisan, just as we hope for nonpartisan behavior from police officers and the people who inspect restaurant kitchens.

Yet, as we see in this chapter, American judges and executives (not just presidents and governors but also the people who head and work in government agencies) are party identifiers. Many presidents and governors behave like party leaders, and although the writers of the Constitution designed an independent federal court system with lifetime appointments, hoping to protect courts from partisan controversy, it has never been possible to design judges who are free of party identification. As a result, the nominations of U.S. Supreme Court justices and most other federal judges now provoke heated partisan conflict.

In many ways, partisanship has penetrated more deeply into the executive and judicial branches in the U.S. than in other Western democracies. As discussed in Chapter 2, the push for popular democracy in the U.S. led to the election of public officials who would be appointed to their jobs in most other nations, such as state school superintendents and local judges. When administrators and judges are elected, partisanship can influence their elections. Even when these officials are appointed, party affiliation is often a criterion for their appointment.

If partisanship affects their selection, wouldn't it also influence the ways in which administrators and judges do their jobs? If so, does this reflect party organizations' efforts to influence the behavior of executives and judges? Or is it simply that most people feel closer to one party than the other, and people who consider themselves Republicans tend to share similar attitudes toward political issues, whether they are voters, police officers, or judges, and the same is true of those who identify as Democrats?

Presidents and Governors as Party Leaders

In a closely divided nation, most presidents hope to locate the sweet spot of broad agreement on major policies; it isn't easy to govern with the support of half the nation and the opposition of the other half. Barack Obama began his presidency with an effort to be "post-partisan." But that proved to be impossible to achieve,[1] and Donald Trump didn't even try to claim the mantle of bipartisanship when he took office in 2017. Presidents, like governors, and even bureaucrats and judges, have political attitudes and assumptions that draw them to one party or the other. Although their enthusiasm for partisan activity varies and can be limited by rules and norms, most recent presidents have found that partisan activity is essential to their success.

Several Republican presidents, in particular,[2] have become extensively involved in party activities by helping to recruit and campaign with party candidates and raise money for the party. These efforts have strengthened the bond between presidents and the party colleagues in Congress for whom they campaign. Especially in the current polarized atmosphere in Washington, and in many state capitals and when the party division in the legislature is close, executives nurture ties with their party's legislators to get the votes needed to pass their policies.

The President as Campaigner-in-Chief

Presidents can't "govern by themselves."[3] They are much more successful in getting their initiatives passed when their co-partisans are in the majority in Congress. To help achieve that, presidents have become vitally important campaign fundraisers for congressional candidates of their party. Presidents also grant campaign endorsements to candidates who can help them politically. Endorsements don't always work the way a president expects, however. Researchers found that President Trump's endorsements of 80 U.S. House and Senate candidates in 2018 increased the fund-raising of endorsed candidates—but also that of their opponents. And the endorsements must be strategically placed; candidates Trump endorsed in 2018 were less likely to win than were those he didn't endorse.[4]

Presidents can do a great deal more for their party organizations. The state or national party organization often finds itself in the difficult position of trying to convince an attractive but reluctant prospect to run for a governorship, or urging an eager candidate not to oppose a party favorite in a primary. Presidents can be very persuasive recruiters or "decruiters," especially when their public or party approval is high. In 2018, for instance, President Trump tweeted about the Nevada congressional races that,

> It would be great for the Republican Party of Nevada, and it's unity if good guy Danny Tarkanian [a Republican who had announced he planned to run against the Republican incumbent senator, Dean Heller, in the primary election] would run for Congress and Dean Heller, who is doing a really good job, could run for Senate unopposed!

Tarkanian took the hint and dropped out of the Senate primary race.

The President as the "Top of the Ticket"

Even when the president doesn't campaign actively for them, a president's actions and successes can affect the prospects of other party candidates.

Coattail Effects   The most direct link between presidential success and party victories has been explained by the metaphor of coattails. Presidents ran "at the top of the ticket," the explanation goes, and the rest of the party ticket came into office clinging to their sturdy coattails. This coattail effect was very common in the 1800s when the parties printed their own ballots, so a voter usually had to cast a ballot for an entire party ticket.

Coattail effects declined from the end of World War II through the early 1980s.[5] Members of Congress became very talented at cultivating their constituency by attending closely to its interests and providing services to individual constituents. This helped to insulate them from outside electoral forces, including presidential popularity.[6] Incumbents gained big advantages over their challengers in fund-raising, especially in House races.

However, the relationship between presidential and congressional election results has reemerged since the early 1990s, as the parties have become more polarized. As congressional expert Gary Jacobson writes, "Highly nationalized, president-centered midterm elections have become the norm in this century."[7] Coattail effects can reach into nonfederal races as well.[8]

Coattails without the Coat   Presidents can influence election results even when they are not on the ballot. As congressional races have become more nationalized, voters' approval of the president's job performance affects their support for candidates of the president's party in midterm congressional elections.[9] In the 2018 midterms, for instance, 34 percent of poll respondents said their vote for Congress was meant to express opposition to the president. Fewer people (26 percent) said they were voting to register their support for President Trump. That made Donald Trump a bigger force in voters' midterm choices than any other president in three decades.[10]

This helps explain why the president's party has almost always suffered a decline in its share of House seats in the midterm election.[11] Most presidents' public approval ratings have dropped by the midpoint of their terms, and the president's declining popularity can drag down congressional candidates of his or her party or discourage attractive party candidates from running.[12] People who disapprove of the president's performance are more likely to vote in midterm elections than those who approve, and their disapproval can lead them to vote for the other party's candidates.[13]

The 1998 and 2002 elections broke this pattern of midterm losses by the president's party. In both years, presidential popularity was either holding steady or increasing. Although President Bush had begun his first term with fairly low approval ratings, his popularity soared to almost 90 percent after the September 11 terrorist attacks and remained above 60 percent as the 2002 election approached. His 90 percent approval among Republicans, in particular, made a difference in close campaigns.[14] But the traditional pattern returned beginning in 2006. Party identifiers—both Republicans and Democrats—increasingly express strong disapproval of presidents from the other party.

In sum, whether or not they choose to act as party leaders, presidents' popularity and success can affect the likelihood that other candidates of their party will win their races. This happens especially if the candidates' advertising stresses their connection with the president and if the president campaigns actively for them. It gives presidents a potential source of influence over the legislative party colleagues they helped elect.[15]

Party Leadership and Legislative Relations

Presidents and governors can gain legislative support for their programs in several ways. Executives use their ability to attract media coverage, their public approval (if it is substantial), and the coattails and favors they may have provided to individual legislators. Chief executives also have legislative liaisons: staff people who work with party leaders and other members of Congress or state legislatures to encourage support for the executive's proposals. A president's "legislative shop" can make a big difference in calming an angry committee chair or providing key information to a wavering supporter.

It helps that members of the executive's party know that if they make him or her look weak, they might weaken their own reelection chances. This can encourage them to rally around the president or governor on important votes, even if they would prefer to vote differently. Consider the example of Rep. Francis Rooney, who represented a Florida congressional district that had supported President Trump by 60 percent in 2016. When Rooney told friends that he might be open to the possibility of impeaching the president in 2019,

> The blowback from the people in Southwest Florida was something. I mean, I had people down here in the local Republican leadership mad at me, yelling at me, telling me nothing should happen to make me waver in my support of Donald Trump. *Nothing*,

Rooney retired from Congress in 2020—after voting against impeachment.[16]

Legislative Support for Executives

Congress members are clearly aware of the close connection between the president's popularity and their own reelection prospects. Popular support is a key resource for the chief executive in getting Congress to go along with his or her programs. That was painfully evident to President Obama, when his steady but low approval ratings undermined his ability to gain congressional consent for his initiatives (see Figure 14.1).

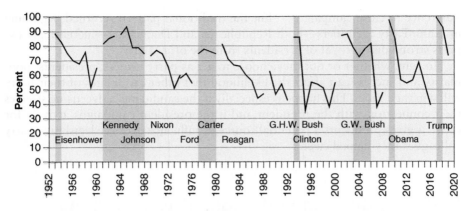

FIGURE 14.1 Presidential Success in the U.S. Congress, 1953–2019

Note: The entry for each year is the percentage of time members of both the House and the Senate voted in support of the announced position of the president. Years that are shaded are those in which the president's party controlled both houses of Congress (unified government).

Source: CQ Magazine, January or February issues.

Presidents do better when their party controls both houses of Congress; these periods of time—the early years of the Eisenhower, Kennedy and Johnson, Carter, George W. Bush, Obama, and Trump administrations—are typically the president's greatest opportunities for success on legislation. Presidents Obama and Trump got historic levels of support during their first two years, when their party controlled both the House and the Senate. Both were careful to take public positions only on legislation they felt they could win. After Republicans regained control of the House in 2011, Obama's success rate plummeted, as it did in the Senate once Democrats lost control in 2014. Trump's experience was similar; his success rate dropped by 20 percentage points once Republicans failed to keep the House in the 2018 elections (see Figure 14.1), though he took clear positions on only a small number of issues.[17]

Even unified party control of Congress does not *guarantee* success for presidents' programs. Splits in the president's congressional parties may still threaten the passage of his or her proposals. President Trump had Republican majorities in both houses for the first two years of his term, yet several of his signature legislative proposals failed to pass because of opposition from small groups of Republican House and Senate members.

And the party polarization in Congress makes it unlikely that presidents will get votes from the other party. During the two years when President Obama had Democratic majorities in both houses, many of his most important legislative accomplishments were passed with no (or almost no) Republican votes. Republican legislators had good reason to vote "no" on the president's proposals because he was unpopular in their districts; in recent years, a huge "public approval gap" has opened between Democratic and Republican identifiers' support of the president.

Public reactions to President Trump set records with respect to party polarization; the gap between Democrats' and Republicans' approval of Trump has been the widest in the history of modern polling, averaging at least 84 percent approval among Republicans compared with 7 percent among Democrats.[18] As a result, very few congressional Democrats could expect to gain constituent support by voting for Trump's policies. And the president's party colleagues who represent "swing" districts, in which both parties are competitive, could endanger their reelections if they vote in lockstep with the president. The bigger the president's legislative majority, the more of his party's legislators are likely to come from swing districts.

In addition, the institutional rivalries designed into a separation of powers system help to ensure that the president's party in Congress will not surrender all its powers to the co-partisan in the White House. Polarized politics has weakened this safeguard, however, as House Republicans' unified support of President Trump in the 2019 impeachment debate indicated.

Divided Control of Government   Presidents generally get much less support, of course, when at least one house of Congress is in the hands of the opposing party, as the unshaded areas of Figure 14.1 show. Unhappily for modern presidents, divided government has been the norm during the past five decades. Almost all of the states have also experienced divided party control of the legislature and the governorship at some point during this time.

With a divided government, executives have two main choices. They can try to negotiate successfully with at least some legislators of the other party—and in fact, some researchers find that a divided government is as likely to produce significant policy change as is a unified government.[19] Or they can try to brand the other party as the "party of no," the roadblock in the way of progress, hoping that voters will respond by giving the president's party a majority in the next election.

In times of both divided and unified party control, governors have some advantages over presidents in gaining support from their legislative party. In state legislatures that do not use seniority rules, governors can take an active part in selecting committee chairs and party floor leaders. Most governors have greater control over party rewards and incentives than a president does. On the other hand, governors are not as visible as presidents are, so their coattails and prestige are normally less influential than those of presidents.

Party Influence in Executive Agencies

Presidents get the media coverage, but the White House is only one part of the executive branch. The people who work in cabinet-level departments such as Education and Agriculture and in other agencies such as the Environmental Protection Agency (EPA) are responsible for carrying out the laws Congress passes. These executive agencies regulate vast areas of the economy—pollution, food safety, and prescription drugs, for example—under congressional mandates that require a lot of interpretation. The administrators and bureaucrats who implement these laws, then, shape policy by applying it. It is they who determine whether the milk you drank was inspected for spoilage, or how much mercury your local power plant is permitted to dump into your air.

How might partisanship (or the chief partisan in the White House) affect the people who work in these executive agencies? Do we see evidence of partisan behavior in federal agencies?

How Is Presidential or Party Influence Exercised?

Partisanship can affect federal agencies because the heads of the largest agencies—cabinet-level departments such as the Department of Defense and the Department of Veterans Affairs—are appointed by the president and can be removed by the president as well. These agency heads have often had a long history of party activity. Most presidential cabinet appointees have been long-time members or activists in the president's party. Presidents no longer use these positions as rewards for loyal *party* service; instead, they look for loyalty to the president's *own* aims. Nevertheless, most presidential appointees have been active partisans whose values and political careers have been shaped to a significant degree by their party.

Modern presidents can make only a few thousand of these high-level political appointments, however—fewer appointive positions than some governors have—to try to gain control of an executive branch employing about 2.1 million civilians. Many of these political appointees are newcomers with little time to "learn the ropes" and little hope of gaining the necessary support of the career bureaucrats who serve under them.[20] Below this top level, agency officials are less likely to have party experience. These officials are chosen primarily for their administrative skills and only secondarily for their political credentials. And most of the remaining agency employees are selected using civil service exams, not party screening procedures.

Another powerful segment of the executive branch is the large number of federal regulatory agencies such as the Food and Drug Administration (FDA). Many of these were established during the Progressive era of the late 1800s and early 1900s. The Progressives worked hard to limit party influence in these agencies, including the influence of the president. For instance, many regulatory agencies are required to be headed by commissions that include members of both parties.

These agencies, like the cabinet departments, deal with highly complex, technical issues. To decide how much mercury can be allowed in your community's air, for example, EPA staffers must be able to understand complicated scientific findings on the effects of mercury on human health and the impact of cleanup costs on the power plant's bottom line. Party loyalty does not provide this technical competence (though it may well affect an agency head's interpretation of the technical findings).

Another limit on presidential or party influence over the bureaucracy is that just as individual legislators pay attention to their constituents' needs, administrators have demanding constituencies as well. The EPA works closely with the many industries whose pollution it regulates, as well as with a variety of professional and citizen groups.[21] If the EPA's rulings in applying the Clean Air Act outrage electric power companies or big environmental groups, the EPA will be in political trouble. Presidents may try to give their agency heads protective cover at these times, but they can't always protect against the impact of a well-financed constituency group, and they may choose not to do so.

Changing Partisan Perspectives in the Federal Bureaucracy

In spite of these limits on party and presidential control, the federal bureaucracy does respond to partisan forces over the long run. As the federal government expanded in the 1930s, President Franklin Roosevelt drew people into the career bureaucracy who were committed to his programs. They then resisted later efforts to weaken these programs, especially as they got promoted to more senior positions in their agencies.

Decades later, the federal bureaucracy still had a pro-Democratic slant. By 1970, Joel Aberbach and Bert Rockman found that nearly a majority of these career bureaucrats said they normally voted Democratic and only 17 percent usually voted Republican. In federal social service agencies, even the administrators who were not Democrats said that they favored liberal policies. So Republican President Richard Nixon, in office at that time, faced a federal bureaucracy that had little sympathy for his conservative agenda. His administration spent a lot of time trying to control the bureaucracy by appointing Nixon loyalists to top bureaucratic positions.[22]

By 1992, however, the bureaucratic environment had changed. Republicans had held the White House for all but four years between 1972 and 1992. When Aberbach and Rockman returned to interview career administrators in comparable positions to those they interviewed in 1970, they now found slight Republican pluralities. As older civil servants retired, a new generation, less committed to New Deal and Great Society programs, had been recruited into senior executive positions. Changes in civil service laws further allowed positions formerly reserved for career employees to be filled by political appointees who could be carefully screened by the White House. The bureaucracy was no longer as hostile to Republican initiatives.[23] The Reagan, Clinton, and George W. Bush administrations made serious efforts to put their own stamp on the federal bureaucracy, sometimes resulting in complaints of partisan bias in federal agencies' activities.[24] By 2020, top federal executives regarded several federal agencies as leaning toward the conservative side, including the FBI, the defense, intelligence, and law enforcement agencies.[25]

In short, partisanship does influence executive branch agencies. But most presidents and governors use their party leadership role to promote their own programs and reelection, not their party's programs.[26] To the extent that the executive's goals are similar to those of his or her party, then the party's program benefits. For most American executives, however, the goals and interests of their party organization are secondary to their own policy goals and political careers.

Traces of Party in the Courts

Courts and judges are affected by party politics as well. Most American judges—even most justices of the U.S. Supreme Court—are political men and women who took office after careers that involved them in some aspect of partisan politics (see box "The Partisan Backgrounds of U.S. Supreme Court Justices" on page 329). Party conflict increasingly plays a role in the appointment and election of judges. Because of the nature of the judiciary, however, party influence can be subtle.

Judicial Voting Along Party Lines

Judges appointed by Democratic presidents tend to be more liberal on issues such as civil rights and liberties, crime, labor issues, and regulation of business than are those appointed by Republican presidents.[27] An environmental research group reported that federal judges appointed by Democratic presidents were much more likely to rule in favor of environmentalists than Republican-appointed judges were.[28] U.S. District Court judges have tended to uphold redistricting plans enacted by their party more than those enacted by the opposing party.[29] And court rulings on states' voter identification laws (see Chapter 8) closely reflect whether the court's majority was nominated by Democratic or Republican officials.[30] These are the kinds of differences we would expect to find when comparing the views of Democrats and Republicans outside the courtroom.

It is not easy to distinguish the impact of judges' partisanship from other influences, including their career goals, law school training, and desire to protect their professional reputations. Judges show much less party cohesion than legislators do. Yet under some circumstances, it is clear that Democratic judges rule differently from their Republican colleagues, especially in higher appeals courts that deal with the most contentious and complex cases.

What Causes Partisan Behavior on the Courts?

Very little of this apparent partisanship is due to active efforts by Democratic and Republican Party leaders to influence court decisions. That wouldn't be acceptable in most communities now. A much better explanation for the impact of party on judges' behavior is simply that judges have some discretion in applying the laws to specific cases, just as bureaucrats do. Judges, like the rest of us, have developed views on political issues and on how flexible the law should be. And among the most fundamental of those views are party identifications.

Just as the two parties reflect different sets of values, so do their identifiers, including those who become judges. Two judges might vote together on the regulation of business because of values they share about the proper role of government. Those values may have led them to identify with the same party years earlier or were developed out of experience in that party. People who want to be judges often join networks of liberal or conservative lawyers, such as the American Constitution Society (liberal) and the Federalist Society (conservative). Increasingly, these partisan values structure a judge's environment. Supreme Court justices, for

The Partisan Backgrounds of U.S. Supreme Court Justices

Justices nominated by Republican Presidents

John Roberts (chief justice; nominated by G. W. Bush) was an aide to the attorney general and White House counsel in the Republican Reagan administration. He was the principal deputy solicitor general in the Republican G. H. W. Bush administration.

Clarence Thomas (G. H. W. Bush) served on the staff of Missouri's Republican attorney general and as assistant secretary for Civil Rights and director of the Equal Employment Opportunity Commission in the Republican Reagan administration. Thomas's wife was a senior aide to former House Republican Majority Leader Dick Armey.

Samuel A. Alito, Jr. (G. W. Bush) was assistant to the solicitor general and deputy assistant to the attorney general in the Republican Reagan administration. Republican G.H.W. Bush nominated him to the U.S. Court of Appeals before G.W. Bush nominated him to the Supreme Court.

Neil Gorsuch (Trump) was nominated for the U.S. Court of Appeals by Republican President George W. Bush after serving as Bush's Principal Deputy Associate Attorney General at the U.S. Department of Justice. Gorsuch is a Republican "legacy": his mother, Anne Gorsuch Burford, was Republican Ronald Reagan's appointee as administrator of the Environmental Protection Agency.

Brett Kavanaugh (Trump) worked for the George W. Bush campaign in 2000 before becoming Bush's White House Staff Secretary. Earlier, he was on the staff of Independent Counsel Kenneth Starr, assessing evidence for the impeachment of Democratic President Bill Clinton. Bush nominated him to the U.S. Court of Appeals for the D.C. Circuit in 2003.

Amy Coney Barrett (Trump) clerked for late Supreme Court Justice Antonin Scalia (nominated by Reagan) and served three years as judge on the 7th U.S. Circuit Court of Appeals, having been nominated by President Trump.

Justices nominated by Democratic Presidents

Stephen G. Breyer (Clinton) was a special assistant to the assistant attorney general under Democratic President Lyndon Johnson and special counsel and then chief counsel to the Democratic-led Senate Judiciary Committee.

Sonia Sotomayor (Obama) served as a New York County assistant district attorney, nominated by a Democratic governor. She was recommended for a federal judgeship by a Democratic senator and nominated by both a Republican (G.H.W. Bush) president and a Democratic (Clinton) president.

Elena Kagan (Obama) was appointed U.S. Solicitor General by Democratic President Obama and as domestic policy adviser by the previous Democratic president, Bill Clinton. She clerked for Democratic justices and judges and interned for two Democratic U.S. House members.

instance, are now more likely to hire law clerks—lawyers who do much of the work of the Court and help shape its rulings—consistent with their partisanship: conservatives hire Republican clerks and liberals hire Democrats.[31]

When presidents and governors nominate or appoint judges, the nominees' value systems are foremost in their minds. They know that judges have flexibility in deciding some cases and that the choices they make may reflect, at least in part, the judge's own beliefs and experiences. When President Obama nominated Sonia Sotomayor to the Supreme Court, for instance, she argued that her life experience as a Latina could add to the Court's breadth of understanding, and her confirmation hearings focused intently on her background and beliefs. In most debates over judicial nominations, especially for higher courts that receive the most challenging cases, Congress members and interest groups now devote major attention to the values and attitudes of the possible nominees. That was especially true in the 2018 confirmation battle over the nomination of Brett Kavanaugh, a strong conservative who moved the Supreme Court's median to the right after replacing its longtime swing justice, Anthony Kennedy.

Federal Judges   If you were president, you would want to nominate federal judges and Supreme Court justices who would uphold your policies, not strike them down. Prospective judges' party and ideology are among the clues you would use to predict how they would rule once in office. Thus, every American president for the past century has made at least 80 percent of his judicial appointments from within his own party. The average is higher than 90 percent.

President Reagan, both Bush administrations, and President Trump took special care to screen candidates for their dedication to conservative principles.[32] As a result, their appointees were even more ideologically distinctive (and more likely to have been active in party politics) than average among recent presidents—more than in the Bill Clinton administration, for instance.[33] This has produced intense ideological battles between Republican-appointed conservative judges and liberal judges appointed by Democratic presidents. It has become routine for Democratic-appointed and Republican-appointed appeals court judges to attack one another's decisions in their own rulings using terms such as "unconscionable," "absurd," and "alarming."[34]

Senate action on the president's nominations to federal judgeships has become more partisan as well. Early shots were fired in the 1980s and early 1990s, when Senate Democrats and their allies waged major battles over the confirmation of two conservative nominees to the Supreme Court: Robert Bork and Clarence Thomas. (In fact, the former case gave rise to a new verb. When an intense, partisan campaign has been mustered against a nominee, he or she is said to have been "Borked.") By the end of the Bill Clinton administration, the level of partisan animosity over judicial appointments was so high that Republican Senate leaders were refusing to schedule debate on some of the president's nominees.[35]

The atmosphere surrounding judicial appointments has become more and more hostile as ideological groups of various kinds use these nominations to fire up their core supporters in the public. Senate Democrats first used the so-called "nuclear option" to end the minority party's right to filibuster a president's federal court nominees in 2013, as a means of keeping Republicans from stalling President Obama's nominations. When Republicans retook control of the Senate, they upped the ante by eliminating filibusters on Supreme Court nominations as well and refused to act on large numbers of Obama's nominations.

Their strategy was rewarded when President Trump was elected in 2016. Trump was able to fill a Supreme Court vacancy that Senate Republicans had left empty when Obama had the right to fill it. Trump later made a second appointment to the high court and so many district and federal appeals court nominations that by the end of his third year in the White House, he had appointed as many circuit court judges as Obama was able to appoint in eight years. By 2020, his appointments had created Republican majorities in a majority of federal appeals courts. And half of Trump's appointees were under the age of 50, so they could be expected to influence court rulings for decades (see box "The Struggle to Reshape the Federal Courts" on page 332).[36]

State Court Judges   State court judges, in contrast, are often elected rather than appointed—a practice used almost nowhere else in the world. Candidates for at least some types of judgeships must run in partisan elections in about a third of the states. Some states use a nonpartisan ballot for judges' races, though party organizations may still endorse their own candidates publicly. In these elections, candidates for judge routinely accept campaign contributions, often from lawyers and groups who will be bringing cases to their courts for a ruling. The contributors, of course, are not donating out of love for the judiciary; they have interests that they want heard.[37] These contests have become more and more costly, especially since *Citizens United* (see Chapter 12). Some have been as acrimonious as nominations to the U.S. Supreme Court.

Even when judges are appointed to their posts, partisanship can still play a role. In many states, party leaders may advise on the nominations of prospective judges. A number of states have moved toward a "merit appointment" system in which nominating commissions screen prospective judges or recommend a shortlist to the governor or another official. In these cases, the appointee usually has to run in a retention election within 4–12 years of his or her appointment. Reformers hoped that these long terms and the likelihood that the appointee would be reelected (thanks to incumbency) would free judges from party pressures, or even pressures from the governor or president. But partisanship is so often already internalized in the judge's values and preferences that a long-term judgeship merely allows them to flourish.[38]

Even in these retention elections, the partisan stakes have risen in recent years. State supreme courts make crucial decisions on policy, and a variety of interest groups have realized that it is much cheaper to affect those policies by changing the composition of the court than to try to change the party balance in the state legislature. Spending in these state supreme court contests does not approach that for congressional races, but during the past two decades, these contests have attracted over half a billion dollars in spending, much of which comes from interest groups. Data show "the transformation of these elections from sleepy low-dollar contests into costly races awash in dark money."[39]

The Struggle to Reshape the Federal Courts

For several years, many important Supreme Court cases were decided by 5–4 votes. Five of the Court's justices had been appointed by Republican presidents and were considered conservative votes, and four were known to be liberals. Then, one of the conservatives, Justice Antonin Scalia, died suddenly. Within hours a bitter partisan fight broke out. Many Republicans claimed that it was undemocratic for Democratic President Barack Obama to nominate Scalia's successor because Obama was in his last year of office. Democrats pointed out that there was no such rule or tradition, and that it was the president's constitutional responsibility to fill any Court vacancy. Republican senators refused to consider Obama's nominee, and the vacancy remained until President Donald Trump was elected and appointed a conservative Republican to the high court. Trump's nominee was quickly confirmed by the Republican-dominated Senate.

It would be hard to find a clearer example of the influence of party on the courts. When he ran for president, Trump promised to reshape the judiciary, which he regarded as biased toward liberals. The strategy was to speed young, very conservative appointees through Senate confirmation, especially in states that

Trump had won in 2016 but were represented by Democrats up for reelection. The wheels were greased by the Senate's vote to require only a majority to end any filibuster of a Supreme Court nominee; previously it took 60 votes to stop a filibuster, which would normally require some votes from the minority party to achieve. And because the Senate Republican majority during the Obama administration had refused to act on Obama's judicial nominations, Trump had the advantage of a very large number of judicial vacancies.

The partisan character of judicial appointments became even more apparent when the leader of the Court's liberal bloc, Justice Ruth Bader Ginsburg, died in September, 2020. But Senate majority leader Mitch McConnell no longer argued that it was undemocratic for a new Justice to be confirmed in the final year of a president's term. Instead, McConnell stated that the Senate would confirm President Trump's nominee right away; in fact, Republicans claimed they had the votes to confirm, even before the president announced his nominee. He nominated Judge Amy Coney Barrett eight days after Ginsburg died, and the Senate moved quickly to confirm her.

Sources: Melissa Quinn, "Senate Confirms Trump's 100th Judicial Nominee," *Washington Examiner*, May 2, 2019, https://www.washingtonexaminer.com/policy/courts/senate-confirms-trumps-100th-judicial-nominee (accessed August 25, 2020); Charlie Savage, "Courts Reshaped At Fastest Pace in Five Decades," *New York Times*, November 12, 2017, p. A1.

Massive campaigns have been waged in Wisconsin, West Virginia, North Carolina, Kansas, and other states as interest groups and parties sought to influence the ideological composition of their Supreme Courts. And in 2018, some Republican legislators tried to impeach state Supreme Court justices who ruled against a plan to gerrymander legislative districts to favor Republicans.[40] Voters' choices in these elections, even in ostensibly nonpartisan contests, have often closely correlated with their votes for president.[41]

Many European countries choose judges differently. Someone prepares to be a judge by studying judgeship, apprenticing, and then scoring well on a special exam. In the U.S., in contrast, there is no special training process for judges—no exam to take, no advanced degree in judging. Any lawyer can be a judge if he or she can win election or appointment to the job. But although the specialized training process required for judgeships in many European nations limits the impact of party organizations and partisan elections, those who become judges will still have political preferences, many of which will have been shaped by their partisanship.

The Party within the Executive and the Judge

The best explanation for party influence on executives and judges is that, like other officeholders, executives and judges hold political beliefs, and the fact that judges and administrators have to interpret laws when applying them allows these beliefs to affect their behavior in office. Democrats usually hold different beliefs about government and the economy than Republicans do, and Democratic judges and bureaucrats, similarly, hold different views from Republican judges and bureaucrats. These party differences are reinforced by partisan aspects of the process by which presidents and governors, top executive officials, and most judges are chosen. We rarely see much evidence of direct influence by the party organization on bureaucrats and courts. The parties don't have the means to enforce party discipline in the executive or judicial branches.

Reformers have tried to take partisan considerations out of the selection process for judges and bureaucrats. When citizens suspect that partisan forces are affecting courts and administrative agencies—for instance, when judges campaigning for reelection get big campaign contributions from lawyers and groups whose lawsuits they will later decide—public confidence in courts and administrative agencies declines.[42] But there is no way to eliminate individuals' beliefs and values, including their partisanship, from their selection as administrators or judges or from their behavior in office.

Notes

1 Sidney M. Milkis, Jesse H. Rhodes, and Emily J. Charnock, "What Happened to Post-Partisanship?" *Perspectives on Politics* 10 (2012): 57–76.
2 See Daniel J. Galvin, *Presidential Party Building* (Princeton, NJ: Princeton University Press, 2010).
3 Brendan J. Doherty, "Presidential Party Fundraising in Hopes of Not Having to Govern by Himself," *The Forum* 12 (2014): 81–101.
4 Andrew O. Ballard, Michael Heseltine, and Hans J.G. Hassell, "Be Careful What You Wish For," Legislative Studies Quarterly (2020), forthcoming.

5 James E. Campbell, "Predicting Seat Gains from Presidential Coattails," *American Journal of Political Science* 30 (1986): 164–183.

6 See Bruce Cain, John Ferejohn, and Morris Fiorina, *The Personal Vote* (Cambridge, MA: Harvard University Press, 1987).

7 Gary C. Jacobson, *Presidents and Parties in the Public Mind* (Chicago, IL: University of Chicago Press, 2019), pp. 168, 190. See also John H. Aldrich, Jamie L. Carson, Brad T. Gomez, and David W. Rohde, *Change and Continuity in the 2016 & 2018 Elections* (Los Angeles, CA: Sage, 2020), pp. 302–304.

8 See Marc Meredith, "Exploiting Friends-and-Neighbors to Estimate Coattail Effects," *American Political Science Review* 107 (2013): 742–765.

9 See Gary C. Jacobson, "It's Nothing Personal," *Journal of Politics* 77 (2015): 861–873.

10 Pew Research Center, "Voters More Focused on Control of Congress – and the President – Than in Past Midterms," June 20, 2018, https://www.people-press.org/2018/06/20/voters-more-focused-on-control-of-congress-and-the-president-than-in-past-midterms/ (accessed August 25, 2020).

11 The classic statement is Angus Campbell, "Surge and Decline: A Study of Electoral Change," in Campbell, Philip E. Converse, Warren E. Miller, and Donald E. Stokes, eds., *Elections and the Political Order* (New York: Wiley, 1966), pp. 40–62. See also Robert S. Erikson, "Congressional Elections in Presidential Years," *Legislative Studies Quarterly* 41 (August 2016): 551–574.

12 See James E. Campbell, "The Midterm Landslide of 2010," *The Forum* 8 (2010), issue 4, article 3.

13 Pew Research Center, "Political Polarization in the American Public," June 12, 2014, https://www.pewresearch.org/politics/2014/06/12/political-polarization-in-the-american-public/ (accessed August 25, 2020).

14 See Paul R. Abramson, John H. Aldrich, and David W. Rohde, *Change and Continuity in the 1992 Elections* (Washington, DC: CQ Press, 1994), p. 196.

15 Governors can have coattail effects too: Robert E. Hogan, "Gubernatorial Coattail Effects in State Legislative Elections," *Political Research Quarterly* 58 (December 2005): 587–597.

16 Tim Alberta, "Who Will Betray Trump?" *Politico*, November 8, 2019, https://www.politico.com/magazine/story/2019/11/08/trump-impeachment-republicans-congress-229904 (accessed August 25, 2020).

17 "2019 Vote Studies: Presidential Support—House," *CQ Magazine*, February 24, 2020.

18 Amina Dunn, "Trump's Approval Ratings So Far Are Unusually Stable – and Deeply Partisan," August 1, 2018, https://www.pewresearch.org/fact-tank/2018/08/01/trumps-approval-ratings-so-far-are-unusually-stable-and-deeply-partisan/ (accessed August 25, 2020).

19 See David R. Mayhew, *Divided We Govern,* 2nd ed. (New Haven, CT: Yale University Press, 2005).

20 Hugh Heclo, *A Government of Strangers* (Washington, DC: Brookings Institution, 1977).

21 Hugh Heclo, "Issue Networks and the Executive Establishment," in Anthony King, ed., *The New American Political System* (Washington, DC: American Enterprise Institute, 1979), pp. 87–124.

22 Joel Aberbach and Bert A. Rockman, "Clashing Beliefs Within the Executive Branch," *American Political Science Review* 70 (1976): 456–468.

23 Joel D. Aberbach and Bert A. Rockman, "The Political Views of U.S. Senior Federal Executives, 1970–1992," *Journal of Politics* 57 (1995): 838–852.

24 Sanford C. Gordon, "Assessing Partisan Bias in Federal Public Corruption Prosecutions," *American Political Science Review* 103 (2009): 534–554.

25 Mark D. Richardson, Joshua D. Clinton, and David E. Lewis, "Elite Perceptions of Agency Ideology and Workforce Skill," *Journal of Politics* 80 (January 2018): 303–308.

26 Kenneth S. Lowande and Sidney M. Milkis, "'We Can't Wait': Barack Obama, Partisan Polarization, and the Administrative Presidency," *The Forum* 12 (2014): 3–27.

27 See Lee Epstein, William M. Landes, and Richard A. Posner, *The Behavior of Federal Judges* (Cambridge, MA: Harvard University Press, 2013), and James F. Spriggs II and Thomas G. Hansford, "Explaining the Overruling of U.S. Supreme Court Precedent," *Journal of Politics* 63 (November 2001): 1091–1111.

28 Juliet Eilperin, "Environmental Group Cites Partisanship in the Judiciary," *Washington Post,* October 9, 2004, p. A2. See also Thomas J. Miles and Cass R. Sunstein, "Do Judges Make Regulatory Policy?" *University of Chicago Law Review* 73 (2006): 823–881.

29 See Randall D. Lloyd, "Separating Partisanship from Party in Judicial Research," *American Political Science Review* 89 (1995): 413–420.

30 See Robert Barnes, "Partisan Fissures Over Voter ID," *Washington Post*, December 25, 2007, p. A1.

31 Adam Liptak, "Clerks Highlight Supreme Court's Polarization," *New York Times,* September 6, 2010, p. A1.

32 Sheldon Goldman, "The Bush Imprint on the Judiciary," *Judicature* 74 (1991), 294–306.

33 Sheldon Goldman, Elliot Slotnick, Gerard Gryski, and Gary Zuk, "Clinton's Judges," *Judicature* 84 (2001): 244, 249.

34 R. Jeffrey Smith, "The Politics of the Federal Bench," *Washington Post*, December 8, 2008, p. A1.

35 See Sarah A. Binder and Forrest Maltzman, "Senatorial Delay in Confirming Federal Judges, 1947–1998," *American Journal of Political Science* 46 (2002): 190–199.

36 Christina L. Boyd, Michael S. Lynch, and Anthony Madonna, "Nuclear Fallout," *The Forum* 13, Issue 4 (February 2016): 623–641.

37 Beth Carter Easter, "Tipping the Scales of Justice," Ph.D. Dissertation, Indiana University, 2014; Melinda Gann Hall, *Attacking Judges* (Stanford, CA: Stanford University Press, 2015).

38 See Melinda Gann Hall, "State Supreme Courts in American Democracy," *American Political Science Review* 95 (2001): 315–330.

39 Douglas Keith, Patrick Berry, and Patrick Velasco, "The Politics of Judicial Elections, 2017–18," Brennan Center for Justice, December 11, 2019, https://www.brennan-center.org/our-work/research-reports/politics-judicial-elections-2017-18 (accessed August 25, 2020).

40 See Meghan E. Leonard, "State Legislatures, State High Courts, and Judicial Independence," *Justice System Journal* 37 (#1 2016): 53–62.

41 Emily Rock and Lawrence Baum, "The Impact of High-Visibility Contests for U.S. State Court Judgeships," *State Politics & Policy Quarterly* 10 (December 2010): 368–396.

42 James L. Gibson, *Electing Judges* (Chicago, IL: University of Chicago Press, 2012).

CHAPTER 15

The Semi-Responsible Parties

As recently as 40 years ago, Americans' attitudes toward abortion were not strongly related to their party identification.[1] Both parties were split on the controversy. Large numbers of Democrats favored a ban on all abortions, and a substantial number of Republicans were pro-choice.

Since that time, abortion has become a deeply partisan issue; the Republican Party's shift to a pro-life stance reflects the growing strength of evangelical Christians within the Republican ranks, and the Democrats' move in the opposite direction parallels the decline in evangelical and Catholic support for Democratic candidates. But there are still pockets of pro-life sentiment within the Democratic Party; while 82 percent of Democrats said in a recent poll that abortion should be legal in all or most cases, 17 percent said no, and among Republican respondents, 36 percent wanted abortion to be legal in all or most cases, though their party's platform disagrees.[2]

If both national parties have some internal disagreement on abortion, then shouldn't both parties' platforms say, "Believe whatever you want about abortion; we won't take a stand"? There's a powerful argument in favor of parties taking clear and opposing positions on issues, however, even if their identifiers aren't totally on board: Political parties are the most effective means we have of holding elected officials collectively responsible for their actions. When parties simplify and clarify our political choices (among other services; see Chapter 1), they make it easier for you to predict what will happen when you make your choices in the voting booth. That, in turn, makes it easier for citizens to hold the awesome powers of government accountable to their preferences. If the American parties can't take clear stands on this important issue and hold their candidates accountable, then is it even possible for individuals to keep government responsive to our needs?

For many years, critics complained that the two major parties were not clear *enough*, and not different enough from one another, on how they would handle big issues. Even now, although the two parties differ dramatically on major questions such as climate change, immigration, and LGBTQ rights, some argue that both parties are controlled by moneyed special interests. Thus, they argue, both major parties serve well-financed minorities—corporations, labor unions, single-issue groups—rather than the people.

These critics come from different perspectives, but at heart they make the same point. They both want the parties to offer clearer and more detailed stands on issues and for the winning party to put its promises to work in public policy. One possible answer is to create a system of truly "responsible parties."[3] The governing party in this system would translate a coherent political philosophy into government action and would then be held responsible for the results.

To some extent, their demands have been met. The parties clearly differ now on a number of important issues. The Democratic Party is more uniformly liberal today than it was a few decades ago, and the Republicans are more consistently conservative. People's party ID is a much better predictor of their political attitudes now than is their age, race and ethnicity, gender, educational level, or religion.[4] In fact, many Americans currently think that the gulf between the parties has become *too* wide; more than half of Americans describe the Republican Party as "too extreme," and a smaller proportion say the same about the Democrats.[5] Has this party polarization made the Democrats and Republicans into "responsible" parties, and does it improve their ability to serve the needs of a democracy?

The Case for Responsible Party Government

The idea of *responsible parties*, also called party government, offers a vision of democracy very different from the traditional American commitment to limited government and the equally traditional American hostility to powerful political parties. Champions of party government believe that we need a strong and decisive government to solve social and economic problems. Our political institutions, they feel, may have been well suited to the limited governing of the early years of American history but do not serve us well today, when we need more vigorous government action against challenges ranging from terrorism to climate change.

Yet the public must be able to keep this strong government under control. Individuals rarely have the time, information, or desire to play an active political role or even to find out what their elected representatives are doing. Candidate-centered elections can reduce public control as well; it is much harder for voters to monitor hundreds of different candidates than to judge the performance of one governing party.

How Would Party Government (Responsible Parties) Work?

To solve these problems, party government advocates say, we should structure the political system so that voters could more effectively hold parties and elected officials accountable.[6] The parties would take the lead in organizing the government and, in the process, reinvigorate the other institutions of popular democracy. Here's how party government would work:

- Each party would draw up a clear, detailed statement of the principles and programs it favors. It would pledge to carry out those programs if the party wins.

- The parties would nominate candidates loyal to their party's program and willing to push for it if elected.
- Each party would run a campaign that clarifies the policy differences between the two parties, so voters would grasp these differences and vote on that basis.
- Once elected, the party would hold its officeholders responsible for carrying out the party program. Voters could then determine whether they liked the results and decide whether to keep or defeat the governing party at the next election.

In this system of responsible parties, then, winning elections would not be an end in itself. The party's main focus would be on the policies it has pledged to put into effect. Nominations and elections would become no more—and no less—than a means to achieve certain public policy goals. *For this to happen, all the elected branches of government would have to be controlled by the same party at a particular time.* The party would bind the divided institutions of government into a working whole, as happens in parliamentary democracies.

What qualifies the party to play this crucial role? A prominent party scholar wrote that "the parties have claims on the loyalties of the American people superior to the claims of any other forms of political organization. ... The parties are the special form of political organization adapted to the mobilization of majorities."[7] So parties would hold a privileged position in politics compared with interest groups, their major rivals as intermediaries between citizens and government.[8]

Those who argue for party government do not always agree on the purposes they feel a strong federal government should serve. Many conservatives, once suspicious of a powerful central government, grew to like it better when conservative Presidents Reagan, Bush, and Trump used their power to urge Congress to eliminate liberal programs. Liberals frustrated by the separation of powers developed greater enthusiasm for the principle when Congress proved capable of checking some of Reagan's, Bush's, and Trump's initiatives. Party government sounds like a better idea, it seems, when your party is in charge. In any case, party government advocates feel that a government pulled together by strong parties would let citizens direct their government more effectively than they do now, and with less investment of citizens' time and effort.

The Case against Party Government

Most American political scientists remain unconvinced of the benefits of party government. Their concerns take two forms. Many argue that party government would not produce desirable results. Others claim that it simply would not work in the American context.[9]

It Would Increase Conflict

First, the skeptics fear that the nature of party government—its dedication to providing clear alternatives on major issues—would provoke even more political conflict. Legislators, they say, would be bound to a fixed party position and would no longer be free to represent their own constituents and to negotiate mutually acceptable solutions. That would weaken the deliberative character of American legislatures.

Critics of party government also fear that a system that makes parties the main avenue of political representation could undercut the rich variety of interest groups that now exist. Without these other means of representing groups and views, the two major parties might be seriously overloaded. Minor parties would pop up, further fragmenting American politics. In short, critics fear that legislatures would be dominated by rigid, dogmatic political parties unable to resolve problems—even more than is the case today.

It Wouldn't Work in American Politics

The second major argument against responsible parties is that the idea conflicts with the American government's design. The responsible parties model eases the path to majority rule. But the American founders set up a system that limits majority rule in important ways. They divided constitutional authority among the various levels and branches of government, using the principles of separation of powers and federalism, to prevent tyranny. The separation of powers allows voters to give control of the executive branch to one party and the legislative branch to the other. Federalism permits different parties to dominate in different states. Equal representation of states in the U.S. Senate advantages residents of the smaller states. Any change in these and other anti-majoritarian features of the American government would require fundamental revision of the Constitution. Frances Lee also points out that the Senate's use of filibusters and other aspects of the American constitutional system require supermajorities rather than just majorities to pass policies,[10] so even a majority may not be enough to win.

American voters have made enthusiastic use of the separation of powers in recent years. Since 1950, in contrast with earlier times, we have had a **divided government** most of the time, so that a president has faced at least one house of Congress controlled by the other party (see Table 15.1). State governments have often been split by party as well, though in very recent times, single-party control over a state's executive and legislative branches has become more frequent.

Divided government makes responsible party government impossible. When both Democratic-controlled and Republican-controlled parts of the government have their fingerprints on every major piece of legislation, voters find it hard to figure out which party is responsible for bad policies. Without that ability, voters can't throw out the guilty party and replace it with the opposition.

To party government advocates, divided government helps to explain why the federal government has failed to respond effectively to a number of major concerns from federal spending to climate change. The critics disagree. They argue that unified party government doesn't necessarily produce more significant legislation; that the federal government has a lot of practice in coping with shared party power,[11] and even that American voters prefer it that way.[12]

TABLE 15.1 Party Control of the Federal Government, 1951–2020

Party Control	Number of Years
Unified	26
Democrats control the presidency and both houses of Congress 1951–1952 (Truman), 1961–1968 (Kennedy, Johnson), 1977–1980 (Carter),1993–1994 (Clinton), 2009–2010 (Obama)	18
Republicans control the presidency and both houses of Congress 1953–1954 (Eisenhower), 2003–2006 (G. W. Bush), 2017–2018 (Trump)	8
Divided	46
Democratic president, Republican House and Senate 1995–2000 (Clinton), 2015–2016 (Obama)	8
Republican president, Democratic House and Senate 1955–1960 (Eisenhower), 1969–1976 (Nixon, Ford), 1987–1992 (Reagan, G. H. W. Bush), 2007–2008 (G. W. Bush)	22
President's party controls one house of Congress 1981–1986 (Reagan), 2001–2002 (G. W. Bush),* 2011–2016 (Obama), 2019–2020 (Trump)	16

Note: The names of the presidents during these years are in parentheses.

*The Senate was Republican controlled for the first five months of 2001 until Senator James Jeffords left the Republican Party and the Democrats gained majority control.

Source: Updated from Harold W. Stanley and Richard G. Niemi, *Vital Statistics on American Politics 1999–2000* (Washington, DC: CQ Press, 2000), pp. 34–38.

The Gingrich Experiment: A Temporarily Responsible Party

Americans got at least a whiff of party responsibility starting in the mid-1990s. Spearheaded by House Republican minority leader Newt Gingrich, the great majority of Republicans running for House seats in 1994 signed a statement called a "Contract with America." It pledged that if the voters would give Republicans a House majority, they would guarantee a vote on each of ten pieces of legislation, all embodying conservative principles, within the first one hundred days of the next Congress. The statement concluded, in words that would gladden the hearts of party government advocates: "If we break this contract, throw us out. We mean it."

The Republicans did win a majority of House seats in 1994. They delivered on their promise; once in office, the new Republican leadership used its iron control of the House agenda to vote on each of the bills before the self-imposed deadline. House Republicans were more unified on these bills than they had been in decades. That, however, is when party government stalled. The Senate Republican majority had not committed itself to the Contract with America and did not feel bound to consider these bills promptly or to pass them. The House Republicans' efforts were further stymied by the divided government; a Democratic president had the power to veto any legislation that made it through both houses.

What can we learn from this experiment? First, the separation of powers is a mighty roadblock in the path of responsible parties. Even the commitment of a legislative party to a set of clear and consistent principles is not enough to produce a responsible party government, as long as the president and/or the other house of Congress are not willing to go along. Most voters may not have appreciated the experiment, either; although Republicans kept their House majority in the next election year, so did the Senate Republicans who had not signed the Contract with America, and the Democratic president was reelected as well.

Even when the same party controls the White House and both houses of Congress, there are obstacles to achieving party government. Because the parties' candidates are chosen by voters in primary elections, parties cannot force their candidates to be loyal to the party's program. Candidates who break with their party on important issues can still run, and win, as long as their constituents keep voting for them. Critics of the responsible parties model also claim that most American voters are not issue oriented enough to see politics only through ideological lenses, that the major parties are not centralized enough to enforce a single set of issue positions on all their officeholders, and that Americans distrust parties too much to let them try. In short, the idea of responsible parties seems to its critics to ask too much of the voters, the parties, and the institutions of American government.

Party Cohesion and Ideology

Although genuine party government is unlikely in the U.S., the parties are occasionally nudged toward greater accountability. Some observers suggest that this is happening now, in the only way that would be consistent with the American system of separated powers: Each party's voters, its party in government, and its party organization have become more willing to agree voluntarily on a clear party program. But there are limits to the parties' cohesiveness on issues.

Are the American Parties Ideological?

An **ideological party** is one with clear and consistent principles on a wide range of issues, from the purpose of government to the essence of human nature. Examples include the old-style Communist parties and the Muslim fundamentalist parties that have arisen in Middle Eastern nations. The principles of an ideological party offer answers to questions such as these: What values should a government try to achieve? Who deserves to have power, and under what conditions do they forfeit that right?

Throughout their long histories, however, the American parties have tended to be more pragmatic than ideological, focusing on concrete problems rather than on the purity of their principles. Ever since their founding, each party has been a blend of its own original tradition (the egalitarian tradition of the Democrats and the Republican tradition of order and industrial capitalism) with those of other groups that associated with it because of personal ties, geographic nearness, or simple expectations of political gain.[13]

There are several reasons why the major American parties aren't ideologically "pure." Most important, there are only two of them to divide up a tremendous array of interests in American politics. In a system with several parties, a party can cater to one ideological niche in the voting public and still hope to survive. In a big and diverse two-party system, with so many different interests and people to represent, such specialized appeals can be made only by minor parties—or by a major party willing to risk self-destruction.

Do They At Least Offer Clear Choices?

Yet even though the two major parties are not as ideological as those in many other democracies, they now differ greatly in their stands on specific issues. This can increase voters' ability to hold them responsible. We can see these differences in the platforms they adopt every four years at their national conventions (see box "Party Differences on Major Issues" on page 343) and in the policies they pursue when they win. It would have been hard, for example, to mistake the stands taken by Donald Trump and other Republican candidates in 2020 on health care, gun rights, and women's rights for those expressed by Joe Biden and other Democrats. "Republicans mostly believe that the role of government is to foster greater individual economic achievement, even if it leads to more economic inequality," one perceptive analyst writes. "The Democratic philosophy is that the government should provide a safety net, even if it leads to economic inefficiency."[14] These differences, especially the Democratic commitment to fund federal social programs and the Republican desire to limit them, have animated the parties since the 1930s. They have been expanded more recently by Republicans' commitment to traditional cultural values and Democrats' openness to a diversity of values.

Each major party has become more unified in its stands during the past few decades as well as more different from the other party—in short, more polarized. A major contributor was the issue of civil rights. When racial justice became an important focus of national policy in the 1960s, national Democrats took a clear position in favor of civil rights laws and national Republicans took the opposite stance. In response, white, segregationist southerners shook off their traditional Democratic loyalty in increasing numbers and took with them into the Republican Party their more conservative views on many other issues. (This story is told more fully in Chapter 7.) This lowered the biggest barrier to unity within the Democratic Party on several issues.[15]

The Ronald Reagan presidency during the 1980s further polarized the parties. Reagan, who strongly identified with the religious, neoconservative wing of the Republican Party, demonstrated the appeal of a simple vision based on one major idea: less government. His assault on the role of government as it had

Party Differences on Major Issues: The 2020 Party Platforms

Limit Abortion?

Republicans: We assert the sanctity of human life and affirm that the unborn child has a fundamental right to life which cannot be infringed. (p. 13)

Democrats: ...every woman should be able to access high-quality reproductive health care services, including safe and legal abortion. (32)

Allow Family Planning?

Republicans: We renew our call for replacing "family planning" programs for teens with sexual risk avoidance education that sets abstinence until marriage as the responsible and respected standard of behavior. (34)

Democrats: We recognize that quality, affordable comprehensive health care; medically accurate, LGBTQ+ inclusive, age-appropriate sex education; and the full range of family planning services are all essential to ensuring that people can decide if, when, and how to start a family. (32)

Repeal "Obamacare"?

Republicans: Any honest agenda for improving health care must start with repeal of the dishonestly named Affordable Care Act of 2010: Obamacare. (36)

Democrats: ...we will give all Americans the choice to select a high-quality, affordable public option through the Affordable Care Act marketplace. (28)

Role of Religion in Public Life

Republicans: We support the public display of the Ten Commandments as a reflection of our history and our country's Judeo-Christian heritage and further affirm the rights of religious students to engage in voluntary prayer at public school events. (12)

Democrats: Democrats celebrate America's history of religious pluralism and tolerance, and recognize the countless acts of service of our faith communities, as well as the paramount importance of maintaining the separation between church and state enshrined in our Constitution. (48)

Protect Gun Rights?

Republicans: We uphold the right of individuals to keep and bear arms. We oppose ill-conceived laws that would restrict magazine capacity or ban the sale of the most popular and common modern rifle. (12)

Democrats: Democrats will enact universal background checks, end online sales of guns and ammunition .... Democrats will ban the manufacture and sale of assault weapons and high capacity magazines. (47–48)

Protect Voting Rights?

Republicans: ...we support legislation to require proof of citizenship when registering to vote and secure photo ID when voting. (16)

Democrats: We stand united against the determined Republican campaign to disenfranchise voters through onerous voter ID laws, unconstitutional and excessive purges of the voter rolls, and closures of polling places in low-income neighborhoods, on college campuses, and in communities of color. (55)

Immigration?

Republicans: ...we support building a wall along our southern border... (26)

Democrats: Democrats believe it is long past time to provide a roadmap to citizenship for the millions of undocumented workers, caregivers, students, and children .... (62)

Finance Student Loans?

Republicans: The federal government should not be in the business of originating student loans. (35)

Democrats: For those earning less than $125,000, we support forgiving all undergraduate tuition-related federal student debt from two- and four-year public colleges and universities. (70)

Public or Private Education?

Republicans: We support options for learning, including home-schooling, career and technical education, private or parochial schools, magnet schools, charter schools, online learning, and early-college high schools. (34)

Democrats: Democrats oppose private school vouchers and other policies that divert taxpayer-funded resources away from the public school system... (67)

Fossil Fuels or Clean Energy?

Republicans: ...coal is an abundant, clean, affordable, reliable domestic energy resource. [Miners] should be protected from the Democratic Party's radical anti-coal agenda. (19)

Democrats: Democrats commit to eliminating carbon pollution from power plants by 2035 through technology-neutral standards for clean energy and energy efficiency. We will dramatically expand solar and wind energy deployment ... (51)

Limit Labor Unions?

Republicans: We support the right of states to enact Right to Work [antiunion] laws (8)

Democrats: We will repeal so-called "right to work" laws ... (14)

Reduce Corporate Taxes?

Republicans: [We support] lowering the corporate tax rate to be on a par with, or below, the rates of other industrial nations (1)

Democrats: Corporate tax rates, which were cut sharply by the 2017 Republican tax cut, must be raised, and "trickle-down" tax cuts must be rejected. (22)

Deal with Discrimination?

Republicans: Merit and hard work should determine advancement in our society, so we reject unfair preferences, quotas, and set-asides as forms of discrimination. (9)

Democrats: [Democrats] recognize that race-neutral policies are not sufficient to rectify race-based disparities. (40)

Keep the Death Penalty?

Republicans: The constitutionality of the death penalty is firmly settled by its explicit mention in the Fifth Amendment. (40)

Democrats: ...Democrats continue to support abolishing the death penalty. (38)

Excerpted from the parties' platforms at https://www.demconvention.com/wp-content/uploads/2020/08/2020-07-31-Democratic-Party-Platform-For-Distribution.pdf and https://prod-cdn-static.gop.com/media/documents/DRAFT_12_FINAL[1]-ben_1468872234.pdf (both accessed August 25, 2020). Note that the Republicans in 2020 chose not to adopt a new platform and to run instead on the party's 2016 platform.

developed since the New Deal gave a more ideological tone to American politics than had been seen in decades. Since then, more issue-oriented leaders have been selected in both parties,[16] and political issues—purposive incentives—have become more prominent in bringing people into party activism. As Chapter 13 showed, both congressional parties vote more cohesively on issues now than they have in decades. State parties are polarizing in a similar way,[17] especially since 2010, when several newly elected Republican governors and state legislatures have promoted major cuts in social programs and limits to collective bargaining for state employees.

The party polarization has not always led to a clearer liberal vs. conservative division between the parties. Rather, Donald Trump's increasingly strong influence in in the Republican Party has led to a Trumpification of the party's issue stands. Trump's devotion to tariffs in foreign trade shifted his party away from a decades-long commitment to free trade. His anti-immigration policies have made his party more nativist, or anti-immigrant, than are the conservative parties in Britain or Australia.[18]

In fact, the RNC in 2020 broke with the party's long history of approving a new platform at its national presidential convention. The party announced that it would continue to campaign on its 2016 platform and that its agenda would henceforth be set by President Trump. As columnist Dan Balz wrote, "...this convention is Trump's show. He is the inspiration, the reality TV impresario, and, of course, the star of the week. The rest of his party is along for the ride."[19] Party platforms normally express the policy stands of the current presidential candidate. But this extraordinary delegation of the party's agenda to the president's judgment clearly indicated that at least at the national level, the Republicans had truly become the Party of Trump.

But Internal Divisions Remain

These clear differences on major issues, however, do not add up to the all-encompassing political philosophies that are found in genuinely ideological parties. Consider, for instance, the interesting relationship between each party's stand on economic policy and its position on issues such as abortion and pornography. As Chapter 1 mentioned, Democrats have long stood for an activist federal government in promoting individuals' social welfare but very limited government power over individuals' decisions on abortion. Republicans generally want to loosen the federal government's grip on the economy and environmental regulation but argue for government activism in banning abortion. Nimble advocates could probably construct a rationale as to why these sets of positions are actually consistent. But in reality, these stands coexist within each party's platform because the major parties, as they always have, adjust their policy positions to attract groups of potential supporters—in this case, when Republicans found common cause with conservative Christians and Democrats reached out to pro-choice women—even at the cost of internal consistency.

In addition, because the major American parties are pragmatic and vote seeking above all, neither party has stayed completely true to the principles it articulates.[20] For instance, the Republican platform has long pledged to bring smaller government. Yet after winning control of the presidency in 2016, Republican Donald Trump presided over larger federal budgets, and much larger budget deficits, than had his Democratic predecessor. The Republicans' aim was to gain support from voters who value tangible economic benefits more than abstract principles. And although Democrats have long been aligned with the resource-poor, Democratic members of Congress have not been shy about backing tax breaks for businesses and wealthy interests in their districts. In addition, both parties continue to deal with internal dissent.[21]

What about party voters? Is it true, as some ideologues charge, that most Americans are committed to ideological principles and want the Democrats and Republicans to provide more clearly defined choices? Or are party voters bored with, or even put off by, the programmatic concerns of many party activists?

Ideology and the American Voter

Media reports of election results frequently use the terms "liberal" and "conservative" to describe voters' choices. The question is more complicated for political scientists, who have long debated the structure of citizens' political attitudes.

How Ideological Is the American Public?

An ideological voter, like an ideological party, would not just hold clear attitudes toward some individual issues but would also connect those attitudes into a coherent structure. However, careful study of American political attitudes raises serious doubt whether most voters can be described as "ideological" or even as very consistent in their political beliefs.

Many individuals with conservative attitudes on, say, government spending may express moderate or liberal attitudes on other issues, such as gay rights or the environment.[22] People do not necessarily hold a set of fixed stands, such as an unqualified "yes" on abortion rights and a firm "no" on taxes. Rather, they might feel that taxes are a great burden *and* that they can be necessary at times. They can be pulled toward one of these views under some conditions and toward another view under other conditions. In fact, a number of survey respondents who call themselves "conservative" use the term to refer to lifestyle preferences rather than to political issues. Some of these might be considered "identity conservatives," in that their conservatism has more to do with their opposition to "political correctness," Democrats, and former President Obama than to acceptance of the conservative philosophy, and who may even express liberal views on some policies.[23] In short, most people have ambivalent attitudes toward at least some issues[24]—a sharp contrast with a more ideological thinker.

This ambivalence allows many of us to hold sets of beliefs that might drive an ideologue to drink. For instance, large numbers of survey respondents say that they want a smaller government with lower taxes *and* a government that provides more services in areas such as health care and education. That is understandable; most people would like to pay less while getting more. But it is not a firm foundation for consistent thinking.[25]

A lot of people termed "moderates" by pollsters are simply people whose views, which may sometimes be extreme, don't fit the liberal-conservative mold. Some Americans, for instance, combine a desire for more government social services with a belief that government should also uphold traditional moral values; these can be called "populists." And as you saw in Chapter 2, libertarians want less government involvement in both of these spheres.[26]

Even in elections when voters are offered clear choices, many voters tend to focus on more pragmatic considerations instead. Reagan campaigned for president in 1980 as a principled conservative, yet many voters supported him in spite of his conservative policies, rather than because of them. In fact, in both 1980 and 1984 most voters preferred the policy stands that Reagan's opponent stood for, though Reagan won both elections handily.[27] Voters' judgments turned more on their *retrospective evaluations* of presidential performance—their general feelings as to whether the most recent presidency had turned out well—than on Reagan's stances on specific issues. Because many voters tend to be results oriented, parties and candidates try to stitch together winning coalitions by appealing to a range of qualities—candidates' personal characteristics, group interests, and feelings about the party in power—rather than by stressing ideological differences.

It is important to note, however, that ideology has played a bigger role in recent elections. Analysts disagree on the nature of the change. Some argue that Americans have become more extreme in their views, with fewer moderates and more conservatives and liberals.[28] Others claim that voters remain as pragmatic and non-ideological as ever, but that political debate *appears* to be more ideological now because of **partisan sorting**, in which most liberal Republicans have switched to the Democratic Party and most conservative Democrats have become Republicans.[29]

Partisan Sorting or Ideological Polarization?

There is no doubt that partisan sorting has taken place. We saw in Chapter 7 the remarkable degree to which conservative whites in the South and liberals in the Northeast and West have moved to the "correct" party since the 1960s.

That partisan sorting has affected the ideological character of the parties. Democrats are now more inclined to call themselves liberals and Republicans to consider themselves conservatives. In the process, the Republican Party has become more homogeneous than the Democrats are. In 2020 Democratic poll respondents were fairly evenly divided between liberals (47 percent), on the one hand, and moderates (38 percent) or conservatives (14 percent) on the other.[30] Republicans, on the other hand, almost universally call themselves conservatives. That ideological distribution seems likely to continue; most Republicans say they want their party to become more conservative, whereas a slim majority of Democrats would like to see their party move in a more moderate direction.[31]

Individuals are also becoming more consistent in their views—less likely to hold a mixture of liberal attitudes toward one issue and conservative stances on another. Again, Republican identifiers have long shown more ideological consistency than Democrats, but as Figure 15.1 shows, consistency among Democrats has taken a recent jump.[32] And age matters: millennials in recent years have become both more liberal and more consistent in their liberal attitudes than baby boomers have.[33]

One means by which individuals' attitudes have become more polarized by party and more consistent is *conflict extension*.[34] Party identification is a strong enough force that when an issue becomes prominent, at least under some conditions, partisans tend to bring their previous views into line with their party's view. Their partisanship is extended to guide their stands on other issues so that they become or remain consistent with their party.

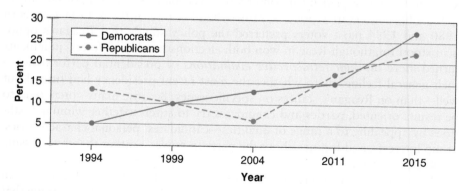

FIGURE 15.1 Partisans' Views Have Become More Consistently Liberal or Conservative, 1994–2015

Note: Data points show the percentage of Democrats with consistently liberal views on issues and the percentage of Republicans with consistently conservative views.

Source: Adapted from Pew data reported in "A Wider Ideological Gap Between More and Less Educated Adults," April 26, 2016, https://www.people-press.org/2016/04/26/a-wider-ideological-gap-between-more-and-less-educated-adults/ (accessed August 25, 2020).

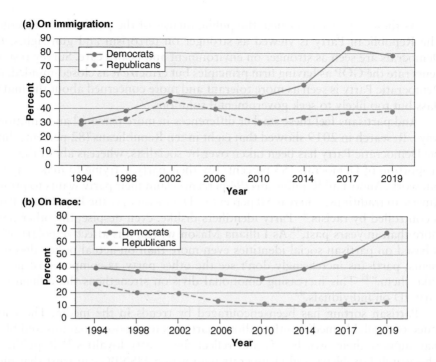

FIGURE 15.2 Republicans and Democrats Hold Increasingly Different Views on Race and Immigration, 1994–2019

Note: In part (a), the data points are the percentage of each party's identifiers who agree that "immigrants strengthen the country because of their hard work and talents." Part (b) shows the percentage of each party's identifiers who say, "Racial discrimination is the main reason why many black people can't get ahead these days."

Source: Adapted from Pew Research Center, "In a Politically Polarized Era, Sharp Divides in Both Partisan Coalitions," December 17, 2019, https://www.people-press.org/2019/12/17/in-a-politically-polarized-era-sharp-divides-in-both-partisan-coalitions/ (accessed August 25, 2020).

So when immigration or climate change hits the headlines, partisans' opinions become more similar to those of their party. Thus you can see in Figure 15.2 that partisans' attitudes toward immigration and race have moved further apart in the past 25 years consistent with the two parties' stands. In fact, the gap between Democrats' and Republicans' positions on these and other issues is much larger than that between blacks and whites, men and women, young and old, and other major determinants of political attitudes.[35]

The two parties' identifiers differ especially in their attitudes toward guns, environmental policy, and race.[36] In recent polls, for instance 73 percent of white Democrats and 95 percent of black Democrats agreed that "white people benefit from advantages in society that black people do not have," whereas only 23 percent of white Republicans concurred.[37] Partisans also differ in the importance they attach to various issues. In a 2020 survey, Democrats were much more likely than Republicans to say that climate change, economic inequality, and racism were major problems, whereas Republicans were much more concerned with illegal immigration.[38]

As these gaps have opened, the public images of the parties have diverged. The Republican Party is viewed as stronger on terrorism and gun rights; the Democrats are seen as stronger on environment and health care. Survey respondents rate the GOP as having firm principles but criticize it as closed-minded; the Democratic Party is seen as more tolerant and more concerned about the middle class but too likely to seek governmental solutions.[39]

And partisans feel these starker differences in more personal and emotional ways. Research in 2019 showed that eight in ten Republicans (82 percent) think the Democratic Party has been taken over by socialists, whereas about the same proportion of Democrats (83 percent) say their party is trying to make capitalism work. Almost all Republicans (94 percent) claim their party wants to protect American traditions, whereas 80 percent of Democrats say the Republican Party is controlled by racists.[40] Party identifiers dislike, even despise, the other party more than in years past.[41] As Lilliana Mason writes, this affective polarization is based on partisan social identities even more than on actual policy disagreements; partisans increasingly don't see the other party as composed of people "like them."[42] This increasing emotional division strengthens the influence of party ID on individuals.[43]

Partisan sorting has been encouraged by trends in the media. The wider range of available media outlets allows partisans to choose programs and blogs that support their own beliefs and reflect their party loyalties.[44] Republicans who watch Fox News and Democrats who watch MSNBC can trust that most of what they see will agree with their partisan views. Even if they are exposed to more diverse sources—as can happen on social media, for instance—people are more likely to remember facts consistent with their partisanship and to resist information that challenges their preconceptions.[45]

The change is not limited to partisan sorting. Some ideological polarization—greater extremism in people's views—seems to have occurred at about the same time. The proportion of all respondents, regardless of party, who tell posters that they are very conservative or extremely conservative, and very liberal or extremely liberal, rose markedly from the early 1970s to the present, and especially since 1994.[46] These voters tend to be more interested and engaged in politics, so we can guess that these terms have some meaning for them. The proportion of Americans who are policy-ambivalent—who take roughly equal numbers of liberal and conservative stands on issues—has dropped, while the share of the public that is ideologically consistent, though not large, has grown a lot in the past decade, especially among more educated people.[47] These changes improve many voters' ability to meet the demands of the responsible parties model.

In sum, Americans have become more polarized in *both* ideological and partisan terms. Evidence suggests that party sorting is the stronger of the two trends; although ideology and partisanship are strongly correlated, party seems to have more power in motivating people's opinions than do ideological principles.[48] It is true that many political activists tend to exaggerate the nature of this polarization.[49] Republicans and Democrats don't differ in their factual beliefs as much as they do in their expressive "team loyalty" toward their party.[50] The trend toward greater polarization may not last forever; people who came of age during the Obama presidency show some signs of greater moderation and liberalism, even among Republican identifiers, in part because younger people in the 2020s are more diverse in race and ethnicity than earlier generations of Americans. And a lot of people have managed to sit out these conflicts altogether. Paul Allen Beck refers to "two electorates—one partisan and about evenly divided, the other estranged from party politics."[51]

Differences among Voters, Activists, and Candidates

Much of the party sorting among voters has come in response to the increasing polarization of party leaders, activists, and party platforms.[52] The gap between Democrats and Republicans in their attitudes toward candidates and issues is much deeper among party leaders and political activists than among people who are less politically engaged.[53] For instance, there's a huge divide between politically engaged Democrats and Republicans on whether government should ensure access to health care; among people who are not politically engaged, the gap is much smaller. And politically engaged Republicans are much more likely to express anger at the federal government than are Republicans who are not politically engaged.[54]

This can pose a challenge for candidates and officeholders. It is not unusual for candidates to find themselves caught in between: closer to the left or right than the party's voters, but not as extreme as its activists. How do candidates respond? If they try to muffle their conservative or liberal views, they risk alienating their party's activists.[55] They know that more strongly ideological members of Congress, for instance, have more followers on social media than moderates do.[56] But if they appeal to those activists, more moderate voters may be turned off.[57] It is no wonder that many candidates prefer to remain vague when asked about issues, at least when they speak to general audiences.

These differences can aggravate the tensions among the party organization, the party in government, and the party's voters. Ideologues in both parties complain that at least some parts of the party in government are too moderate. Liberal Democrats objected to what they saw as President Obama's "sellout" on climate change and budget cuts, and right-wing conservatives felt betrayed by some Republican congressional leaders' failure to cut federal spending to the bone, as they had allegedly promised. Bipartisan behavior in a politician seems to disgust strong partisans (who are most likely to vote), whereas weak identifiers and independents claim that they reward bipartisanship in their elected officials.[58]

The dilemma of ideology, then, is not whether the American parties can become genuinely ideological parties. That is not likely. The problem is whether the increasing ideological commitment of their activists and of many of their elected officials can be sustained without alienating their more pragmatic supporters.

The parties already face a deep well of public suspicion. Much of the public dislikes the parties' attachment to organized interests, their affinity for negative campaigns, and their failure to keep their promises.[59] Voters have often felt more moderate than the choices they've been given; they see Republican candidates as more conservative, and Democratic candidates as more liberal, than the voter him- or herself.[60] But this may be changing as party polarization continues; moderate candidates no longer have an electoral advantage over extremist candidates,[61] and local party leaders, especially among Republicans, increasingly see extremists as more likely to win elections than moderates are.[62] If so, as one writer put it, moderates may become more convinced that "politics no longer speaks to them, that it has become a dialogue of the deaf, a rant of uncompromising extremes."[63]

When Is Party Government Most Likely?

Responsible parties are hard to achieve. Even the British Parliament, so often cited as a model of party government, has not always had the cohesion and the binding party discipline that a "pure" responsible party government would require.[64] Under what conditions have the American parties come closest to the ideal of responsible parties?

When There Is Strong Presidential Leadership

At times, a strong president—Ronald Reagan and George W. Bush in their first terms are good examples—has been able to push Congress to enact important parts of the platform on which he ran for office. That is especially likely, of course, when the president's party controls both houses of Congress by more than a narrow margin. Party-oriented presidents can also draw voters' attention to party differences. But the result will probably be "presidential government" rather than party government; voters are likely to respond to the president's performance rather than that of the party as a whole.

In Times of Crisis

At critical times in American history, the parties have divided in ways that were, if not truly ideological, at least very policy oriented. In the 1936 presidential election, for example, the Democrats and the Republicans offered dramatically different solutions to a nation devastated by the Great Depression. The hardships of that economic collapse probably focused voter attention to an unusual degree on the possible remedies that government could provide. Combined with a campaign centered on the pros and cons of the Roosevelt program for economic change, this may well have produced something close to a mandate in the election for both the president and Congress.[65] When strong presidential leadership is combined with crisis conditions, then a degree of responsible party government might be achieved for a time.

When the Parties' Supporting Coalitions Are Reshaped

When the parties' supporting coalitions of social groups have undergone major change—sometimes called "realignments" (see Chapter 7)—American politics seems to have most closely approached the requirements for party government. At these times, the parties have divided more clearly on a single, riveting set of issues, and party leaders, activists, and voters have reached high levels of agreement with one another and major differences with the other party.

These changes in the party system typically produce a unified federal government, with one party controlling both houses of Congress, the presidency, and a judiciary that, through the president's appointment power, comes to reflect the new majority. On only five occasions in American history has one party enjoyed control of Congress and the presidency continuously for more than a decade; each time, this control was first established during a realignment. Party cohesion in Congress has been especially high at the beginning of a new party system. So it is not surprising that major bursts of comprehensive policy change followed the realignments of the parties' coalitions after the Civil War and again during the Depression.

Even at these times, it is hard to see the American parties as fully responsible. At the time of the Roosevelt New Deal as well as currently, both parties remain collections of varied interests even when they are able to unite on a few central goals.

When You "Get What You Wished For"

The major American parties behave more like responsible parties now than they have in a long time—perhaps ever—in the sense that each party in Congress hangs together more fully. There is a marked difference between the Republican Party organizations and activists and those of the Democrats on basic principles of public policy, both at the federal level and in increasing numbers of states. Many reformers think this is cause for celebration. When parties stand for clear principles and voters are offered clear choices in elections, they say, citizens are better able to hold government responsible for the policies it produces. That may make for a stronger and more vibrant democracy. On the other hand, widespread public distrust of government[66] and growing public hostility toward the people and policies of the other party suggest that more responsible parties can bring us problems as well as benefits.

It is not likely that the American parties and voters will ever meet all the demands of the responsible parties model. If the parties are to become more accountable, more like responsible parties in a system of party government, these differences on issues and greater organizational strength are not enough. There must be some set of basic principles that can connect different issues into a single logical structure for each party, some means by which voters and leaders are able to distill the large number of policy issues into one major dimension or a few, so that voters can easily understand and predict the party's stands.

Too many powerful forces stand in the way of achieving that much structure and coherence in the party system. Because of the separation of powers and the federal system of government, voters will always be able to divide power between the parties. No matter how much money they raise, American party organizations still won't be able to choose their own candidates; voters will make that choice in primary elections. As a result, candidates will always have some degree of independence from their party organizations. Without basic changes in the American political structure, including moving to a parliamentary system, the parties will remain semi-responsible. The consequence is that the American government will remain semi-accountable to the public.

Notes

1 Donald Granberg, "Abortion Attitudes, 1965–1980," *Family Planning Perspectives* 12 (#5 1980): 250–261.

2 "Public Opinion on Abortion," Pew Research Center, August 29, 2019, https://www.pewforum.org/fact-sheet/public-opinion-on-abortion/ (accessed August 25, 2020).

3 Committee on Political Parties of the American Political Science Association, *Toward a More Responsible Two-Party System* (New York: Rinehart, 1950).

4 Pew Research Center, "In a Politically Polarized Era, Sharp Divides in Both Partisan Coalitions," December 17, 2019, https://www.people-press.org/2019/12/17/-in-a-politically-polarized-era-sharp-divides-in-both-partisan-coalitions/ (accessed August 25, 2020).

5 CNN/ORC poll reported in Ariel Edwards-Levy, "Republican Party Too Extreme, Majority Of Americans Say: Poll," *Huffington Post*, December 6, 2017, https://www.huffpost.com/entry/republican-poll_n_2337757 (accessed August 25, 2020).

6 See Austin Ranney, *The Doctrine of Responsible Party Government* (Urbana, IL: University of Illinois Press, 1964), Chapters 1 and 2.

7 E. E. Schattschneider, *Party Government* (New York: Rinehart, 1942), p. 208.

8 E. E. Schattschneider, *The Semi-Sovereign People* (New York: Holt, Rinehart, and Winston, 1960).

9 See John Kenneth White and Jerome M. Mileur, eds., *Challenges to Party Government* (Carbondale, IL: Southern Illinois University Press, 1992).

10 Frances E. Lee, "Parties as Coordinators: Can Parties Unite What the Constitution Divides?" in Marjorie Randon Hershey, ed., *Guide to U.S. Political Parties* (Los Angeles, CA: Sage, 2014), Chapter 3.

11 John J. Coleman, "Unified Government, Divided Government, and Party Responsiveness," *American Political Science Review* 93 (1999): 821–835, and David R. Mayhew, *Divided We Govern*, 2nd ed. (New Haven, CT: Yale University Press, 2005).

12 Richard Born, "Split-Ticket Voters, Divided Government, and Fiorina's Policy Balancing Model," *Legislative Studies Quarterly* 19 (1994): 95–115.

13 A. James Reichley, *The Life of the Parties* (Lanham, MD: Rowman & Littlefield, 2000), Chapter 6.

14 David E. Rosenbaum, "Bush to Return to 'Ownership Society' Theme in Push for Social Security Changes," *New York Times*, January 16, 2005, p. 20.

15 Edward G. Carmines and James A. Stimson, *Issue Evolution* (Princeton, NJ: Princeton University Press, 1989).

16 Jason M. Roberts and Steven S. Smith, "Procedural Contexts, Party Strategy, and Conditional Party Voting in the U.S. House of Representatives, 1971–2000," *American Journal of Political Science* 47 (2003): 305–317.

17 Charles Barrilleaux, Thomas Holbrook, and Laura Langer, "Electoral Competition, Legislative Balance, and American State Welfare Policy," *American Journal of Political Science* 46 (2002): 415–427.

18 See Glenn Kefford and Shaun Ratcliff, "Republicans and Democrats Are More Polarized On Immigration Than Parties in the U.S. or Australia," *Washington Post*, August 16, 2018, https://www.washingtonpost.com/news/monkey-cage/wp/2018/08/16/republicans-and-democrats-are-more-polarized-on-immigration-than-parties-in-the-u-k-or-australia-heres-why/ (accessed August 25, 2020).

19 Dan Balz, "Trump and Republicans Attack Biden, Stick to Grievances," *Washington Post*, August 25, 2020, p. A1.

20 See David Karol, *Party Position Change in American Politics* (New York: Cambridge University Press, 2009).

21 Robin Kolodny, "Moderate Party Factions in the U.S. House of Representatives," in John C. Green and Daniel M. Shea, eds., *The State of the Parties*, 3rd ed. (Lanham, MD: Rowman & Littlefield, 1999), pp. 271–285.

22 The seminal study is Philip E. Converse, "The Nature of Belief Systems in Mass Publics," in David Apter, ed., *Ideology and Discontent* (New York: Free Press, 1964), pp. 206–261.

23 Christopher Ellis and James A. Stimson, *Ideology in America* (New York: Cambridge University Press, 2012).

24 John Zaller and Stanley Feldman, "A Simple Theory of the Survey Response," *American Journal of Political Science* 36 (1992): 579–616.

25 See Pew Research Center, "Beyond Distrust: How Americans View Their Government," November 23, 2015, www.people-press.org/2015/11/23/beyond-distrust-how-americans-view-their-government/ (accessed August 25, 2020).

26 See Edward G. Carmines, Michael J. Ensley, and Michael W. Wagner, "Why American Political Parties Can't Get Beyond the Left-Right Divide," in John C. Green, Daniel J. Coffey, and David B. Cohen, eds., *The State of the Parties*, 7th ed. (Lanham, MD: Rowman & Littlefield, 2014), pp. 55–71.

27 Paul R. Abramson, John H. Aldrich, and David W. Rohde, *Change and Continuity in the 1984 Elections* (Washington, DC: CQ Press, 1986), Chapter 6.

28 Alan I. Abramowitz, *The Disappearing Center* (New Haven, CT: Yale University Press, 2009).

29 See Matthew Levendusky, *The Partisan Sort* (Chicago, IL: University of Chicago Press, 2009), and Seth J. Hill and Chris Tausanovitch, "A Disconnect in Representation?" *Journal of Politics* 77 (2015): 1058–1075.

30 Hannah Gilberstadt and Andrew Daniller, "Liberals Make Up the Largest Share of Democratic Voters, But Their Growth Has Slowed in Recent Years," *Pew Research Center*, January 17, 2020, https://www.pewresearch.org/fact-tank/2020/01/17/liberals-make-up-largest-share-of-democratic-voters/ (accessed August 25, 2020).

31 Pew Research Center, "Public's 2019 Priorities," January 24, 2019, https://www.people-press.org/wp-content/uploads/sites/4/2019/01/PP_2019.01.24_political-priorities_FINAL.pdf (accessed August 25, 2020).

32 Yphtach Lelkes and Paul Sniderman, "The Ideological Asymmetry of the American Party System," *British Journal of Political Science* 46 (2016): 825–844.

33 Pew Research Center, "A Wider Ideological Gap between More and Less Educated Adults," April 26, 2016, https://www.people-press.org/2016/04/26/a-wider-ideological-gap-between-more-and-less-educated-adults/ (accessed August 25, 2020).

34 Geoffrey C. Layman and Thomas M. Carsey, "Party Polarization and 'Conflict Extension' in the American Electorate," *American Journal of Political Science* 46

(2002): 786–802. See also Corwin D. Smidt, "Polarization and the Decline of the American Floating Voter," *American Journal of Political Science* 61 (2017): 365–381.

35 "The Partisan Divide on Political v Values Grows Even Wider," October 5, 2017, http://assets.pewresearch.org/wp-content/uploads/sites/5/2017/10/05162647/10-05-2017-Political-landscape-release.pdf (accessed August 25, 2020).

36 Pew Research Center, "Election 2020," August 13, 2020, https://www.pewresearch.org/politics/2020/08/13/important-issues-in-the-2020-election/ (accessed August 26, 2020).

37 J. Baxter Oliphant, "Views about Whether Whites Benefit from Societal Advantages Split Sharply along Racial and Partisan Lines," *Pew Research Center*, September 28, 2017, https://www.pewresearch.org/fact-tank/2017/09/28/views-about-whether-whites-benefit-from-societal-advantages-split-sharply-along-racial-and-partisan-lines/ (accessed August 25, 2020).

38 Amina Dunn, "As the U.S. Copes with Multiple Crises, Partisans Disagree Sharply on Severity of Problems Facing the Nation," July 14, 2020, https://www.pewresearch.org/fact-tank/2020/07/14/as-the-u-s-copes-with-multiple-crises-partisans-disagree-sharply-on-severity-of-problems-facing-the-nation/ (accessed August 26, 2020).

39 Pew Research Center, "Partisan Antipathy," October 10, 2019, https://www.people-press.org/2019/10/10/partisan-antipathy-more-intense-more-personal/ (accessed August 25, 2020).

40 "Fractured Nation: Widening Partisan Polarization and Key Issues in 2020 Presidential Elections," PRRI, October 20, 2019, https://www.prri.org/research/fractured-nation-widening-partisan-polarization-and-key-issues-in-2020-presidential-elections (accessed August 25, 2020).

41 See Shanto Iyengar, Gaurav Sood, and Yphtach Lelkes, "Affect, Not Ideology," *Public Opinion Quarterly* 76 (2012): 405–431.

42 Lilliana Mason, "Losing Common Ground," *The Forum* 16 (#1 2018).

43 David C. Kimball, Bryce Summary, and Eric C. Vorst, "Political Identity and Party Polarization in the American Electorate," in Green, Coffey, and Cohen, *The State of the Parties,* 7th ed., pp. 37–54.

44 See Markus Prior, *Post-Broadcast Democracy* (New York: Cambridge University Press, 2007).

45 Jennifer Jerit and Jason Barabas, "Partisan Perceptual Bias and the Information Environment," *Journal of Politics* 74 (2012): 672–684.

46 Pew Research Center, "A Wider Ideological Gap."

47 Pew Research Center, "A Wider Ideological Gap."

48 Michael Barber and Jeremy C. Pope, "Does Party Trump Ideology?" *American Political Science Review* 113 (February 2019): 38–54.

49 See Douglas J. Ahler, "Self-Fulfilling Misperceptions of Public Polarization," *Journal of Politics* 76 (2014): 607–620.

50 John G. Bullock, Alan S. Gerber, Seth J. Hill, and Gregory A. Huber, "Partisan Bias in Factual Beliefs about Politics," *Quarterly Journal of Political Science* 10 (2015): 519–578.

51 Paul Allen Beck, "A Tale of Two Electorates," in John C. Green and Rick Farmer, eds., *The State of the Parties,* 4th ed. (Lanham, MD: Rowman & Littlefield, 2003), pp. 38–53. On less involved Americans, see Donald Kinder and Nathan Kalmoe, *Neither Liberal Nor Conservative* (Chicago, IL: University of Chicago Press, 2017).

52 Nolan McCarty, *Polarization* (New York: Oxford University Press, 2019), p. 14. See also Jordan Kujala, "Donors, Primary Elections, and Polarization in the United States," *American Journal of Political Science* 64 (2020): 587-602.

53 For example, see Seth E. Masket and Hans Noel, "Serving Two Masters," *Political Research Quarterly* 64 (2011): 1–20. See also Kyle L. Saunders and Alan I. Abramowitz, "Ideological Realignment and Active Partisans in the American Electorate," *American Politics Research* 32 (2004): 293, and Marjorie Randon Hershey, Nathaniel Birkhead, and Beth C. Easter, "Party Activists and Political Polarization," in Mark D. Brewer and L. Sandy Maisel, eds., *The Parties Respond,* 5th ed. (Boulder, CO: Westview Press, 2013), pp. 75–102.

54 See, for example, Pew Research Center, "Beyond Distrust." "Politically engaged" is defined as the 48 percent of Republicans and 34 percent of Democrats (including leaners) who say they are registered to vote, vote regularly, and follow politics most of the time.

55 See Seth E. Masket, "It Takes an Outsider," *American Journal of Political Science* 51 (2007): 482–497.

56 Adam Hughes and Onyi Lam, "Highly Ideological Members of Congress Have More Facebook Followers Than Moderates Do," *Pew Research Center*, August 21, 2017, https://www.pewresearch.org/fact-tank/2017/08/21/highly-ideological-members-of-congress-have-more-facebook-followers-than-moderates-do/ (accessed August 25, 2020).

57 See Brandice Canes-Wrone, David W. Brady, and John F. Cogan, "Out of Step, Out of Office," *American Political Science Review* 96 (2002): 127–140. This can also be true of the many candidates who, according to Larry M. Bartels, are even more extreme on important issues than are their party's core supporters. See Bartels, "Failure to Converge," *The Annals* 667 (2016): 143–165.

58 Laurel Harbridge and Neil Malhotra, "Electoral Incentives and Partisan Conflict in Congress," *American Journal of Political Science* 55 (2011): 494–510.

59 John R. Hibbing and Elizabeth Theiss-Morse, "Process Preferences and American Politics," *American Political Science Review* 95 (2001): 145–153.

60 John H. Aldrich, Jamie L. Carson, Brad T. Gomez, and David W. Rohde, *Change and Continuity in the 2016 & 2018 Elections* (Los Angeles, CA: Sage, 2020), p. 174.

61 Steven M. Utych, "Man Bites Dog," *Journal of Politics* 82 (2020): 392–396.

62 David E. Broockman, Nicholas Carnes, Melody Crowder-Meyer, and Christopher Skovron, "Why Local Party Leaders Don't Support Nominating Centrists," *British Journal of Political Science* 49 (2019): 1–26.

63 David Von Drehle, "Political Split Is Pervasive," *Washington Post*, April 25, 2004, p. A1.

64 Leon D. Epstein, "What Happened to the British Party Model?" *American Political Science Review* 74 (1980): 9–22.

65 On presidential mandates, see Julia R. Azari, *Delivering the People's Mandate* (Ithaca, NY: Cornell University Press, 2014).

66 See "Government Gets Lower Ratings for Handling Health Care, Environment, Disaster Response," *Pew Research Center*, December 14, 2017, http://assets.pewresearch.org/wp-content/uploads/sites/5/2017/12/14104805/12-14-17-Government-release.pdf (accessed August 25, 2020).

CHAPTER 16

The Place of Parties in American Politics

A change in party control of government affects your life in so many ways. It helps to determine how much you'll pay in taxes and receive in benefits. It affects the ease with which you could buy a gun or have an abortion. It can say "yes" or "no" to LGBTQ couples who want to adopt children or to programs that forgive student loan debt. Even your friendships and family relationships can be affected: in 2020, almost half of poll respondents said they've stopped talking about politics with someone, reflecting the bitter polarization of current politics.[1] The government, and therefore the two major parties that drive it, leaves its mark on everything you do, whether you vote or not, and even whether you realize it or not.

Throughout this book you have seen big changes over time in the ways the parties organize for action, the policies they promote, and the relationships they maintain with voters and candidates. The major parties fund their campaigns much differently now than they used to. Joe Biden and Donald Trump ran for office in 2020 using tactics that Thomas Jefferson and Abraham Lincoln could not have imagined. The media environment, the nature of the population, and the forms of transportation are light-years distant now from what they were early in the republic's existence. But the parties have adapted to this changing landscape and remain a fundamental part of American political life.[2]

This chapter will sum up these changes in relation to a simple but important truth: Political parties are powerfully shaped not only by the people who lead and participate in them but also by the environment in which they act. They are profoundly affected by election and campaign finance rules, immigration rates, changing educational levels, and instances of terrorism, just as they influence the response to these forces. To understand the changes in party power and behavior over time, we should explore the relationships between parties and their environment.

Parties and Their Environment

The Democrats and the Republicans have done a lot to shape American politics over time. Political parties promote public policies in response to citizens' beliefs, demands, and fears. They recruit individuals into active roles in politics

TABLE 16.1 Environmental Forces Influencing the American Parties	
Types of Influences	**Examples**
1. Nature of the electorate	Changes in the right to vote, citizens' political interest and knowledge, social characteristics of the electorate (age, race, income)
2. Political institutions and rules	
(a) Institutions	Federalism, separation of powers, single-member districts
(b) Electoral processes	Direct primary, nonpartisan elections
(c) Laws and regulations	Laws governing campaign finance, structure of party organization, voter ID and voter suppression laws
3. Social forces	
(a) National events and conditions	State of the economy, pandemics, terrorism
(b) Other political intermediaries	Types of other organized interests, media
(c) Political culture	Attitudes toward parties and politics

and government. Through their communications and performance, parties affect public attitudes about the Democrats and Republicans and about politics more generally. Party organizations and the parties in government structure their own environment even more directly as well: They make the rules governing who will get their names on the ballot and who is allowed to cast a vote.

In turn, their environment helps to shape the parties' nature, activities, and effectiveness. Three types of environmental forces have been especially important in influencing the American parties as well as those in other Western democracies: the nature of the electorate, the nation's basic governmental institutions and rules, and the forces that affect the broader society (Table 16.1).[3]

The Nature of the Electorate

Media coverage in recent years has focused a great deal on the changing political attitudes of white voters without a college degree. Between 2010 and 2018, whites without college degrees grew from 50 to 59 percent of Republican voters, while whites who did finish college fell from 40 to 29 percent of Republican voters. Why? For some analysts the answer has to do with less-educated whites' fear that their life chances are shrinking without a college degree, while those of other groups, especially minorities, are gaining.[4]

Concerns such as these influence a party system. The societal "fault lines" that divide voters into opposing groups—race is one of the clearest and most persistent examples in American politics—help to define the parties' issue agendas. So do the social characteristics that make some groups more likely to vote than others.

Legislatures and courts have greatly expanded the right to vote in the U.S. From an extremely limited suffrage—the small proportion of white male adults who owned property—it now includes the great majority of citizens over the age of 18. Political information has expanded as well. The Internet and other media have made information about politics much more accessible. More citizens have the advantage of higher education, which helps them find and understand the information. We have a lot of tools to affect politics now: primary elections, referenda, recall elections, and Internet access to public officials. Yet most people's interest in politics and their feelings of political effectiveness and trust have not increased. So at the same time as these opportunities for participation expanded, voter turnout dropped. Turnout remains lower in the U.S. than in most other industrialized democracies.

Turnout has not declined to the same degree among all groups in the population. Lower-income Americans' voting rates have declined more steeply than those with greater wealth.[5] At the same time, the income gap between the very wealthy and the rest of the population has grown larger in the U.S. than in most other industrialized democracies.[6] And as we saw in Chapter 8, the turnout rate of young Americans, though it rose in recent elections, still lags far behind the turnout rate of adults over 65. It is no surprise, then, that Social Security and Medicare are much more frequent campaign issues than are college loans. Those who participate are more likely to be heard.

Political Institutions and Rules

The second set of environmental influences on the parties includes the nation's basic framework of political institutions: whether the government is federal or unitary, whether it is parliamentary or has separated powers, and how its positions of power are structured. Then there are the laws that regulate the parties, ranging from the secret ballot and nonpartisan local elections to state laws governing mail-in ballots and federal laws regulating campaign spending.

American political institutions differ in many ways from those of most other democracies.[7] Most democratic nations do not divide governmental powers so insistently among different branches and levels of government. Few other democracies choose most of their leaders in single-member districts with plurality rules (see Chapter 2) or stagger the terms of different types of officials. The direct primary limits the party organization's role in selecting candidates to a degree unknown in most other democracies (see Chapters 9 and 10). American party organizations are regulated more heavily than are other nations' parties. The effect of this regulation—and in most cases its intention—is to restrict the development of the party organizations. An unintended effect is to boost the power of the party in government relative to that of the party organization.

As a result, the major American parties differ in important ways from parties in most other democracies.[8] In particular, the American parties are more decentralized; just as state and local governments have powers independent of the national government, so do state and local party organizations relative to the national party.[9] The two-party system is due in large part to the impact of American political institutions. The strength of the party in government means that the party organization's leaders have few effective tools to keep party legislators in line with the party's stands. To survive independent of a strong party organization, candidates must raise and spend much larger sums of money from private interests than do their counterparts in other democracies. With the important exceptions of the direct primary and the secret ballot, however, these rules have changed less dramatically over time than has the nature of the electorate, so they are less well able to explain changes in the parties.

Societal Forces

Events in the larger society also affect politics at a particular time. Terrorist attacks, the controversy over building a wall between Mexico and the U.S. to stop undocumented immigration, and disinformation spread on social media platforms have powerfully affected what we talk and think about. Thus, they have become part of the parties' agendas. They affect the parties' appeals and supporting coalitions.

These societal forces also include the organized interests in the nation, the media, and other means of representing interests. If people find effective ways to pursue their political goals outside of the parties, they will use them. If an interest group speaks more loudly in opposing abortion or backing LGBTQ rights, then why should an individual try to achieve those political aims through a party? The nature of the parties at any given time, then, depends partly on the available alternatives to parties and the competition among them.

All these elements of their environment have contributed to the unique character of the American parties. As this chapter summarizes the dramatic changes that have occurred in the parties' structure, supporting coalitions, and strength during the past four decades, we will pay special attention to the effects of their environment—including the unprecedented impact of the corona virus pandemic in 2020—and above all to changes in the electorate.

Party Decline in the 1960s and 1970s

A fundamental feature of the American parties is that the three party sectors are bound together only loosely. The party organization does not involve large numbers of party identifiers in its structure and activities, nor has it been able to direct the campaigns or the policy-making of the party in government. The party decline that was becoming apparent in the 1960s affected the three sectors very differently.

The Parties in the Electorate

Voters' loyalty to the parties weakened during the late 1960s and 1970s, a time of upheaval in many aspects of American life. What caused the decline? Many voters at this time, especially in the South but also in the Northeast and Mountain West, reacted to the parties' changed stances on race and other issues. These shifts undermined the strong Democratic loyalties of white southerners. Many began to think of themselves as independent "leaners" rather than as strong party identifiers. And just as the growing conservatism of the national Republican Party attracted many white southerners and some westerners, it repelled many liberal and moderate New Englanders who had long considered themselves Republicans. Overall, the early phase of this big coalitional change weakened the party loyalties of a lot of formerly strong partisans, and the parties found themselves with smaller numbers of less loyal identifiers.

Those who remained attached to a party no longer took their party's advice in elections as often as they once did. Ticket splitting surged. By 1968, almost half of the respondents in national surveys said they had voted for more than one party's candidates in state or local elections. In 1974 that figure topped out at 61 percent. The number of congressional districts selecting a presidential candidate of one party and a congressional candidate of the other party exceeded 30 percent for the first time in history in 1964 and reached 44 percent early in the next decade.[10]

In this turbulent period, some voters were stimulated by the issue-oriented candidacies of the time. The campaigns of Barry Goldwater in 1964, Eugene McCarthy and George Wallace in 1968, and George McGovern in 1972 spurred many people's awareness of issues such as the Vietnam War, the environment, and racial tensions. Television was used more heavily in campaigns, and the images and action conveyed on TV screens evoked some of the support that party symbols once commanded.

Increasingly, then, voters responded to candidates as individuals rather than as members of a party. Some independent candidates ran credible races for president and governor. Because candidates and issues change far more often than parties, the result was a less stable pattern of voting.

Party Organizations

The last of the great party machines were fading by the 1960s and 1970s. The famous Daley machine in Chicago was ripped apart in a series of tumultuous struggles. Party organizations could no longer depend on the patronage and preferments that once were so vital in recruiting party activists. Instead, more people were being drawn into party activism because of their commitment to particular issues. These were better-educated people, and they demanded greater participation in the party's decisions. Some of these new activists felt that standing on principle was more important than winning an election. If their party did not satisfy their ideological goals, they stood ready to leave it for other groups—candidates' campaigns and single-issue organizations—which were more narrowly targeted to meet their needs.

Other aspects of the party organization were under stress as well. As the direct primary came to dominate presidential nominations, party organizations gave up their control over nominations to whoever voted in the primary. By the time a primary season had ended, the party's presidential nominee had been determined, so its nominating convention no longer played a truly independent role. Grassroots activists took much of the party organization's own decision-making away from party leaders. This was particularly true of the Democrats, who in 1972 and 1976 nominated presidential candidates well outside the mainstream of their own party.

In addition to their declining influence over nominations, by the 1960s and 1970s, the party organizations had lost their central role in campaigns more generally. To run in primaries, candidates now had to build their own campaign organizations and raise their own campaign money. The knowledge and resources they once received from local party organizations could now be obtained directly from pollsters or campaign consulting firms that were, in effect, "rent-a-party" agencies. These professionals offered more sophisticated campaign skills than the party organizations could provide. The national parties began to develop greater technological expertise during the 1970s and to share their resources with state and local parties, but consultants had already established a beachhead. And campaign finance reforms gave candidates an incentive to raise nonparty money at a time when the technologies for doing so were becoming more effective.

Even with this new vigor in the national committees, the party organizations in the 1970s remained more decentralized than did life and politics in the U.S. Voters were looking more and more to national political leaders and symbols, but the party organizations still tended to be collections of state and local activists.

The Party in Government

In the 1960s and 1970s, elected officials began to rely more than ever on direct appeals to voters. With enough money, candidates could buy media time to speak to their constituents. In primary elections, and because of the increased split-ticket voting in general elections, candidates could not rely as much on voters' party ID to generate support. Through personal style, personal appeals, and personally raised funds, they developed a "personal vote" independent of party.[11]

The personal appeals worked. Incumbents' reelection rates rose. That deterred attractive challengers from running. When they did, party organizations were not vigorous enough to provide challengers with the campaign resources they so desperately needed. Holding public office became more of a profession—a lifetime career—even at the state and local levels, where political professionals were once rare.

As incumbents became more secure electorally (even though many did not feel that way), members of Congress gained greater freedom from their party organizations. Legislative party leaders found it harder to convince their members to vote for the congressional party's bills. The Democratic Party in Congress was especially diverse, divided between the remaining southern conservatives and northern moderates and liberals. This made congressional Democrats reluctant to grant much power to their legislative party leaders; neither southern nor northern Democrats could trust that legislative party leaders would serve the needs of *all* members of their congressional party. Senate and House Republicans were a varied group as well. So party-line voting in Congress fell to a new low at this time. However, it was a perverse kind of freedom. Protected from the demands of party leaders, legislators were more exposed to other pressures, mainly from growing numbers of interest groups.

Without much competition from unified legislative parties, presidents and governors could exercise greater leadership. Presidents did not depend on their party organizations for much; in fact, with the help of federal campaign money after 1974, presidential candidates could run their campaigns free of obligation to the party organization at any level. By that time, however, divided government had become the norm. That undercut executives' power by permitting the opposition party to block their initiatives.

Shifting Power Centers Inside the Parties

These changes produced a major shift of power inside the parties. The party organizations had lost power not only to the individual members of the party in government but also to other intermediaries, especially interest groups and the media. Party organizations and leaders became even more vulnerable to suspicions that they were run by bosses plotting in smoke-filled rooms. Visions of "boss rule" were as much alive in the 1960s and 1970s as they were in the early 1900s, even though, ironically, the party organizations no longer had the resources that could have made boss rule possible.

The result was a peculiar kind of political party. A party organization is the only sector of the party whose interests go beyond winning individual elections. It is the party organization that sustains the party when its candidates lose their races. It is the organization that links the party's officeholders and office seekers and calls them to collective action of the type that parties were created to achieve. Without it, party candidates are individual entrepreneurs seeking individual goals in a political system that requires collective decisions. The decline of the party organizations was a major force in the decline of the parties more generally.

Party Renewal since the 1980s

This marked decline was not the end of the story, however. The American parties responded to these challenges, just as they have adapted to changing circumstances at other times. The steady decay of the parties was stopped and reversed, but some of the changes that took place in the 1960s and 1970s continue to leave their imprint even now. The parties have had to adjust to new roles in American politics.

Change in the Parties' Electoral Coalitions

The slow, steady change in the parties' supporting coalitions since the 1960s (see Chapter 7) also changed the nature of the party system. The most striking elements

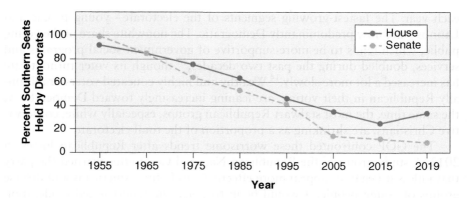

FIGURE 16.1 Eroding Democratic Strength in the South: U.S. House and Senate Seats, 1955–2019

Note: Data points are the percentage of U.S. senators and House members from the 13 southern states (Alabama, Arkansas, Florida, Georgia, Kentucky, Louisiana, Mississippi, North Carolina, Oklahoma, South Carolina, Tennessee, Texas, Virginia) who are Democrats.

Source: Data for 1955–1995 from *Congressional Quarterly Weekly Report*, November 12, 1994: 3231. Data for 2005, 2013, 2015, and 2019 compiled by the author from www.Senate.gov and www.House.gov (accessed April 7, 2020).

of this coalitional change have been the movement of white southerners into the Republican Party, which led to a dramatic decline of Democratic strength in the South (see Figure 16.1), and the growth of almost universal Democratic identification among black Americans. Other demographic characteristics not normally associated with the party division have taken on a partisan tinge. Religious conservatives, both Catholic and Protestant, are now a major force within the GOP. Marital status and sexual orientation have become related to partisanship; unmarried people (especially women) and LGBTQ people now identify mainly as Democrats. The urban–rural split has taken on partisan implications, with rural voters more Republican and suburban voters less Republican.[12]

These coalitional changes have transformed a Democratic-dominated political environment into one of close party competition in national politics. In the 1990s and at times in the 2000s, Republicans came closer to parity with the Democrats in both party ID and election results than they had since the 1930s. In the past decade, both Democrats and Republicans have held the presidency and majorities in the U.S. House. Republicans won unified control of the national government in 2016, only to lose it in 2018. The three states that tipped the Electoral College vote to Trump in 2016 by very small margins—Wisconsin, Michigan, and Pennsylvania—all went Democratic in 2018 and 2020. Both parties can dream of victory.

Which Party Will Gain the Advantage?

The close party division at the national level has made election results very volatile. On the one hand, the groups that favor Democratic candidates are expanding each year. The fastest-growing segments of the electorate—young people and Latinos—are now predominantly Democratic. The nonwhite share of the voting public, which tends to be more supportive of government social programs and services, doubled during the past two decades,[13] though its voter turnout rate has increased a lot more slowly.[14] Wealthy and highly educated voters, traditionally Republican in their voting, are leaning increasingly toward Democrats. At the same time, the most stalwart Republican groups, especially white, conservative Christians, are shrinking as a proportion of the total electorate.

The GOP confronted these worrisome trends after Republican losses in 2012. A study group of the Republican National Committee warned the party that unless it began to appeal more effectively to Latinx Americans and diverse groups of young people, it would be in trouble. The report urged moderation in the party's position on immigration: "If Hispanic Americans perceive that a GOP nominee or candidate does not want them in the United States (i.e. self-deportation), they will not pay attention to our next sentence." It cautioned the party against intolerance."[15]

But four years later, Republican presidential nominee Donald Trump took the opposite direction. Trump's strong stand against illegal immigration and rock-bottom approval ratings among African Americans and young people cut the ground from under the RNC's 2012 recommendations. In fact, the report can no longer be found on the party's website. Pressure had increased in the meantime from the party's base of strong conservatives and white evangelical Christians. The Tea Party Republican faction charged that in its desire to gain power, the Republican Party had sacrificed its principles (small government in particular).

The Republican party dealt with these challenges in the short term. The Republican base, energized by hostility toward President Obama, dominated the 2014 midterms, contributing to the biggest Republican House majority in 60 years. And Donald Trump's victory in 2016 gave new energy to the party. His winning coalition mobilized a larger proportion of whites without a college degree than have other recent Republican presidential candidates, which convinced some analysts that the Republicans could rely on socially conservative, nativist appeals indefinitely.

That is a risky bet, given the inexorable march of demographic change. It is a demographic fact that the groups the current Republican coalition depends on—whites, especially those without college degrees; evangelical Christians, rural people, and older men—are shrinking as a share of the American population relative to people of color, secular people, and younger people.[16] Trump's strategists have doubled down on getting more of these groups to the polls, by intensifying their uneasiness about living in a multi-cultural world and perhaps even being dominated by it. But that is likely to work only for the next decade or two. If the Republicans are to remain viable in the longer term, they will need to expand their appeal to the very groups that President Trump has been disparaging.

No matter how the parties in the electorate evolve, however, clearly we are now in a different party system from that of the New Deal. In contrast with the relatively quick political changes that accompanied the Depression of the 1930s, the more recent shifts in party coalitions have developed over several decades and continue to evolve. Neither party has a clear edge at the national level, though most states lean toward one party. Polls show very little public enthusiasm for either major party or, for that matter, many other aspects of American politics.

The events of the 1960s and 1970s produced an ongoing challenge to party loyalties. Large numbers of voters now rely on sources other than the parties, such as cable TV, blogs, and single-issue groups, for their political information. Sometimes these sources reinforce partisan views; in other cases, they don't.[17] Yet even with this formidable competition, parties remain important landmarks on most people's political maps. Levels of party identification rebounded beginning in the 1990s, and partisanship is now at least as strong an influence on people's voting as it was before the 1960s.[18] Split-ticket voting, especially as measured by the number of districts voting for a presidential candidate of one party and a congressional candidate of the other, is now uncommon.[19]

The Rise of More Cohesive Parties in Government

Well before the current revival of partisanship among voters—and one likely cause of it, the parties in government had begun a revival of their own. By the mid-1970s, the long decline in party unity in Congress had stopped and the organizational seeds had been sown for greater party strength. By the 1980s, the congressional parties were becoming more cohesive than they had been in a century. The slow, steady movement among voters from the Democratic "solid South" to a largely Republican South left both congressional parties more homogeneous, which in turn made it easier for each party to offer clear alternatives on big issues.

Demographic changes as well as redistricting caused more and more congressional districts to become safe for one party. By 2020, very few Congress members represented states or districts where their party was in the minority.[20] As a result, the main threat to their reelection would come from more extreme elements within their own party, in the primary, rather than from the other party. Forces pushing Republicans to become more conservative and Democrats more liberal drowned out pleas for bipartisanship and moderation. Especially "for the overwhelming majority of House Republicans, the largely white, resolutely conservative electorate that Mitt Romney relied on [in 2012]... is all they need to ensure reelection" to their House seats.[21] State legislative parties were also becoming more unified and polarized on issues.

Partisanship became more important in the executive branch as well. The Reagan administration came into office in 1981 as the most ideologically committed in decades. Reagan's leadership placed conservative principles at the top of the GOP's agenda and solidified the hold of his brand of conservatives on the party. The Democrats became more unified in response. By the mid-1990s, there was intense partisan conflict between a programmatically committed, Republican-led Congress and an activist Clinton White House. The battles have continued, resulting in a level of incivility and gridlock that can bring Congress to its knees. Consider one House member's recollection of a new member orientation program in which a Democratic leadership staff member suggested the importance of getting to know Republican legislators. One of the new Democrats replied, "Why would we want to do that?"[22] The bitter impeachment fight in 2019 and 2020 illustrated the massive gulf between Democrats and Republicans in the House and the Senate in their issue positions as well as the vanishingly small interest in bipartisan cooperation.

The New "Service Parties"

The party organizations have revived just as dramatically. Facing an environment of candidate-centered campaigns, both parties retooled their national organizations to provide services to the party's candidates. They have used their increased funding and staffing to help state and local parties, recruit candidates, provide resources, and step up their role in campaigns, compared with the 1960s and 1970s.

The new service party, however, differs a great deal from the grassroots organizations of earlier years. Because its main role is to support candidates, it is not very visible to voters, nor can it always make a major impact on campaigns. In the big-spending world of campaign finance, party organizations do not bring enough money to the table to be able to dominate political campaigning in most races. The service party is one of many forces trying to win the attention of candidates, influence elected officials, and mobilize citizens.

The party organizations, in short, are more vigorous now than they have been in years. There is a greater balance of power between the national and state and local parties. Party organizations have adapted to new conditions by taking on a new form: the service party. However, as service parties, the party organizations are no longer as distinctive as they used to be in the sense of providing campaign resources that no other group could deliver. Both national parties have created massive databases of information on voters. But so have a variety of other organizations.

The two national parties are not mirror images of one another. Although they have both transformed themselves into service parties and become more internally cohesive and more different from one another in their policies, they have followed different paths in doing so.[23] As Chapter 10 showed, the parties strengthened their national organizations for different reasons and in different ways. Although party polarization has led both parties in Congress to grant more power to their parties' leaders, the polarization has been asymmetric: the Republican Party in Congress has moved further to the right than the Democrats have moved to the left.[24] And many observers see the two parties as distinctive in their ideological styles, with Republicans more ideologically oriented and Democrats more focused on the needs of constituent social groups.[25]

The Future of Party Politics in America

These trends affect us because the future of the U.S. as a democratic system is not guaranteed, and political parties can help preserve a democracy. Parties can enable political leaders to work together toward shared interests over time. They can provide cues that help voters make decisions on candidates and issues with relatively little effort. They can bring voters to the polls, which helps legitimize a democracy. Perhaps most important, parties organize majorities, which are necessary for governing. Interest groups such as super PACs can effectively represent intense minorities, but there are not many alternatives to the parties for organizing lasting and predictable majorities.

Will Party Polarization Cool?

During past catastrophes, such as world wars and major terrorist attacks, bipartisanship has replaced intense partisan divisions—for a time.[26] But the corona virus pandemic did little to cool the party polarization that has developed such force in recent decades. Perhaps because there was no visible foreign enemy to blame, partisans aimed their fire and frustration at the other party instead. Democratic activists denounced President Trump and several Republican governors for not responding in time to contain the virus, given that cases had appeared in the U.S. in January, but the president largely played down the crisis until mid-March, and some governors had still not ordered lockdowns of their states by mid-April. Republicans claimed that it was the Democrats' fault for spending so much time on impeaching the president until February 5.

Party polarization infected even the mechanics of voting. Public health authorities warned that the pandemic spreads when people gather in crowds. One logical response for state governments, then, was to reduce crowds at polling places by increasing voting by mail. Mail balloting and absentee ballots have long been used in American elections; even before 2020 began, five states had conducted their balloting entirely by mail for years, and military personnel have typically voted by mail.[27] Although a big expansion of any voting system can cause challenges, turnout increases when voters can cast a ballot by mail.[28]

Yet a big shift toward voting by mail was opposed by some Republican leaders. President Trump complained to Fox News that if vote-by-mail were adopted nationally, "You'd never have a Republican elected in this country again."[29] He charged, without evidence, that mail voting was full of fraud and that the election results would therefore be "rigged."[30] At the same time, the president's newly-appointed Postmaster General implemented new cost-saving rules that slowed down mail delivery nationally.[31] Mailed-in ballots in many state primaries were not received in time to be counted. Democrats feared that the new rules were intended to obstruct votes cast by mail, on the assumption that a higher voter turnout would hurt President Trump's reelection.

Several Republican state party chairs broke with the president's stand. Many of their party's voters, they said, were echoing the president's claim that voting by mail was a bad idea. If so, that might dissuade many Republicans from requesting mail ballots, which could reduce Republican turnout in November. And in fact, the controversy rested on a mistaken assumption; research has found no evidence that Republican candidates are disadvantaged by all-mail elections or absentee balloting.[32] Even a national health crisis, then, was fed into the meat grinder that polarized politics had become in the 2020s.

A Changing Intermediary Role

Party politics can try people's patience even in the best of times. But democracies have never yet been able to survive without political parties. Elections require voters to make large numbers of choices, even though most voters don't know much about most candidates. Parties serve as efficient guides. The value of the party label in elections is probably greatest when a mass electorate has just begun to develop and has serious need for information. As the electorate matures, its needs change. One explanation for American voters' decreased reliance on party loyalties in the 1960s and 1970s was that voters had become better educated by then and could sift through a broader range of political messages without the need for party labels as a guide.[33]

It is interesting, then, that although education levels have continued to increase since the 1960s, party identification has reasserted its influence on voters' choices. Why should partisanship help citizens who have so many other sources of information about candidates and issues? Perhaps it is *because* they are exposed to so much information. Without this simple guide, the blizzard of political messages could confuse voters rather than inform them. At the same time, the fact that the two major parties have drawn farther apart from one another on important issues lends even more value to the party labels for politically engaged citizens. Added to the heightened party competition in the 2020s and the resulting intensity of campaign messages, an individual's party tie often becomes more meaningful to him or her than any other political cues.

The parties face greater competition now from organized interests and the media. A century ago, someone concerned about environmental quality would probably have had to pursue his or her goals through a political party; not many groups focused specifically on energy or water pollution. Now, however, along with the growing reach of government into most aspects of private life, a huge array of organized interests has developed permitting individuals to establish a "designer link" with the political system. If someone prefers to see politics entirely from the perspective of climate change, or gun rights, several groups can make that possible. There is no need to compromise or support a coalition of other groups' needs and a range of candidates, as a party loyalty would encourage.

In this fractured political world, parties take on greater significance as a means of broadening individuals' perspectives and improving their ability to hold elected officials accountable. The parties have long struggled with hostile environmental forces, from a system of separated powers that is inhospitable to strong parties to a political culture suspicious of all parties. However, as we have seen throughout this book, the parties are adaptable. They are not the intermediaries they were in 1900 or 1950, but for large numbers of Americans and for the policy-making process, the major parties remain the most important intermediaries.

The Need for Strong Parties

Although we need parties, we don't like them. We don't even like to admit that they influence us. Most of us claim that issues and candidates' personal qualities have the biggest impact on our votes. Yet it's clear that partisanship is closely related to our attitudes toward issues and candidates and is the source of much of their influence.

Democracy is unworkable without parties.[34] The U.S. has probably come closer to testing that principle than any other democracy; much of American local politics has been, at least officially, nonpartisan for some time. But when parties are reduced to playing a smaller role in politics, the quality of democracy can be weakened.

Consider the role strong parties can play in Congress and state legislatures. As a representative body, Congress is structured to permit legislators to give their constituents what they want: short-term, tangible benefits such as disaster relief and tax breaks. Legislators facing reelection seek the Holy Grail of constituent service: a project such as a new highway or a change in the tax code that benefits their own constituents but whose costs are paid by taxpayers all over the country. But if the individual voter and the individual legislator are motivated to pay close attention to the benefits they can get for their district, who is motivated to think about the collective cost? Very few voters support the idea of raising their own taxes to pay for benefits to others, or even to pay for benefits to themselves.

Strong legislative parties have an incentive to take responsibility for the collective costs.[35] Some legislative party members can gain personal career advantages by becoming leaders of their congressional party. When the party's members in Congress are elected from similar districts and hold similar views, they can afford to trust these legislative party leaders with greater power to structure the choices they will make. Members realize that although their own reelection needs are primary, they also need coordination within the legislature to pass bills and to help with the endless tasks of legislative life.

By using the carrots and sticks discussed in Chapter 13, legislative party leaders can induce their party colleagues to make truly national policy, not just "Christmas tree" legislation that consists of government-spending ornaments for particular interests. By holding their legislators to this party program, legislative party leaders can create a favorable brand name for their party in elections, which voters can come to recognize and associate with their own district's candidate. In the absence of strong parties, it is difficult to imagine where this collective responsibility might come from. Without strong parties, individual members of Congress and state legislatures have every reason to behave in ways that conflict with their collective interest and that of their constituents.[36]

In a society dominated by interest groups and other intermediaries, most people would not be as well represented. Among the many links between citizens and government, only the parties have the incentive to create majorities to win a wide range of elections over a long period. In turn, that gives the parties, to a greater extent than interest groups or even elected officials, a reason to pay attention to those citizens who are not activists or big campaign contributors. As political scientist Walter Dean Burnham has written, parties are the only devices that can "generate countervailing collective power on behalf of the many individually powerless against the relatively few who are individually—or organizationally—powerful."[37]

It is the parties that can mobilize sheer numbers against the organized minorities that hold other political resources. The parties do so in the one political arena where sheer numbers count most heavily: elections. Because of that, parties traditionally have been the means by which newly enfranchised but otherwise powerless groups gained a foothold in American life. The old-style urban machines, for example, provided the instrument with which immigrants won control of their cities from the more established Anglo-Saxon Protestant elites.

In a less party-driven politics, well-organized minorities with critical resources—money, insider knowledge, and technological expertise—would have even greater advantages than they do now. As we have seen from research on nonpartisan elections, eliminating the party symbol often makes it tougher for citizens to hold their representatives responsible.[38] That may be one reason why voter participation has declined more sharply in recent decades among poorer and less educated Americans; they may feel less represented by a politics in which the parties are no longer preeminent,[39] even if they fail to see party change as the cause.

Finally, weakened parties would rob the political system of an effective means of governing. Without at least moderately strong parties, it is harder to mobilize majorities to pass legislation. Individual candidates, freed from party loyalties, would have to recreate majorities for every new legislative proposal. The result could be even greater gridlock, in which legislatures splinter into conflicting and uncompromising groups.

It is true that the congressional parties have not distinguished themselves in resolving contentious issues recently. As Frances Lee points out, the frequent changes of party control in Congress combined with greater polarization have motivated the congressional parties to behave irresponsibly, to make points rather than to make policy.[40] But in practice, it is hard to imagine 535 House members and senators reaching any agreement at all without parties. Laws and policies could continue to be made only by shifting coalitions of elected officials, campaign contributors, and interest groups. Because these coalitions would be less permanent and less identifiable to the public, it would be much harder for citizens to hold them accountable.

How to Make the Parties Stronger

Because parties bring so much value to American democracy, some analysts have considered ways to expand the parties' role in political life. The most effective solutions—ending the separation of powers, the direct primary, and the anti-party sentiment engrained into the political culture—are not on the table, of course. But there are less dramatic ways to strengthen the parties.

One survey showed that most respondents would like the parties to be more active in helping people deal with the government. Its authors propose, among other ideas, that party organizations could create "mobile units" to help citizens in areas where the U.S. (and perhaps the state) representative is from the other party. That would allow the party organization, not just members of the party in government, to perform constituent service. They note that this idea was especially attractive to survey respondents who described themselves as alienated from politics. By providing attractive nonpolitical benefits such as low-cost health insurance, as many interest groups do now, parties could help to build long-term loyalty among their volunteers.[41] Parties could also renew their connection with citizens by airing campaign ads promoting the party as a whole, not just individual candidates. These ads could strengthen the meaning of party by stressing the link between the party's stands and individuals' daily lives. And more states could join those letting taxpayers contribute to a party organization through the state tax system.

Conclusion: The Parties' Prospects

The American parties have never lacked interesting challenges. The electorate has become more varied. Some traditional group ties have broken down. New groups, ranging from those opposing transgender rights to those favoring for-profit prisons, are tilling the ground that the major parties once owned. Most voters still identify with a party, but they also respond to candidates, issues, and national trends. The result is a more diverse, complicated politics that frustrates elected officials, party leaders, voters, and nonvoters.

The parties can't meet every political need. We can't expect the parties in government to get along if we elect candidates who boast of their refusal to compromise. Parties find it hard to offer policy alternatives in campaigns without engaging in the conflict that many Americans find so distasteful. It is difficult for parties to unite their officeholders and office seekers on a single agenda while giving candidates the independence to choose their own appeals and meet their own districts' needs. Parties can't provide accountability to a public that wants to choose candidates individually.

Americans will continue to challenge the parties with these conflicting expectations and criticisms. The parties' distinctive character has sustained them longer than any other tool of democratic politics. For the sake of representation, effective policy making, and accountability in governance, even the most independent-minded citizens have a stake in sustaining vigorous party politics in the U.S.

Notes

1 Mark Jurkowitz and Amy Mitchell, "A Sore Subject," *Pew Research Center*, February 5, 2020, https://www.journalism.org/2020/02/05/a-sore-subject-almost-half-of-americans-have-stopped-talking-politics-with-someone/ (accessed August 27, 2020).

2 See Seth E. Masket, *The Invincible Party* (New York: Oxford University Press, 2016).

3 The classic source is Robert Harmel and Kenneth Janda, *Parties and Their Environments* (New York: Longman, 1982).

4 Thomas B. Edwall, "We Aren't Seeing White Support for Trump for What It Is," *New York Times*, August 28, 2019, p. A1.

5 See Sean McElwee, "Why the Voting Gap Matters," October 23, 2014, https://www. demos.org/research/why-voting-gap-matters (accessed August 27, 2020).

6 Kay Lehman Schlozman, Sidney Verba, and Henry E. Brady, *The Unheavenly Chorus* (Princeton, NJ: Princeton University Press, 2012).

7 See Stephen K. Medvic, *Campaigns and Elections* (Boston, MA: Wadsworth, 2010), pp. 312–314.

8 See Paul Allen Beck, "Parties in the American Political Environment," in Marjorie Randon Hershey, ed., *Guide to U.S. Political Parties* (Los Angeles, CA: Sage, 2014), Chapter 5.

9 Robert Harmel, Matthew Giebert, and Kenneth Janda, *American Parties in Context* (New York: Routledge, 2016), Chapter 4.

10 Harold W. Stanley and Richard G. Niemi, *Vital Statistics on American Politics 1999–2000* (Washington, DC: CQ Press, 2000), pp. 44 and 133.

11 Bruce E. Cain, John Ferejohn, and Morris P. Fiorina, *The Personal Vote* (Cambridge, MA: Harvard University Press, 1987).

12 See Katherine J. Cramer, *The Politics of Resentment* (Chicago, IL: University of Chicago Press, 2016).

13 William H. Frey, "U.S. White Population Declines," *Brookings Institution*, June 22, 2018, https://www.brookings.edu/blog/the-avenue/2018/06/21/us-white-population-declines-and-generation-z-plus-is-minority-white-census-shows/ (accessed August 27, 2020).

14 Bernard L. Fraga, *The Turnout Gap* (New York: Cambridge University Press, 2018).

15 Shushannah Walshe, "RNC Completes 'Autopsy' on 2012 Loss, Calls for Inclusion Not Policy Change," March 18, 2013, https://abcnews.go.com/Politics/OTUS/rnc-completes-autopsy-2012-loss-calls-inclusion-policy/story?id=18755809 (accessed August 27, 2020).

16 Ronald Brownstein, "Trump's Coalition Is Narrowing," CNN.com, August 25, 2020, https://www.cnn.com/2020/08/25/politics/gop-future-after-trump-isolation/index. html? (accessed August 25, 2020).

17 See Robert Huckfeldt and Paul Allen Beck, "Contexts, Intermediaries, and Political Activity," in Lawrence C. Dodd and Calvin Jillson, eds., *The Dynamics of American Politics* (Boulder, CO: Westview Press, 1994), Chapter 11. On the other hand, organized interests have become more polarized by party since the Reagan years; see Jack L. Walker, Jr., *Mobilizing Interest Groups in America* (Ann Arbor, MI: University of Michigan Press, 1991), Chapter 8, and media coverage frequently refers to party; see Marjorie Randon Hershey, "If 'The Party's in Decline,' Then What's That Filling the News Columns?" in Nelson W. Polsby and Raymond E. Wolfinger, eds., *On Parties* (Berkeley, CA: Institute of Governmental Studies, 1999), pp. 257–278.

18 In 2016 and 2020, about nine in ten voters chose a presidential candidate consistent with their party identification.

19 Thanks to Bruce Oppenheimer for calculating this information.

20 John H. Aldrich, Jamie L. Carson, Brad T. Gomez, and David W. Rohde, *Change and Continuity in the 2016 & 2018 Elections* (Los Angeles, CA: Sage, 2020), pp. 332–333.

21 Alex Isenstadt, "Logic of House GOP Intransigence," *Politico*, December 28, 2012, www.politico.com/story/2012/12/the-logic-of-house-gop-intransigence-85546.html?hp=110 (accessed August 27, 2020).

22 Rep. Daniel Lipinski, "Navigating Congressional Policy Processes," in Lawrence C. Dodd and Bruce I. Oppenheimer, eds., *Congress Reconsidered*, 9th ed. (Washington, DC: CQ Press, 2009), p. 344.

23 See Daniel Galvin, *Presidential Party Building* (Princeton, NJ: Princeton University Press, 2010).

24 See Matt Grossmann and David A. Hopkins, "Ideological Republicans and Group Interest Democrats," *Perspectives on Politics* 13 (2015): 119–139.

25 Yphtach Lelkes and Paul Sniderman, "The Ideological Asymmetry of the American Party System," *British Journal of Political Science* 46 (2016): 825–844. See also Matt Grossman and David A. Hopkins, *Asymmetric Politics* (Oxford: Oxford University Press, 2016).

26 Marjorie Randon Hershey, "The More Things Change…: Did Partisanship Decline As a Result of September 11?" in Dennis L. Dresang et al., eds., *American Government in a Changed World* (New York: Longman, 2002), pp. 93–113.

27 Darrell M. West, "How Does Vote-By-Mail Work and Does It Increase Election Fraud? Brookings Institution, June 22, 2020, https://www.brookings.edu/policy2020/votervital/how-does-vote-by-mail-work-and-does-it-increase-election-fraud/ (accessed August 27, 2020).

28 R. Michael Alvarez, Dustin Beckett, and Charles Stewart III, "Voting Technology, Vote-by-Mail, and Residual Votes in California, 1990–2010," *Political Research Quarterly* 66 (September 2013): 658–670.

29 Elise Viebeck, Amy Gardner, and Michael Scherer, "GOP Fights Efforts to Ease Voting During Pandemic," *Washington Post*, April 5, 2020, p. A2.

30 Wendy R. Weiser and Michael Ekeh, "The False Narrative of Vote-by-Mail Fraud," April 10, 2020, https://www.brennancenter.org/our-work/analysis-opinion/false-narrative-vote-mail-fraud (accessed August 27, 2020).

31 Daniel Cassady, "Postmaster General Said To Admit To Imposing Rules That Would Slow Delivery Of Mail," Forbes, August 6, 2020, https://www.forbes.com/sites/danielcassady/2020/08/06/postmaster-general-said-to-admit-to-imposing-rules-that-would-slow-delivery-of-mail/#2244969a7d68 (accessed August 27, 2020).

32 West, "How Does Vote-By-Mail Work."

33 See Ronald Inglehart, *Culture Shift* (Princeton, NJ: Princeton University Press, 1990), Chapters 10 and 11.

34 John H. Aldrich, *Why Parties? A Second Look* (Chicago, IL: University of Chicago Press, 2011), p. 3; and Nancy L. Rosenblum, *On the Side of the Angels* (Princeton, NJ: Princeton University Press, 2008).

35 David R. Mayhew, *Congress: The Electoral Connection* (New Haven, CT: Yale University Press, 1974), especially pp. 141–149.

36 See Marjorie Randon Hershey, "Political Parties as Mechanisms of Social Choice," in Richard S. Katz and William Crotty, eds., *Handbook of Party Politics* (London: Sage, 2005), pp. 75–88.

37 Walter Dean Burnham, *Critical Elections and the Mainsprings of American Politics* (New York: Norton, 1970), p. 133.

38 See Gerald C. Wright and Brian F. Schaffner, "The Influence of Party," *American Political Science Review* 96 (2002): 367–379.

39 See Steven J. Rosenstone and John Mark Hansen, *Mobilization, Participation, and Democracy in America* (New York: Macmillan, 1993), Chapter 8.

40 Frances E. Lee, "Parties as Coordinators: Can Parties Unite What the Constitution Divides?" in Hershey, ed., *Guide to U.S. Political Parties*, Chapter 3.

41 Larry J. Sabato and Bruce Larson, *The Party's Just Begun* (New York: Longman, 2002), pp. 156–160. See also James Zogby, "Invite Independents into the Process," *Washington Post*, February 28, 2020, Outlook p. 1.

INDEX